The Blackstone of Military Law

Colonel William Winthrop

Joshua E. Kastenberg

Martin Gordon, Consulting Editor

THE SCARECROW PRESS, INC.
Lanham, Maryland • Toronto • Plymouth, UK
2009

SCARECROW PRESS, INC.

Published in the United States of America
by Scarecrow Press, Inc.
A wholly owned subsidiary of
The Rowman & Littlefield Publishing Group, Inc.
4501 Forbes Boulevard, Suite 200, Lanham, Maryland 20706
www.scarecrowpress.com

Estover Road
Plymouth PL6 7PY
United Kingdom

British Library Cataloguing in Publication Information Available

Library of Congress Cataloging-in-Publication Data

Kastenberg, Joshua E., 1967–
The Blackstone of military law : Colonel William Winthrop / Joshua E. Kastenberg.
p. cm.
Includes bibliographical references.
ISBN 978-0-8108-6177-0 (pbk. : alk. paper) — ISBN 978-0-8108-6301-9 (ebook)
1. Winthrop, William, 1831–1899. 2. Judge advocates–United States–Biography. 3. Lawyers–Massachusetts–Boston–Biography. 4. Lawyers–Minnesota–Biography. I. Title.
KF368.W58K37 2009
340.092–dc22
[B] 2008050013

™ The paper used in this publication meets the minimum requirements of American National Standard for Information Sciences—Permanence of Paper for Printed Library Materials, ANSI/NISO Z39.48-1992.
Manufactured in the United States of America.

Contents

Preface

1956: During a heated questioning session in the Supreme Court, James Lee Rankin, the solicitor general of the United States, argued for a greater expansion of military jurisdiction to include civilian spouses and Defense Department contractors residing on overseas military bases. An offended Associate Justice William O. Douglas passed to Associate Justice Hugo Black a note that read:

> We have been listening to the arguments in *Covert* and *Kruger*, and I am surprised that the Court is not subjecting Rankin to more penetrating questioning. Here are some items from my memorandum which he undoubtedly cannot satisfactorily explain. Why not hit him with Winthrop, with English precedent before 1789, and with early American law.

That two of the court's foremost civil rights advocates turned to William Winthrop, a scholar of military law who believed in the necessity of a separate, more austere code than the civil law, is in and of itself interesting. Over time, a number of conservative justices have turned to Winthrop's work in upholding the military's separate legal system to include the efficacy of military trials of captured enemy insurgents accused of violating the law of war.

"Hit him with Winthrop": In the spring of 2000, while serving as a senior Air Force trial counsel, I prosecuted a colonel charged with sexually assaulting his young female executive officer. The charges against him included not only that assault but also a number of maltreatment allegations against other women, as well as the unique military offense of conduct unbecoming an officer and a gentleman. Regarding this last

charge, the colonel had made a number of sexually solicitous comments to female subordinates, as well as a few heavy-handed threats. It was, as attorneys describe, a "heated fully litigated trial." His lead defense counsel, a retired judge advocate and nationally noted litigator, objected to the conduct unbecoming an officer and a gentlemen charge. The defense counsel argued not that the charge, listed under the 133rd Article of the Uniform Code of Military Justice, was in and of itself unconstitutional; rather, he argued it was unconstitutional in this particular case because his client did not have the appropriate notice that his behavior was so discrediting to the Air Force as to render it criminal. After all, in domestic state laws, sexual harassment may be grounds for a civil suit, but it is not a criminal matter.

In defending the charge, I turned to *Military Law and Precedents*, a century-old treatise written by Colonel William Winthrop. I argued to the judge that, in the historic context, the Air Force colonel's behavior was precisely the type of conduct befitting the Article 133 charge against him. Winthrop's treatise placed the colonel on notice that his conduct was detrimental to the military's public reputation and the good order and discipline required by the military. Officers set an example, I argued, and if the colonel were to go uncharged for his conduct, it would become the norm in the military. If the behavior became the norm, then it would significantly degrade the Air Force. I conceded that, of course, the court-martial could find the colonel not guilty, but at least the higher command believed the colonel's behavior merited a prosecution.

The defense counsel responded in two distinct yet related arguments. First, Winthrop's work was so antiquated as to be of no use to the court. Counsel's specific dismissive words were, "This court should take no interest in a hundred-year-old book." This argument was somewhat ironic since he used Winthrop's work to defend another client in an appellate case a few years earlier, but the duty to zealously defend a client often overrides a desire for consistency in one's professional life. His second argument was that the behavior the Air Force charged his client with, something akin to sexual harassment, was not enumerated as a specific offense. As a result, his client could not possibly know that his conduct, while perhaps boorish, was of a criminal nature. The military judge overruled these arguments, and the colonel was, in addition to the sexual assault type charges, found guilty.

Since that trial, I wondered about who Colonel Winthrop was. I attempted to research Winthrop's life, but only a few short articles on him existed, as there never had been a biography written about him. I assumed that his personal correspondences had been lost to history, but they were not; a number of his letters exist at Yale University, some at the New York Archdiocese, and others at the Library of Congress and

National Archives. This biography is a first, and it is my hope that it serves its readers a number of purposes. For military historians, this biography is not merely an addition to the large shelf of Civil War and late nineteenth-century military history. It explains how the army came to not only collectively approach courts-martial, but also its constitutional place in the American democracy. From the late nineteenth century and into the twentieth century, military officers were trained primarily at the United States Military Academy and at such service schools as Fort Leavenworth. They were taught military law according to Winthrop through his texts and lectures. Although some officers decried the weak constitutional role of the Army and many lamented American society's disinterest in military affairs, Winthrop educated his fellow officers that the military's place was constitutionally set for a purpose. He also took advantage of society's disinterest in military affairs to internally professionalize the military's legal system.

For legal historians, this biography is both a study on how military law evolved alongside its civil counterpart and an analytic contribution on civil–military relations at the turn of the last century. For practitioners of military law, public international law, or constitutional law, it is a contextual document. So much of each legal field is historic, or, as international law denotes, "customary." The United States military has a culture of professionalism, a codified law, and an accompanying *lex non scripta*, or unwritten common law. Winthrop's was the last comprehensive work on that subject, but to Winthrop, military law was more than courts-martial—it was the body of law, both constitutional and international, that governed the profession of arms in the American democracy.

Acknowledgments

This book could not have been written without the help of a number of people. Dr. Martin Gordon at the Scarecrow Press not only edited out so much of the legalese that the public finds difficult to read, but also his revisions kept the biography focused and cogent. The librarians at the Library of Congress's manuscripts division were particularly helpful. My wife's support of this project was critical for its completion, and she helped in finding hidden yet essential sources. The enthusiasm for this project of Darren Eicken, a fellow judge advocate, resulted in great discussions generating ideas and travel to various historic collections. Andrew Williams and Seth Deam, two judge advocates who I worked alongside at the Air Force's Operations Law directorate in the Pentagon, provided invaluable ideas and patient proofreading. I particularly owe a tremendous debt to three others: I have never met two finer legal minds than Eric Merriam, also a judge advocate, and Russell Leavitt, a former judge advocate and current federal attorney. Both are outstanding public servants working in the nation's defense, and neither truly had the personal time to do what I asked. Yet they did. There is something of Winthrop in both of them. I have never met a more conscientious and well-versed individual in the Civil War than Mrs. Cheryl Chasin, who is also a public servant. I have called Mrs. Chasin an "expert without portfolio" because she does not possess a Ph.D. As a knowledge base on the war, and on the tax laws of this country, she has no equal. But whatever mistakes exist in this book are mine.

I dedicate this book to my son, Matthew Ari Kastenberg, for one reason alone: He is my son, and I love him.

1

A Privileged Lineage

We have called Colonel Winthrop . . . The Blackstone of Military Law.

—United States Supreme Court majority in *Hamdan v. Rumsfeld* (2006)

Born August 3, 1831, in New Haven, Connecticut, to one of the most prominent families in United States history, William W. Winthrop was a soldier, a scholar, a public servant, and a man of letters. He fought in the Union army, on the Peninsula, at Second Manassas, Antietam, and Fredericksburg. In those battles he withstood his own fears and witnessed the horrific mangling and killing of soldiers on both sides of the conflict. He also witnessed the suffering of noncombatants. Winthrop suffered just as the common soldier in any war suffered: he survived a bullet through his chest, repeatedly faced disease, and carried the debilitating effect of each through his life. He also saw two fellow officers he admired court-martialed on specious grounds. Though both were acquitted, the experience reinforced Winthrop's determination to bring fairness to the administration of military justice.

After the war, Winthrop served as a judge advocate, he taught law at the United States Military Academy, and he wrote *Military Law and Precedents*, a key foundation of modern military law. Through his scholarship and advice to commanders, Winthrop contributed to the professionalizing of military law, and in doing so, the professionalizing of the officer corps. He has been called "a giant in military law."[1] His scholarship is still cited by international law jurists, a variety of appellate courts, and the United States Supreme Court. Indeed, in deciding a significant question of international criminal jurisdiction, in 2004, the Supreme Court turned to Winthrop.[2] And in 2006, the Court adopted his guidance in a decision defining a subject no less constitutionally important than the limits of executive authority in time of war (*Hamdan v. Rumsfeld*, 548 U.S. 557).

Winthrop's influence does not end with his treatises on the laws of war. Indeed, this body of law was only one of three major areas about which Winthrop wrote. Military justice was, until the past two years, the subject in which Winthrop's influence appeared strongest. During the past century, a number of appellate courts turned to Winthrop for guidance in matters of jurisdiction, as well as the nature of defining purely military offenses. While less quantifiable, the contemporary practice of courts-martial owes a great deal to Winthrop. He advocated for a system in which the fairness of military law was judged by comparison to its domestic civil counterpart and foreign military legal systems.

Yet, Winthrop was not merely a legal scholar in matters of military justice. He was a complete military scholar. In order to advance his theories on military discipline, he had to convey his knowledge of the profession of arms and its place in a democracy. In this later regard, Winthrop was also an astute military historian. If Winthrop were simply an advocate and military scholar, his influence might not have lasted as long as it has. But he was more than an advocate or historian. Winthrop was perhaps the first American soldier to effectively articulate an interrelationship between the law of war, military discipline, and achievable strategy.

Winthrop's writings directly influenced the relationship between the government, its represented people, and the military. In his thirty-four years of military service, Winthrop directly advised the great commanders of his day including Ulysses Grant, William Sherman, Philip Sheridan, and John Schofield. Through his scholarship and personal service, he taught and influenced a generation of commanders who served in both world wars. He lived in an age of great evolution, where the nation transitioned from slavery to emancipation, and from possessing a relatively homogeneous population to having an increasingly diverse demography. The America into which Winthrop was born was largely agrarian and isolated from overt European influences, such as overseas imperialism. By his death in 1899, the United States possessed an industrial capacity and capitalist economy that was well on its way to surpassing its European rivals. Moreover, the nation gained an overseas empire after defeating Spain.

Winthrop's primary topic of scholarship—though he had others—was the military, and even this arena underwent dramatic changes during his life. Warfare, for instance, evolved from lineal formations of men in 1861 to the total warfare of 1865, and beyond into the roots of twentieth-century industrial war. A number of prominent officers in the post–Civil

War army believed the military should incorporate the institutions of the Prussian military system to the fullest extent possible. Winthrop stood as a barrier to this change, arguing for the military's absolute submission to the constitutionally elected executive and its complete respect for the other two government branches.

Winthrop chose to spend most of his life in the army after serving in it during the greatest period of strife in United States history, the Civil War. But he did not initially set out as a young man to do so. Had the war never come, he would likely have been a successful New York attorney dabbling in local politics and teaching a college course or two, and remembered as a patron of local culture, supporting libraries, museums, and art centers.

To most of the public, military law is a small field relegated to questions of administering discipline in the ranks. Military law practitioners and scholars know otherwise. The field encompasses not only military criminal law and discipline but also the constitutional foundations of civil and military relations, as well as a large body of international law. United States military law is, in effect, all of the domestic and international law that affects the existence and efficiency of the military, as well as the military's place in a democratic society.

That Colonel Winthrop became the leading scholar of military law in the late nineteenth century is unsurprising. A brief review of his educational background evidences the ability to master such a broad field. Coming from one of the wealthiest families in the northeast, he attended both Yale Law School and Harvard Law School, and prior to college was educated in one of the better secondary schools in Connecticut.

What is surprising is his choice of vocation, a life in the profession of arms. Today, as in much of America's history, the wealthiest members of American society seldom serve in the military, opting for the less opulent to guard the nation and fight its wars. However, Winthrop's lineage and the values passed to him are, in large measure, precisely what motivated him to enter the military during America's most critical moment and remain there for most of his life. While much of what Winthrop and others believed about the original American Winthrops was self-enforcing to those values, and not necessarily historically accurate, his exposure to these stories shaped his early life, as well as his desire to make the American profession of arms his vocation. The United States was his country, and he saw a personal stake in it.

And yet, it was not merely his family lineage that made Winthrop believe he had a responsibility to fight to preserve the Union. As a classically educated young man, he mastered Greek, Roman, and European political philosophy, and he was fluent in a number of foreign languages, including ancient Greek. Winthrop had an Athenian view of political and social responsibility. He believed that the wealthiest and most powerful members of society had a duty to serve on the front lines of conflict in times of national danger and be prepared to do so during times of peace.

For reasons just touched on, William Winthrop's family background requires study in order to understand Winthrop himself, since that heritage is a key to his early decisions and lifelong values. His lineage also provides a background of the development of American military law prior to Winthrop's life in that arena. Not surprisingly, his ancestors had an early role in the evolution of that law.

His extensive family background also presents a backdrop to his later independence from it. During his life, Winthrop departed from some of the very values, in particular the Puritan mores, with which he early on had aligned. These included, most visibly, his marriage to a Catholic in a Catholic Church, as well as his egalitarian principles of law and secular beliefs in its utility. But there were other, more subtle values such as joining an abolitionist movement in the late 1850s, against the wishes of a prominent relative, as well as a sojourn to the northern wilderness frontier of Minnesota without the comforts of New Haven and Boston.

Winthrop grew up in a family whose members were involved in politics and befriended a number of the early nineteenth-century political icons such as Henry Clay, Daniel Webster, and William Henry Seward. In Winthrop's early adult years, his personal friends included Joseph Choate, who later represented the United States as ambassador to Great Britain as well as to The Hague Conference of 1907, and Robert Gould Shaw, the commander of the colored 54th Massachusetts Regiment. His family politics were anti-Jacksonian in nature; that is, the Winthrops were Whigs. But along with his older brother Theodore, Winthrop found the mainstream Whig view of conciliation toward slavery an amoral response to an immoral institution; so much so, that in 1861 both he and his brother joined the army to fight not only secession, but also slavery, a minority ideology in that era.

He was not only a very educated man but also a lively writer. He frequently interspersed his correspondence with German, French, and even Greek. Winthrop wrote and published poetry, usually with a martial flavor, in the magazines and literary journals of his day. His siblings and nieces were avid writers as well, and it is evident that they shared their insights and gave assistance to each other's writing efforts.

Winthrop was not a stiff Victorian, but he was a serious scholar in a number of subjects. His letters to his family are replete with humorous stories, something his scholarship was rightfully devoid of. Although he was intellectually ambitious, he did not use this ambition to attain the highest rank. He could have done so; his backers included General John McAlister Schofield; Joseph Holt, the judge advocate general during most of the Civil War; and at least one secretary of war, William C. Endicott. Instead, he disliked officers who engaged in personal aggrandizement at the expense of the army. Although Winthrop seldom disparaged others, there were four soldiers he expressed his personal disgust toward: General Daniel Sickles; Colonel Hiram Berdan, the commanding officer of the First United States Sharpshooters; and two judge advocates, Thomas Barr and Asa Bird Gardner. Winthrop found Gardner unethical and believed his actions in a highly visible court-martial of an African American cadet to be both unjust and a discredit to the army.

These aspects of Winthrop have been absent from the few, often inaccurate sketches of his life found in military and law journals. So, too, has Winthrop's early life and the role of his legal education been ignored. His egalitarian approach in the first court-martial of a black cadet at West Point, his prosecution of a sitting United States congressman, and the impetus for his publishing several long-lasting influential works on military law have all been absent from these biographical sketches. The best biography—written in 1956 by George Prugh, a World War II veteran and later the judge advocate general of the army from 1971 to 1975—stated a truism about Winthrop: "The writers of great legal treatises usually fade into obscurity while their work remains unchallenged."[3]

This biography brings Winthrop out of obscurity. The early chapters detail Winthrop's life and legal development through the Civil War. Later chapters encompass his contributions to the development of the modern military. Dissecting his individual contributions requires both a thematic and chronological approach, which is how the latter chapters are formatted. As a result, there is some overlap between the chapters detailing later parts of his life.

Because Winthrop's work is so important to the field of military law, his two principle treatises, *Military Law* and *Military Law and Precedents*, are analyzed throughout the second half of the biography, both for their accuracy as to the time he wrote them, as well as their continued relevance. His legal philosophy partly reflected a jurisprudential school dominated by Oliver Wendell Holmes and partly reflected an internationalist and comparative law school, while still addressing the unique disciplinary needs of the army.

William Winthrop's traceable family roots date back to before the European discovery of America, but it is in colonial America where the Winthrop family first rose to high prominence. The first Winthrop in America, John Winthrop (1588–1649), was also the first colonial governor of Massachusetts. He was a devout Puritan and a university-trained lawyer. Chosen as governor in 1629, from the start he sought to enlarge the colony's population with the crown's blessing. In 1630, he led a fleet of eleven ships carrying over seven hundred passengers to what was then called the New World. The main, but not only, reason behind his drive to bring people to the Massachusetts Colony was to establish a haven for beleaguered Puritans. In effect, Winthrop wanted to establish a "new Zion," established on faith and Christian rules.[4] During John Winthrop's life, it was unclear whether Protestantism would survive at all. In the first hundred years after Martin Luther began the Reformation, Europe was replete with wars and atrocities committed between Catholic and Protestant forces. At the same time as the religious infighting infested Europe, a series of parallel conflicts arose in Britain with almost equally destructive results.

John Winthrop was known, in his day, for authoring a particular sermon titled, "City on a Hill," or "Model of Christian Charity." The contents of that sermon present a theme that characterized the Winthrop family through its generations down to William Winthrop and his siblings. In that sermon, John Winthrop stressed a covenant with the new world and its Christian community, forgiveness and love to an enemy, charity to the poor, and public service. Historians in William Winthrop's time characterized John Winthrop as practicing these mores in his personal life and leadership, and expecting his family to do the same.[5]

The histories of early Massachusetts published during William Winthrop's early life portrayed John Winthrop as instrumental in the survival of the Puritan faith and the colonies. In W. H. Carpenter's 1853 *The History of Massachusetts, from Its Earliest Settlement to the Present Time,* Winthrop had "in the midst of dangers from without and civil dissensions from within, remained firm and steadfast to the best interests of the colony." Likewise, John Barry, in his 1855 *History of Massachusetts,* wrote, "God entrusted to John Winthrop the leadership of the colony." Barry further characterized John Winthrop as "dignified, yet unassuming; learned, yet no pedant . . . benevolent, cordial, he was the man for the colony, every way elaborated and perfected for its purposes." And, in an 1831 school textbook lauding John Winthrop, the text stated, "Winthrop was distinguished for his talents and virtues; his wealth and affluence, hospitality, piety, and integrity. He was a lawyer by profession and he relieved the needy."[6]

John Winthrop's son, John Winthrop the Younger (1606–1676), was the first colonial governor of Connecticut. Early on, the younger Winthrop shone not only as a political leader but also as a man of science, arts, and letters. He published treatises on the geography and flora of the northeast which were so well received that he gained enough prominence to be admitted into the prestigious Royal Society.[7] Included in the list of the Royal Society's membership were such contemporaries as Francis Bacon, Christopher Wren, Samuel Pepys, and Sir Isaac Newton. Later, the same society included Benjamin Franklin. During a trip to Britain in 1634, Winthrop the Younger was commissioned by the crown to build a fort on the mouth of the Connecticut River and was appointed as the Connecticut Colony's first governor for a one-year term.

Three years later, war broke between settlers and their Mohegan and Naranganset Indian allies on one side, and the Pequot Indian tribe on the other. The war ended in a disastrous defeat for the Pequots. In popular lore, the Pequots were portrayed as the aggressors, yet the war appears to have occurred as part of a struggle between the tribes and settlers for economic gain. But the war's combatants each justified their participation in the war on the ground of self-defense.[8]

Although Winthrop the Younger was in Massachusetts at the time of the conflict, it did not prevent him from influencing military policy during and after the war. Nor did it prevent his father from providing guidance to the settlers on dealing with the remaining Pequots. The victorious settlers wholly disbanded the Pequots, selling some into slavery in the West Indies and others to local Mohawk tribes. The elder Winthrop brought some of the captured Pequots into his house to work as servants, sparing them from deportation to the Barbados. Included in this number was a family, as the elder Winthrop could not countenance splitting up a whole family for the purpose of slavery.[9] As to the rest of the Pequots, their conditions in the Mohawk tribes so offended the younger Winthrop, he argued for them to be brought back to their lands, earning him a reputation for justice among his contemporaries. Forty years later when war broke out between the Colonists and a number of other Indian tribes, the Pequots allied with the Colonists.[10] In 1657, the younger Winthrop was reelected governor by the colony, and he served in that capacity until his death.

As in the case of the elder Winthrop, the younger son was heroically portrayed in a number of histories in publication during William Winthrop's life. In 1838, historian Edward Lambert, in a history of New Haven, credited the younger Winthrop with bringing an "amicable peace and tranquility" to the union of the New Haven and Connecticut colonies. W. H. Carpenter's *The History of Connecticut from Its Earliest Settlement* labeled the younger Winthrop as "wise and patient with Connecticut owing its tranquility to him." At the same time, G. H. Hollister's *History of Connecticut* described the younger Winthrop as "one of the finest chemists of his age, an excellent physician, and as a diplomatist he had no superior in his day."[11]

The younger John Winthrop's children continued in public service and also took a leading role in a war far more dangerous to the survival of the colony than the Pequot conflict. His eldest son, John Winthrop III, or "Fitz-John" Winthrop (1639–1707) as he became known, commanded colonial militia against French and Indian forces in North America. He also commanded forces in Scotland and served in the court of William III. In 1698, Fitz-John Winthrop was elected as governor of the Connecticut Colony, bringing with him, according to W. H. Carpenter, "three years of uninterrupted tranquility."[12]

A second son, John Wait Still Winthrop (1643–1717), served as both a major general in the Massachusetts colonial militia and as an admiralty judge. Toward the end of his life, he became the chief justice of the Massachusetts colonial courts. In this capacity, he was a jurist during the notorious 1692 Salem witch trials.[13]

John Winthrop the Younger participated in King Philip's War, though Winthrop the Younger did not live to see its full termination. The war was fought in a particularly vicious manner, in part because the settlers believed their survival, and that of Christianity, hinged on their complete victory.[14]

Despite the war, most of the Winthrop line remained attracted to careers in law and politics, rather than the profession of arms, though a number would continue to serve in militias. A number of Winthrops commanded militia units during both King William's War (1689–1697) and Queen Anne's War (1702–1713) against France and its Indian allies. Wait Still's eldest surviving son, John Winthrop IV (1681–1747), served as a jurist in the Massachusetts Colony after graduating from Harvard in 1700. John Winthrop IV spent a life in academia as well, teaching at Harvard and researching topics in natural sciences such as the trajectory of Venus and the causes of earthquakes. Like his grandfather, he was admitted into the Royal Society; contributions in astronomy, math, and physics gained Winthrop IV this honor. He was considered one of the foremost astronomers of his day.[15]

John Winthrop IV's children were active in the administration of Harvard University and local government in Massachusetts. A number of Winthrops fought on the Colonists' side during the Revolutionary War against the British Crown, but then returned to their political and legal occupations. Thomas Lindall Winthrop (1760–1841), one of the younger John Winthrop's great-grandsons (and William Winthrop's great-great uncle), became the lieutenant governor of the state of Massachusetts. His son, Robert Charles Winthrop (1809–1894), was also a career politician.

First elected to Congress as a Whig in 1840, Robert Charles Winthrop rose to become the Speaker of the House of Representatives. Robert Charles was also a family historian, authoring a number of volumes on the life of the early Winthrops. A contemporary of Daniel Webster, Robert Charles was appointed to fill Webster's Senate seat when Webster moved on to become the secretary of state in 1850. As a young adult, Robert Charles had apprenticed in Webster's law office. Robert Charles was unable to hold onto the seat, losing it in a primary election, though he remained politically important in Boston long after he retired from politics. However, Robert Charles later made unfortunate political alliances, campaigning for Millard Fillmore in 1856, John Bell in 1860, and George McClellan in 1864.[16] He also advocated for unpopular and—in William Winthrop's opinion—immoral causes after leaving politics, such as the accommodation of slavery.

Robert Charles was a benefactor to William Winthrop in the 1850s, when, for a three-year period, Winthrop lived in Boston, studied at Harvard, and then practiced law there. This brought Winthrop into contact with Webster, Clay, and other prominent Whigs. Moreover, Winthrop's early letters mention Robert Charles and his opinions on politics as important to his own views. A search of Winthrop's correspondence yields no indication of affinity between the two men, nor any evidence of animosity. There is, however, a break in ideology between the two which occurred on the eve of the war. Robert Charles remained a conservative Whig at heart, long after the party disappeared, while Winthrop embraced the Republican Party.

Like Robert Charles Winthrop, William Winthrop traced his ancestry through John Still Winthrop. John Still was the eldest son of John Winthrop IV. His second-born son, Francis Bayard Winthrop (1754–1817), was a Yale graduate and wealthy New Haven mercantilist. Francis Bayard's second-born son (William Winthrop's father) was also named Francis Bayard (1787–1841). This Francis Bayard followed in his father's footsteps and attended Yale, earning a degree in law. He also inherited some of his father's mercantile business. His business interests were both in New York and New Haven. This Winthrop branch appeared to abandon the family tradition of political leadership, but in its place sought positions in the legal profession as well as academia.[17]

Through his mother Elizabeth Woolsey, Winthrop's lineage also included an impressive array of men involved in the shaping of the United States. Elizabeth Woolsey descended from Jonathan Edwards (1703–1758), a prominent Puritan minister who sought to reverse a trend of blandly teaching religion and a return to faith with passion. It is interesting to note that Edwards himself descended from John Winthrop the elder, as well as through Cotton Mather, another seventeenth-century religious giant.[18] His mother was also a cousin to George Hoadly (1826–1902), Ohio's thirty-sixth governor. Hoadly's father had been the mayor of New Haven, Connecticut, and then moved the family to Cleveland. Although not documented in any surviving letters, the fact that Hoadly and Salmon Chase were law partners in the 1850s, and lifelong friends after, gave Winthrop a possible avenue into government service.

One of Elizabeth Woolsey's great uncles, Timothy Dwight IV (1752–1817), was a president of Yale University. Her brother, Theodore Dwight

Woolsey (1801–1899), also served as president of Yale University from 1846 to 1871. After the death of Francis Bayard Winthrop, Theodore Woolsey became one of the two most important influences in William Winthrop's life. Woolsey was active in the Anti-Slavery Association and the African Improvement Association of New Haven.[19] The Improvement Association included both whites and blacks in an attempt to overcome racial prejudices in the city.[20] Later, Woolsey denounced both the Fugitive Slave Act and the Kansas-Nebraska Act as an evil affront to civilization.

In nineteenth-century academia, just as it was common for grandfathers to pass along business interests to sons and grandsons, so too were professional relationships passed along and intertwined across family lines. Dr. Woolsey's international law scholarship brought him into a friendship with another renowned scholar, Professor Francis Lieber, who wrote the first law of war model code for Union forces in the Civil War.[21] Together, Lieber and Woolsey advised President Lincoln on the "Alabama Affair," a significant international law issue implicating relations with Britain and France during the Civil War.[22]

Dr. Lieber's son, Norman G. Lieber, became the judge advocate general of the army in 1884, with William Winthrop serving as his deputy. An additional interesting connection to the military and the Dwights—and by implication Winthrop—existed at this time. The father of the future commanding general of the Army of the Potomac, George Brinton McClellan, had been a student of Theodore Dwight, and the latter was an enormous influence on the father.[23] But this was not the only thread connecting Winthrop to McClellan. The Winthrop family and McClellan shared a mutual friendship with the steamship magnate William Aspinwall.[24]

Francis Bayard and Elizabeth Woolsey married in 1816, with Theodore Woolsey presiding at the wedding. Francis Bayard had been married once before, to Elsie Rogers, and fathered three children. Two of his children grew into adulthood. One son, Edward, became a prominent Episcopal clergyman in New York. Francis Bayard Winthrop's first wife died in 1814, and he remarried two years later.

Francis Bayard and Elizabeth Woolsey had three daughters and two sons who grew into adulthood. Their eldest child, Elizabeth Woolsey, lived the longest, until 1907, and became a family historian. Their second daughter, Laura Winthrop, was born in 1825 and became a writer and poet, publishing a child's story in 1854 and a collection of poetry titled *Poems of Twenty Years* in 1874 under the pen name of Emily Hare. Her short stories and poetry were printed in the popular nineteenth-century journals *Scribner's* and the *Atlantic*. She also published a poetry collection of her brother, Theodore, after he was killed in the Civil War. In 1846, she married William Templeton Johnson and moved to New York shortly after.[25] A third daughter, Sarah Chauncey, was born to Francis and Elizabeth in 1834 and married Theodore Weston, whose younger brother Roswell served alongside William during the Civil War.[26]

Born on September 22, 1828, Francis and Elizabeth's eldest son, Theodore, had the most promising literary future in the family, and after Theodore's death, William Winthrop expended considerable energy maintaining his brother's literary efforts in public view. By all accounts from his siblings and other observers of the family, he was the promising star of the family; boisterous, intelligent, and fearless. Theodore Winthrop matriculated at Yale University as a sixteen-year-old and graduated with high standing as well as achieving the prestigious Clark Scholarship. While at Yale, he excelled in Greek and metaphysics, although he was expelled for one semester for throwing a brick through a window. His best friend in college was a native of South Carolina, and on the eve of war, the two promised not to shoot each other. After college, Theodore traveled through Europe and returned in 1852 to study law as an apprentice to a Staten Island attorney. While he lived in Staten Island, he resided at his sister Laura's house. The law bored him and he traveled frequently, joining an expedition to Panama, as well as venturing through the Pacific Northwest and back across the country, where he met Brigham Young.[27]

Theodore was the first young Winthrop to completely break free of the family's Whig ideology, though William eventually followed. Theodore was involved in early Republican Party politics. He worked on John C. Fremont's campaign for the presidency in 1856.[28] Fremont must have appealed to Theodore as a fellow adventurer since, at the time, Fremont was perhaps best known for his western explorations. But the draw of Republican politics to a New Englander also meant one thing above all others: the abolition of slavery. Fremont ran on a platform that was first and foremost hostile to the institution of slavery.[29]

Theodore was fluent in Greek and earned money in a trip across Europe by tutoring the children of wealthy Americans he met along the way. He was known for magazine articles he authored on the eve of the Civil War, but these mainly had to do with travels and his brief life in the army. After Theodore died in 1861, his sister Laura and brother William discovered a number of his writings, took on the onus of editing three novels and other stories, and sought to have them published through family friends. William also took it upon himself to see that Theodore lived on, in name instead of in body. But in doing so, he also ensured Theodore would remain the more popular of the two during his life. This makes sense when one considers William's character. He was modest and throughout his military life sought no public laurels for his bravery in battle.

Little is known about William's youth in New Haven other than the schools he attended and the town he lived in. Like Theodore, William was educated at the Stiles School. Francis Bayard Winthrop took a detailed interest into his sons' education and augmented their school readings with selections from his vast library. He also shared with his sons his love of nature. Francis took his sons on various travels, including one trip to Georgia. He also imparted to them the meaning of the name *Winthrop*. It was a name which conveyed tremendous prestige. However, Francis Bayard could not spend all of his time with his sons. His legal and commercial interests brought him to Staten Island on a regular basis, and the family joined him during the summers in New York. Both boys and Sarah Winthrop also played with Lillie Blake and the four developed an early friendship.[30]

Francis Bayard also reared his sons in the Whig political philosophy. As a wealthy merchant, this made sense. The exposure to Whig politics was not borne out of any intent to have the boys enter political life. Both parents strongly advocated a classical education and literary excellence, over public oratory. It may be the case that William initially embraced Whig ideology from a number of different sources of exposure, including Robert Charles Winthrop, as well as the town of New Haven itself. However, even in New Haven a new anti-slave movement had taken root, likely as a result of a cargo of African slaves accidentally appearing in the town.

In the 1830s, New Haven was a small, geographically isolated town, although it was the largest town in Connecticut. Its population was homogeneous, mainly composed of English descendants. It remained an American Puritan, Congregationalist town. However, to boys valuing formal education or desiring knowledge of a world outside the town, it probably was not stifling, since its main feature was Yale University. The Winthrops and Woolseys were intimately tied to the university, receiving their education at Yale and serving on boards of trustees, if not the faculty, there.

New Haven's economy partly relied on sea and canal commerce that brought in a number of sailors and other tradesmen from around the world. One of the more significant events to occur during William's youth had to do with the arrival of Africans who had seized control of a Spanish slave ship, the *Amistad*, in 1839. The legal and political questions arising from this incident dominated the town, as it did the presidency of Martin Van Buren and the Supreme Court. The incident occurred when William Winthrop was eight years old, and while there is no surviving correspondence indicating he knew of the *Amistad* or formed an opinion of it at that early age, he possibly joined Theodore in visiting the Africans, bringing them food, clothing, and bibles.[31]

For reasons later touched on, as a youth, William Winthrop probably accepted a uniquely Northern Whig view that condemned slavery as an evil, but viewed the abolition of it by federal decrees an equal evil. Later in life when he embraced the Republican platform seeking the abolition of slavery, Winthrop looked back on the *Amistad* incident as proof of the institution's immorality, as well as the law's ability to right a wrong.

New Haven also had an industrial base. Eli Whitney, a Yale graduate and inventor of the cotton gin, established an arms factory in the northern part of the town. Southern cotton was essential to the New England economy, and Connecticut had a number of "Cotton Whig" politicians who viewed slavery as an amoral economic necessity.

But the town was inconvenient for travel to other areas of the United States. Until 1848, New Haven and New York were a day's journey apart. That year, a rail line connected the two, reducing the journey to a few hours. In 1830, the census listed New Haven as having a permanent residency base of 10,678. Ten years later, the population climbed to 14,390.[32] In comparison to the crime rate in New York and Boston, New Haven's crime rate remained relatively low, and patterns of immigration, including the growing influx of Catholics, which were then occurring in New York and Boston, had not impacted New Haven to a similar degree. It was essentially a small town which embraced its Protestant faith and, at the same time, looked on the growth of executive power as undesirable.

During William Winthrop's youth, New Haven politics, like the rest of Connecticut, was almost dominated by the Whig Party. From the election of 1844 onward, the state reliably voted Whig in every election until the demise of the party in 1852. But New Haven's Whig loyalties ran deeper than most of the rest of the state. In 1836, Martin van Buren edged the Whig challenger, William Henry Harrison, by a count of 19,291 votes to 18,754 in Connecticut. In New Haven, Harrison took 3,476 votes to van Buren's 3,420.[33] Four years later when the two candidates were in an election rematch, Harrison's candidacy was backed by 5,100 New Haven votes to van Buren's 4,013.[34] This trend continued through to the last national election involving a Whig Party candidate in 1852. New Haven also showed another ideology involving antislavery as a political as well as religious movement. In the election of 1848, New Haven voters gave Whig candidate Zachary Taylor 5,273 votes, and Democrat Louis Cass, 4,517. However, a Free Soil candidate, the former Democrat president Martin van Buren, earned 806 votes.[35]

In 1856, three years after William left for Massachusetts, Connecticut favored the nascent Republican Party, voting for its first presidential candidate, John C. Fremont, over the Democrat James Buchanan, 42,717 votes to 34,997. The third party candidate, Know-Nothing Millard Fillmore, received 2,615 votes. New Haven was no different. Fremont won 7,975 votes to Buchanan's 7,315, with Fillmore barely registering.[36]

Most of New Haven's residents appeared to support the *Amistad* Africans rather than the various claims of a number of owners. The state's politicians tended, however, to campaign on temperance, antigambling, and bankruptcy reform. New Haven witnessed a number of "Congregationalist revivals" as part of America's "Second Great Awakening," which likely contributed to the support of the *Amistad* Africans. By the 1820s, New England Protestant evangelical movements tended to be abolitionist. As of 1830, nativism had yet to affect Connecticut politics to any cognizable degree.[37] Catholicism did not gain a foothold in Connecticut until the late 1830s, and very few foreign-born residents lived in the state, though New Haven may have been an exception as a port town.[38]

Through his tenth year in New Haven, the forces which shaped William's life were his family's ideology, which was not simply a political ideology, but also a social and economic set of values as well. He was wealthy and had the advantage of a prominent family, but he was not entirely shielded from the whole of the New Haven population, or that of the country. His family was entirely Whig in their orientation, although for reasons noted in the following chapter, this label meant more than a political alliance. Still, as a youth, Winthrop met with, and was influenced by, some of the leading Americans of his day: Daniel Webster, Henry Clay, Robert Charles Winthrop, and Theodore Dwight Woolsey.

NOTES

1. Andrew S. Effron, "Military Justice: The Continuing Importance of Historical Perspective," *Army Lawyer*, June 2000, 4.
2. See, for example, *Hamdi v. Rumsfeld*, 542 U.S. 507 (2004).
3. George Prugh, "Colonel William Winthrop: The Tradition of the Military Lawyer," *American Bar Association Journal* 42, no. 2 (May 1956), 126. In his article, General Prugh compares Winthrop to Thomas Cooley, one of the early commentators on American Tort Law. However, the federal appeals courts continue to cite Winthrop with regularity. This is not the case with Cooley.
4. Francis J. Bremer, *John Winthrop: America's Forgotten Founding Father* (London: Oxford, 2003), 181–184.
5. See, for example, William H. Carpenter, *The History of Massachusetts, from Its Earliest Settlement to the Present Time* (Philadelphia: J.B. Lippincott, 1853), 111–112; John Stetson Barry, *The History of Massachusetts: The Colonial Period* (Boston: Phillips Sampson and Co., 1855), 184.
6. Carpenter, *The History of Massachusetts*, 111. Carpenter also proclaimed Winthrop "devoted his own personal efforts to maintain the purity of the religious tenets he espoused." See also, Barry, *The History of Massachusetts*, 184, and *Conversations of the History of Massachusetts from Its First Settlement to the Present Period for the Use of Schools and Families* (Boston: Munroe and Francis, 1831), 45–46.
7. James Grant Wilson, ed., *Appleton's Cyclodpaedia of American Biography*, vol. VI (New York: D. Appleton and Co., 1887), 547.

8. See Steven Katz, "The Pequot War Reconsidered," *New England Quarterly* 64, no. 2 (June 1991), 208; Alex Axelrod, *America's Wars* (New York: Wiley and Sons, 2002), 18.

9. Bremer, *John Winthrop*, 273; see also, "Trumbell's History of Connecticut," *The North American Review* 8, no. 22 (1818), 93.

10. Katz, "The Pequot War Reconsidered," 233.

11. Edward R. Lambert, *History of the Colony of New Haven, Before and After the Union with Connecticut* (New Haven: Hitchcock and Stafford, 1838), 31; William H. Carpenter, *The History of Connecticut from Its Earliest Settlement to Its Present Time* (Philadelphia: J. B. Lippincott, 1854), 122; G. H. Hollister, *The History of Connecticut from the First Settlement of the Colony to Its Present Constitution* (New Haven: Durrie and Peck, 1855), 299.

12. Carpenter, *The History of Connecticut*, 137.

13. See, for example, Marion L. Starkey, *The Devil in Massachusetts: A Modern Inquiry into the Salem Witch Trials* (New York: Dolphin Press, 1949), 152.

14. Philip Ranlet, "Another Look at the Causes of King Philip's War," *New England Quarterly* 61, no. 2 (June 1988), 94–95.

15. Daniel J. Boorstin, *The Americans: The Colonial Experience* (New York: Vintage, 1958), 245.

16. Sean Wilintz, *The Rise of American Democracy: Jefferson to Lincoln* (New York: W.W. Norton and Co., 2005); Stephen Sears, *George B. McClellan: The Young Napoleon* (New York: Da Capo, 1999), 378–382.

17. Benjamin W. Dwight, *The History of the Descendants of John Dwight of Dedham Mass*, vol. 1 (New York: John F. Throw and Son, 1874), 253. As in the case of the inheritors of early descendants of wealth, this book was commissioned as a family history, to show the "lineage of the best and early Religious families of New England." See also, Elbridge Colby, *Theodore Winthrop* (New York: Twayne Publishers, 1965), 17.

18. Francis J. Brenner, *The Purtian Experiment: New England Society from Bradford to Edwards* (Hannover, MA: University Press of New England, 1995), 228–229.

19. George A. King, *Theodore Dwight Woolsey: His Political and Social Ideas* (Chicago: Loyola University Press, 1956), 43–46; Wilson, *Appleton's Cyclopaedia*, 12.

20. Robert Senior, *New England Congregationalists and the Anti Slavery Movement* (Ann Arbor, MI: University Microfilms, 1954), 36–39; Robert Austin Warner, *New Haven Negroes: A Social History* (New York: Arno Press, 1969), 46–47.

21. Joseph Henry Thayer, "Theodore Woolsey, Reminisces," *Atlantic Monthly* 64 (October 1889), 559.

22. John A. Bolles, "Why Semmes of the Alabama Was Not Tried," *Atlantic Monthly* 30 (July 1872), 88.

23. Ethan S. Rafuse, *McClellan's War: The Failure of Moderation in the Struggle for the Union* (Bloomington: Indiana University Press, 2005), 12–13.

24. For McClellan's connection to Aspinwall, see Stephen Sears, ed., *The Civil War Papers of George B. McClellan: Selected Correspondence, 1860–1865* (Boston: Ticknor and Fields, 1989), 365. In 1862, McClellan wrote to Aspinwall seeking advice on his postwar civilian career.

25. Eugene Woolf, *Theodore Winthrop: Portrait of an American Author* (Washington, DC: University Press of America, 1981), 8.

26. Lawrence Mayo, *The Winthrop Family in America* (Boston: Massachusetts Historical Society, 1948), 273.

27. Woolf, *Theodore Winthrop*, 8–10; Frank Moore, ed., *The Portrait Gallery of the War: A Biographical Record* (New York: D. Van Nostrand and Co., 1865), 97–99.

28. Dumas Malone, ed., *Dictionary of American Biography*, vol. 20 (New York: Charles Scribner's Sons, 1936), 417.

29. James Grant Wilson and John Fiske, eds., *Appleton's Cyclopaedia of American Biography*, vol. VI (New York: D. Appleton and Co., 1889), 577; Malone, *Dictionary of American Biography*, 417.

30. Grace Farrell, *Lillie Devereux Blake: Retracing a Life Erased* (Amherst: University of Massachusetts Press, 2002), 7–13.

31. Woolf, *Theodore Winthrop*, 9.

32. Colby, *Theodore Winthrop*, 19.

33. Michael J. Durbin, *United States Presidential Elections, 1788–1860: The Official Results by County and State* (Jefferson, NC: McFarland and Co., 2002), 62.

34. Durbin, *United States Presidential Elections*, 73.

35. Durbin, *United States Presidential Elections*, 98.

36. Durbin, *United States Presidential Elections*, 135–137.

37. Jarvis M. Morse, *A Neglected Period of Connecticut's History: 1818–1850* (New Haven: Yale University Press, 1933), 123–125.

38. Morse, *A Neglected Period*, 286.

2

From Youth to Yale: The Making of a Legal Mind

To further my studies in the law of nations as I find trover uninteresting in comparison.

—William Winthrop to his sister Sarah Winthrop

William's youth consisted of the normal activities one might expect of a boy born into his family's social station. In addition to his elite private school program, he freely traversed New Haven with his friends and his brother, Theodore. He attended the social engagements of the upper tier of New Haven society, though his youth was not entirely spent in frivolous, opulent social affairs. His parents imparted a love of nature and literature on William as they had done with Theodore. However, he did not spend his entire youth in New Haven or with Theodore. With the death of his father, his mother decided it was best for William to be raised in a house which had a father figure. Beginning in 1841, he was sent to his Aunt Sarah and Uncle Charles's house in Owego, New York. At the same time, Theodore spent some time with his older half-brother, Edward Winthrop, an Episcopal clergyman in Marietta, Ohio.

In 1835, Elizabeth Woolsey Winthrop's sister, Sarah W. Woolsey, married Charles F. Johnson, a prominent New York attorney. Johnson's father, Robert Charles Johnson, who was also an attorney, owned considerable tracts of land around Owego, which he probated to Charles F. Johnson. Likewise, the Woolseys owned large tracts of land in the surrounding area. Winthrop's aunt and uncle parented two sons and a daughter, all younger than William. Charles F. Johnson likely picked up Winthrop's education where Francis Bayard had left it. Like the Winthrops, the Johnsons possessed a large library. Charles Johnson was not merely an attorney; he was also an inventor who patented an atmospheric dock for raising ships, as well as a tumbler lock. At some point, he gained a mastery of Latin and translated a book of Roman poetry. His two sons mirrored his academic pursuits. The older son, Charles Frederick Johnson Jr., became a professor of literature at Trinity College, and William Woolsey Johnson, a professor of draughting at the United States Naval Academy.[1]

Situated in Tioga County on the Susquehanna River, the lightly populated upstate New York town was surrounded by forested hills. Evidence for the exact date of Winthrop's departure to Owego is unclear, and his cousin Lillie Blake's diary only mentions her playing with Theodore and Sarah Winthrop in New Haven. Clearly William was absent from New Haven after his tenth year.[2]

Owego was established in 1788 from land taken from the Iroquois Confederation. Its economy consisted mainly of farms, and like many small towns it had a church school, a town doctor, and a small legal practice. In the early 1840s, Owego was isolated from many of the influences of large urban areas such as New York. The small town had a homogeneous white Protestant population. New York City was a two-day journey by horse. On foot, it took considerably longer. It was not until 1849 that Owego was connected to New York City by rail.

A number of wealthy New York and New England families owned land in Tioga County and collected rents from tenant farmers, who composed the bulk of the population. As the Winthrops were involved in Whig politics, so too were the Johnsons. However, unlike New Haven, Tioga County was a Democrat-leaning area. In 1836 and 1840, its voters gave Martin van Buren a sizeable majority over Whig William Henry Harrison. The first time its residents favored a Whig candidate was in 1848, when 1,782 of its residents voted for Zachary Taylor over 1,683 for Democrat Louis Cass, and 789 for the Free Soil candidate van Buren. It may be the case that van Buren received some of these votes as a "favorite son" from upstate New York instead of for his Free Soil politics. On the other hand, Free Soil politics were welcomed by many of the farm renters for the simple fact that these renters believed Southern slavery placed them at an economic disadvantage.

In 1852, the Democrat candidate Franklin Pierce received 2,815 votes to war hero Winfield Scott's 2,234.[3] Scott did not run an energetic campaign and the incumbent Whig president Millard Fillmore did little to help Scott. The 1852 election was the last time the Democrats took a majority in Tioga County until the turn of the century. In 1856, John C. Fremont, the Republican candidate, prevailed over Buchanan—3,331 votes to 2,154. Nativist Millard Fillmore received 435 votes in the same election.[4] It may have been the case that by 1856 the Tioga County voters transferred their antipathy of Whig elitism to an antipathy toward the Southern Democrat slave-owning class and their Northern Douglas Democrat allies, who were also viewed as oppressive elites. Support to Fremont might also have been part of a process of increasing Free Soil politics. Free Soilers viewed slavery not only as an immoral institution, but also an economic injustice to non-slaveholding white farmers. From 1856 through the end of the century, Tioga County remained largely Republican.

Throughout his time in Owego, Winthrop remained a Whig, largely as a result of his family's influence over him. Like a number of other Northern Whigs, Winthrop may have viewed slavery as immoral but did not join a third party such as the Free Soil or Liberty parties. Moreover, his interests were focused on his studies and in the nature surrounding him.

Although William's letters indicate he was well cared for in a warm home, he was not always happy to be away from his immediate family in New Haven. In particular, he found the town school unchallenging and unfriendly. In more than one instance, he concluded his letters with a dour note on the "foolish Presbyterian schoolmaster." His commentary on the social life of the area was bleak, and describing a "little juvenile party at Ms. Platt's over the way," he concluded with the statement, "but I did not have much fun." To his younger sister, Sarah, he provided the encouraging words, "I think, though I want to say for certain, that you will grow up to be a fine woman if you obey ma and Cousin Charles."[5]

As he grew into adulthood, Winthrop continued to write to his mother and sisters in New Haven and New York, and unsurprisingly his letters became more descriptive of the people and events in his life. If he felt lonesome or disappointed in his family separation, Winthrop did not show it, and he always ended his letters with a statement of affection for his mother. Sometimes he wrote with a hint of sarcasm, ending his letters with commentary such as "my love to Grandma and the rest of the domestic department." He surrounded himself with animals, his favorite being a horse named Phoenix that he boasted "galloped harder than any horse I ever rode on."[6] William also occasionally shared a room with his cousin, Robert Charles Winthrop Jr., the son of the Speaker of the House of Representatives. He and the younger Robert Charles developed a friendship which lasted at least to the Civil War.[7]

Aunt Sarah ensured Winthrop's social life was lively as he attended a number of parties and other social events. When he described these events, he did so in assuring detail for his mother, writing of one, "the repast was a singular one. I thought of as 'mixture or conglomerate.' It consisted of the following articles—bread, tea, plum sweetmeats, custards, pickles, curds, mushrooms, and something else that I cannot remember just now."[8] His letters do not display a hint of unhappiness with his surroundings. Still, despite the warmth of his aunt and uncle, as well as his love of upstate New York, he must have felt a longing for something more than a small Presbyterian school and a home that, while it welcomed him, was not his own. On the other hand, he immersed himself in books while living in Owego, mastering German and French, a skill that thirty years later assisted his military law studies as he investigated the military disciplinary systems of Prussia and France.

William frequented Owego as a young adult, even while he attended Yale. Writing to Laura in 1849 prior to his departure to begin his junior year at Yale University, Winthrop noted that during the summer, he and a friend named George Watson had studied together, partly out of fear that they would lose "all our classical knowledge." But his studies were not merely relegated to classroom requirements. On his own, Winthrop "roamed about in the woods, sometimes ascending high hills in search of birds of prey." He maintained his independent interest in the study of nature, describing the forests "of dense bushwood" and "the Susquehanna as it flows by in silent majesty through its channel." In addition to his nature observations, Winthrop hunted small game, writing that he bagged "some red squirrels, and a woodchuck." Whatever his feelings on hunting small game, he wrote of an instance where he shot a hawk; "taking deliberate aim, it fell to the ground with a crash." In a telling instant which later repeated itself on his view of taking human life in the Civil War, he wrote, "I shan't forget his dying look, it was one of mingled rage and offended vanity and I was not glad I shot him."[9] He also wrote openly of his interest in the local women, describing one as "quite countrified" and another who's expression reminded him of "Rosa," but "could not at all compare with her."[10]

In addition to living in Owego, Winthrop also spent a good deal of time in the nearby town of Geneva, New York, with his other relatives. Unlike Owego, Geneva appears to have been a vacation spot for the Winthrop family, rather than a home. His sister Laura and her husband, William Templeton Johnson, owned a summer home in Geneva. Winthrop celebrated his birthday with a long horseback ride through the Finger Lakes area with a young woman named Charlotte Morse. At the same time, he compared his riding companion with another young woman, likely known to his sisters, named Rosa. One had bright eyes, and the other did not. But his main thoughts were with the prior term at Yale, where he spent all of his time "cramming for examinations," which he "got through well and better than expected." He was not completely out of physical contact with his family. Winthrop concluded this letter with a brief report on Laura's infant child as looking "prettier and prettier every day."[11]

Winthrop was admitted to Yale in 1848, the same year that his brother was expelled for acts of vandalism. Yale University was dominated by its president, his uncle Theodore Dwight Woolsey. Woolsey entered Yale at fifteen years of age and was the valedictorian of the class of 1820. He became a paid tutor in law at Yale in 1825, a professor shortly after, and the university president in 1848. Prior to his assumption of the school presidency, he was ordained a Congregationalist minister. Woolsey taught Greek and history, but international law and political science were his primary focus. In 1860, he authored a treatise on international law titled *Introduction to the Study of International Law,* which became a common text in United States colleges. Like William, Woolsey's legal treatises have been cited by the Supreme Court. He also wrote for *The Independent,* a Congregationalist journal William was to contribute to a half century later.[12]

Unlike students of its rival in Cambridge, Massachusetts, Yale's students were increasingly antislavery and this may have been the result of Woolsey's influence. He was active in the Anti-Slavery Association and championed Free Soil politics. He did not possess a staunch allegiance to the Whig Party, though he tended to support their anti-Jacksonian platforms. He took a leadership role in the African Improvement Association of New Haven, where he worked alongside freemen and considered race no bar to equality. Woolsey ensured the Yale administration stood against the Fugitive Slave Law. Woolsey publicly argued that the Kansas-Nebraska Act was unconstitutional, and he may have had a role in helping a group of students purchase Sharps Rifles for distribution to antislave factions in Kansas. When the Republican Party came into being, Woolsey developed an allegiance to it, backing every Republican candidate from Fremont through Benjamin Harrison. If Woolsey influenced a generation of Yale students, he clearly was instrumental in forming Winthrop's belief in the immorality of slavery as well as racial equality.[13]

Under Woolsey, Yale University demanded its students maintain their devotion both to their Protestant faith and their studies. In the 1840s, a student was expelled for advocating "freethinking" beliefs. Publicly stated doubts on the existence of an almighty were not tolerated. In the early 1850s, Lillie Blake and George Hastings, an undergraduate student and close friend of William's, were involved in an amorous relationship creating a scandal which led to Hastings' expulsion from the university. The expulsion did not destroy William's friendship with Hastings. Indeed, the two men served alongside each other in combat during the Civil War.[14]

During his presidency, Theodore Woolsey drove the school to improve the undergraduate program by making it more rigorous. Greek and Latin were required subjects as was metaphysics. Woolsey brought science studies to a level of prominence not before reached by developing courses of study in chemistry, astronomy, and mineralogy. He supported the development of literary organizations such as the *Yale Literary Magazine*, and he founded a graduate studies program, bringing Yale to a status parallel with Harvard and the prominent European institutions of the day. William obtained a mastery over many of these subjects.

For all Woolsey's views on the immorality of slavery, the school was largely conservative on other issues. It did not admit Catholics, and it remained wedded to its original Puritan ideals. There was a demographic statistic of significance in the student body as well. The influence of Southern students was not as great as Harvard University. In 1850, there were seventy-two Southern and border-state students out of a total of over five hundred. Woolsey's beliefs on slavery undoubtedly contributed to a precipitous decline in this number: in 1860, there were only thirty-three students from the Southern and border states enrolled as undergraduates. During the Civil War, twenty-five Yale graduates were generals in the Union army, none in the Confederate army.[15]

William Winthrop stood out among his peers as a scholar while at Yale. He was a member of the Phi Beta Kappa honor society. During his junior and senior years, he served as a tutor in Latin and French. He also was named as the Berkeleian Scholar of his class at his graduation. Berkeleian Scholars were almost always chosen on the basis of talent.[16] Winthrop pursued his education with an intense passion that he often captured in his letters. Writing home his first year, he described his performance in the front of the class completing mathematics exercises on a blackboard. "With a firm step he crosses the floor and mildly seizes the chalk. He begins to inscribe upon the blackboard 'figures that speak of plusses and minuses that burn.'"[17] William also admitted that his first year was an imperfect performance: "I made one bad mistake and in Greek."[18] To show his brother, Theodore, his mistake, he copied an exam answer in Greek on the front of a letter. In the same letter, he begged Theodore to convince his mother to purchase him a neck-handkerchief, pleading poverty. At the end of his first year, Yale awarded him a prize for being the best Latin translator in the class.[19]

He approached the spring semester of his sophomore year with the same hard-nosed determination that he utilized during the previous three semesters. He wrote of his success in mathematics and Greek, but admitted this foreign language took a good deal of effort to learn. Winthrop also defended a professor who "people thought a fool, but is rather a first rate teacher and speaker." Winthrop assured his family that he exercised regularly, though he wanted to go on vacation to Philadelphia and visit a "chocolate manufacturing firm." He also noted that he intended to return to Owego in the summer, and to him this was a necessary trip since, "Rosa will just be coming back and I shall have to be with her."[20] Rosa, as it turned out, was not his only interest, and he developed a relationship with a younger girl named Sophie whom he met in Owego and maintained contact with. Although this relationship continued past his time at Yale and Yale Law School, his letters from Yale only briefly mention her.

In late 1849, William briefly considered pursuing a career in the ministry. In this matter he was similar to Theodore, as he turned back to the law as his goal. He translated a series of epistles and delivered an oration to the class, "every part of the epistle pleased them very much, except me." It appears President Woolsey steered Winthrop away from pursuing the ministry and toward a legal career. Winthrop did not actively join Woolsey's antislavery movement while he attended Yale, but he was aware of the growing belief in slavery's immorality.

In 1851, Yale awarded Winthrop the Townsend Prize for authoring the leading nonfiction essay of that year. Titled "The Republic of Holland," his essay advanced the Dutch State of Holland as a model for the United States. Taking into account the Winthrop family history, it is not surprising he favored the Netherlands. After all, the middle-class Dutch Calvinist state had harbored British Puritans from persecution in England.

The essay provided a concise political and demographic history of the Netherlands from the sixteenth century to the 1850s. The essay also described the system of governance throughout the Netherlands, paying attention to the checks and balances between the central government in each state and the various city counsels. Winthrop drew similarities between the United States government and the Dutch, though he pointed out the Dutch office of Staadholder was quite different than the executive branch of the United States. He also commented that the Dutch office of Grand Pensionary, which served as a check on the Staadholder's power, had no equivalent in the United States government.

Winthrop considered the Dutch state of Holland as the most enlightened and free area of Europe, and he encouraged Americans to look to Holland as an example of democracy. As a result of the Netherlands' unique history, freeing itself from "the oppressive Spanish yoke," it produced an unparalleled array of intellectuals, artists, and statesmen in relation to its small population. Moreover, intellectuals fleeing Spain and Italy found a home in the Netherlands. Winthrop noted that the long duration of its internal war to free itself of Spanish rule, as well as wars with its neighbor, France, caused considerable suffering. After all, beginning in the middle of the sixteenth century, the Netherlands warred with Spain for an almost continuous eighty-year period.

Winthrop argued these wars provided the foundation of Dutch Republicanism much in the way the American Revolution shaped the early United States. However, instead of a war against a British sovereign of like faith, to William, the Dutch Rebellion was a "glorious struggle for the liberty of conscience against the bigotry and slavery of Romanism."

He also fashioned the Dutch independence struggle as "the vindication of Protestantism."[21] The Eighty Years' War was clearly a religious conflict, though Spain had, under medieval law, a rightful title to the Dutch states. It was also a conflict typical of the Protestant Reformation in which the warring sides paid scant regard to the laws of war or other humanitarian aspects. For example, in 1576 Spanish soldiers sacked Antwerp, killing eight thousand civilians.

Winthrop believed the United States possessed the same intellectual capabilities as Holland because of the similarities between Dutch history and their system of governance, and those of the United States. He engaged in an anti-Catholic commentary, perhaps reflecting a Northern Whig anti-immigration political view. A number of Whigs were beginning to migrate to anti-immigration politics such as the American Party. Although it is unclear as to whether Winthrop joined any of these movements, his prominent relative Robert Charles Winthrop had political allies in the nascent anti-Irish, anti-Catholic parties. Winthrop ended his essay with a tribute to Holland writing, "No country has ever done more for freedom and the result of its efforts was the irrevocable guarantee of civil and religious liberty."[22]

Interestingly, Winthrop's primary example of a leading thinker was Hugo Grotius. Grotius was, long before Winthrop's time, considered as the master of international law. Indeed, Grotius was known for his treatise on the law of war during his own lifetime, which spanned much of the Thirty Years' War. It has been noted that one of the warrior kings of that war, Gustavus Adolphus of Sweden, carried Grotius' treatise with him during the war.[23] Winthrop's use of Grotius may have been the first indication of his interest in military law, but if this were the case, his interest went into dormancy until 1861. It may also reflect the influence of Theodore Dwight Woolsey on Winthrop, since the Yale president had begun by this time to write on international law. On the other hand, Winthrop later cited Grotius a number of times in his classic treatises, *Military Law* and *Military Law and Precedents*.

In addition to his academic writing, Winthrop also dabbled in poetry. While at Yale, Winthrop wrote at least two poems which survive today and perhaps more which do not. One of the poems, a tribute to Nestor, the old warrior found in Homer's *Iliad*, was written in ancient Greek—a testament to Winthrop's abilities at mastering foreign languages. In it, Winthrop praised Nestor's unrivaled wisdom, diplomacy, and courage. It was, according to Homer, Nestor who penetrated through Agamemnon's arrogance and forced the Greek king to see reason.

Winthrop's second Yale poem, written in English, regarded the siege of Belgrade. In 1456, Hungarians and other Balkan Christians held off an Ottoman army bent on capturing Belgrade. The Ottomans had steadily defeated Christian armies, but Belgrade was able to stem the Islamic advance. In each poem, Winthrop lauded military leadership traits he later found lacking in a number of Union army commanders such as John Pope and George McClellan. Moreover, he may have found in Nestor a role model for himself to later follow.

Later in life, Winthrop published a short story in a California literary magazine in which he criticized Union generals with the same candor that he approached Agamemnon or the Turkish generals outside of Belgrade. But while at Yale, just as in the case of his prized essay, Winthrop only showed a passing interest in martial affairs. As a student, he clearly did not seek to make a career of the military.

Winthrop earned his first leadership position at graduation, when the graduating class unanimously elected him class secretary. The position required Winthrop to maintain a correspondence with the other graduates so that three years after graduation, in 1854, an annotated roster could be published. The roster, titled *Statistics of the Class of 1851, of Yale College*, not only evidences William Winthrop's literary capabilities, but it also is a demographic snapshot into the student body. The roster was published by John Wilson and Son of New Haven and presented to the class on their reunion at the Tontine Hotel, New Haven, Connecticut.[24]

It is very clear that in looking back three years since his graduation, Winthrop felt a strong affinity toward Yale and the value of the education he received. He prefaced the roster with an introduction: "We are stretching forward free and far upon our broad noon. We have reached the age of experiment, or trial, of waiting. We have become men. The professions of life have been entered upon. Wives have been married. Children have been born. We are citizens,—husbands,—fathers." William professed that the societal standing of his classmates was based in their "Alma Mater whose *storge* is so precious to us all."[25] And, he argued, "we are conscious of what a want it would have been to have grown up without any claim to a membership in such a fraternity as a college class."[26]

The class roster included George Hastings, who later served alongside Winthrop as an officer in the Sharpshooters during the Civil War. Hastings took part in the Peninsula Campaign, Second Manassas, Antietam, Fredericksburg, and Chancellorsville, where he was severely wounded and invalided out of the service. For a short duration after his injuries, Hastings also served alongside of Winthrop as a judge advocate, reviewing the records of military trials over civilians. Like Winthrop, after Yale Hastings pursued a law degree at Harvard, and he later practiced law in New York. Hastings may have owed a debt to Winthrop and other classmates. He did not graduate from Yale in the technical sense, leaving class before completing his senior year. The roster indicates that after staunch lobbying on the part of his friends, the university administration conferred a degree on Hastings.[27] Another friend of Winthrop's whose life later intersected with his was Asher Robbins Little. Little studied law at Yale after a year-long circumnavigation of the world by clipper ship.[28] Little and William briefly became law partners on the eve of the Civil War, and during the war, Little taught law at the Naval Academy. After the war, Little became a patents commissioner in Washington, DC; resided in Saint Anthony, Minnesota; and eventually became a director of the Astor Library, the forerunner of the New York Public Library.[29]

As a Yale student, Winthrop had campaigned for Whig candidates in Connecticut. His affiliation with the Whig Party is unsurprising in the sense that elite New Englanders tended toward that party over the opposing Democrat Party. An individual of Winthrop's socioeconomic class in New England was likely to be a Whig. The roots of the Whig Party bear mention in a biography of William Winthrop, not simply because he was a member of the party, but also because the fundamental political beliefs he held—namely, the immorality of slavery—were wrapped up in the party's demise.

This party was deeply entrenched in his family. Francis Bayard Winthrop was a Whig, as was Robert Charles Winthrop, a rising political star when William was in his youth. Charles F. Johnson, Winthrop's brother-in-law, was a Whig. Moreover, the Johnson and Winthrop men campaigned for Whigs, and Winthrop was no different. Theodore Dwight Woolsey initially was at least a nominal Whig, though this likely was a result of his contempt toward Andrew Jackson for Jackson's disregard of the Constitution's system of checks and balances, as well as Jackson's antielitism. There were other Whigs and former Whigs of importance in William's professional life. The list included Abraham Lincoln, William Henry Seward, George Brinton McClellan, and William McKee Dunn, the assistant judge advocate general under Joseph Holt and later the judge advocate general immediately after Holt's retirement.

By 1840, Whig support tended to come from wealthy businessmen, professionals, and Southern planters. In addition, artisans and merchants voted Whig, in response to a Democrat alliance to cheap immigrant labor. The Whig Party was in some respects an alliance between the inheritors of the Puritan traditions and commercial interests. Its members tended to be more nativist than the Democrats. In contrast, the Democrats attracted subsistence farmers, immigrants, Catholics, and "others who resented the self-righteous morality of dominant protestant groups."[30]

From the beginning, the Whig Party suffered a structural weakness. It was formed, in part, by elites angry with Andrew Jackson. The party did not establish a platform of unification outside of economic interests. Southern Whigs were slaveholders, and a number of Northern Whigs, the so-called Cotton Whigs, supported the Southerners for reasons of economic theory. Other Northern Whigs—particularly the younger Whigs and those involved in the second revival—were known as Conscience Whigs and felt slavery an immoral institution. Abolitionism first reappeared in strength in New England as part of the Second Great Awakening. The fact that the majority of Conscience Whigs were traditional Protestants is not merely coincidental. But the Whig problems ran deeper than the slavery issue, though that issue alone was likely to tear the party apart. The Whig Party was hardly unified on issues of nativism and immigration as well. Some Whigs believed the growth of the Catholic Church a moral corruption. Other Whigs, such as William Henry Seward of New York, combated nativists in the party.[31]

Although there were a number of minor fault lines that caused dissent in the Whig Party, it was slavery which tore the party apart. In 1846, Congress debated a proviso named for one of its originators, Pennsylvania Democrat David Wilmot, which would bar the extension of slavery into any territory annexed by the United States from Mexico. Some Whigs supported the proviso and others vehemently fought against it. Many Whigs did not support Polk's Texas annexation policy, which clearly would lead to war with Mexico. For these Whigs, the proviso became a proverbial line in the sand. Although antislavery politicians from both parties supported the proviso, a number of these supporters were simply racist and voted for the proviso as a means of keeping blacks out of their state or territory. Indeed, Wilmot called his proposal "the White Man's Proviso."[32] William Winthrop supported the proviso and did not view it in terms of black exclusion.

Other Northern Whigs initially supported the proviso, but then reversed positions when it became clear that the party could sectionalize over the issue. The proviso was hotly debated and never obtained enough support for passage in its original form. In fact, in 1850, Congress repudiated the proviso with the Compromise of 1850. Robert Charles Winthrop was part of this process. He initially supported the proviso but withdrew his support when it threatened to tear apart the Whig Party and the country as a whole. He also supported the war with Mexico, while a number of his Massachusetts Whig peers, such as Charles Sumner, did not. On the eve of the war with Mexico, Sumner declared, "Slavery is the source of all meanness, from national dishonesty to tobacco spitting." But by then the Massachusetts Whigs had fallen into two unbridgeable camps over slavery. Indeed, Robert Charles Winthrop terminated all connection with Sumner over their differences.[33]

Related to the issue of slavery was the Whig Party's inability to develop a cohesive definition of citizenship. Robert Charles Winthrop believed that only whites could be citizens. Charles Sumner and the other Conscience Whigs argued the opposite; that persons born within a jurisdiction were the citizens of that jurisdiction. This difference in views had an effect not only on the arguments over slavery but also on the issue of who could become a citizen of the United States, which led to another weakness in the Whig Party: its view of curtailing immigration. Southern and midwestern Whigs did not, as a rule, embrace anti-immigration positions or temperance. These issues were mainly confined to New England and New York, and they worked to the detriment of the party. However, just as Northern Cotton Whigs accommodated slavery for party unity and economic growth, Southern Whigs supported the Northerners' anti-immigration platform.

In 1844, the Whigs nominated Clay as their presidential candidate, but placed alongside him Theodore Frelinghuysen of New Jersey for vice president. Frelinghuysen's nomination was problematic. He was a prototypical Northern nativist who previously railed against Catholic immigration. That year, the Liberty Party, a third party fashioned around antislavery, captured fifteen thousand votes in New York. Considering that Clay's Democrat opponent, James K. Polk, won New York by five thousand votes, it is likely the combination of Frelinghuysen's presence on the ticket and the Whig silence on slavery cost Clay New York. Had he won New York, he would have won the presidency.[34]

William's great uncle Robert Charles Winthrop serves as an example for the decline and fall of the Whig Party. He was first elected to the Massachusetts state House of Representatives in 1834, with the support of Daniel Webster. In 1838, he became the speaker of the state house. In 1840, he was elected to Congress as a Whig. He vigorously campaigned for Henry Clay in 1844. Robert Charles Winthrop found the nativists too demogogic for his tastes in the 1840s, but this did not detract from his support to Clay (in the 1856 election, he supported the Know-Nothing candidate). In this light, he fulfilled many of the detrimental working-class expectations of Whigs. He acquiesced to slavery interests for economic reasons, and he supported temperance as well as curbing Catholic immigration. Yet he did not acquiesce on matters he felt to have a moral base. For instance, he had opposed Andrew Jackson's removal of Cherokee Indians from Georgia as an extreme exercise in executive authority.[35]

In 1846, Robert Charles Winthrop was chosen as the Speaker of the House of Representatives by the Whig majority. But, like the party, he was ill prepared for the issues of the day. The Whig Party was divided on the issue of Texas annexation or any territorial acquisition which would likely spread slavery. He did not envision the growth of nativism, abolitionism, or third parties such as the Free Soil or Liberty parties as threatening the existence of the Whigs.[36] Nor did he envision that in 1844, James Knox Polk would defeat Henry Clay for the presidency and launch the United States into a war with Mexico. Many Whigs condemned the war and saw it as an attempt to expand slavery into the conquered territories. Ironically, the two chief military commanders of the war, Zachary Taylor and Winfield Scott, were Whigs, and in the case of Scott, the candidate was lukewarm to the war, despite his dynamic campaign from Vera Cruz to Mexico City. In 1849, with slavery increasingly at the forefront of congressional politics, Southern Whigs blocked Robert Charles Winthrop's attempt to gain reelection as House Speaker, while in the North, a small but growing number of antislavery Whigs arrayed against him.[37]

By 1850, the Whig Party and the nation stood at a crossroads between continuance and dissolution. The Wilmot Proviso proved unworkable, and as the nation expanded after the victory over Mexico, the issue of slavery stood as divisive as ever. Conservative Whigs believed further attacks on slavery would cause Southern Democrats to secede from the Union; enough Southern politicians, both Whig and Democrat, hinted as much. Conscience Whigs began to defect from the party into third parties. However, enough Americans desired the continued existence of the United States that fire-eaters on both sides were curbed when the old Whig Henry Clay sought a compromise between abolitionists and pro-slavery politicians.

Calling it the Compromise of 1850, Clay fashioned a series of separate territorial issues, each with underpinnings of slavery, into a single program to appease the interests of each side. For instance, California was to be admitted as a free state, and the sale of slaves forbidden in Washington, DC. Popular sovereignty would decide whether slavery would exist in the western territories taken from Mexico. Although Texas was reduced in its size, the federal government took over its $10 million debt to foreign and commercial entities. However, the new Fugitive Slave Law (which William Winthrop found repugnant and campaigned against) bound Northern officials to return captured runaway slaves, and these slaves were not entitled to challenge the veracity of their bondage before state courts. Clay's compromise was attacked by parties on both sides, including John C. Calhoun and William Seward, whom William Winthrop later campaigned for in his 1860 bid for the Republican nomination. However, on July 9, 1850, President Zachary Taylor died and was replaced by his vice president, Millard Fillmore. Fillmore backed Clay's proposal, and by September, each of these compromise measures was passed into law. At the time of its passage, the Compromise of 1850 was hailed as saving the Union. It did not do anything of the sort, and at best, it delayed Southern secession for a decade. At its worst, it signified the beginning of a quick death for the Whig Party.[38]

In the absence of Whigs taking a unified stand on slavery, third parties began to form in the 1840s. In 1848, antislavery men from both the Whig and Democrat parties formed the Free Soil Party and nominated Martin van Buren for president. Free Soil candidates captured 14 percent of the Northern vote in that year, but in 1852 their percentage declined to 6.6 percent. The Free Soil antislavery platform did not catch on for a number of reasons, including the fact that a number of Northern Conscience Whigs initially remained loyal to the Whig Party. Their number included William Seward, Horace Greeley, Abraham Lincoln, and William Winthrop.[39] Additionally, Free Soil leaders employed economic arguments against slavery, often over the moral issue of the institution. In contrast to the Free Soil Party, the Liberty Party was founded in 1839, specifically as a moral attack on slavery. Its leaders stressed slavery's immorality through biblical scripture, and it reflected the second revival more than any other party.[40] The Liberty Party performed less successfully than the Free Soil Party, though it lasted roughly as long.

Another third party, noted further in the following chapter, rose as an indirect challenge to Whig authority in the North. In response to an increase in Irish Catholic immigration, a number of Northern Whigs and some Democrats formed third parties. Prior to 1854 nativism was not a centralized political force. That is, no single party rallied around the anti-Irish banner in the same manner that a single party had, prior to the Whig formation, rallied around an opposition to masonry. Anti-immigration and anti-Catholicism movements shared some of the puritanical elements found in New England Whigs. There was no inconsistency between abolitionism and nativism, particularly where slavery was viewed as a crime against Christianity. By the time the anti-immigration movements coalesced into a single party under the Know-Nothing banner, the Whig Party had already entered into its death throes. Certainly, the nativist impetus in New England affected the Whig Party in that it could not attract Catholics.[41]

In the 1850s, Northern Cotton Whig leaders showed more animus to the Free Soil Party than to the Democrats. Robert Charles Winthrop made the Free Soilers an object of derision claiming, "The typical [Free Soil] speech consisted of one third Missouri Compromise to repeal, one third Kansas Outrages, and one third disjointed facts, misapplied figures, and great swelling words of vanity."[42] By this time William had Free Soil leanings.

William Winthrop's transition from Whig into Republican politics began while at Yale's Law School. To some extent, his Republicanism began during his undergraduate course of study in the sense that he was exposed to Conscience Whig, the antislavery branch of the party, politics. Given Winthrop's socioeconomic station, it was unlikely he would have subscribed to a third party such as the Free Soil or Liberty parties. His writings, even through law school, evidence that his belief in the immorality of slavery was not so great as to call for bloodletting or revolution to end the institution. Theodore differed from William, appearing the more radical of the two brothers. However, it was through William's legal training that he found not only a passion for international law (including an appreciation for the importance of basic internationally recognized individual rights), but also a belief that slavery had to be defeated and equality guaranteed through the law.

By the nineteenth century, Yale University was already competing with Harvard for top national academic honors. However, Yale's law school did not enjoy the same status as the university. Indeed, in the 1840s, Harvard and Columbia were viewed as having the best law schools.[43] Part of Yale Law School's difficulties had to do with its origins. Yale University was founded in 1701. Its first move toward the establishment of a law school was its creation of a law department in 1801. Yale did not possess a formal law school until the mid-1820s. By then the law schools at Harvard and Columbia were already established. Another difficulty for Yale's law school had to do with the nature of entering the legal practice in the mid-nineteenth century. Formal legal education was only one means of entry into the practice of law, and it was, in William Winthrop's time, the minority means for doing so. A Yale law degree, in and of itself, was not a guarantee of well-remunerated employment.

Most attorneys in the nineteenth century were admitted into the profession through an apprenticeship program. Under this system, a young man interested in the practice of law served as an understudy to a licensed attorney and learned the law through example. The apprentice copied legal documents, drafted filings, and accompanied the attorney to court. Usually, at some point, the apprentice sat for an exam in front of a local judge. Upon passing the exam, the apprentice was licensed to practice law.[44] There was an increase in the numbers of attorneys in proportion to the population during Jackson's presidency, and this reflected the egalitarian view of Jacksonians that the professions were best served when open to the common man.

The counter belief to the Jacksonian view of the common man may have spurred an increase in the emphasis in formal law school training as a mechanism for differentiating elites from their pedestrian attorney peers. On the other hand, Henry Clay, one of the more prominent Whigs in the first half of the century, studied the law as an apprentice. Daniel Webster also entered into the law through the apprenticeship system, although both Clay and Webster were apprenticed to nationally prominent jurists. Robert Charles Winthrop learned the law apprenticing to Daniel Webster. William Winthrop's second commander in the Judge Advocate General's Department, General William McKee Dunn, entered into the practice of law in Indiana having apprenticed to a local Indianapolis attorney. Indeed, most of the older Whigs who practiced law learned through the apprentice process.

Initially, municipal governments administered the process of licensing attorneys with very little oversight from state governments or professional associations. However, in the 1830s the states increasingly wrested control over this process from the local municipalities. The increased control by state governments did not end the apprenticeship system, but it did lead to a more professionalized rigor in the practice of law.[45] As a result of this trend, there was a growth in the numbers of university and proprietary law schools. The typical proprietary law school was established by already practicing attorneys, and the course of study was modeled on the apprentice system. It was a practical education, but it did not lend itself to training lawyers as legal intellectuals. The foremost of these proprietary schools was established in Litchfield, Connecticut, and the school influenced the methods of teaching law during Winthrop's education, in particular at Yale. Indeed, more than any other institution, Yale's law school was likely the primary beneficiary of Litchfield's influence.

Yale's law school was not always welcome to the university. The university had granted undergraduate degrees for a century and a half without involving itself with a law school. Despite its affiliation, the law school first offered a degree in 1843, nineteen years after it joined Yale.[46] Like Litchfield, it taught law as a profession, rather than as an academic study. The law school's mission and the university's mission were viewed as so incompatible that the administration gave serious thought to dissociating the university from the law school in 1845 and again in 1869. In 1845, the relationship between the law school and the university was salvaged by a deal between a number of local attorneys and the university. These local attorneys agreed to raise money for a school law library, provided they had access to it. For all his efforts to enhance Yale's academic reputation, Theodore Dwight Woolsey did little for the law school. He expected it to make its own way.[47]

A Yale law historian noted that the university's attitude toward its law school was not unusual. Princeton University and Indiana University both shuttered their law schools in the mid-nineteenth century.[48] However, Yale's administrators did not close the law school down or disassociate it from the university. Instead, the law school maintained its course of instruction, seemingly mired as a second-rate institution in comparison to its main competitor, Harvard. What made it a second-rate institution was only partly attributable to the occasional animus between the university faculty and administrators and those of the law school. Its curricula and faculty simply did not favorably compete with Harvard's.

Yale's law school somewhat departed from the Litchfield method of wholly teaching law by lecture, though some of this method remained in the Yale curriculum. Instead, the law school adopted the "text and recitation method" of instruction. The administrators of the law school propounded, "It is the conviction of the faculty . . . that definite and permanent impressions concerning the principles and rules of any abstract science are best acquired by the study of standard textbooks in private, followed by examinations and explanations in the recitation room."[49] This method was already in place in the undergraduate classical education at Yale. Blackstone remained a standard text under this system, but it was augmented with American legal treatises. After an extensive faculty search in 1847, Yale settled on its third choice, Clark Bissell, to head the school. The university also hired Henry Dutton, a Connecticut Supreme Court justice, and Thomas Osborne, a former Congressman, as assistant faculty members. Other faculty served as part-time instructors, augmenting the curriculum with their expertise in areas such as admiralty and the law of nations.[50] While Yale Law School did not provide the best legal education available in the United States, it did provide a complete and competent course of study.

Winthrop had displayed an enthusiasm for the law from an early age; upon entering the study of law at Yale, his enthusiasm changed to outright passion. For example, he humorously advised family members on causes of action they might take against one another. During his first semester at school, Winthrop wrote his sister regarding her legal status resulting from her seventeen years of age, beginning with "you are not as well acquainted as you might be with the rights and liabilities which the law in all its majesty (and courtrooms) has imposed on your enlivening age." These rights and liabilities Winthrop listed included drafting a will, entering into marriage, and accepting the role as executrix, and in a joking manner, he wrote of her status under the criminal law as "the extreme likelihood of your being confined in a house of correction before you are a month older."[51]

He described his legal schooling, in part, as though it were a series of moot courts. His first case, an action in trover, he considered to be easy.[52] His next case involving a brokerage stoppage was more complex, but he described the two teams, "Ridgely and Jerome for the plaintiff, Rounds and Winthrop for the defendant," in the exercise as "the best speakers in the school." However, over time, he yearned for a greater challenge than Yale had to offer. This is not to suggest that he was bored with the law.[53]

Winthrop also maintained an interest in foreign relations, and this continued into his Yale law studies, where he sought to study international law, then called the law of nations. One area he found fascinating and studied with zeal was the foreign policy of the United States toward Austria. Technically a dual kingdom of Austria and Hungary after 1848, their government was largely Germanic to the exclusion of other ethnic groups, and it was dominated by one of the world's oldest monarchies, the Habsburgs. In an era of revolts, the Habsburg government spent considerable energy repressing ethnic minorities rather than granting them rights.

An incident in 1849 altered the relationship between the United States and Austria. The Habsburg government intercepted and read a diplomatic note from Secretary of State John M. Clayton to the United States envoy in Austria, Dudley Mann. The note expressed support for a Hungarian revolutionary named Louis Kossuth. It did not offer Kossuth aid or weaponry, and his revolution had been crushed. By the time the letter was intercepted and read, Daniel Webster had replaced Clayton as secretary of state. Johann George Hulsemann, the Austrian chargé d'affaires, protested to Webster that the letter from Clayton to Mann was offensive to Austria, and he threatened Webster with "acts of retaliation" in response to the American interference in Austria. Hulsemann's threat was problematic. Clearly the Austrian government violated custom when it intercepted and read a United States government communiqué between its employees.[54]

On the other hand, Webster had to respond to the Austrian threat as well as defend American actions in supporting Kossuth. Instead of ameliorating the growing strain between the two governments, Webster responded with a long, bombastic public letter notifying the Austrian government that the United States stood ready to fight a war "if Austria chose to engage in one." Webster went on to deride Austrian military capabilities in contrast to those of the United States. He may have foreseen Austria as a weakening state, rather than a great power. Nine years after the Kossuth exchange, the French Army and their Piedmontese allies defeated the Austrian Army at the Battle of Solferino. Eight years after the Battle of Solferino, the Prussian Army crushed Austria at Koniggratz. But it is more likely the case Webster took a risk that Austria could not back up any threats due to distance and a lack of a navy. He also argued that there was nothing inherently wrong with a neutral government such as the United States morally supporting an internal revolution occurring in another state, provided the support was not overtly physical. Webster pronounced the actions of Clayton and Mann as "wholly unobjectionably and strictly within the rule of the Law of Nations."[55] Thus, Webster claimed the rights of Americans to express their support for freedom or revolutionary movements consistent with international law. At the same time, Webster argued the United States had the right to resort to armed force against a foreign nation which challenged the right to express support to a revolutionary movement. This was a view which Winthrop later cautiously agreed with, but in his youth gave his full endorsement.

During this time, Kossuth fled from Austria to the Ottoman Empire, where he sought entry into the United States. The Turkish government was placed in an almost untenable position. The Ottoman Empire had a great deal to fear from its neighbors, Russia and Austria, and very little to gain from siding with the United States. The United States and the Ottoman Empire were even more distant than the United States and the Habsburg monarchy. The Austrian and Russian governments demanded Kossuth's extradition. The United States government welcomed Kossuth's immigration. Webster ensured that the Turkish minister to the United States was treated as royalty, and he caused Hulsemann's pithy antidemocratic correspondence to be published in several newspapers. In the end, the Turkish government permitted Kossuth to emigrate to the United States, where he caused a number of embarrassing gaffes, such as demanding American support for a new Hungarian revolution. He was not alone in this. In 1852, Webster expressed sympathy for the Hungarians in a public speech, attacking the Austrian emperor and claiming "no nation can be happy living in a country belonging to someone else," and that the Hungarians "had a hereditary love of liberty." Webster concluded with a toast to Hungarian independence. Hulsemann opted to have the last word on the matter, seeking an audience with President Fillmore and demanding Webster be removed from government. This information became public and was seen as an affront to democracy, adding to Webster's popularity.[56]

Winthrop embraced Webster's jingoism and argued Austria had trammeled Kossuth's rights. From Yale, he wrote a letter supporting both Webster and Kossuth. He noted that the high point of his 1851–1852 academic year was briefly meeting Kossuth, and he asked his sister if she met and kissed Kossuth as well. Winthrop did not leave to history his reasons for supporting Webster and Kossuth. True, up to this point, he remained a Whig, and Robert Charles Winthrop likely supported Webster. But Webster's bombast could have placed the United States on a course toward conflict with a country it had no quarrel or competition with. Moreover, Webster may have used the incident as a cipher to detract attention away from the more divisive issue of slavery. Still, the incident left Winthrop with a desire to further his studies in the law of nations, finding "trover uninteresting in comparison."[57]

That Webster may have used the incident to divert attention from the growing sectionalism in domestic politics did not appear to Winthrop. He may have simply gotten caught up in a moment of jingoistic bluster. The souring of relations with Austria did affect United States foreign policy. When, during the Civil War, the French emperor Napoleon III installed a nominal Habsburg, Maximilian, on the Mexican throne, the U.S. government saw the act as a provocation that could lead to war with France. From the end of the Civil War through 1917, the United States had little to do with Austria, and in 1917, when the United States went to war against Germany, the U.S. government also declared war against Austria, Germany's ally. In 1918, the great internationalist President Woodrow Wilson spearheaded an effort to dismember the Habsburg empire into small independent countries based on nationality. This partly fulfilled Webster's earlier vision of providing independence to the Hungarians and other minorities.

Winthrop ultimately was confronted with an issue both Webster and Robert Charles Winthrop avoided: how could one argue for the liberty of oppressed Hungarians and ignore Southern slavery? The only possibility to avoid this question was to look at Africans as less than human, and this was something Winthrop could not find in himself to do.

NOTES

1. LeRoy Wilson Kingman, *Early Owego* (Owego: Tioga County Historical Society, 1987), 33–341. A reprint, the original title for the book was *Some Account of the Early Settlement of the Village in Tioga County, Called Ah-Wa-Ga by the Indians Which Name Was Corrupted by Gradual Evolution into Owego* (1907).

2. Neither Grace Farrell nor Katherine Devereux Blake (Lillie's daughter) mentions William Winthrop when discussing Lillie's childhood. It may be that Lillie was drawn to Theodore as he was likely the family's center of attention with his demeanor and penchant for writing. Still, given Winthrop's youth in Owego, his absence from her diary provides context to his youth as well.

3. Michael J. Durbin, *United States Presidential Elections, 1788–1860: The Official Results by County and State* (Jefferson, NC: McFarland and Co., 2002), 115.

4. Durbin, *United States Presidential Elections*, 144. In contrast, New Haven gave Fremont 7,975 votes; Buchanan 7,315 votes; and Fillmore 410 votes. In Massachusetts, Fremont received 108,190 votes to Buchanan's 39,240 votes, or 64.76 percent to 23.5 percent.

5. William Winthrop, letter to his sisters, Laura and Sarah, July 10, 1845 (YALE).

6. William Winthrop, letter to his sister Laura, September 1849 (YALE).

7. Although their differences over the issue of slavery and Republican politics appear to have caused an estrangement in their relationship, Robert Charles Winthrop Jr., authored the complimentary entries for Theodore and William Winthrop in James Grant Wilson and John Fiske, *Appleton's Cyclodpaedia of American Biography* (New York: D. Appleton and Co., 1889).

8. Winthrop, letter to Laura, September 1849.

9. Winthrop, letter to Laura, September 1849.

10. Winthrop, letter to Laura, September 1849.

11. William Winthrop, letter to his sister Sarah, August 11, 1850 (YALE).

12. George King, *Theodore Dwight Woolsey: His Political and Social Ideas* (Chicago: Loyola University Press, 1956), 8–25; Brooks Mather Kelly, *Yale: A History* (New Haven: Yale University Press, 1974), 171–172.

13. Kelly, *Yale*, 196

14. Grace Farrell, *Lillie Devereux Blake: Retracing a Life Erased* (Amherst: University of Massachusetts Press, 2002), 15.

15. Kelly, *Yale*, 196

16. Lawrence Mayo, *The Winthrop Family in America* (Boston: Massachusetts Historical Society, 1948), 374; Kelly, *Yale*, 175. The Berkeleian scholarship enabled a student to continue academic study past graduation. However, as in Winthrop's

time hardly any Yale students came from the lower economic strata, the scholarship prize undoubtedly went to a wealthy student.

17. William Winthrop, letter to his mother, Elizabeth, 1847 (YALE).

18. Winthrop, letter to Elizabeth, 1847.

19. I. Maltby, ed. *The Yale Literary Magazine* (New Haven: Yale University Press, 1848), 332.

20. Winthrop, letter to Elizabeth, 1847.

21. William Winthrop, "The Republic of Holland," *Yale Literary Magazine*, July 1851, 342.

22. Winthrop, "The Republic of Holland," 342.

23. George B. Davis, *A Treatise on the Military Law of the United States, Together with the Practice and Procedure of Courts-Martial and Other Military Tribunals* (New York: John Wiley and Sons, 1915), iv.

24. William Winthrop, *Statistics of the Class of 1851, of Yale College* (New Haven: John Wilson and Son, 1854), 6; Kelly, *Yale*, 196.

25. In ancient Greek, *storge* (στοργή) is the word for familial love.

26. Winthrop, *Statistics of the Class of 1851*, 12–14.

27. Winthrop, *Statistics of the Class of 1851*, 23.

28. Winthrop, *Statistics of the Class of 1851*, 27.

29. *Addresses of the Living Graduates of Yale College* (New Haven: Yale University Press, 1872), 40–41. According to the *Addresses*, in 1872 there were only four graduates residing in the South. In contrast, four resided in Europe and two in the Ottoman Empire.

30. David Potter, *The Impending Crisis, 1848–1861* (New York: Harper, 1976), 236; Michael F. Holt, *The Rise and Fall of the American Whig Party: Jacksonian Politics and the Onset of Civil War* (New York: Oxford University Press, 1999), 83.

31. Michael F. Holt, *The Fate of Their Country: Politicans, Slavery Extensions, and the Coming of the Civil War* (New York: Hill and Wang, 2004), 74; Holt, *The Rise and Fall*, 982–984.

32. Holt, *The Fate of Their Country*, 27.

33. Robert Remini, *Henry Clay: Statesman for the Union* (New York: W.W. Norton, 1991), 725; Kinley J. Brauer, *Cotton versus Conscience: Massachusetts Whig Politics and Southwestern Expansion, 1843–1848* (Lexington: University of Kentucky Press, 1967), 106–108, also 209; Charles Sumner, letter to Samuel G. Howe, in Wilson Beverly, ed. *The Selected Letters of Charles Sumner*, vol. 2 (Boston: Northeastern University, 1990), 345.

34. Remini, *Henry Clay*, 663; Holt, *The Rise and Fall*, 205–206; Sean Wilentz, *The Rise of American Democracy: Jefferson to Lincoln* (New York: W.W. Norton, 2005), 323–324.

35. Wilentz, *The Rise of American Democracy*, 695–697.

36. Holt, *The Rise and Fall*, 156.

37. Potter, *The Impending Crisis*, 90; Brauer, *Cotton versus Conscience*, 219; Wilentz, *The Rise of American Democracy*, 637–638. The Democrats had a marginal plurality in the House of Representatives, but there were twelve Free Soil Congressmen and one nativist independent who would generally support a Whig for speaker over the Democrat pro-slavery congressman, Howell Cobb of Georgia. However, as Winthrop opposed the Wilmot Proviso, he lost their support.

Moreover, Southern Whigs distrusted Winthrop since he originally supported the proviso before withdrawing his support.

38. Wilentz, *The Rise of American Democracy*, 637–643; Holt, *The Rise and Fall*, 550–552; Holt, *The Fate of Their Country*, 69–70.

39. Potter, *The Impending Crisis*, 227.

40. Eric Foner, *Free Soil, Free Labor, Free Men: The Ideology of the Republican Party before the Civil War* (Oxford: Oxford University Press, 1970), 78–80; James M. McPherson, *Battle Cry of Freedom: The Civil War Era* (New York: Oxford University Press, 1988), 61–61.

41. Ira Leonard and Robert Parmet, *American Nativism, 1830–1860* (New York: Van Nostrand, Reinhold and Co., 1971), 70–73; McPherson, *Battle Cry of Freedom*, 139–144.

42. Foner, *Free Soil*, 43.

43. See, for example, Mark Bartholomew, "Legal Separation: The Relationship between the Law School and the Central University in the Late Nineteenth Century," *Journal of Legal Education* 53 (September 2003), 368–401.

44. Lawrence Friedman, *A History of American Law* (New York: Simon and Schuster, 2005), 606; Kermit Hall, *The Magic Mirror: Law in American History* (New York: Oxford University Press, 1989), 211–212; also, Robert Stevens, "History of the Yale Law School: Provenance and Perspective," in *History of the Yale Law School*, ed. Anthony Kronman, 9 (New Haven: Yale University Press, 2004).

45. Hall, *The Magic Mirror*, 212.

46. John M. Raymond and Barbara Frischholz, "Lawyers Who Established International Law in the United States," *American Journal of International Law* 76, no. 4 (October 1982), 816; Kelly, *Yale*, 201.

47. Kelly, *Yale*, 201.

48. John H. Langbein, "Blackstone, Litchfield, and Yale: The Founding of Yale Law School," in Kronman, *History of the Yale Law School*, 17.

49. John H. Langbein, "Law School in a University: Yale's Distinctive Path in the Later Nineteenth Century," in Kronman, *History of the Yale Law School*, 57; see also, Steve Sheppard, "Casebooks, Commentaries, and Curmudgeons: An Introductory History of Law in the Lecture Hall," *Iowa Law Review* 82 (1987), 573.

50. Langbein, "Law School in a University," 57–60.

51. William Winthrop, letter to his sister Sarah, December 9, 1851 (YALE).

52. In common-law, trover is a theory of liability in lawsuits involving the wrongful taking of private property. It is an action which seeks not the actual replacement value of the property, but rather the market value of the property plus the economic loss incurred by its taking. For example, a carter whose wagon is stolen might, under the theory of trover, recover the market value of the wagon and whatever economic loss he suffered while unable to work.

53. Robert Remini, *Daniel Webster: The Man and His Life* (New York: W. W. Norton, 1997), 700–710.

54. Holt, *The Rise and Fall*, 600–601; Robert Remini, *Daniel Webster: The Man and His Life* (New York: W.W. Norton, 1997), 700–704.

55. Remini, *Webster*, 700–704; Robert Charles Winthrop Jr., *A Memoir of Robert Charles Winthrop: Prepared for the Massachusetts Historical Society* (Boston: Little, Brown, 1897), 144.

56. Remini, *Daniel Webster*, 703.

57. Winthrop, letter to Sarah, December 9, 1851.

3

Bostonian Lawyer with Stirrings of Abolitionism

Not at the expense of sacrificing the Puritan Faith of my Fathers.

—William Winthrop to his mother, Elizabeth Woolsey Winthrop, 1854

William Winthrop left New Haven for Massachusetts to further his law studies at Harvard University in the summer of 1853. He resided in a Cambridge house whose family owners, the Greenleafs, rented him a room. He was not the only renter in the house either, as six other Harvard law and medical students obtained similar arrangements. Describing the Greenleafs as "a respectable good-natured family," Winthrop was puzzled at the concept of renting rooms, writing "many families in Cambridge, in a way unaccountable to me because we have never kept boarders, survive this way in Cambridge." Winthrop noted that the house was a one-minute walk from the law school and near the public offices and town center. To his family, he described his room furnishings as consisting of "a somewhat dilapidated but comfortable sofa, several chairs of different grades of ease of form (one with rockers which sways back with mingled feelings of curiosity and dread) two small tables, a fireplace, shelves for books, and a bed, six by three and a half feet." He drew for his mother's benefit the evening dinner table arrangement in which the Greenleafs placed him at the head of the table. Winthrop inscribed a meal of pate, turbot fish, and onions, in an assurance to his mother that he was eating well.[1]

Three of the other boarders studied medicine, and Winthrop befriended each, although he pointed out that one of the medical students had "the appearance of a cadaver." The other three boarders were law students, none of whom he befriended, opining "none of them particularly congenial." Winthrop's living quarters were better than most Americans possessed, but the comfort level was clearly less than he previously enjoyed in New Haven or Owego. Still, his letters home were filled with promises of hard work and study in the school library, as well as optimism for his future. He wrote of learning secret conveyances and property rights, as well as participating in difficult moot court cases. In his free time, he walked "great distances," including frequent thirty-three-minute treks to the coastal town Nahant. Of Nahant, he reported that he "could live there forever."[2] His mother had previously written to him about her plans to travel to Philadelphia, where her mother fell ill. Winthrop expressed a concern for the health of both women and encouraged his mother to keep him informed. He also expressed his sorrow at not being home.[3]

Winthrop entered a one-year program designed for experienced students who had already attended another law school, or were admitted to practice in another jurisdiction. The normal course of study for new students was two years.[4] He assured his family that he made a number of friends at Harvard, listing their names: Lew, Coolidge, Real, Eustis, the "three Choates," Thorndike, and Baker. Future Supreme Court justice Melville Fuller also attended Harvard at the same time as Winthrop. Winthrop had no regrets on the decision to leave New Haven for Boston, writing, "I am very glad I came here. What a boy I would have been if I had bulged forth into practice instead of waiting to learn and study for some longer time in this legal atmosphere." He also noted that not every student was a friend, describing some as "hard students . . . digs as they are vulgarly called."[5]

His studies departed from the traditional law formula he experienced at Yale, and he clearly felt he was receiving a superior education because of Harvard's emphasis on students practicing law in moot courts. Harvard owed its early educational model to a number of influences, but one of the more prominent of these was Associate Supreme Court Justice Joseph Story, a scholar whom Winthrop admired throughout his professional life. In 1829, while serving as a Supreme Court justice, Story accepted an appointment as a professor of law at Harvard. He brought the concept of education by moot court into the forefront of Harvard.[6]

Harvard gave young men such as Winthrop a purpose beyond training for a profession. Its graduates tended not to remain in Boston, as its education was geared toward a national practice. In Harvard Law School's first fifty years, roughly one-third of its graduates migrated to the western territories or the South. Joining a model "House of Representatives," and serving on its Committee on Foreign Relations, he participated in resolving international disputes, while other students drafted a model constitution for the Nebraska territory, should it become a state. Interestingly, during Winthrop's tenure as a law student, Louis Kossuth was feted as a hero at the law school during a visit.[7]

Although not formally part of the Nebraska group, Winthrop maintained an interest in its work and occasionally provided his thoughts on their project. However, the burning issue of slavery surrounding the Kansas and Nebraska territory in 1853 was absent from the student draft. William noted, "Last term the slavery question was the cause of savage conflict, and Judge Parker has prohibited this year all themes except those which are not to some extent legal."[8] This is a curious description since at the heart of the debate on slavery was the inherent constitutionality or illegality of it. Moreover, since the 1820s, Congress, and increasingly the state legislatures, drafted laws defining the extent and meaning of slavery.

The prohibition on debates over slavery reflected the faculty's desire to maintain peace and stability on the campus, rather than a strong political ideology. Harvard's students were from the upper tier of America, but they came from all areas of America. As a result, a number of the students were from Southern plantation families.[9] Winthrop did not befriend any of these students, and their attitudes on slavery resulted in his drift toward abolitionism.

That drift became final in an explosive antislavery issue. In 1854 Anthony Burns, a fugitive slave, was discovered in Boston and arrested by a local marshal. Before any hearings began, a number of antislavery supporters unsuccessfully attacked volunteer police guarding Burns. Judge Edward G. Loring, a prominent Bostonian jurist and part-time Harvard faculty member, ruled Burns had to be returned to his Virginia owner. During the trial, Loring shut the entire courthouse down and its other routine functions were abated. Fearing a second abolitionist attempt to free Burns, a number of Southern students volunteered to protect Burns' owner. This was an unnecessary gesture as President Pierce deployed United States marines to guard Burns' transfer to Virginia. In response to a student outcry, the Harvard Board of Overseers elected to discontinue Loring's status as a part-time faculty member. In 1855, pro-Loring students in the model Congress passed a resolution condemning the removal. This did not occur without an outbreak of physical violence between pro-slavery students and their abolitionist counterparts.[10]

By the time Burns was captured and brought to trial, Winthrop had graduated Harvard's law school and worked in an office next door to Burns' chief defender, Richard Henry Dana, a noted abolitionist attorney. He assisted Dana in defending Burns' extradition to a slave owner. Winthrop did not remain publicly silent in his opinions on the Burns case, and he departed from the position held by Robert Charles Winthrop. However, like his great uncle, Winthrop did not approve of

Burns' freedom through mob violence. Writing to his uncle, Winthrop stated, "Loring is a resolute gentleman . . . a man of fearless justice, and integrity. If he decides that the slave is to be remanded, I for my part should acquiesce entirely."[11]

At some point during the first semester, Winthrop along with Joseph Choate joined "The Coke Club," named after Sir Edward Coke, a prominent sixteenth-century English jurist. The Coke Club was one of the two most distinguished law student organizations.[12] During Winthrop's tenure, the Coke Club included, in the words of one of its members, the Reverend Charles C. Grafton, "Langdell, the two Choates (one of whom was afterwards Ambassador), Chandler (afterwards Senator for New Hampshire), Carter (afterwards the leader at the New York bar), Shattuck (afterwards a noted lawyer in Boston), and, I believe, Felton (afterwards of sonic note in California)."[13]

Two of the issues which interested Winthrop were of importance to the nation as a whole. The first matter had to do with United States and British foreign relations over the issue of fishing rights off eastern Canada. The British government placed naval warships off Canada to discourage American fishing vessels. Acting under Secretary of State Daniel Webster's guidance, President Fillmore dispatched the frigate *Mississippi* to the region in response. Fortunately, the naval commanders of both parties agreed that their ships were present to contain their own nationals from becoming overly aggressive. Although the two sides quietly let the matter fade, the fisheries dispute presented a compelling question of international law, and it was brought to the forefront of Harvard Law School's international legal studies. Winthrop believed that the United States had the right to send a naval vessel off another nation's coastline to protect its economic interests.

The second issue revolved around deteriorating relations with the Austrian Empire. In his last term as secretary of state, Daniel Webster had alienated the Habsburg government with his jingoistic approach over the Kossuth affair. He had argued that the United States government possessed the right to express sympathy for oppressed people wherever they may reside. Although the Austrian government eventually let the matter die, the United States government did not, and a new opportunity for disagreement arose in 1853.

Martin Koszta, a Hungarian revolutionary, immigrated to the United States in 1848 after a failed revolt for independence from Austria, and by 1850 he had begun to seek citizenship. In 1853, Koszta went on personal business to the Turkish city of Smyrna, where the Austrian navy seized him. In turn, a United States naval officer, Captain Duncan N. Ingraham, commanding a sloop of war, threatened the officer in command of the

Austrian vessel to release Koszta or be fired on. The Habsburg Austrian government took exception to Ingraham's threatened actions. In response, William Marcy defended the right of the United States government to express its support to foreign movements and protect American residents. Koszta was not a citizen of the United States, and Austria considered him within its proper jurisdiction.

The Austrians released Koszta to the French chargé d'affairs. Although relations with Austria were all the more strained over the matter, the French government ultimately mediated the dispute to the satisfaction of the United States.[14] Winthrop argued to his fellow students and the Harvard faculty that the United States was legally justified in its response to Austria.

While Winthrop saw these issues as matters for academic debate and moot government exercises, his participation in them was a part of his legal development. This is particularly important in the area of international law, one of the three areas Winthrop concentrated on in his later military scholarship. And, although in the United States diplomacy and foreign affairs are the province of the elected government, particularly the executive office and the Senate, Winthrop later opined that any understanding of the laws of war could only be achieved where the general international law of nations was understood. It was in these contemporary debates and mock governments where he obtained his first hands-on learning experiences. In both the Canadian fisheries dispute and the Koszta affair, Winthrop felt the United States' response to be legally sound and justifiable.[15]

In addition to the international law activities, Winthrop participated in moot courts with other students. Writing his mother in November of 1853, Winthrop described a probate exercise where he served as senior counsel mentoring a young student named Fitzgerald. "Think of me next Thursday afternoon, arguing with a mature demeanor and wild, but impressive utterance." He informed his mother that he would be unable to return home for Christmas as he intended to press home his studies, writing, "I am really beginning to feel like I am learning something and I am afraid I will lose too much if I go home at Christmas." Although he felt it unwise to take a holiday, he asked for news of his grandmother's health, as well as another relative, Lyndall Winthrop, who apparently fell ill in China. He assured his mother of his love for her despite his focused studies, concluding the letter with, "do not think, admirable parent, that though comfortable here among friends, I can ever forget you, oft I yearn for you all, your frequent letters are the joy of my existence."[16]

Winthrop's passion for the law was distracted by a personal matter involving a young woman named Sophie Deveraux. This is unsurprising given the amount of attention he placed on women in his earlier writing. Perhaps the absence of a father for much of his formative youth, or perhaps being surrounded by women during his rearing, was the reason for Winthrop's apparent fixation on the "fairer sex." His letters from both Yale and Harvard were replete with allusions to female relationships, interspersed with commentary about law and family matters.

In the summer of 1853, Sophie and her mother relayed to a number of people that William and Sophie were betrothed. This news reached Elizabeth Woolsey by way of a forged letter purporting an engagement proposal from William to Sophie, and it did not accord well with the Winthrop family. It is difficult, if not impossible, to know the reason for this disapproval. Perhaps Sophie was considered beneath William's station. A biographer of Theodore Winthrop considered the Winthrop family to be snobbish to their "social inferiors."[17]

Perhaps Elizabeth Woolsey did not approve of Sophie for personal reasons. Winthrop had alluded to his mother having a personal disdain for both Sophie and her mother. However, the basis of the disdain is absent from any surviving letters, and its existence is only recorded. "For me to think of marriage for another 5 or 6 years would be pure folly and imprudence, but most of all, absurd recklessness," Winthrop argued to his mother. "As to Sophie; while, ever since I was with her in the summer of '51, I have felt more or less concern about her; and while I have now and then written her letters of encouragement and advice in answer to appeals from her, it is impossible that I ever should have ever written a word that could be construed by anybody into an offer!"[18]

Winthrop reassured his mother that all other aspects of his life were going well. Whatever rift between him and his mother the issue with Sophie may have caused, it was quickly healed. Writing to his mother in late November 1853, he addressed her as "My dear and mellow parent." He lampooned Theodore, imagining his brother's tall tales of adventure at the Thanksgiving table. Theodore had earlier published his western travel experiences, during which he met with Brigham Young, Modoc Indians in California, and frontiersmen. Winthrop satirized his brother regaling the family while he carved a Turkey, calling it the "Sublime Porte," as a play on the Ottoman Empire. Next, William imagined Theodore would "pass along the Dalles," referring to a small post along the Oregon Trail, then offer up to the guests, "some Mormon" followed by "a little emigrant," and then, "a Puget." At the same time, Winthrop reassured his mother he was well, though he included in his letters his personal observations of the young women of Cambridge that he was "becoming fast acquainted with," such as "the lovely and pleasing Miss Storer of White Mountains," and the "incomparable Miss Collins."[19]

Winthrop himself, in fact, celebrated Thanksgiving at three separate homes, including his boarding lodge and the home of Robert Charles Winthrop Sr. He conversed with his great uncle Robert Charles and another prominent jurist named Horace Gray, whom Winthrop described as "a glorious fellow."[20] Winthrop would later have a brief association with Gray's half brother, John Chipman Gray, a prominent jurist and confidant of Oliver Wendell Holmes Jr. During the Civil War, Winthrop and John Gray served together in the Judge Advocate General's Department under Joseph Holt's command. After the Civil War, John Gray departed the service and became a leading scholar in American property law and a noted Harvard Law professor, while Horace Gray served as a justice on the Massachusetts Supreme Court and was later appointed to the United States Supreme Court by President Chester Alan Arthur. Winthrop's circle of prestigious friends grew during his time in Cambridge, thanks in large part to the influence of Robert Charles.

And yet, Harvard offered Winthrop opportunities to meet with prominent politicians and jurists independent of his prominent great uncle. In the winter of 1853, he met with Judge Lemuel Shaw, the chief justice of the Massachusetts Supreme Court. In addition to obtaining career advice from Justice Shaw, Winthrop also befriended Richard Dana, the noted lawyer who defended Burns and authored *Two Years before the Mast*. During and after the Civil War, Dana taught international law at Harvard. Dana took an interest in helping Winthrop succeed and introduced him to Senator Charles Sumner, the Whig turned Free Soiler and ardent abolitionist opponent of the former House Speaker.[21]

In January 1854, Winthrop gained admission to the Massachusetts bar, but still intended to finish his course of study at Harvard first.[22] He celebrated by drinking "Whiskey Punch," and in letters to his family, he included copies of the *Boston Atlas*, the *Courier*, and the *Commonwealth*, noting his admission to the bar. In passing the bar, he did more than to become eligible to practice law in Massachusetts. His bar examiners publicly commended his performance, and he took a great deal of personal pride in the accomplishment, conveying to his sister, "I am very glad that it has been my privilege to come out first in the cleanest bar in the United States. You notice Rufus Choate's name very near mine."[23]

Winthrop finished his year of study in May 1854 and moved into a Boston house in living conditions similar to what he experienced in Cambridge. The room cost $3.50 per week and included breakfast and tea as well as a Sunday meal. However, he suffered a temporary shortage of funds to begin his career, and he felt it necessary to ask his mother to borrow $120. His prospects for employment were very good as a result of both his family connections and those he made on his own at Harvard.

According to the newspapers, Winthrop was something of a rising star in the law. By the end of summer, he interviewed with the prominent firm Hubbard and Watts. William J. Hubbard, the senior partner in the firm, was the son of a Massachusetts Supreme Court justice with judicial aspirations of his own. Despite Winthrop's family connections to the firm, he realized he had to prove his intellect to Hubbard, a former judge, writing, "I shall do all I can to prove to Hubbard that I am reliable."[24]

But Winthrop may have had a personal connection to Hubbard that opened the door to the partnership. Hubbard initially studied at Yale under the tutelage of Timothy Dwight and studied alongside Theodore Dwight Woolsey. He was active in the administration of a Presbyterian congress. Hubbard also served as a chairman of the Prudential Committee of the American Board of Commissioners for Foreign Missions, a Congregational organization which placed American missionaries in overseas posts, an organization which Winthrop's family were involved with as well.[25]

William spent the summer and fall of 1854 with an optimistic outlook for his future. By the end of the year, he entered into a partnership with Hubbard. Hubbard's junior partner, a young attorney named Suter, had planned to leave the firm. With the prospect of Winthrop taking Suter's place, Hubbard, according to Winthrop, wanted to speedily effectuate the move. Hubbard tendered two offers of employment. The first offer was to serve as a salaried assistant at the rate of four hundred dollars per year. Salaried assistants copied legal documents, drafted and entered court filings, and conducted research. But Winthrop chose the more ambitious offer, which was to join Hubbard as a limited partner. "The senior has his own private peculiar business, and the junior has his, but there is an intermediate business in which both share business," Winthrop described. The shared business occurs "when the senior needs the assistance of the junior, or when the junior needs the senior's advice and superior momentum." On the other hand, this relationship was one of even cost sharing between the two for the upkeep of their legal office, including heating coal, books, and other expenses. Having decided to enter into the relationship with Hubbard as a copartner, Winthrop had to ask his mother for a "temporary allowance" to buy a desk, account books, and signs. In this request, he argued that a partnership with Hubbard would give him, "position, status, and consideration."[26]

Winthrop then stressed to his mother an allegiance to his family lineage. Hubbard had objected to Winthrop's "Episcopalian elements in the office." He acquiesced to Hubbard by removing candlesticks and religious artifacts from the office but refused to undertake any action "at the expense of sacrificing the Puritan Faith of my Fathers." In terms of professional success, by October 1854 Winthrop had won two large settlements, including one in an admiralty trial. In that case, he represented the owner and captain of a vessel he described as "a weather beaten old mariner," and prevailed, winning damages and an additional twenty dollars, as well as his fees. He assured his mother that he longed for the whole family, and in particular Theodore, whom he had not heard from in some time.[27]

In addition to his law practice, William wrote articles on the upcoming 1856 elections for the *Boston Atlas*. As his brother-in-law William Templeton Johnson resided in Staten Island, Winthrop believed Templeton would know personal details of the local Republicans, including Hamilton Fish, John A. King, and William Seward. He caveated his letter that, although he believed Seward was a likely candidate for the 1856 presidential election, Robert Charles Winthrop thought otherwise. What Templeton provided in return is unknown, but Winthrop's interest in the three candidates was not misplaced, as all three of them held high state and federal offices, though none of them ever occupied the White House. Of the three, Seward was the most successful and had a personal connection to Robert Charles, which later benefited Winthrop's entry into the Judge Advocate General's Department.[28]

It was becoming apparent to Winthrop that the practice of law only partially fulfilled him and he felt restless. In 1856, Robert Charles Winthrop and his peers campaigned for Millard Fillmore's candidacy and brought Winthrop grudgingly along. In 1850, Fillmore ascended to the presidency by succession rather than election, serving as vice president in Zachary Taylor's administration when Taylor died in office. Fillmore failed to gain his own party's nomination at the Whig Convention in 1852, in part because he signed into law the Fugitive Slave Act. This act earned him the enmity of a number of Northern Whigs. Although a Northerner himself, Fillmore had little support in the North. He was no longer a national candidate, and his support was largely from pro-slavery Southern Whigs.[29]

There were a number of other reasons for Fillmore's unpopularity among many former Northern Whigs, in addition to his third-party candidacy under the Know-Nothing banner in 1856. Essentially a nativist political movement, Know-Nothings demanded reform, while at the same time espousing anti-immigrant, in particular anti-Irish, leanings. Many Know-Nothings were also abolitionists, but an antislavery platform in no way unified the Know-Nothing Party. Know-Nothings ran a number of successful elections between 1852 and 1858 capturing the mayoral races in Chicago, Philadelphia, Baltimore, and San Francisco, as well as the Massachusetts and Maryland governorships. By 1854, the Know-Nothings had effectively killed the Whig Party in Massachusetts. Robert Charles Winthrop had, in fact, been offered a leadership post in the Know-Nothing Party, but declined.[30] But with the emergence of the Republican Party, the Know-Nothings began to fade almost as quickly as they rose after the death of the Whigs. Like the Whigs, the Know-Nothings were likely doomed from the start to a short life span. In American history, it is difficult to make overt and violent hate nationally respectable for a length of time, and the Know-Nothings attempted to do just that. But, during a vacuum of power, it is possible to discern how old family Americans, particularly Northern old families such as the Winthrops, would find a brief attraction to the Know-Nothings. There was no other party to attach to until 1856.[31]

Winthrop found Fillmore's politics distasteful, but thought him a better candidate than James Buchanan. To Winthrop, Buchanan was another Jacksonian Democrat who supported slavery. The Boston Winthrops, however, could not support Fremont, the Republican candidate, and as long as William lived among them, he seems to have felt the necessity of going along with their views. Many later Republicans, including Ulysses Grant, supported either Buchanan or Fillmore over Fremont. The reason behind Fremont's lack of appeal may have been nothing more than his lack of experience, but a number of fellow officers found Fremont personally unacceptable. He was feted at Harvard during the election campaign. Yet in a letter to Theodore, William expressed support for Fremont, believing that the Republicans would run him again in 1860. William compared Fremont's 1856 campaign to Andrew Jackson's 1824 efforts, writing that "just as Jackson was the candidate of the Democrats from the first days of Adams' administration till the election in 1830—so do the Republicans see now the beauty of giving a point and coherency to their efforts by looking to Fremont, and making his name the rallying cry."[32]

Winthrop's political interests rivaled his interest in the law. Perhaps this was natural since the law and politics often intersect, and in the case of the 1850s elections, law and politics had the potential to dictate sweeping legal changes to a degree not seen since at least the election of 1828. Still, Winthrop understood that the law provided him a living and politics, a diversion. Of all the cases of which he wrote, the most detailed was a medical malpractice case involving an omnibus driver. His client, the driver, had broken his "radius and ulna" in an accident, and a doctor performed, in Winthrop's estimation, an unnecessary and harmful surgery. Describing the doctor's expert witness as "a German physician who was ignorant and stupid of the operation performed" and the surgery as "a kind of butchery or 'incomprehensible experimentation,'" William relayed that he won the case for the plaintiff.[33] The financial award is absent from his letter. However, in the nineteenth century, a medical malpractice case was, in and of itself, a significant undertaking, favoring the medical professional. But Winthrop prevailed in this case, convincing the jurors the doctor erred.

Of all Winthrop's cases from his tenure in Boston, only one, *Swain v. Minzer*, survives in the appellate record. He represented a plaintiff at both the trial and appellate portions of a debtor dispute case which centered on the question of police authority to enter into a private dwelling. A police officer in the process of executing a civil process smashed through the door of a private dwelling. The law forbade marshals and peace officers from entering the dwelling of a private owner or renter for the purpose of serving a civil process. The plaintiff's particular house was subdivided, giving the officer an impression that the front door was a street entry into a number of private apartments when in fact the plaintiff occupied all rooms in the structure. At trial the jury found for the plaintiff and awarded damages against the officer, who then appealed. The basis of the officer's appeal was that tenement apartments were distinguishable from private homes. Winthrop argued to the Massachusetts Supreme Court that the law did not distinguish in the quality of the construction of dwellings. The state court agreed, stating such tenements were "entitled to the privilege and protection the law affords to the habitations of men."[34] Perhaps the case was unexceptional, but it did show Winthrop could side with working-class clients as well as wealthy ones. And yet, this appears to be the only case during his Boston tenure in which Winthrop represented such a client. Later, in Minnesota and then in the army, Winthrop represented poor and unpopular clients with zeal.

NOTES

1. William Winthrop, letter to his family, September 21, 1853 (YALE).
2. Winthrop, letter to his family, September 21, 1853.
3. Winthrop, letter to his family, September 21, 1853.
4. Charles Warren, *History of the Harvard Law School and of Early Legal Conditions in America*, vol. 2 (New York: Da Capo reprint, 1970), 345.
5. Winthrop, letter to his family, September 21, 1853. Winthrop was also a member of the Blackstone Club, along with his friend Joseph Choate, named in the above letter. Winthrop's relationship with Choate, a fellow wealthy New Englander with colonial roots, was unsurprising given the nature of Harvard law in the mid-nineteenth century. Choate eventually became a noted diplomat, serving as ambassador to Great Britain; a gifted attorney; and an international law expert. In his career, he ably represented Indian tribes and attacked anti-Chinese legislation. In 1878, he successfully defended Fitz-John Porter, a disgraced Civil War general under whose command Winthrop served. Choate represented a diverse array of clients, from a common laborer who was injured by the actions of a wealthy New York icon to Stanford University. He took an interest in foreign

trials as well, arguing that the French prosecution of Emile Zola in 1898 was an affront to basic rights. Eight years after Winthrop's death, Choate represented the United States at the 1907 Hague Peace Congress that attempted to lessen international conflict and reduce the horrors of war. One of Choate's assistants in 1907, Major George B. Davis, was previously an assistant to Winthrop while he taught at West Point.

6. Arthur Sutherland, *The Law at Harvard: A History of Ideas and Men, 1817–1967* (Boston: Harvard-Belknap, 1967), 75.

7. Warren, *History of the Harvard Law School*, 182.

8. Winthrop, letter to his family, September 21, 1853. In 1853 the Harvard model Congress was disrupted with threats of violence over the slavery issue. See Carla Bosco, "Harvard University and the Fugitive Slave Act," *New England Quarterly* 79 (June 2006), 240–241.

9. Violence among the Harvard law students had occurred in the 1850s, arising specifically from the slavery issue. The campus violence reflected a growing anger between pro-slavery adherents and abolitionists. In May 1854, Congress passed the Kansas-Nebraska Act, and it was shortly signed into law by President Pierce. The act effectively nullified the Missouri Compromise of 1820 by permitting slavery to expand north of the 36-30 line, should popular sovereignty so dictate. As a result of the act, a number of pro-slavery interests as well as abolitionists entered into the Kansas Territory armed. Violence immediately ensued as the population of settlers rose from eight hundred in 1854 to eight thousand in 1855. See Nicole Etcheson, *Bleeding Kansas: Contested Liberty in the Civil War Era* (Lawrence: University of Kansas Press, 2004), 28.

10. For a detailed overview of the legal case involving Burns, see Samuel Shapiro, "The Rendition of Anthony Burns," *Journal of Negro History* 44, no. 1 (January 1959), 34–51; also Bosco, "Harvard University and the Fugitive Slave Act," 227.

11. Shapiro, "The Rendition of Anthony Burns," 43, citing W. W. Winthrop to Judge Winthrop, May 27, 1854. Shapiro labels William Winthrop as a young antislavery lawyer. This label is perhaps premature for this time. While in Boston, Winthrop believed slavery an immoral, but constitutionally permissible institution. It was not until after Winthrop left Boston for Minnesota that he espoused slavery as unconstitutional.

12. Warren, *History of the Harvard Law School*, 175.

13. Charles C. Grafton, *The Works of the Rt. Rev. Charles C. Grafton*, vol. 4, ed. B. Talbot Rogers (New York: Longmans, Green, 1914), 21–53.

14. William Winthrop, letter to his mother, Elizabeth, November 27, 1853 (YALE).

15. Winthrop, letter to Elizabeth, November 27, 1853.

16. Winthrop, letter to Elizabeth, November 27, 1853.

17. Elbridge Colby, *Theodore Winthrop* (New York: Twayne Publishers, 1965), 17.

18. Winthrop, letter to Elizabeth, November 27, 1853.

19. Winthrop, letter to Elizabeth, November 27, 1853.

20. Winthrop, letter to Elizabeth, November 27, 1853.

21. John M. Raymond and Barbara J. Frischholz, "Lawyers Who Established International Law in the Untied States," *American Journal of International Law* 76, no. 4 (October 1982), 813. Although Winthrop did not record it at the time, his asso-

ciation with Joseph Choate, Horace Gray, Lemuel Shaw, and Richard Dana likely boosted his own transformation from supporting Whig politics to embracing the early Republican antislavery platform. Too, by 1856 Theodore Winthrop was an ardent Republican campaigning for Fremont. Certainly William's circle of friends consisted of future Republican leaders, and it is not difficult to draw a line from his later legal writing to the views held by the men in this circle. In particular, the concept of equality under the law was a view shared by these men, although this did not translate into an equality in practice for all of them. Despite their declarations of equality, old stereotypes died hard, and in many cases a patrician attitude toward freemen was evident.

22. William Winthrop, letter to his sister Sarah, January 8, 1854 (YALE).

23. Winthrop, letter to Sarah, January 8, 1854.

24. William Winthrop, letter to his mother, Elizabeth, May 7, 1854 (YALE).

25. John E. Todd, *Sketch of the Life and Character of the Hon. William J. Hubbard, Delivered at His Funeral* (Boston: Suffolk County Bar, 1864), 1–16.

26. William Winthrop, letter to his mother, Elizabeth, October 15, 1854 (YALE).

27. Winthrop, letter to Elizabeth, October 15, 1854. He also notified his mother of a new romance with one "Ms. Eliza H.," but since this was only a singular reference, it can easily be assumed his stated marital intentions did not materialize.

28. William Winthrop, letter to William Templeton Johnson, March 25, 1856 (YALE).

29. David Potter, *The Impending Crisis, 1848–1861* (New York: Harper, 1976), 236–263.

30. Michael F. Holt, *The Rise and Fall of the American Whig Party: Jacksonian Politics and the Onset of Civil War* (New York: Oxford University Press, 1999), 889; Robert Charles Winthrop Jr., *A Memoir of Robert Charles Winthrop: Prepared for the Massachusetts Historical Society* (Boston: Little, Brown, 1897), 168.

31. James M. McPherson, *Battle Cry of Freedom: The Civil War Era* (New York: Oxford University Press, 1988), 157–159.

32. William Winthrop, letter to his brother, Theodore, November 18, 1856 (YALE).

33. William Winthrop, letter to his brother, Theodore, March 30, 1857 (YALE).

34. *Swain v. Minzer*, 74 Mass. 182, 186 (Mass. 1857).

4

Frontier Lawyer in the Minnesota Territory

Being much interested in carrying through my surprise abolition movement.

—William Winthrop to his sister Laura Winthrop Johnson

While Winthrop's Boston law practice included a diverse range of advocacy, involving criminal law defense, slander, estate drafting, and business and property disputes, it was not enough to sustain his interest. His clients were not from all levels of society, but rather, they were mostly a select few of Boston's elite, though he had assisted Richard Dana in the Anthony Burns rendition case. By 1856, his correspondence with his family contained statements suggesting boredom and a longing for adventure.

Although involved in Boston's politics, he did not approve of the upper-crust Whigs. Nor was he enamored of the Know-Nothings. To be sure, Winthrop harbored many of the typical negative views of Protestant Americans, in particular toward the new Irish immigrants. But he viewed prejudice by law and exclusion by decree as equal anathemas, and he refused to join any nativist societies. A number of his peers migrated to the Know-Nothing Party.

Winthrop coupled his education with his desire for adventure. He wanted to remain a practitioner of the law, but at the same time break free from what must have been for him a stifling and rigid Bostonian practice. He chose to become a frontier lawyer, whose clients came from a broad spectrum of society. In the 1850s, the American frontier was vast, stretching from the Pacific Coast where Theodore traveled, across the Rocky

Mountains to the Great Plains. It was in the cold northern plains of the Minnesota Territory that Winthrop found his adventure and fulfillment.

Originally called the Wisconsin Territory until 1848, the region consisted of modern-day Wisconsin, Minnesota, and parts of the Dakotas. When the eastern part of the territory achieved statehood and took the name Wisconsin, the remaining territory adopted Minnesota as its name. This territory offered more than land. In the 1850s, an economic boom created employment opportunities in timber, fur trading, and agriculture. In turn there was a need for banking, medical, and legal services to support the growing population. The population was a hodgepodge of Irish, German, and Scandinavian immigrants; eastern speculators and timber men; and a smattering of Southerners.[1]

There was a wide range of languages and accents, as well as values; and, despite the vast differences of the settlers, whether by ethnicity or class, there was a shared common struggle against nature's elements. Winthrop had never before been exposed to this type of diversity. In the 1850s, the territory was relatively peaceful, though in 1862 the Sioux Indians and settlers engaged in open warfare. With the possibility of statehood, there were political opportunities as well.

The territory was not newly discovered. Europeans had explored Minnesota at around the same time as John Winthrop the Younger served as governor of the Connecticut Colony. It was the French who first crossed over the territory and came into contact with the Sioux and the Ojibwe Indians. Fur trading was the French settlers' primary enterprise, although exploration for other natural resources remained a constant feature. The city and county names still echo the French and Indian heritage of the territory: Duluth, Hennepin, Minneapolis, Mendota. But the French never attempted to settle the area in large numbers or displace the native Indians, preferring to trade with them instead. This remained the case with the British, who after their victory in the French and Indian War gained control over the eastern part of the territory. For the most part, good relations existed between the Europeans and Indians of all tribes.[2]

The United States first came into possession of the western part of the territory as a result of the Louisiana Purchase from Napoleon in 1803. Ownership of the eastern and northern sections of the territory was disputed between the United States and Great Britain until 1818, when the governments of both countries agreed on a boundary separating Minnesota and Canada. The following year, the army constructed an outpost which came to be known as Fort Snelling. The outpost was designed to enforce treaties between the government and the Sioux and Ojibwe. In the 1830s, a trickle of settlers arrived. In 1842, the British and United States governments settled all other outstanding boundary issues with the signing of the Webster-Ashburton Treaty. In the 1840s and 1850s, a number of agreements and treaties with the diverse Indian tribes were signed and most of their land was ceded to settlers in exchange for monies. As a result of a number of unscrupulous failures by territorial authorities and land speculators to live up to the terms of the treaties, a feeling of ill will accumulated among the tribes which later led to a bloody uprising.[3]

The territory's size was reduced by almost a third with the establishment of the state of Wisconsin in 1848. However, Minnesota's population grew from 4,000 that year to over 150,000 a decade later. In 1849, the territory passed its first set of laws which liberally granted a free public education to any person between the ages of four and twenty-one years. Land sold for $1.25 per acre, and by 1856 the government had sold over 1 million acres.[4] Equally important was the territory's prohibition on slavery. The first mass antislavery meeting was held in St. Anthony, Minnesota, in 1855. Although bound by the Fugitive Slave Law of 1850 to return slaves on demand, Minnesota became a haven for runaway slaves. This fact was highlighted in the infamous 1857 *Dred Scott* decision, in which the majority of the Supreme Court ruled an African was not a citizen under the Constitution, and a slave could not shed his slave status without his owner's consent. Scott resided in the Minnesota Territory and many considered him a free man. However, he left the territory for St. Louis and challenged his slave status there. Had he remained in the Minnesota Territory, he might have maintained his freedom. The decision occurred on the eve of Minnesota statehood and upset many of the state's constitutional convention delegates. Minnesota was clearly an antislavery enclave, though not necessarily one populated by ardent abolitionists eager for war.[5]

The same year *Dred Scott* was decided, Congress passed the Minnesota Enabling Act. This act set in motion the legal mechanisms for achieving statehood. It dictated that in June 1857, the territory would elect delegates to a convention to decide whether the residents wished to join the United States as a state or remain a territory. If the convention decided for statehood, it was then charged with the duty of drafting a state constitution, consistent with its federal counterpart. Once the state constitution was accepted by the people of the state, it then had to be considered for ratification by the United States Senate. If the Senate ratified the state constitution, statehood was effectively achieved. However, political divisions in the territory did not lend uniformity of purpose to the process.

In the 1850s, as Minnesota moved toward statehood, slavery dominated most of the internal debates. The territory was divided into two almost numerically equal political camps. In St. Paul and the other large towns such as St. Anthony, the Democrats held a slight majority. Outside of the cities, the majority of the easterners were loyal Democrats, but at most shared a plurality with the other residents who tended toward the

Republican Party. Minnesota Democrats tended to look to Stephen A. Douglas as their leader, even though he had not set foot in the territory. Like Douglas, Minnesota Democrats viewed slavery as an evil, but federal termination of it as an equal evil. In essence, these Democrats professed local sovereignty as the cornerstone of democracy. Most Minnesota Democrats also believed that slave owners possessed pecuniary rights in their property, no matter how vile the institution of slavery was.[6]

Opposed to the Democrats were the emerging Republicans, and Winthrop joined this political group within a short time of his residency there. Consisting of former Whigs, religious abolitionists, and German and Scandinavian immigrants who obtained the right to vote locally, the Republicans sought an end to slavery nationwide, though with differences among themselves as to timing and methods. The division between Republicans and Democrats resulted in acrimonious debate during the 1857 state convention, which became so contentious that each side created its own independent convention and declared the other side's efforts as illegitimate.[7]

The Democratic territorial governor, Willis Gorman, accused Republicans of cheating in the numbers of delegates eligible to attend the convention, as well as in the numbers of persons voting for the appointment of delegates. Democrats also accused Republicans of desiring war against the South, as well as a dissolution of the Union to rid the remaining states of slavery.[8] A local Democrat newspaper derisively referred to the Republicans as "black Republicans, who were willing to have their daughters marry niggers."[9] Yet, despite the two conventions, each side drafted a proposed state constitution remarkably similar to the other side, with a number of minor differences in wording being the only issues. On October 15, 1857, the state constitution was adopted by a vote of 30,555 to 571. It was a singularly lopsided vote which, in and of itself, did not speak to the year-long acrimonious debate.[10]

The results of the first legislative and gubernatorial elections were not without controversy. In November 1857, Democrats narrowly won the governorship and control of the legislature. Republicans claimed the results tainted as a result of illicit voting by United States soldiers and imported Irish laborers. Winthrop fully believed that the Democrats engaged in chicanery at the election polls.[11]

Ultimately, the Minnesota Constitution prohibited slavery in any form except as a punishment for convicted criminals. The state constitution also enumerated many of the same rights as its federal counterpart, but unlike its federal counterpart the state constitution contained a clause allowing for the eventual enfranchisement of black males. Moreover, there was a prohibition of discrimination based on religious belief or ethnicity. It was, for its time, a liberal guarantee of rights. In the end, the Minnesota

Constitutional Convention and transition to statehood were more peaceable than "Bleeding Kansas," but the rhetoric in the debates consisted of outright denunciations of Republicans for their attempts to overturn the Fugitive Slave Act, and these denunciations added fuel to the growing sectionalist debates.[12]

In the three years between 1857 and 1859, the territory offered a number of new opportunities for a restless or politically ambitious man. If the young man were already politically connected, the opportunities were all the more readily available. Winthrop arrived in Minnesota with two great assets. The region had a need for lawyers, and his Boston law background clearly was a benefit in a place such as Minnesota. Additionally, he possessed the asset of having his lineage. As an emerging Republican and a man with the Winthrop name, he could open doors to a political career if he so chose. Indeed, he met with Alexander Ramsey, the leading Republican in the territory. But Winthrop went to Minnesota to become a frontier lawyer and represent people, rather than to lead them in a state house or in Congress.

On January 22, 1857, William told his brother that he had made up his mind to move to Minnesota. He asked Theodore to remain quiet until he decided to announce his intentions. "I have said nothing to RCW or the snobs. . . . I pretty much make up my mind," he noted. As a possible reflection of his own life, Winthrop talked of his Boston law practice, commenting on defending a weak case: "I did what I could for them." On the other hand, he was amused by an instance where one of his "learned brethren" was unable to shake the testimony of a simple girl.[13] The month following the letter, William packed his belongings and headed to Minnesota. He traveled by rail as far as Cleveland. From there he continued his journey on horse across the Midwest and into the northern plains in search of a home.

Located alongside a set of falls on the west bank of the Mississippi River, across from Minneapolis and north of St. Paul, was St. Anthony, a third town vying for prominence. Named after the patron saint of lost possessions and travelers, the town shared the same name with the falls. In 1872, Minneapolis absorbed St. Anthony, but this was twelve years after Winthrop departed from the state. In 1849, a traveling New England minister preached the beauty of St. Anthony's Falls to his Connecticut flock, proclaiming, "I had views of the greatness of my country, such as I have never had in the crowded capitals and the smiling villages of the east. Far in the distance did they seem to be, and there came over the soul the idea of greatness and vastness, which no figures, no description, had ever conveyed to my mind." Detailing to his flock the region's bluffs, river basin, islands, forests, and prairies, the minister concluded, "God who did all of this, that he might prepare it for the abode of a civilized and Christian people."[14] Whether Winthrop heard this sermon is unknown, but it reflected his own initial thoughts about St. Anthony and Minnesota. At this time, Minnesota experienced an economic boom and St. Anthony's population reflected the boom.

When Winthrop first arrived in St. Anthony in May of 1857, it was second in population to St. Paul. Its position on the Mississippi River was not as accessible to river traffic as was St Paul or Minneapolis. However, it had access to land routes that the other towns did not. St. Anthony also had a feature typical of frontier towns: a handful of elder businessmen controlled much of the local economic and political power as a result of having bought up hundreds of acres in land speculation before immigrant waves arrived. In the case of St. Anthony, the local magnate was a man named Franklin Steele. Mr. Steele owned the largest island on the river as well as a number of land parcels in the town. He was also the director of a sawmill critical to the local economy. Steele had hoped to create a "Lowell of the west" by expanding the mill and tapping into the river for power.[15] Steele had also obtained lines of credit from eastern banks in order to finance his plans for St. Anthony's growth. He donated land and a building for the eventual establishment of a state university.[16]

Steele had hoped to be nominated as a Republican senatorial candidate in 1858 but did not receive the party's endorsement, though he had Winthrop's support. More than any other St. Anthony resident, Steele had a vested interest in seeing the town independently succeed. In this, he ultimately failed. Still, St. Anthony's residents felt the city could grow into the capital of the territory, when and if the territory became a state. Moreover, St. Anthony had the promise of a city on the rise, with a planned university, schools, churches, and banks. Fittingly, for Winthrop, the first two churches in the city were of Presbyterian and Congregationalist denominations, each a variant of the original Puritan movement.[17] But in 1857, when Winthrop arrived, St. Anthony must have been a rough-hewn frontier town. Locally, the main political issue revolved around the grog shops, prostitution, and a temperance movement. Connected with the grog shop issue was the presence of violent crime. A number of unsolved murders and assaults were usually blamed on Irish immigrants.[18]

This blame coincided with the lingering presence of Know-Nothing influence as well as the normal prejudices of the day. At the constitutional convention, there were a few Know-Nothing adherents of little consequence, but they did tend to vocally oppose Catholic and Irish influences as immoral.[19] St. Anthony possessed a red light district, with crime conditions so bad that in 1857 the town's residents formed a vigilance committee. The committee, composed of six hundred men, marched into the district and attempted to force saloon proprietors and prostitutes out of the town. Although the committee succeeded in their goals by smashing up saloon furniture and forcefully removing the owners and prostitutes, it was only a temporary reprieve, and by the end of the year these businesses returned.[20]

At times while in Minnesota, Winthrop espoused prejudice against the Irish, but he supported the Constitution's guarantee of rights regardless of faith or nationality. Since he drank whiskey, he sided with the saloon owners against prohibitionists. Moreover, the St. Anthony Brewery, one of the town's leading businesses, was also an occasional client. Winthrop thought St. Anthony a coarse frontier town, lacking amenities, writing that "it is a real luxury in this town for a man to even secure a good room."[21] He also wrote home after a year in the state, that in order to succeed one must "blow and bully about, and not be suave and benign." Indeed, in relating to the locals, William felt the use of profanity to be a valuable asset.[22] But he showed an enthusiasm for his new surroundings unlike in any previous time in his life. Moreover, he had achieved a degree of the personal freedom that he had earlier sought.

It was the territory itself which most attracted Winthrop. "This beautiful country . . . greenly flow the grass and trees on the Minneapolis side. How feathery, light, and delicate the beeches and elms on Niblet Island. How the prairie sparkled with gosling flower and yellow of the goldeneye and blue violet," he told his family.[23]

He also set out on explorations of the territory, encountering men from the various Indian tribes, claiming "every day I become more identified with this country, seeing men from St. Cloud, and the Sioux, the Minnetouka . . . etc."[24] In contrast to his occasional swipes at the Irish, Winthrop's letters to his family do not contain any aspersions against Indians, but rather, when he mentions them, there is a sense of admiration for their toughness.

Describing his law offices as comfortable and well furnished, Winthrop presented an optimistic view of the future in his letters. But he also displayed competitiveness in regard to his law practice. Writing of a fellow attorney and New Haven native named Joice, he characterized him "as a man of no remarkable parts, but a gentleman and an agreeable fellow." Winthrop also described his first case titled *Hewes & Noble v. Poncin*, in which he represented a plaintiff against a stable owner for an injury to the plaintiff's horse. Describing the case outcome, he wrote, "Verdict $50, which was all we asked—Annihilated Secombe, the atty on the other side."[25]

Secombe was unlikely a worthy opponent. In 1856, the territorial supreme court found that Secombe did not possess the requisite fitness of character to continue the practice of law. Having been effectively disbarred for ethical violations, Secombe petitioned the United States

Supreme Court for relief. The Supreme Court declined to reverse the territorial court's determination, issuing a brief decision.[26] Secombe's legal career did not permanently cease. At some point he was readmitted to the territorial bar. In 1858, Secombe found his way into the United States Supreme Court once more. He had earlier sued Franklin Steele in a case involving a contested land transaction. The case wound its way through the appeal process to the Supreme Court, where that court sided with Steele.[27] In a sense, Winthrop was lucky to have Secombe as a business competitor. There were only a handful of attorneys in St. Anthony and competing for clients against an attorney with a sullied reputation must have made Winthrop's practice all the better. Surprisingly, by 1860, Secombe's reputation recovered enough for him to be appointed as a delegate to the Republican National Convention.[28]

By June 1857, Winthrop's law practice paid enough for him to move from a boarding house to a small home he obtained from a Swedish music teacher. He filled his new home with the "appendages of refined culture," including books. At the same time, he asked his family to send more books, hoping to build a personal library. He continued to praise the flora and fauna of Minnesota, especially the "blueness of the lakes," writing, "Never have I gazed across such exquisitely blue water." Winthrop concluded the letter with, "Business very good, we have the best set of clients of any law firm here on the whole north."[29]

Through the summer of 1857, Winthrop remained convinced the fortunes of his law practice would continue, writing that "business has been uniformly good and piquant during the whole summer." Alexander Ramsey continued to invite Winthrop to St. Paul. In Winthrop's letters, he mentioned visiting Governor Ramsey a few times during the summer and fall, but did not mention any topics of conversation. Later, when Ramsey served as secretary of war in President Rutherford B. Hayes' administration, Winthrop still served as a judge advocate. But Winthrop never benefited from his relationship with Ramsey. President Hayes, acting on James Garfield's wishes, jumped a junior officer over Winthrop to become the judge advocate general.

When not trying cases, William hunted small birds and game with a group of friends. And he continued to attend church, becoming increasingly active in church administration, as well as a religiously based abolitionist group.[30] He remained interested in the Kansas Territory that was then suffering through a number of violent upheavals. But Kansas must have seemed too distant for him to become directly involved with its antislavery movement.

Winthrop described hunting birds, "shooting them on the wing," as well as exploring the northern lakes and sometimes swimming in them. One of his clients brought him to a northern land claim after a court victory to hunt game. In addition to describing court cases and clients, he continued to vividly describe the flora and fauna of Minnesota, writing of the "rock elm," as the "finest feature, large and lofty," as well as the "grandeur of blossom oaks and maples." He also continued to remind all of his family members to take care of his mother, sometimes writing, "coddle ma," "my affection to ma," or "check in with mother."[31]

He sent some twenty dollars to Sarah in September 1857, telling her to spend it on "dress, drink, and maraschino," and reminded her to remember him during her indulgence. In his free time, Winthrop had taken up hunting for quartz crystals and other gemstones. After finding a number of "perfect cornelians"—a type of quartz—Winthrop polished them for the purposes of giving them to his sisters as presents. Winthrop continued to believe the fortunes of his law practice would hold even with a depressed economy on the horizon, which began in New York. But there was a shortage of United States currency in the territory as a result of the economic depression. The economy increasingly relied on scrip. Inside of the territory, scrip had some value, depending on the issuer. Outside of the territory, scrip was worthless. William did not immediately see the impact of this shortage of currency on his fortunes. In late 1857, the territory entered into the economic depression by then affecting the whole nation.[32]

Although Winthrop leaned toward Republican politics, this did not stop him from socializing with some of the leading Democrats such as Willis Gorman and Henry Sibley. Indeed, he considered the Sibleys as his "best friends" in the territory.[33] It may be the case that Winthrop felt a degree of kinship with Henry Sibley for reasons of family pride. Although Sibley was twenty years older than Winthrop, the two shared a family connection. Sibley was a descendant of a Puritan family who came to Massachusetts with the first John Winthrop.[34] When South Carolina's militia fired on Fort Sumter and the state seceded from the Union, Sibley and Gorman put aside their dislike of the Republican Party and fought for the Union. In the end, it was the common belief in the sanctity of the Union as well as the bonds of friendship between Minnesotans, which often stretched across political party lines, that mattered more than the political differences between Republicans and Democrats.

By the late fall of 1857, the law firm's fortunes had declined, although Winthrop maintained high spirits. There were a number of reasons, including those mentioned, for the decline in business, none of which had to do with the practice itself. The area experienced the economic downturn then affecting the country as a whole, and when cold weather set in, peoples' reluctance to travel for any reason was a factor. Scrip remained problematic for those with debts outside of Minnesota. Moreover, Minnesota banks ceased issuing specie in October 1857, and a number of them collapsed. Many professionals had a difficult time securing a living and turned to farming or migrated out of the territory. It was not, as one state historian noted, uncommon for a doctor to double as a pharmacist, teacher, or farmer. Lawyers became increasingly involved in property foreclosures, a practice Winthrop found distasteful.[35]

With free time on his hands, Winthrop explored the area more and traveled often into St. Paul. He also made friends with "one Dutton," who Winthrop conveyed had "been born in South America, educated in England, made a personal fortune in hardware manufacturing in New York, and been broken in a California swindle." Dutton was not his only friend, either. He befriended George Nourse, a fellow attorney and erstwhile Republican politician. Unlike Secombe, Nourse impressed Winthrop with his abilities. The two tried some cases together, and Winthrop mused in his letters on the possibility of a law partnership. Though this did not occur, the two men remained friends and hunting partners. Nourse went on to a successful political career and President Lincoln later appointed him United States attorney for the state. Winthrop also had time to improve his German speaking and writing, understanding that this was important to communicating with prospective clients.[36] Many, if not most, of his clients were immigrants, a complete change from his Boston practice. Winthrop's interaction with his clients brought him into an environment where he met with all economic classes of people. This may have played a part in fostering his later egalitarian view of military law.

Despite the decline in plaintiff's work, criminal cases did not cease, and these cases kept Winthrop gainfully employed through the winter and spring of 1858. In one of these cases, Winthrop apparently held affection for one of his clients, Mrs. Emily Burlingham. She was accused of committing an assault with the intent to kill by a man named J. Kraft. William described her to his sister Laura as a "light haired fair complexioned woman, full of pluck." Kraft trespassed on Burlingham's property, which he claimed to own. The timing of Kraft's trespass was suspect; it occurred during the absence of Emily's husband on a logging trip. When Kraft refused to leave, Emily turned a gun on him, threatening him and chasing him well past her property line. Kraft convinced the prosecutor to charge Emily with trespass, larceny, and assault. Winthrop wrote that the prosecutor objected to his "vivid" closing arguments, but the jury acquitted Emily. Winthrop recorded the courtroom scene: "In the presence of a full candle lit court room we won our triumph, and around the discharged prisoner crowded all her woman friends."[37]

Despite the seriousness of the criminal cases and his increasing involvement in abolitionism, Winthrop's letters did not lose their continual humor. Writing to his mother, he described an incident where the church minister's horse was boarded in a stable alongside a calf, and the hungry calf chewed off the hair on the horse's tail. His interest in the fairer sex remained as strong as before, too. To his sister, Winthrop expressed his interest in a St. Paul woman and suggested that he might move to that city for the convenience of both.[38]

Winthrop's foremost problem during this time was not a lack of clients, but rather a lack of paying clients. He complained to his family of being remunerated in scrip, seething at "town, country, territorial, state scrip. University scrip, bridge scrip." To augment his income, William attempted to teach university students in law and German. He befriended a Reverend Charles Woodward, who had been hired by the university as a foreign language instructor. In turn, Winthrop was able to teach some German. The teaching position augmented his law salary, but even this pay came in the form of scrip. He concluded his tirade against the payments with, "Scrip sir is your Pay!"[39]

One of Sarah's former beaux, a Polish immigrant named Joseph Karge, planned on venturing from the east to teach at the university as well. The tone of William's letter suggests a personal dislike of Karge, predicting, "Utterly alone and desolate will be Karge here if he should come. And some drizzly morning at the foot of a bluff, on the brow of which the university stands, will be found the corpse of Joseph Karge in its Sunday garments, smelling strongly of cigars and liquor."[40]

The ultimate fate of Joseph Karge was far from William's prediction. Karge had been a cavalry officer in the Prussian Army before immigrating to the United States in 1828. Although a professor of languages, Karge remained a cavalryman at heart. He commanded the First and Second New Jersey Cavalry during the Civil War, seeing action in Tennessee and Alabama. He acceded to the chair of the language department at Princeton University and died of natural causes in 1892.

On May 10, 1858, Winthrop celebrated his one-year anniversary in Minnesota and by his own account, it had been a successful year. In a letter to his sister Laura, he reflected that he had seen the Wild West, met the Chippewa Indians, found agate stones, and attended church regularly. He also celebrated Minnesota's statehood, writing, "Now we are a state and many political and pecuniary doubts and difficulties growing out of our semi state, semi territory condition are solved by act of admission." It was at this point in his life where Winthrop took his only step toward a political career. Winthrop went to the 1858 Republican Convention as a delegate from St. Anthony. He did so to support Alexander Ramsey in his attempt to achieve the governorship. Describing to Laura his reasons for going to the convention as "being much interested in carrying through my surprise abolition movement," he also expressed more interest in his increased administrative duties at the local Congregationalist church. From all objective respects, Winthrop was on his way to becoming a pillar of the local community. And yet, the same restlessness that had caused personal unhappiness reappeared, as he wrote Laura, "Why have I not been happy?"[41]

As the spring turned to summer, Winthrop's law fortunes remained in a depressed state. To his brother, Theodore, he expressed an interest in a Miss Patterson, even considering moving to St. Paul so that the two might be together. Increasingly attuned to politics, he expressed an interest in two Republicans running for the presidency, Chase and Blair. To Winthrop at this time, Lincoln was probably unknown. But, like many in the nascent party, he saw possibilities in Seward, Blair, and Chase. These three men were far more obvious candidates for the executive office in 1860 than the almost unknown Illinois attorney. Winthrop spent his free time in a variety of pursuits, domino games with Dutton, church activities, exploring upriver, reading, and recording for his family the nature of a land he passionately loved. But it also became clear to Winthrop that as much as he had a passion for Minnesota, he had a greater longing for his family. Writing to Theodore, he concluded his letter by stating, "Some of you write, I don't care whom."[42]

Of all of his Minnesota cases, Winthrop's most lasting legacy in the state was a defeat before the state supreme court. In late 1858, Winthrop defended a Ramsey County sheriff on appeal before that court. The sheriff had seized a debtor's property and sold it at auction. The sheriff did not have the jurisdiction to seize the property and it was returned to the debtor after the auction, leaving the purchaser bereft of both the property and his payment. The sheriff claimed he provided a caveat emptor statement to the purchasers, but this was disputed. At a trial court, the sheriff, represented by another lawyer, lost the case and was ordered to repay the plaintiff. Representing the sheriff, Winthrop argued that the state supreme court should reverse the verdict since the original court did not have jurisdiction to try the case. While the state supreme court agreed that the original court might not have had jurisdiction, the sheriff waived the argument at trial and therefore forfeited any appeal remedy. As a result, Minnesota adopted the basic rule of civil procedure that jurisdictional defects are a matter of waiver if either party to a lawsuit fails to timely object.[43]

In January 1860, Winthrop began to prepare to leave Minnesota. He informed his mother of his intention to move to New York and perhaps join Theodore who had already begun a law practice in Staten Island. Winthrop noted that he did not mind the Minnesota weather, commenting that while the thermometer had dropped below minus twenty-five degrees, there was an absence of snow. But he also noted that he was "surrounded by sick and dying people." He continued to pursue Miss

Patterson, but did not expect her to reciprocate. He also related to his mother that he continued in the church's abolition movement, but opined that clerics "lacked backbone." As a humorous twist to his opinion, he added, "Why are clerical gentlemen always a little shaky on the stronger points of opinion? In my utopia, chaps destined for the cleric profession are apprenticed to a pirate for four years."[44]

Winthrop left behind a positive impression of his contributions in the shaping of Minnesota law and court procedure. In 1904, five years after Winthrop's death, in a book titled *Pioneer Sketches*, a surviving Minnesota Territory pioneer wrote, "We doubt, however, if there be any brighter legal minds now represented than were found on this list of men who were at first instrumental in shaping court proceedings, no matter how complicated the case: Charles E. Vandenburgh, David A. Secombe, . . . W. W. Winthrop."[45]

In 1860, Winthrop departed Minnesota for Staten Island, New York. His interest in Miss Patterson had ended. Theodore had set up a legal practice there with another friend, and the twin prospects of returning to his family and working in a secure economic environment appealed to Winthrop. He did not tire of Minnesota, and his last letter home spoke of sunsets with the appearance of "a sea of melting gold" and rocky outcroppings resembling a ghost battlefield, "the towers, minarets, and jaggedness where stood the fighting men, and alarm bells ringing, blazed with fire and flame." He saw Minnesota, in his own words, as a continuous passion, "the passion of love, the passion of sunset, the passion of a midnight, moonlit, tempest ocean." But at the same time, he wrote of the world as "a young man's Bohemia," and in it, his "willingness to drift anywhere."[46] Winthrop had gone to Minnesota for adventure and to see and study the land and its people. This he accomplished. But his restlessness did not abate. Like a number of men in the 1850s, Winthrop searched for an outlet to channel his restlessness. It was in New York where this outlet would first appear, not in the law, but in the divisive politics then ripping the country apart.

NOTES

1. Theodore Blegen, *Minnesota: A History of the State* (Minneapolis: University of Minnesota Press, 1963), 175.
2. William E. Lass, *Minnesota: A History*, 2nd ed. (New York: W.W. Norton, 1998), 68
3. Blegen, *Minnesota*, 168–169.
4. *Minnesota, a State Guide*, American Guide Series (New York: Hastings House, 1947), 51; William Watts Folwell, *A History of Minnesota*, vol. 1 (St. Paul: Minnesota Historical Society, 1922), 352.

5. Lass, *Minnesota*, 101–120; Folwell, *A History of Minnesota*, 375.

6. See, for example, Lucius Hubbard and Return I. Holcombe, *Minnesota in Three Centuries*, vol. 3 (St. Paul: Publishing Society of Minnesota, 1908), 36.

7. Blegen, *Minnesota*, 222–223.

8. See, for example, Francis Smith, "Conduct of the Republicans," July 23, 1857, in *The Debates and Proceedings of the Minnesota Constitutional Convention Including the Organic Act of the Territory: With the Enabling Act of Congress, the Act of the Territorial Legislature Relative to the Convention, and the Vote of the People on the Constitution*, 17–29 (St. Paul: Earl S. Goodrich, Territorial Printers, 1860); also Lass, *Minnesota*, 126.

9. Folwell, *A History of Minnesota*, 394.

10. See, e.g., Folwell, *A History of Minnesota*, 394; also Kenneth Stampp, *America in 1857: A Nation on the Brink* (New York: Oxford University Press, 1990), 247.

11. Stampp, *America in 1857*, 257. Winthrop engaged in ethnic stereotyping against "the greasy, sleepy, noisome Irish paddy who sued a warmhearted bricklayer," in one case. After winning the case for the bricklayer, Winthrop described the plaintiff as "slick as Bengal offending cartridge grease," making an illusion to the Sepoy Rebellion having recently occurred in India. William Winthrop, letter to his brother, Theodore, June 11, 1854 (YALE).

12. Folwell, *A History of Minnesota*, 418.

13. Winthrop, letter to Theodore, January 22, 1857 (YALE).

14. Wesley J. Bond, *Minnesota and Its Resources: To Which Are Appended Camp-Fire Sketches, or, Notes of a Trip from St. Paul to Pembina and Selkirk Settlement* (New York: Redfield Press, 1853), 149.

15. Bond, *Minnesota and Its Resources*, 155.

16. Hubbard and Holcombe, *Minnesota in Three Centuries*, 525.

17. Donald Marti, "The Puritan Tradition in a 'New England' of the West," *Minnesota History* 40 (June 1964), 5–8.

18. Bond, *Minnesota and Its Resources*, 153. See also Lucille Kane, "Governing a Frontier City: St. Anthony 1855–1872," *Minnesota History* 33 (September 1956), 117.

19. Hubbard and Holcombe, *Minnesota in Three Centuries*, 31–32.

20. Blegen, *Minnesota*, 205–206.

21. William Winthrop, letter to his brother, Theodore, June 11, 1857 (YALE).

22. William Winthrop, letter to his sister Sarah, April 14, 1858 (YALE).

23. William Winthrop, letter to his brother, Theodore, May 20, 1857 (YALE).

24. Winthrop, letter to Theodore, May 20, 1857.

25. Winthrop, letter to Theodore, May 20, 1857.

26. *Ex parte Secombe*, 60 U.S. 9 (1856).

27. *Secombe v. Steele*, 61 U.S. 92 (1858).

28. Hubbard and Holcombe, *Minnesota in Three Centuries*, 38.

29. William Winthrop, letter to his brother, Theodore, June 11, 1857 (YALE).

30. Winthrop, letter to Theodore, June 11, 1857.

31. William Winthrop, letter to his sister Sarah, September 28, 1857 (YALE).

32. Winthrop, letter to Sarah, September 28, 1857.

33. Winthrop, letter to Sarah, September 28, 1857.

34. Winthrop, letter to Sarah, September 28, 1857.

35. Blegen, *Minnesota*, 208; Folwell, *A History of Minnesota*, 363.

36. William Winthrop, letter to his sister Sarah, August 11, 1857 (YALE).
37. William Winthrop, letter to his sister Laura, May 20, 1858 (YALE).
38. Winthrop, letter to Laura, May 20, 1858.
39. Winthrop, letter to Laura, May 20, 1858.
40. William Winthrop, letter to his sister Sarah, April 14, 1858 (YALE).
41. Winthrop, letter to Laura, May 20, 1858.
42. William Winthrop, letter to his brother, Theodore, August 2, 1858 (YALE).
43. *Tullus v. Brawley*, 3 Minn. 277 (Minn. 1859).
44. William Winthrop, letter to his mother, Elizabeth, January 20, 1860 (YALE).
45. Frank G. O'Brien, *Minnesota Pioneer Sketches: From the Personal Recollections and Observations of a Pioneer Resident* (Minneapolis: H.H.S. Rowell, 1904), 197.
46. Winthrop, letter to his sister Sarah, 1860 (YALE).

5

The Winthrop Brothers Go to War

William and I will stand through and, see the end of this business.

—Theodore Winthrop to William Templeton Johnson, April 1861

New York had a wealthier base of clients than Minnesota, and these clients were more likely to pay cash instead of credit for legal services. Together with his Yale classmate Robbins Little, Winthrop opened a law office at 43 Wall Street, Manhattan. Gone would be the days of relying on scrip and barter for legal work. For Winthrop, the move to New York City had an additional benefit beyond financial stability. Manhattan provided him proximity to his family. In addition to seeing his sister and brother-in-law, Laura and William Templeton Johnson, he was able to spend time with his brother, Theodore. The summer of 1860 found Theodore employed as a lawyer in Staten Island as well, though he spent much of his time secretly writing novels. Still, the Winthrop brothers remained attracted to the outdoors, and the two spent the summer of 1860 exploring the nooks of the island. They also campaigned for Republicans in the 1860 election.[1]

New York's favorite son, William Henry Seward, was roundly believed by many, including the Winthrops, to be the Republican presidential candidate. In stark contrast to Fremont, Seward was a seasoned politician whose antislavery views mirrored those of Charles Sumner. Thus, New York also offered something that Minnesota did not in terms of Republican politics and antislavery beliefs. If the Republicans were to succeed nationally, they would have to succeed in New York and New England, capturing the bulk of the population's loyalty there to counterbalance the Democrats' stranglehold on the South.[2]

Legal historian Kermit Hall writes that by the Civil War, there were three basic divisions among the antislavery movement: radicals, moderates, and Garrisonians. The radicals held that slavery was illegitimate everywhere and rejected the notion that local laws could prevail over the natural right of freedom for all persons. Moderates, who were in the majority of the Republicans and included Salmon Chase, Lincoln, and Seward, sought to prevent the spread of slavery, but felt that the federal government lacked the power to destroy the institution. Garrisonians, named after William Lloyd Garrison, believed that the issue of slavery transcended even the Constitution. To Garrison and his followers, slavery was a sin and if the Constitution supported it, it was "a covenant with death and an agreement with hell."[3]

The Winthrop brothers were clearly not Garrisonians, and as adherents to the Constitution, they subscribed to the moderate position. There was, however, one exception to this position regarding the constraints on federal power: they believed that if an insurrection occurred, the federal government had the right to suppress it through all armed means. After all, Andrew Jackson threatened just that during the first South Carolina secession crisis. Moreover, many moderate Republicans believed that should war occur and the South lose, the Northern victors would have the constitutional right to terminate slavery once and for all through the law.[4]

Theodore and William were also part of a circle of friends that met regularly to discuss the politics of the day. Their number included Robert Gould Shaw and the publisher George Curtis. Robert Shaw was ten years Theodore's junior and eight years William's. Born into a wealthy Unitarian Boston family, Shaw traveled to Europe and shared a love of adventure. He was educated in a Jesuit Catholic school in New York as well as in a prestigious school in Switzerland. Like William, Shaw attended Harvard. In an interesting twist, while Shaw studied for admission to Harvard, his tutor was Francis Barlow, a former Harvard valedictorian who eventually rose to brigadier general in the Army of the Potomac. Barlow later commanded a New York regiment which fought alongside Winthrop's company near Malvern Hill in 1862. Barlow later complimented Winthrop's Sharpshooter company in an official dispatch to George McClellan.

After Harvard, Shaw moved to Staten Island in the later 1850s.[5] He befriended the Winthrop brothers during their stay in Staten Island, but based on the content of Shaw's letters home to his mother and father, it appears his parents knew Elizabeth Woolsey Winthrop. These letters contained such language as: "The Winthrops are both well and send their regards," and "The Winthrops have me to say again that they are both well."[6] The religious orientation of the Winthrop brothers differed from

Shaw's, but their affinity for abolitionism and their worldliness were the common denominators of their friendship. Shaw's abolitionism began with his parents, who had joined the Anti-Slavery Society in 1838. His father's closest friend, Sidney Howard Gay, was the editor of the *Anti-Slavery Standard*. In 1856, Shaw's parents moved to Staten Island, and his father campaigned for Fremont. During the 1856 presidential campaign, both Robert and his father were introduced to George W. Curtis, who later published Theodore's novels. Curtis was also an abolitionist.[7] Thus, there were a number of connections between the Shaws and the Winthrops, but it is unclear as to which one of the connections began the friendship.

The Winthrop brothers also had contact with Hamilton Fish, a prominent local Republican who later became secretary of state in Grant's administration, and a number of their circle of friends, including William, campaigned locally for Seward and then for Lincoln in the summer and fall. When South Carolina militia fired on Fort Sumter and the state seceded from the Union, Theodore and William felt it necessary to take part in suppressing the rebellion. But the two did not merely join to fight for reunification. In the words of George Curtis, the Winthrop brothers enrolled in the army to fight injustice in the nation, and emancipate its black population.[8] Like Theodore, William had grown to detest slavery, and if the war ended with emancipation, he found it a matter of justice.

On April 12, 1861, South Carolina militia fired artillery at Fort Sumter, and eventually forced its surrender. On April 15, 1861, President Lincoln issued a call to the Northern state governors for seventy-five thousand militia to preserve order in the Union and protect Washington, DC. Early on, it became apparent that the security of the capital was in doubt. Washington's population included many Southern sympathizers. Virginia, the most populous slave state, buttressed the government seat just across the Potomac River. Even the War Department's employees could not promise absolute loyalty to the United States. And rumors to the effect of kidnap and murder plots against the president flew. The strangest but apparently most believed of these had to do with a contingent of Texas Rangers lurking in Alexandria in wait for the president. In response to the president's call for militia and in reaction to the impending war, Northern states such as Pennsylvania, Massachusetts, and New York mobilized a number of their respective militia regiments for a ninety-day period of service. Most of the militia commanders and their state governors assumed that if war broke, it would be short.

These militia regiments were anything but uniform and even within the individual states, two regiments might be equipped differently, so as to distinguish one company from another. There was little command and control between the states, and officer positions were largely a product of political patronage. Most state militia regiments seldom drilled, and when they were called to duty, it was invariably to suppress a civil disturbance. The Seventh New York Militia was an oddity, even by the standards of 1861. Divided into eight companies, its members came from the New York elite. Its roster was essentially a "who's who," for the upper crust of engineers, lawyers, and businessmen. Fitz James O'Brien, a popular fiction author, was a member. O'Brien, like Theodore Winthrop, left a written account of the Seventh's march to Washington. On January 1, 1861, it numbered 895 men. By April 18 of the same year, it numbered 1,050, though 100 of these would not make the eventual march to Washington. After Confederate forces fired on Fort Sumter, large numbers of New Yorkers attempted to join, but according to the regiment's official history, most were turned away. There were too many New Yorkers vying for positions in a regiment whose cap could not exceed 1,200 men.[9] However, the Winthrop brothers as well as Robert Shaw were able to join, and they secured enlistments as privates. Theodore went on to the regiment's artillery company while William and Shaw served together in an infantry company and were tent mates.[10] Theodore took on additional employment during this time as a writer for the *Atlantic Monthly*.

The regiment's men wore grey uniforms reminiscent of United States Military Academy cadets. Wearing a unique or even garish regimental uniform, such as the gray, scarlet and blue pantaloon and shirt combination of 11th New York Zouave Firefighters, was not unheard of in the early days of the Civil War. But, as O'Brien recorded, the Seventh's kit was finely tailored in the city's upper cost shops. It had corporate sponsorship from such companies as the mining concern, Phelps, Dodge and Company. The New York Stock Exchange and the Mercantile Exchange each donated one thousand dollars to outfit the regiment. William Aspinwall donated worsted wool jackets for the entire regiment. The Seventh's drum major, standing over six feet in height, was specifically imported from the Prussian Army. The Seventh mustered for a thirty-day period of service instead of the ninety days Lincoln called for. While other regiments marched to Washington, DC, or rode in standard railcars, the Seventh had first-class accommodations. On their way, they ate sandwiches prepared by Delmonico's restaurant and sat on "velvet stools." It was a "champagne" unit.[11]

And yet, the Seventh had a reputation for being the best-drilled regiment in the nation. The regiment was used for ceremonies honoring foreign dignitaries and monarchs. It was the pride of New York. It was also effectively used to suppress civil riots which had plagued New York in the 1840s and 1850s. On January 14, 1861, the regiment's officers presented a petition to Edward D. Morgan, their state governor, indicating their desire to be called to duty if Southern secession occurred. Lincoln's former rival in two elections, Stephen A. Douglas, a native of Illinois, called the unit "that unrivalled regiment of citizen soldiers." By this time Douglas had argued for unity with the president and proclaimed that "every man had to be for the union or against it, a patriot or traitor."[12] He cheerfully endorsed the Seventh's march to war, as did Major Robert Anderson, the hero of Fort Sumter who was present at the Seventh's departure parade through the city.[13]

The long-term patriotism of the regiment's men was not in doubt. Of the men who mustered into service and marched to Washington, DC, in April 1861, 606 later served as officers in other regiments. Of these, 3 became generals; 29, colonels; and 46, lieutenant colonels. Fifty-eight died during the war, and a considerable number were wounded.[14] One of the more famous casualties was Theodore's friend, Robert Shaw, who later served with distinction in the Second Massachusetts at Antietam, and went on to command the Fifty-fourth Massachusetts Infantry, one of the first African American regiments. Shaw later obtained a colonelcy but was killed during an attack on Fort Wagner in South Carolina in the summer of 1863. Thus, while Seventh New York was a "champagne unit," its members were unafraid to serve in combat. The Winthrop brothers were among this category, but Theodore misread the patriotic drive and war fervor of his militia companions. Shortly after arriving in Washington, DC, Theodore wrote to his brother-in-law William Templeton Johnson that both he and William would stand through and "see the end of this business," but doubted the resolve of his fellow New Yorkers in the Seventh. At the same time, Theodore wrote of his desire to obtain a commission and sought Johnson's help, as well as assistance from their mutual friend and Theodore's publisher, George Curtis.[15]

To his friends in New York, Theodore inquired into rumors that a new regiment was being raised in Richmond County (Staten Island). He justified a commission for both himself and William, writing, "I think we can do some good at a time when good men to lead are more wanted than good men to follow." To emphasize his point, he underlined the words "to lead."[16] William Marvel, a Civil War historian, recently argued that during the first year of the war, there was a disparity in the apparent patriotism between the upper and lower classes. Marvel concluded the upper classes did not possess the high level of patriotic commitment to the preservation of the Union as their middle- and working-class counterparts. He based his argument on rates of volunteerism. Although Marvel did not incorporate the idea that there may have remained a strong influence of New England Cotton Whiggism into his analysis, it may have been one of the underlying elements to the absence of upper-class Northern enlistments into the ranks of volunteers. If Marvel's argument is statistically true, and there is little reason to believe otherwise, the Seventh and the Winthrop brothers are exceptions to the norm.[17]

The brothers' commander, Colonel Marshall Lefferts, had been a member of the Seventh through the 1850s but was only elected to command on the eve of the war. In his civilian life, he was a chief engineer for the Western Union Telegraph Company and an ardent abolitionist. Colonel Lefferts commanded the Seventh throughout the war, including during the New York City draft riots in 1862. By April 17, the regiment was fully equipped and the state governor indicated this fact to General Winfield Scott, the commander of the army. In turn, General Scott ordered the Seventh to travel to Washington by rail. On April 19, the regiment departed New York accompanied by a large parade of well-wishers. A mutual friend of the Winthrop brothers and Shaw, Sydney Gay, wrote, "I saw Theodore and Bob Shaw off today, the former looked very grave."[18]

After news of anti-Union rioting in Baltimore became known, the Seventh traveled first to Philadelphia by rail, and then by ship to Annapolis. In Philadelphia, the men of the Seventh were treated to another enthusiastic crowd. Theodore recorded that loaves of bread were struck on his bayonet, and an Irish woman offered him cooked eggs.[19] The Seventh also met its first divisional commander, Major General Benjamin Butler, in Philadelphia. But Butler could not immediately assume command over the Seventh as the regiment had not yet been sworn into federal service.

General Butler commanded the Eighth and Sixth Massachusetts Regiments and was the senior ranking officer among the state militia units. Perhaps outside of Theodore's knowledge, there was almost immediate contention between Colonel Lefferts and General Butler. Shaw may have known of this disagreement. He did not approve of Butler, finding him coarse and uncouth. Butler issued orders to the Seventh, but as neither Butler nor the Seventh had yet been sworn into federal service, the orders were not valid. Butler wanted the Seventh to transit through Baltimore, and Colonel Lefferts chose to travel the regiment by a safer path, to Annapolis, and then overland to Washington.[20]

Departing by ship from Philadelphia on April 24, the regiment arrived in Annapolis. Theodore relished the possible dangers along the way, and based on his writing for the *Atlantic Monthly*, he conveyed the impression William did as well. In his article "Our March to Washington," he penned, "The Sixth and Second Companies, under Captain Nevers, are detached to lead the van. I see my brother Billy march off with the Sixth, into the dusk, half moonlight, half dawn, and hope that no beggar of a Secessionist will get a pat shot at him, by the roadside, without his getting a chance to let fly in return."[21]

Following a forced march and a railroad repair operation, the men entered into the capital on April 25, much to President Lincoln's relief. The Seventh's entry into the city included a march up Pennsylvania Avenue under presidential review. Its first several days in the city were spent securing the defenses and fixing sabotaged rail lines. Its most important role, however, during the first days in Washington was its mere presence. Quartered in the Capitol Building, its men slept on desks and couches. Theodore wrote of the 25th, it was "fun and faithful." In the same prose he described the state militia as "four or five thousand others in the same business as ourselves, drums beating, guns clanking, companies are tramping all the while."[22] Although Theodore was brief in describing the Seventh's living arrangements, Private Robert Shaw wrote to his mother that Theodore obtained the keys to the House of Representatives Post Office and together with William and Theodore, the three slept in privacy.[23]

On April 26, the Seventh's men were sworn into service, beginning their thirty days of required duty. General Irwin McDowell, the unlucky commander of Union forces during the Battle of Bull Run, presided over the ceremony. Theodore observed that while the oath was not as long or poetic as the knights of old, it was both a thrilling and solemn ceremony. One week later, the regiment moved to an area called Camp Cameron. At the center of the camp was a house abandoned by a doctor who had been loyal to the Confederacy. Writing for the *Atlantic Monthly*, Theodore described Camp Cameron as "sybaritic," with "cellars overflowing with edibles and drink." Using William as a model named "Private W," the article described a daily drill of reveille, drill, target practice, and work. In the article, Theodore had Private W musing that "while any man can become a master tactician, generalship is based on something more." In a veiled reference to General Butler, Theodore wrote, "For that you must have genius, and it appears out of Massachusetts."[24]

General Butler was, if anything, a man of action. Like the Winthrop brothers, he was a lawyer. He was also a politician who, in the 1860 Democrat Party Convention, initially supported Jefferson Davis, but only to disrupt the convention's outcome.[25]

Butler did not tolerate secession and found slavery repugnant. He had made a career of defending the poor and working class against the wealthy. Once in uniform, he acted without permission from superior officers or, for that matter, the president. Initially appointed to secure Annapolis, he moved the Sixth Massachusetts and a number of New Yorkers into Baltimore, where he had the wealthiest citizen arrested. Butler's heavy-handed tactics were not done in isolation. Lincoln challenged the authority of the Supreme Court over the issue of the executive branch's authority to detain civilians considered a danger to the Union. This included a defense of Butler's actions. Butler's anger at Baltimore did not occur in a vacuum. Earlier, in the Sixth Massachusetts' April transit through the city, an angry mob fired weapons at the men, killing and injuring a number of soldiers.[26] A large percentage of the city's population supported secession. Throughout the war, Butler was known for heavy-handed civil administration in such places as New Orleans.

General Winfield Scott initially demanded Butler be court-martialed for disobedience, but President Lincoln convinced the commanding general to issue a reprimand and transfer Butler to Fort Monroe, Virginia, where it was assumed nothing significant was likely to occur.[27] Whether the Winthrop brothers fully knew of Butler's specific actions and approved of them at the time is lost to history. But it is possible to discern, based on Theodore's later activities, that he approved of Butler's leadership.

Despite the extensive equipment provided by the Seventh Regiment, Theodore and William continued to receive food and sundry packages from friends and family. In a May 15 letter to Templeton, Theodore asked him to thank a number of people who sent food and other items. He also requested that Templeton send new shoes and clothes. Theodore apologized for not writing opinions on the war, but told of the Seventh's constant drilling. Yet, he expressed his and William's dissatisfaction with the Seventh's station in the capital, writing, "Billy and I both want to be where we can feel more of the hard work of the campaign." He was disappointed in the regiment's leadership, accusing them of having little stomach for a fight. And he reserved his greatest criticism for the regiment's clerks, writing that "each fancies himself a Hannibal and the man to lead armies not to go to the ranks." He closed the letter, still seeking a commission through an unnamed friend's connection to the cavalry.[28]

Through May, Theodore remained unable to secure a commission. In 1861, Secretary of War Cameron was flooded with requests for commissions, and his office could not function effectively in processing these. Many grants of commissions were made for reasons of political expediency at the state and federal levels of government. The War Department was not immune from engaging in patronage either. But Theodore was unable to use his family connections to Secretary Cameron; there were too many like the young author seeking favor. In mid-May, in an effort to secure a commission, Theodore turned to another powerful Republican, William Henry Seward, Lincoln's recent appointment as secretary of state. His letter to Seward indicated that at some recent time, a friend acting on his behalf sought Seward's help in obtaining a commission. Writing, "I am anxious, of course, to engage your combined good will in my application for a post in the New Army of the U.S." Theodore asked Seward for two favors. First, he sought a personal audience with Secretary Cameron. Second, he asked for a captaincy, "if it be consistent with the public interest." At the same time, he sought a commission for "Will." Theodore informed the secretary of state that Hamilton Fish and Mr. George Curtis supported his desire as well.[29]

On May 2, Robert Shaw secured an audience with both Seward and President Lincoln. It is unclear as to whether he attempted to help Theodore gain a commission, or whether he sought one for himself. Theodore's letter suggests Shaw may have been the individual who met with Seward on his behalf but it did not specifically name Shaw. Shaw did not bring Theodore with him to meet with Lincoln or Seward, but he was in a position to pass on Theodore's desire to obtain an audience. Shaw's letter to his mother describing the meeting was more illuminating as it expressed his opinion of Lincoln: "It's too bad they call Lincoln one of the ugliest men in the nation for I have seldom seen a pleasanter or more kind-hearted looking one." He added, "Though you can't judge a man in a five minute conversation, we were much pleased with what we did see of him." Shaw concluded he felt privileged to meet the president, writing, "We got rather ahead of the regiment as none of the others have seen him and we thought we had done a pretty good afternoon's work in calling on the President and Secretary of State both."[30]

On the other hand, it appears Theodore eventually did meet with the president and secretary of state. Shaw may have armed Theodore with a letter of introduction to Seward after his own meeting with the secretary. According to Theodore, he called at Seward's house at a time when Lincoln visited. Theodore recorded the event as though he met a giant, writing, "I lose my hand in his." Theodore described Seward's helpful introduction: "This is Mr. Winthrop, a scholar and a gentleman; you must make a lieutenant of him." However, this did not occur, and Theodore concluded his thought by saying, "In my Uncle's house are many nephews and whether nepotism or my transcendent merit will prevail . . . I have fun, I get experience, I see much, it Pays!"[31]

On May 23, the Seventh advanced into Arlington and fortified the heights overlooking the capital. Theodore wrote of this march that "his individual pride gave way to that of a mighty machine." He continued with a patriotic tone, concluding, "On that day, the Seventh was the fulfillment of *e pluribus Unum*."[32] Still, combat eluded the regiment and the Winthrop brothers. Three days later, with the Seventh's thirty days of service concluded, most of its men decamped and returned to New York. Had the Seventh remained in service for ninety days, its men would have taken part in the Bull Run debacle. If, during the thirty days in Washington, the Winthrop brothers did not see the war up close, they witnessed secession's fervor on both sides of the Potomac. During the march onto the Arlington Heights, the commander of the Eleventh New York, Colonel Elmer Ellsworth, noticed an inn with a Confederate flag draped from its windows. When he went into the house to cut down the flag, the innkeeper shot and killed him. In response, one of the Zouaves returned fire, killing the innkeeper.[33]

Not all of the Seventh's men returned. After an extensive personal lobbying effort, Theodore secured employment on General Butler's staff, resulting in a backdoor path to a commission. Butler had the authority to grant commissions through the War Department. At first, Theodore was commissioned as a captain in the Fourteenth New York and then was brought onto Butler's staff as his aide-de-camp. However, it may have been the case that once Theodore obtained his initial commission, he wanted to remain a line officer. Butler, in turn, used his persuasion to get Winthrop on his staff with a promotion to major. Thus, in less than three short months, with no prior military experience, Theodore jumped from the lowest enlisted rank to that of a field-grade staff officer.

Theodore must have appealed to Butler's political ambitions. He had made a name as a rising author with political connections, and the well-read *Atlantic Monthly* magazine hired him to write about his experiences in the war. In 1892, Butler recorded that Theodore had approached him and he advised "Winthrop to serve out his time with the Seventh, because those were the terms of his enlistment, and then to come to me wherever I was and I would give him a place on my staff." Three decades after Theodore was killed, Butler credited him with asserting that slaves who entered into Union lines became "contraband of war." Although Butler claimed the term was personally distasteful, he also noted Theodore "created an epigram which freed the slaves."[34]

Having Theodore on his staff guaranteed Butler national exposure. In an *Atlantic Monthly* article titled "Washington as a Camp," Theodore specifically credited Butler with "saving Washington from the heels of secession."[35] He did not write that General Scott sent Butler to Fort Monroe as a punishment for his independence and harsh threats in dealing with Baltimore's anti-Union elements. Nor did Theodore appear to comprehend that Butler was in the process of falling out of favor with the military establishment. Butler later got into trouble with the administration over his contraband slave policy by declaring that slaves caught within his command were to be considered as war spoils and freed. Butler's unique approach likely appealed to Theodore. And yet, Butler had been a Democrat state legislator prior to the war and during the party convention in 1860, supported Jefferson Davis and then John C. Breckenridge. On the other hand, General Butler seems to have grown a friendly affection for Theodore, beyond his personal ambitions. Butler had earlier championed the rights and safety of mill-workers and saw in Theodore a kindred spirit.

On June 3, Butler ordered Theodore to board the steamer *Yankee*, traveling to Fort Monroe. Butler directed the commander of the vessel to consider Theodore the commander of all troops on the vessel in his absence, as well as to view orders from Theodore as originating from the commanding general. The *Yankee* carried Theodore and a number of troops to Fort Monroe, located at the tip of a Chesapeake Bay peninsula that, within the year, would become known as "the Peninsula." Theodore would not live to see this peninsula be referred to as such, but he was soon to see his first, and only, battle.[36]

Fort Monroe was secure against attack. Its gun emplacements and three-thousand-man garrison ensured that any attack would be costly in lives. For this reason, the Confederate army ignored Fort Monroe during the war. But northwest of the fort were a number of small Confederate garrisons. One of these small garrisons was stationed at a small crossroads town known as Big Bethel, named for its church. The Virginian forces fortified the area by quickly erecting earthworks. Butler decided to capture the town and destroy the Confederate garrison. In a plan drawn up by Theodore Winthrop, several regiments, numbering 4,400 men, set out from Fort Monroe on the night of June 9. Setting out on two roads, the troops converged on each other, each column of soldiers mistaking the other for the enemy. A few Union soldiers were killed by friendly fire in the exchange, and the Confederate forces under the command of General James Magruder were alerted to the operation.

With Theodore's encouragement, the expedition continued to Bethel, where a series of ineffective charges by the Union forces ensured Union forces suffered in greater numbers than their adversaries. The Battle of Big Bethel was a bungled affair, typical of early battles in the war. Theodore was killed leading one of these charges. Of the Confederates who saw his death, one officer wrote, "He was the only one of the enemy who exhibited an approximation of courage on that day."[37] Theodore did show courage. He led a charge, sword in hand, and rallied his men to the front of the Confederate positions, only to be shot in the heart and killed instantly. Later, there was a story printed, which if true, provided irony to Theodore's death. The rumor had a slave killing Theodore.[38]

Laurels were heaped on Theodore's bravery. General Butler reported to Winfield Scott, "The country has to deplore the loss of Maj. Theodore Winthrop, my acting military secretary . . . who at the moment of his death was engaged in finding the best manner of entering the battery, when he fell mortally wounded. His conduct, his courage, his efficiency in the field, were spoken of in terms of praise by all who saw him." Forty years after the battle, the *Richmond Dispatch* recorded Theodore's last moments: "Gallant young officer, Major Theodore Winthrop, of New Haven, Conn., who was General Butler's private secretary, and who volunteered as an aid on General Pierce's staff for this expedition, while attempting to rally a wavering column, drew his sword, waved it aloft, leaped on the trunk of a fallen tree, and shouted to his men: 'One more charge, boys, and the day is ours!' Alas, for poor Winthrop! It was his last charge. A North Carolinian sent a bullet crashing through his heart, and he fell dead at the head of the column, which retired in great confusion."[39]

On June 3, 1861, William was released from the Seventh New York militia. The unit had returned home, with a good deal of fanfare, but without having fought a battle. Seven days later, news of Theodore's death arrived by an Associated Press Office telegraph directly to William. The telegraph was brief, stating only that Theodore had fallen "mortally wounded into the arms of a Vermont volunteer."[40]

Theodore's death deeply affected the Winthrop family as well as a number of their friends, including Curtis and Shaw, and in their surviving correspondence it is evident Theodore remained in the forefront of their thoughts, even into the twentieth century. Theodore's mother never recovered and spent her life lamenting her lost son. His sister Laura Winthrop Johnson wrote to Butler, "It is a great satisfaction to us to know from Theodore's letters that some of the last acts of his life were kindness to an oppressed race, a race he never forgot as part of the nation whose battle he fought."[41] Robert Shaw, on hearing the news, wrote his father, "I have thought a great deal about poor Winthrop. I think that, if he had expected it, he would not have been sorry, excepting for the sake of his family. Some remarks he made in Washington led me to think so."[42] Three months later, Shaw had not come to terms with Theodore's death, writing, "I think of the house and you all sitting on the porch looking across too. It is hard to realize that Theodore Winthrop is not there too, in the summer evenings."[43]

With Theodore killed, William, safely back in New York, remained Francis Bayard's only son bearing the name Winthrop. But there remained one task to honor the older brother. Laura Winthrop Johnson discovered Theodore's incomplete novels. She and William spent the weeks following Theodore's death completing and editing *Cecil Dreem*, *Edward Brothertoft*, and *John Brent*. For fifty years after Bethel, a number of literary agents and biographers remained fascinated with the details of Theodore's life, his literature, and his death. Some reviewers argued that Theodore's closest friends did not know of his writing, and the existence of his novels came as a surprise to his publisher, Curtis. Their fascination over Theodore existed, in some part, because of William's efforts in keeping Theodore's literary accomplishments alive.[44] Indeed, for the remainder of William's life, he undertook efforts to ensure Theodore's work was serialized and libraries were stocked with Theodore's complete works. Even when William wrote and published his own fiction stories, he referenced Theodore's works. But for William, the world of law and literature was entering a hiatus and the war was just beginning.

On learning of her eldest son's fate, Elizabeth sent William to retrieve Theodore's body. On June 17, 1861, William and Theodore Weston were escorted by Confederate officers to Theodore's casket. According to General Butler, William was given all courtesies. William was also offered a Seventh New York lieutenancy, but declined. Over time, a number of military authors perpetuated the notion that William turned down the offer out of respect for his mother, but none of them elaborated beyond this statement. The notion of his mother's involvement in his early military career is only partly true. Elizabeth Winthrop did not want William to be part of a unit such as the Seventh Regiment that, from all appearances, would sit out the war in New York. As noted earlier, Theodore certainly doubted the Seventh's commitment to fight, and he conveyed these thoughts to family and friends. William also desired to see action against the enemy, all the more so after the enemy took his brother's life.[45] William's quest for combat was realized through a fellow New Yorker, Hiram Berdan, but the opportunity to see combat had its genesis even before William's release from the Seventh.

NOTES

1. Elbridge Colby, *Theodore Winthrop* (New York: Twayne Publishers, 1965), 49.
2. Robert Charles Winthrop Jr., *A Memoir of Robert Charles Winthrop: Prepared for the Massachusetts Historical Society* (Boston: Little, Brown, 1897), 211.
3. Kermit Hall, *The Magic Mirror: Law in American History* (New York: Oxford University Press, 1989), 137–138.
4. Hall, *The Magic Mirror*, 137–138.
5. See Robert Gould Shaw, *Blue-Eyed Child of Fortune: The Civil War Letters of Colonel Robert Gould Shaw*, ed. Russell Duncan (Athens: University of Georgia Press, 1999), 11; Peter Bouchard, *One Gallant Rush: Robert Gould Shaw and His Brave Black Regiment* (New York: St. Martins Press, 1965), 6; also, Russell Duncan, *Colonel Robert Gould Shaw and the 54th Massachusetts Infantry: Where Death and Glory Meet* (Athens: University of Georgia Press, 1988), 1–20.
6. Robert Gould Shaw, letter to his mother, April 27, 1862, and Robert Gould Shaw, letter to his father, May 2, 1862; Shaw, *Blue-Eyed Child of Fortune*, 82, 91.
7. Shaw, *Blue-Eyed Child of Fortune*, 1–3.
8. George William Curtis, "Biographical Sketch of the Author," in *Cecil Dreeme*, by Theodore Winthrop, 14 (Boston: Ticknor and Fields, 1864).
9. William Swinton, *History of the Seventh Regiment, National Guard, State of New York, during the War of the Rebellion: With a Preliminary Chapter on the Origin and Early History of the Regiment, a Summary of Its History since the War, and a Roll of Honor, Comprising Brief Sketches of the Services Rendered by Members of the Regiment*

in the Army and Navy of the United States (New York: Field, Osgood and Co, 1870), 26–27.

10. Shaw, *Blue-Eyed Child of Fortune*, 83.

11. Fitz James O'Brien, "The March of the Seventh Regiment," in *Anecdotes, Poetry, and Incidents of the War of the North and South, 1860–1865*, ed. Frank Moore, 228 (New York: Bible House, 1867); Clarence C. Buell, "The New York Seventh," *Scribners' Magazine* 20 (1880), 69; Shaw, *Blue-Eyed Child of Fortune*, 95; Margaret Leech, *Reveille in Washington* (New York: Harper Brothers, 1941), 66; also, Swinton, *History of the Seventh Regiment*.

12. Buell, "The New York Seventh," 69.

13. David Detzer, *Dissonance: The Turbulent Days between Fort Sumter and Bull Run* (New York: Harcourt, 2006), 282–283.

14. Buell, "The New York Seventh," 72.

15. Theodore Winthrop, letter to William Templeton Johnson, April 30, 1861 (New York Public Library).

16. T. Winthrop, letter to Templeton, April 30, 1861.

17. William Marvel, *Mr. Lincoln Goes to War* (New York: Houghton Mifflin, 2006), 52–53. In examining the degree of patriotism among the economic classes, Professor Marvel uses New Hampshire and Massachusetts as primary case studies. He also focuses on Dartmouth College, where graduates enlisted at a far lower rate than the rest of the nation.

18. Duncan, *Colonel Robert Gould Shaw*, 25; also Shaw, *Blue-Eyed Child of Fortune*, 14.

19. Swinton, *History of the Seventh Regiment*, 43–44.

20. Benjamin F. Butler, *Autobiography and Personal Reminiscences of Major-General Benj. F. Butler: "Butler's Book"* (Botson: A.M. Thayer and Co., 1892), 200–201. Three decades after the war, Butler disparaged the Seventh New York writing that "the Eighth Mass, the farmers, fishermen, and mechanics," did a more meaningful portion of the work. As for the Seventh, "the loss of their velvet covered stools was the only hardship which taught them the horrors of war." For general information, see also Detzer, *Dissonance*, 288.

21. Theodore Winthrop, "Our March to Washington," in *The Oxford Book of American Essays*, ed. Brander Matthews, 18 (New York: Oxford University Press, 1914).

22. Theodore Winthrop, letter to unknown person, possibly to the *Atlantic Monthly*, n.d. (New York Public Library, Misc Files).

23. Robert Gould Shaw, letter to his mother, April 29, 1861, in Shaw, *Blue-Eyed Child of Fortune*, 85.

24. Theodore Winthrop, "Washington as a Camp," *Atlantic Monthly*, June 1861, 103.

25. Dick Nolan, *Benjamin Franklin Butler: The Damnedest Yankee* (Novato, CA: Presidio, 1991), 50.

26. Richard West, *Lincoln's Scapegoat General: A Life of Benjamin F. Butler, 1818–1893* (New York: Houghton Mifflin, 1965), 51.

27. Marvel, *Mr. Lincoln Goes to War*, 67; West, *Lincoln's Scapegoat General*, 60; Nolan, *Benjamin Franklin Butler*, 60.

28. Theodore Winthrop, letter to William Templeton Johnson, May 15, 1861 (New York Public Library).

29. Theodore Winthrop, letter to William Henry Seward, May 1861 (University of Rochester).

30. Robert Gould Shaw, letter to his mother, May 2, 1861, Shaw in *Blue-Eyed Child of Fortune*, 91.

31. Eugene Woolf, *Theodore Winthrop: Portrait of an American Author* (Washington, DC: University Press of America), 19.

32. Winthrop, "Washington as a Camp," 114.

33. Leech, *Reveille in Washington*, 81.

34. Butler, *Autobiography and Personal Reminiscences*, 259.

35. Winthrop, "Washington as a Camp," 105–108.

36. Benjamin Butler, letter to the commander of the *Yankee*, June 3, 1861 (New York Public Library).

37. Marvel, *Mr. Lincoln Goes to War*, 84.

38. H. M. Whitney, "The Analogy between Slavery and Intemperance before the Law," *New Englander and Yale Review* 39, no. 156 (May 1880), 379.

39. *Richmond Dispatch*, October 18, 1901, 1.

40. Associated Press Office, telegraph to W. W. Winthrop, esq. (New York Public Library).

41. Laura Winthrop Johnson to Butler, June 1861, in Benjamin F. Butler, *Private and Official Correspondence of General Benjamin F. Butler*, vol. 1, 136 (Norwood, MA: Plimton Press, 1917).

42. Robert Gould Shaw, letter to his father, June 16, 1861, in Shaw, *Blue-Eyed Child of Fortune*, 109.

43. Robert Gould Shaw, letter to his father, September 5, 1861, in Shaw, *Blue-Eyed Child of Fortune*, 137.

44. John H. Williams, *Winthrop and Curtis: A Reviewer Reviewed* (Tacoma, WA: J.H. Williams, 1914), 7. In this article, Williams asserts that William Woolsey Winthrop made substantial revisions to Theodore's works prior to publication; also, Elizabeth Winthrop Johnson, "Concerning Theodore Winthrop," *Modern Language Notes* 30 (1915), 196–197.

45. Elizabeth Winthrop, letter to Pension Office of Support, undated (probably 1900) (AWPF). Elizabeth Winthrop, *The Life and Letters of Theodore Winthrop* (New York: Henry Holt, 1884), 298.

6

A Sharpshooter on the Peninsula Campaign

Soon the Great Something Will Come

—Lieutenant William Winthrop to his mother,
Elizabeth Woolsey Winthrop

On May 3, 1861, President Lincoln issued a second call for volunteers. Having painfully learned the shortcomings of ninety-day volunteers, even before the Bull Run debacle, Lincoln sought forty-two thousand men to volunteer for three years of service. The need was obvious; the ninety-day volunteer obligation was coming to a close, and the seceding states showed no sign of abandoning their departure from the Union. The Confederacy raised an effective army in short order and threatened Washington. And the border states' loyalty, critical to the Union's solvency, was an open question. Without federal occupation, there was a chance that Maryland, Missouri, and Kentucky might go over to the Confederacy. Sectional conflict had broken out in each. Thus, even before the Union defeat at Bull Run, the need for a long-term army became apparent.

The growing army needed a commander, and Lincoln appointed an individual he initially believed to possess the intelligence, insight, and charisma to lead it—George Brinton McClellan, a man Winthrop initially admired. McClellan had graduated second in his class from the United States Military Academy and served as an engineer during the Mexican-American War. He also observed the Crimean War, fought between France, Britain, the Kingdom of Sardinia, and the Ottoman Empire on one side, and Czarist Russia on the other. Notable in that war was his observation of the siege at Sevastopal, where the British and French made extensive use of their engineers. Although he left the military in 1857 to work for a major railway company, McClellan was thought to possess one of the foremost military minds in the country. At the outbreak of war, McClellan was commissioned as a major general and commanded forces in the Ohio Valley. At thirty-four years of age, he was the youngest commander in the army and only the aged Winfield Scott outranked him; however, on July 26, 1861, when McClellan assumed dual command, of the Army of the Potomac and the commanding general of all Union forces, Scott was forced into retirement. But McClellan had significant shortcomings that were to become apparent through the remainder of that year and into 1862.

The experience of raising volunteer forces was not without precedent. During the War of 1812, the states supplied volunteer militia forces to the fight. In the Mexican-American War, the United States raised a volunteer army in a short time. However, in both conflicts, militia commanders as well as their state governments contested centralized control over volunteers. For a war with the South, Lincoln needed a better degree of control over the armies in the field than any president had before him. The army he set out to build had more than enough eager men fill its ranks, but the men selected to lead the forces were not always competent or able to grasp the changing nature of the war that lay ahead. In Hiram Berdan, Lincoln found a leader who initially seemed able to do both.

Born in 1824 in upstate New York and raised in Michigan, Berdan studied engineering at Hobart College.[1] He was a skilled engineer and inventor who also built political connections. He designed and patented repeating rifles, a machine that separated gold from ore, and an automated bakery. In 1853, he sold a patent for his gold separator for $550,000.[2]

By 1861, Berdan was well-known in both American and British industry and had been mentioned in such journals as *Scientific American,* the country's oldest continually published magazine. He was also known in the decade prior to the war as the best shot in the nation, having won a number of shooting contests. However, popular as he was in industry and among politicians, sportsmen, and hunters, Berdan had a few detractors, including the Springfield Armory director, who labeled Berdan as unscrupulous and unreliable.[3]

Berdan was sympathetic to abolitionism, speaking and writing about the economic evils of slavery. This fact, too, ensured he would have opponents. He was intellectually gifted, but also a showman, and he ultimately caused controversy throughout his military career, first as the leader of a regiment and later as a brigade commander. A number of his junior officers grew to believe Berdan was dishonest and owed his position solely to patronage and a relationship with the president. Indeed, over time some of his men and officers questioned his integrity and accused him of cowardice in combat. His conduct on the battlefield and propensity to exaggerate his "frontline heroism" in official correspondence did not go unnoticed by higher-ranking commanders either. William Winthrop was not, at first, a critic of Berdan, but it is certain he heard grumblings about Berdan and over time grew disillusioned with the colonel.[4]

Without formal military training, Berdan recognized that the linear geometric battlefield formations that had characterized battlefields for the previous three centuries were outdated. Rifles had double the range and increased accuracy over smoothbore muskets. Effective breechloaders, such as the 1859 Sharps model, could fire eight to ten rounds per minute, triple the speed of a muzzle-loading smoothbore. Later breech-loading rifles used by the sharpshooters, such as the Spencer Repeating Rifle, even increased the rate of fire over the Sharps model.[5] Innovations were not limited to rifles. In terms of accuracy and range, rifled cannon surpassed muzzle-loading smoothbores as well. Between advances in rifle and artillery technology, the massed linear formations based on the musket that were required to provide a quantum of firepower simply weren't needed, and worse, presented a larger stationary target to opposing forces. This fact was lost on many Union and Confederate commanders early in the war, to the detriment of the men in combat.[6]

Utilizing these advances, Berdan proposed to create a formation of skilled skirmishers, or sharpshooters, whose purpose was twofold. First, his skirmishers could create gaps in the enemy lines by concentrating firepower on a small but critical area. Through these gaps, the sharpshooters could then sever lines of communication, disable the essential command and control over enemy units, and create confusion and terror in their ranks. Second, these skilled riflemen could target officers and other points, such as artillery, essential to the enemy's ability to exercise supremacy over the battlefield itself.[7] Although snipers had been part of the battlefield for over two centuries, a whole regiment of them was a novel idea in America.

Hiram Berdan began recruiting men for his regiment even prior to receiving official government sanction for it. However, Berdan's confidence in his idea was not misplaced. His past association with a number of politicians, as well as his standing as an inventor and abolitionist, provided the necessary status to push for the regiment's formation. In the fall of 1861, he personally demonstrated his repeating rifle invention to Lincoln, and the president considered him a friend. In a July 20, 1861, *New York Times* article, Berdan stated his desire for eight hundred to one thousand men, capable for rifle marksmanship at "any range." He concluded the article with a forceful request to Congress to fund the regiment.[8]

Unlike a standard regiment, the sharpshooters were to be composed of independent companies so that division, corps, and army commanders could use them to protect a position critical to a defense or spearhead an assault.[9] In Berdan's scheme, the regiment would exist for training purposes only. But, in more than one battle, notably at Malvern Hill and the Second Battle of Manassas, both in 1862, the regiment fought as a complete unit. Berdan also intended that each man would be fully qualified before entering the regiment, proposing a requirement that each man be a capable shot. He also sought to equip the regiment with specialized repeating rifles. The *Scientific American* magazine, which was also used in recruiting the regiment, stated, "Any drafted man who is an experienced marksman, and can prove upon affidavit that he has made five consecutive shots, not exceeding 25 inches, with a target rifle, distance 200 yards, at least, will be admitted to Berdan's Sharpshooting Regiment."[10] In a sense, Berdan's proposal was a forerunner of modern special operations and sniper units.

On June 15, 1861, Secretary of War Simon Cameron ordered Berdan to recruit his regiment and equip it "without expense to the government."[11] Cameron's order provided Berdan a colonelcy, placing him in formal command of the unit. In response, Berdan put out the call to the Northern state governors for volunteers. He also sent out recruiters to advertise the regiment in fall hunting competitions throughout the Northern states, promising recruits the Sharps breech-loading rifle, as well as additional pay over the standard Union infantryman. Winthrop took part in the recruiting effort by displaying his marksmanship to the interested public.

Berdan's recruiting methods were successful, though they would shortly become problematic. A number of promises were made to prospective recruits, including a higher rate of pay than the standard infantry private, which were not kept. When recruiting was completed, the regiment was composed of ten companies of roughly one hundred men in each company. New York furnished four companies; Michigan, three; and Vermont, New Hampshire, and Wisconsin, one each. One New York company was composed of Swiss immigrants, a number of whom had prior military service in the Swiss and French armies and saw combat at Solferino or the Crimea. Shortly after the regiment filled up with qualified volunteers, it became apparent that there were enough interested and qualified men to create a second regiment.[12]

Although Berdan advocated an unconventional tactical method of warfare utilizing advanced rifled firepower, he required his recruits to soldier with precision. And he introduced uniforms consisting of a dark green coat, light blue pants—later exchanged for green—and a black plumed hat. Berdan wanted enemy forces to know when they faced his sharpshooters, although it was also intended to provide some camouflage for the individual soldier serving at a far distance as a sniper.[13]

For all the aplomb of the Sharpshooters, it was a unit that clearly deserved the title "elite." Throughout the war, its men saw action during the 1862 battles on the Peninsula, at Second Manassas, Antietam, Fredericksburg, Chancellorsville, Gettysburg, and in the wilderness.[14]

Both the Confederate and Union armies adopted its basic tactics. Early on, the Confederate press knew of the unit's existence. For instance, while the unit was campaigning on the Peninsula, the *Petersburg Express* reported on the deaths of individual sharpshooters. Even before it saw combat, the Sharpshooters became one of the best-known regiments in the Union army. A favorite of sightseers as it trained in Washington, it attracted the attention of not only Union and Confederate generals, but also foreign observers. For instance, the Swiss military attaché in Washington, DC, frequented the regiment during its training. In June 1862, a Spanish officer, General Juan Prim, spent a day with the regiment. His specific mission was to ascertain if any lessons could be learned for European and colonial warfare.[15]

On October 1, 1861, Winthrop accepted a lieutenant's commission in Company H and along with its commander, his former Yale peer, Captain George Hastings, he recruited men to fill this unit.[16] Another Company H officer, Frederick Tomlinson Peet, detailed an account of life in Company H through the Peninsula Campaign, where he was injured and taken prisoner. Writing forty years after the war, Peet remembered his first meeting with Lieutenant Winthrop and Captain Hastings. In early August 1861 while Peet walked down New York's Montague Street, he encountered Winthrop and Hastings. Peet previously knew Hastings from his brother's law practice. Like Winthrop, Peet earlier served in the Seventh New York Regiment, but the two apparently did not meet during their respective thirty days of duty. Prior to the war, Frederick Peet had been a Brooklyn school superintendent and harbored abolitionist views. Hastings offered Peet a second lieutenancy, which Peet accepted, placing him third in command of Company H. From that point, Winthrop and Peet shared a tent and developed a friendship. Writing to Peet's brother after Peet had been taken prisoner, Winthrop recorded that he always found Peet "generous, honest, and brave."[17]

Whether or not Winthrop knew at the time that Berdan's Sharpshooters were playing a part in the transformation of battle from Napoleonic lines of fire, to "fire and maneuver by squad," he lived through several advances in warfare, science, and industry that significantly altered the battlefield, as well as war itself. These changes had an effect on how the laws of war, as well as military discipline, were shaped and enforced. Winthrop's first-hand experience in the Sharpshooters later directly influenced his legal scholarship, but not just in the field of international law.

Winthrop witnessed a wide range of legal issues, including scope of command authority, indiscipline, and the unique military justice function of convening of courts-martial. Indeed, he found himself at the unpleasant end of the courts-martial process while serving under Berdan, testifying against his commander on behalf of two comrades.

Berdan prepared his men for campaigning a mile outside of Washington, DC, in an area known as the Camp of Instruction, with regular drill including long arduous marches. However, the drill was supplemented with sports such as fencing, boxing, wrestling, and racing. Writing some twenty-five years after Appomattox, the regimental historian Captain Charles Stevens remembered a high esprit de corps among the early volunteers, calling them a "band of brothers."[18]

The regiment had its share of legends and characters who were long remembered for their combat exploits. These included Caspar Trepp, a Swiss immigrant who fought in a number of European conflicts including the Crimean War. Another such character, who amused Winthrop, was a Private Truman Head, nicknamed "California Joe." Private Head was in his forties or perhaps fifties when he enlisted in the Sharpshooters. But he was a superb shot and on a number of occasions, picked off Confederate snipers, as well as officers. Stories of Private Head's forays—no doubt embellished by writers—and photographs appeared in a number of magazines, but he was shy of publicity. Winthrop described Truman Head in a letter to his mother as a "refined old character and a crack shot."[19]

Berdan also expected his regiment to comport with the laws of war and treat noncombatants with respect. In May 1862 while campaigning on the Peninsula, Berdan instructed his men to purchase produce and meats from local farmers, rather than forage for sustenance. Moreover, he posted guards at houses to prevent pillage.[20] Forty years after the campaign, Lieutenant Peet remembered that even in the instance of a hostile homeowner, his men asked for bread, rather than demanding it. He also recalled that Berdan ordered his men to protect, rather than consume, the homeowner's wine barrels.[21] On the Peninsula, the Sharpshooters were also ordered to protect property against Union looters from other regiments. In another instance, a sharpshooter threatened soldiers from an Ohio regiment seeking to despoil a farm near Fort Monroe.[22] In any case, Berdan made it clear to his men their responsibility to uphold his orders against pillage, looting, rape, and murder. These orders were part of the overall drill regimen and treated as seriously, if not more, as those forbidding desertion.

Still, there were moments of acceptable levity during training. Winthrop later recalled an instance where nine soldiers named Smith were placed in a large formation together. When a lieutenant from the inspector general's office asked each man his name and the response was

"Smith" from all nine, the lieutenant became apoplectic to the humor of the entire formation. Charles Stevens recorded other humorous exploits. When a new lieutenant with a reputation for arrogance arrived at the camp wearing a personalized cap with the letters "U.S.S.S," on the front, the older veterans shouted, "Unfortunate Soldiers Sadly Sold," again to laughter.[23] One other occasion that was remembered with a good deal of humor occurred during initial training. An enlisted volunteer approached a regular officer, asking him for tobacco with a visible display of informality. The regular officer proceeded to not only swear at the soldier, but also at Colonel Berdan, for "the damnable impudence of the accursed volunteers."[24] Berdan could not bring himself to punish the offending soldier in this instance. One source of humor Stevens omitted from the Sharpshooters history was the men's lampooning of Berdan. For instance, a Swiss soldier of Company A drew an image of two officers wearing baker's attire pulling a sheet out of an oven. On the sheet stood Colonel Berdan in full Sharpshooters attire. The drawing was captioned, "Freshly Baked Officers Available." The picture was posted on the parade ground. Berdan did not find humor in this episode and launched an investigation to find the offender.[25]

Despite the levity, the fall and winter of 1861–1862 were difficult on the regiment's health. Several of the men died and many more were incapacitated from sickness and poor sanitary conditions. Measles were also problematic during the colder months. By December, 72 men out of 745 were considered unfit for duty due to medical reasons.[26] The diet of the army was problematic for the health of the men, as most of the men consumed fried meats and little fruits and vegetables. Appalling sanitation conditions in the camps in and around Washington, DC, contributed to a decline in the health of the Union army in the winter and spring of 1861–1862 as well. Having large numbers of men fall ill was typical of the conditions during the war. During the war, 110,070 men were killed in battle while 249,458 died from disease, from accident, as military prisoners of war, or from other losses, although the dividing line between illnesses caused by battle stress and those caused by disease alone was not well-known or analyzed in the nineteenth century.[27]

The Sharpshooters received their first taste of combat just outside of Washington near Chain Bridge. After the disaster at Bull Run, Confederate forces began to encroach on the city. In response, forces protecting the capital, including the Sharpshooters, began to conduct forays against Confederate sites. On September 27, Companies C and E, along with companies from Vermont, Indiana, and New York, exchanged fire with Confederate forces at Lewinsville. In that action, the Sharpshooters served as skirmishers. Charles Stevens recalled that the Sharpshooters suffered one troop wounded and the Confederate forces retreated from the field. Two days later, both companies engaged Confederates on Munson's Hill in a night firefight while supporting a regiment from California and the Sixty-ninth Pennsylvania Regiment against Virginia militia. Munson's Hill had a signal tower and "cannon" emplaced on it from which the Confederates could see the Capitol Building. Again, the Sharpshooters suffered one casualty, but the man recovered to rejoin the ranks. Charles Stevens recorded the Virginians as having retreated from the area. According to Stevens, these two early actions boosted morale for the whole regiment.[28] However, Stevens did not mention that on taking the hill, two days after the skirmish, Union forces found a number of "Quaker guns," wood, and pasteboard designed to look like cannon left behind by the Virginia troops. Nor did he record that the casualties were a result of friendly fire. Indeed, the discovery of the Confederate abandonment of Munson's Hill proved embarrassing to McClellan.[29]

By the end of 1861, Berdan considered the Sharpshooters fully trained and ready to deploy into combat. They had drilled from 5:45 a.m. to 5:30 p.m., six days per week from October through January. In fact, the Sharpshooters were likely the sole regiment which trained daily in musketry, adding to their unique effectiveness.[30] In what must have seemed like a repeat of Winthrop's first march to defend Washington, the Sharpshooters were reviewed by General Irwin McDowell who judged the unit battle-worthy. By this time, McDowell was perhaps the most unpopular general among the Union forces, and it was not the last time Lieutenant Winthrop's career would be influenced in some way by McDowell. However, the Sharpshooters were not to fall under McDowell's command. Instead, they were sent to join General McClellan's Army of the Potomac on an area known as the Peninsula in the first full offensive campaign designed to defeat the South and restore the Union.

The Peninsula is a relatively flat area. In 1862, as it generally remains today, the Peninsula was dotted with a few small towns and the occasional rise (though today there is an enormous naval base on the southern end and Norfolk and Hampton are considerably more populous than in 1862). To the north, the York River is fed by two smaller rivers—the Mattapony and the Pamunkey—both flowing from central Virginia. On the south side of the Peninsula flows the James River, partly fed upstream by the Appomattox River. Along this system are a number of "landings," or beachheads. In 1862, the Peninsula was a composition of rich farmland, forests, and swamps. The largest of the swamps, White Oak Swamp, rested in the middle. The swamps existed, in part, because of a third river, the Chickahominy, that flowed down the middle of the Peninsula into the lower James. Dividing the Peninsula nearly in half in the northern part of its landmass, the Chickahominy River could only be forded by an army with artillery in certain areas. Along the Peninsula were a series of historic towns, made famous in colonial America. From the eastern end toward Richmond, these towns included Hampton, Yorktown, and Williamsburg. A number of other settlements dotted the area including West Point, City Point, the Bermuda Hundred, New Market, Cumberland, Cold Harbor, Fair Oaks, Gaines Mill, Hanover Courthouse, and Mechanicsville.[31]

At the end of the Peninsula sits Richmond, the capital of the Confederacy and the symbol of its independence. Located only ninety miles south of Washington, DC, Richmond represented, to both President Lincoln and General McClellan, the key to ending the rebellion. Take Richmond, they felt, and the South crumbled. But Lincoln only allowed McClellan troops for the campaign as long as Washington remained adequately defended. Lincoln did not want to leave Washington open to attack while the Army of the Potomac operated over one hundred miles away.

Advancing from a Union stronghold, Fort Monroe, McClellan planned first to take Yorktown, and then Williamsburg and West Point. From there, the Army of the Potomac would fight its way into Richmond, ostensibly ending the war. Along most of the campaign, the Army of the Potomac would have its flanks protected by Union naval forces. Initially, McClellan believed he possessed an army of 140,000 men, but when the defense of Washington was considered, his forces were reduced to roughly 100,000.[32] However, reinforcements of roughly 40,000 men under the command of Irwin McDowell were promised along the way. As a result, McClellan assumed he would have over 150,000 men under his command before attempting to take Richmond. On March 17, the first units in McClellan's army departed the capital for the campaign.

On March 20, 1862, the Sharpshooters broke camp in Washington and proceeded to join General McClellan's command on the Peninsula. For Lieutenant William Winthrop, this meant a return to the site of Theodore's death. Winthrop and the rest of Company H disembarked first at Fort Monroe. Lieutenant Peet recalled Winthrop describing in detail how he had gone into Big Bethel the year before and retrieved his brother's body. Peet also maintained a copy of a report detailing Winthrop's first encounter with rebel forces in combat as a sharpshooter. On March 30, 1862, Winthrop was ordered, along with twenty other Company H men, to join a reconnaissance in force near Big Bethel.

During a night march through the swamps, Winthrop's men encountered no rebel forces, but after reaching the crumbling year-old ramparts blocking the area, they spotted a Confederate cavalry unit. "Our men were first to the ramparts, and shot a rebel horseman," Winthrop recorded. "We pushed several miles further on, had some good shots and killed a few."[33]

The Confederate forces on the Peninsula did not contest the Union landing, opting to retreat into a series of earthworks that stretched fourteen miles in length from Yorktown—of Revolutionary War fame—to the Warwick River. This would be the spot where the Army of the Potomac first engaged the Confederates. The Confederate commander in the field, General John Magruder, who had successfully commanded rebel forces in June 1861 at Big Bethel, constructed a second line of fortifications ten miles behind Yorktown, at Williamsburg. In addition to building earthworks, Confederate forces felled trees to create open fields of fire, as well as booby traps and ambush areas. Additionally, should the second line prove insufficient to withstand a federal assault, the ground behind this line, an area known as White Oak Swamp, would likely slow Union forces while Richmond received reinforcements. For the Army of the Potomac to succeed in capturing Richmond, it would need to act with speed so that its initial overwhelming strength could be used to an advantage. Under McClellan's command, the army had neither of these two essential elements.[34]

On April 1, the Sharpshooters marched toward Yorktown, along with the rest of the Army of the Potomac. At this juncture, the Sharpshooters fell under the divisional command of a McClellan favorite, Fitz-John Porter. After a skirmish near Yorktown on that day, the company next saw action against Confederate forces at Great Bethel on April 4. It was also at this action where Company H suffered its first combat death.[35]

On April 5, Company H went into action near Yorktown again, this time as part of the larger battle then taking place under General Porter's direct command. The company orderly sergeant recalled the experience of battle for Company H that day as follows: "Passing through a hollow before taking a position on a hill, a shower of bullets flew around and over us. We took action double quick and passed safely over to the hill, but many of us had bullet marks in our clothes, the balls also striking the ground in front every step we took."[36]

Writing to Lillie Devereux Blake,[37] Captain George Hastings described Company H's position at the beginning of the siege: "My own company were not at first deployed as skirmishers or in position to give fire, but were stationed with other companies as a support to the defense." This position did not exempt Company H from danger, as Hastings explained: "Twice my position was discovered from the works and they commenced shelling me and I had one man killed at my side." Hastings lauded Company H's performance during the first days of the siege writing, "My men behaved with the coolness of veterans." He noted, in what was to become a continual theme in his letters, that the Sharpshooters were lauded by the division commander which fed "Berdan's vanity which knows no bounds." He also informed Blake that Berdan "seizes upon every vagabond newspaper reporter he can find and fills him with material for publication." While Berdan's vanity offended Hastings, there was another reason Hastings did not approve of publicity. He feared that the Sharpshooters would be specifically targeted by the Confederates.[38]

Winthrop's first letter home was written on April 30 from an occupied plantation known as the Farenholt House, during the siege of Yorktown. At the time, he was "stationed near an artillery battery of five 100 lb and one 200 lb 'Parrot' guns." "When the parrots fired, I felt the ground tremble under me," he told his mother. He wrote gleefully that when the Army of the Potomac appeared at the house, the owner, Amanda Farenholt, fled into a "negro shanty, and what must Amanda Farenholt feel—standing on tiptoe, with her mouth open, a stunning battery in her apple orchard, the enemy is everywhere!" He also described the sharpshooters' battlefield positions, "out from the trenches run saps to advanced rifle pits which we sharpshooters occupy. We have now driven the rebel picket lines gradually back every night by our advancing work."[39] Winthrop also wrote to his family that the Sharpshooters were shelled every night, and that they were living in rainy and muddy conditions.

On May 3, Winthrop told his family, "We are pretty far forward. This and other bold positions increase the frustration, often exaggerated, for the sharpshooters." Describing inaccurate Confederate artillery, he recorded, "All day they kept at our trenches and fatigue parties and batteries. But, all to very little avail. Thus, every hour was full of uproar. But, all to little purpose. Only two men along the whole line were struck."[40] In contrast to the light casualties from Confederate artillery, Winthrop was certain Union artillery killed a large number of Confederates. He witnessed an incident of a Confederate trench mortar blowing up on its crew, "throwing the gunners high in the air." Despite the continual artillery fire, Winthrop was able to communicate with his sister Elizabeth, serving as a nurse aboard the hospital sloop *Daniel Webster*. He also provided a first personal insight into his feelings about the war and its carnage: "All of these noises of shot and shell are hideous to me—they tell of a detestable hateful war undertaken through the dire necessity of self preservation." Winthrop even expressed doubts about the morality of killing: "I find I can't be gleeful as many of our officers are over victims and bloody successes and slayings and mayhem. . . . You should have given me more raw meat when I was weaning."[41]

Confederate and Union infantry forces did not remain static outside of Yorktown, and a number of scouting parties and raids occurred across the lines. Because the Sharpshooters were in a forward position, they occasionally saw enemy parties laboring as well as scouting and took the brunt of Confederate fire. On April 12, a Confederate force attempted to dislodge the Sharpshooters as well as a number of men from the Sixty-Third Pennsylvania Volunteers. General Charles Hamilton, commanding the Third Division, reported that during the Confederate attack, most of the Sharpshooters and Pennsylvanians held their positions and the attack was repulsed. However, a few did not, and some argument ensued between the commander of the Pennsylvanians and Berdan as to whether either of them gave an order to retreat.[42]

Berdan avoided reporting the incident, instead writing that all of his Sharpshooters "displayed the greatest coolness and bravery during the entire action, and manifested their power to use their skill to good advantage under a galling fire." He also claimed to have reconnoitered the ground prior to placing the Sharpshooters in their firing position.[43] Lieutenant Colonel Ripley recollected in his history of Company F that "occasionally a man would be found who, carried away by his enthusiasm, would mount the parapet and with taunting cries seem to mock the Union marksmen, but no sooner would he appear than a score of rifles would be brought to bear and he was fortunate indeed if he escaped with his life."[44]

During the siege, Berdan pulled Winthrop onto the regiment's staff to serve as temporary adjutant. In this position, Winthrop was responsible for conveying orders and ensuring Berdan's expectations were carried out. "I like active company business much better, though I am excused from guard duty and picket duty in bad weather," Winthrop recorded.[45]

On May 4 Yorktown fell into Union hands, and McClellan cabled news of the victory to the capital. General Fitz-John Porter reported, "The sharpshooters under Colonel Berdan were heavily engaged as skirmishers and did good service in picking off the enemy's skirmishers and artillerists whenever they showed themselves."[46] Likewise, Colonel Berdan recorded, "The men displayed great coolness and bravery during the entire action and manifested their skill under a galling fire, which deserves special notice as this was their first engagement."[47] During the siege, Berdan sent companies independently to support other commands. These commands favorably reported the Sharpshooters' service as well. General Porter reported to General McClellan that the Sharpshooters were instrumental in the siege's success and rendered valuable service to other corps as well.[48]

Elation certainly was the case for Winthrop, who jubilantly wrote home, "Last Night our guns and mortars thundered. This A.M. comes an order, Yorktown is evacuated! Cook three days rations and prepare to march at once; Glorious!"[49] Other Sharpshooters were not as happy as Winthrop to enter Yorktown.

The Confederates were, in fact, conducting an orderly retreat to the second defensive line and were nowhere close to being defeated. On May 5, William again saw action near the historic town of Williamsburg. Several Sharpshooters, including Winthrop, supported a beleaguered Union brigade until reinforcements were able to stem the Confederate advance. Once inside Williamsburg, the Union forces, including the Sharpshooters, confronted a similar array of booby traps as at Yorktown.[50]

One of Winthrop's fellow officers, Lieutenant J. Smith Brown recorded, "The enemy charged in splendid style. . . . Three times they advanced yelling like demons, crying out, 'Bull Run, Ball's Bluff.' Eight rods in front of us was a rail fence. Only one man, a Captain crossed it. He fell dead." The next day Lieutenant Brown described reconnoitering the battlefield: "In one place I counted seventy five dead, in another forty-six; the eyes open, staring horribly, hands clenched, body convulsed by the last. strong agony, tongues protruding. . . . Our loss in battle was 2,000—The rebels 2,500."[51]

On May 8, Winthrop's regiment boarded a Union vessel and traveled up the York River to West Point. From there, the regiment marched fifteen miles to a Lee-Custis plantation called White House. Later that week, McClellan and William Seward, the secretary of state, inspected the forces near White House in a rainstorm. Winthrop described himself to his mother with humor as "your champion in a private's dark blue blouse (with shoulder straps) and private's light blue shoddy trousers thrust into high boots—his pistol in his belt—his sword extended at present arms."[52]

The following day, Winthrop claimed his company marched five miles on a circular patrol around White House through bottomless mud with caissons and wagons stuck in the mud once more. The march was so disorganized that companies became intermingled, and then regiments did the same. That evening, the Sharpshooters set a bivouac in newly issued tents. Winthrop took delight in describing these *tente d'abri* to his family, "into which we crawl, like to whom we dress in a measure, and also consume our rations." He concluded his sentiments on the bivouac by saying it was "rough and rude." Unlike his experiences at Camp Cameron with the Seventh Regiment a year earlier, Winthrop longed for a "Sybaris of luxury" and for an end to war to "enjoy some creamy trifles of which now I can only dream." But Winthrop did not take a wholly negative view of his surroundings, describing the White House area as "a beautiful plain of clover." Winthrop concluded his letter with the hope that the Sharpshooters would rest several days at White House.[53]

On May 15 General McClellan reorganized the Army of the Potomac into five corps for what he believed would likely be the final battle of the Peninsula campaign and perhaps the war. With reinforcements to augment the army, his forces totaled 128,000 men, of which 21,000 were left to garrison captured towns, were sick, or were absent without leave. But even this depletion of forces still gave McClellan numerical superiority over the Confederate army. Moreover, the Army of the Potomac enjoyed a high level of morale and confidence that the end of the Confederacy was near. The reorganization of the army into five corps, with two divisions assigned to each corps, was designed to provide optimum command and control of the battle.

It also enabled McClellan to promote Fitz-John Porter and William Franklin, two officers he considered superior, to corps command. But despite the army's high morale and its reorganization, McClellan doubted his army's readiness and believed intelligence reports indicating the forces opposing his army numbered 180,000 men. His intelligence chief, Alan Pinkerton of detective agency fame, told him as much. Moreover, McClellan insisted his opponent's strength was likely to grow. From his location at White House, he and the Sharpshooters could hear church bells in Richmond. McClellan decided that the time to move against the Confederate forces opposing the Army of the Potomac would never be more opportune.[54]

On May 27 Union forces under the command of Fitz-John Porter engaged the Confederates near Hanover Courthouse. General Porter sent the First U.S. Volunteers ahead of his main battle line as skirmishers. With their unparalleled firepower, the Sharpshooters, along with a New York regiment, pushed the Southerners into a scattered retreat. In a one-sided battle, which cost Porter's corps 397 casualties, the Confederates lost more than one thousand men.[55] This battle brought McClellan closer to Richmond than at any point and was the high-water mark of the Peninsula campaign.

Although Winthrop did not leave a written recollection of the battle, a number of other Sharpshooters did. Lieutenant Brown recorded, "Soon we got our force up and the fun began. The left wing of our regiment was on the edge of the woods 500 yards in front of the brass howitzers and they tried to drive us out with grape. Several of the men from Albany Co. and Vermont Co were killed and wounded, but we did not stir. . . . The dead and dying were scattered everywhere." Brown also recorded how the Sharpshooters treated captured Confederates, writing, "A wounded rebel raised up and fired at Bennet. Bennet captured the unregenerate cuss and brought him into the shade where he soon after died. Before he died he gave Bennet his watch and bade him an affectionate goodbye."[56]

Toward the end of the battle, Berdan divided his regiment into two wings, one under the command of Lieutenant Colonel Ripley and the other under the command of Captain Hastings. This act elevated Winthrop to command of Company H. Advancing into a wooded area, one sharpshooter wrote, "Here the fighting was tremendous. Our batteries played on the enemy, and the shell crashing through the treetops. The rebels fought well, but they could not keep the field." The regiment suffered roughly twenty casualties. However, during the battle another significant event occurred, degrading the regiment's efficiency. Colonel Berdan absented himself from the battle, and a number of the regiment's officers began to believe he acted with cowardice. Winthrop was among their number.[57]

No reading of Berdan's report of action after this engagement would receive a hint that the Sharpshooters' commanding officer was disengaged from the battle. Berdan described his role in the battle as actively readying his troops to advance through a woods and leading them in an engagement against a North Carolina regiment. He also claimed that the Sharpshooters killed seventeen North Carolinians, wounded twenty-seven, and took prisoner another thirty-one. At the same time, the Sharpshooters suffered no losses except for one prisoner of war, the regimental surgeon.[58] How it happened that the surgeon was captured was not explained. Winthrop's letters are silent as to this event as well.

Three days after the battle at Hanover Courthouse, the Sharpshooters were engaged once again, this time ten miles south at Fair Oaks, or "Seven Pines." On May 30, General Johnston ordered Confederate divisions under the command of James Longstreet, D. H. Hill, and Benjamin Huger to attack the Union corps closest to Richmond. The battle that ensued was later labeled by Civil War historian Shelby Foote as "unquestionably the worst-conducted large-scale conflict in a war that afforded many rivals for that distinction." Foote's characterization is supported by another historian, James McPherson, who wrote, "From the early morning of battle things began to go wrong for the Confederates."[59] The three Confederate commanders failed to communicate effectively among each other, and with Johnston. Nonetheless, the Confederates made a number of limited gains against the federal lines. The target of the Confederate assault, a corps commanded by General Erasmus Keyes, held on long enough to be reinforced by a second Union corps, commanded by General Edwin Sumner. In a number of subsequent campaigns, the Sharpshooters came under Sumner's command.

Born in 1797 and nicknamed "Bull," Sumner was a veteran of the Black Hawk and Mexican-American wars. Sumner may have been one of the more competent corps commanders, and Winthrop appraised him as such; however, due to Sumner's age—he died the following year—he was unlikely to ever command a full army. (Some of Sumner's contemporaries felt he had been promoted far above his competency). He took command of all forces in the battle including the First U.S. Volunteers and held the line against any further Confederate assaults. But this came at great cost, and one of the regiments in the division to which Winthrop was assigned broke and ran from the battle. By day's end, the Confederates lost 6,134 dead or wounded, and the Union lost slightly less. Although the battle was technically a Union victory, since McClellan still maintained the offensive, a significant event occurred which signaled the beginning of a change for both sides. General Johnston was wounded while reconnoitering near the front lines. His replacement would rise to become one of the top military commanders in U.S. history. Unfortunately for Winthrop, the Sharpshooters, McClellan, the Army of the Potomac, and the country as a whole, General Robert E. Lee was a Confederate.

Hastings conveyed to Lillie Blake that the fight at Fair Oaks was brutal. He described the "constant reconnaissance in front our outpost" and the fact that "we were in constant expectation of an attack remaining under arms night and day."[60] Winthrop recorded the battle conditions as well. Writing home to his family on June 6 from Gaines Mill, Winthrop reflected on the fights at Hanover House and Fair Oaks. "As I understand it, the fight at Fair Oaks seems to have been a pretty fair test," adding, "we were badly punished." Although he maintained faith in the prowess of his regiment, he expressed his disgust at higher command, writing, "Our regiment would not have broken at Fair Oaks, and we have seen a good deal of fighting than some of the division." Winthrop may have sent an earlier letter to his family—now missing—indicating he was sick. In the June 6 letter, he wrote, "I feel better than when I last wrote, but not perfectly well." He also asked his family to inquire as to any officer openings in another regiment, scathing Colonel Berdan in the process: "Though he has always treated me with respect, for I have behaved in such a manner as to compel it, yet his conduct and character generally are such as to make him repulsive to anyone feeling any honor. I say no man as this is as detested, and let this be pretty much over." Winthrop also commented that as an officer, he was not allowed to resign his commission except for a "strong reason." Appointment to another regiment with a "higher rank would constitute such a reason."[61]

On June 6, Company H was formally split off from the regiment and formally moved to the corps under the command of General Edwin Sumner. Shortly after reporting to General Sumner's headquarters, the men were placed in forward positions to counter Confederate picket fire. After discovering the source of the fire, the men of Company H engaged in a brief skirmish and drove their adversaries out of range. "The enemy were soon upon us and we engaged them successfully at Allen's Farm: My company was then deployed as skirmishers and did the service required of them," Hastings recorded.[62]

For almost a month, the opposing armies did little fighting and reconstituted themselves. Fair Oaks appears, in retrospect, to have sapped McClellan's desire for a continued moving offensive, and during the month following the battle, Robert E. Lee assembled a force roughly equal to the Army of the Potomac. Included in this larger force was a corps under the command of Thomas J. "Stonewall" Jackson. Surprisingly, McClellan seems to have had little regard for the abilities of either Jackson or Lee. But McClellan was very concerned about being outnumbered and about having a base of supply running through the middle of the Peninsula. He wanted to have the protection of naval artillery for his supply lines, and he grew more concerned about the Army of the Potomac's health. The army had suffered losses to battle and sickness, not easily replaced in comparison to Lee's forces. Sickness was prevalent throughout the Civil War, but in the war's early stages, there were significant shortcomings in military medicine.

In mid-June 1862, Winthrop experienced military medicine first-hand. On June 11, a doctor examined Winthrop for dysentery. He had suffered a month-long bout of "severe diarrhea," and the doctor noted Winthrop had "lost much flesh and [was] quite enfeebled." The report ended with a doubtful statement on Winthrop's chance for a quick improvement. On June 19, Winthrop was examined again, suffering "bilious diarrhea." Winthrop still had not improved despite constant medical care. Winthrop's condition may have accounted for a break in writing letters home, and, although he returned to Company H on June 26, other events transpired which kept him from corresponding with his family.[63]

On June 25, a division of the Army of the Potomac under the command of General Joseph Hooker moved against Lee's forces and was soundly defeated. The following day, Lee countered with a campaign to drive McClellan off the Peninsula, if not trap the Army of the Potomac and force its surrender.

On June 27, Lee's forces attacked the Union corps under General Porter's command around Gaines Mill. This was the largest Confederate offensive to date in the war, and Porter's corps was in danger of annihilation but was spared this result, in part because Thomas Jackson was unable to bring up reinforcements to the Confederate attack. It was an intense day, costing the Union side over six thousand casualties, while the Confederates lost over eight thousand. The following day, Lee's forces regrouped and launched only minor attacks, but the intensity of Gaines Mill caused McClellan to order a retreat to Harrison's Landing. On June 29, Lee's forces assaulted the Union positions around Glendale and White Oak Swamp. It was on the following day that Company H saw its first hot action in the retreat.

Company H, like the rest of the regiment, had been continually on the march during the Army of the Potomac's retreat from the Peninsula. But it was a fighting retreat. While skirmishing and cannonades were a constant feature for the company, during the Seven Days, the company went into full battle twice, at White Oak Swamp on June 30, and near Malvern Hill the following day. At White Oak, the unit came up against troops commanded by Stonewall Jackson. Along with Companies A and I, they withstood a Confederate artillery barrage and frontal assault, losing twelve of their men. Captain Hastings later reported that at the Battle of White Oak Swamp, "the men stood nobly in the field . . . under a terrific fire of musketry from an enemy concealed in the woods." Hastings concluded his report stating that "the enemy far outnumbered the Sharpshooters, but were unable to push the Sharpshooters off the field."[64] One unfortunate result of the battle that fell entirely out of the control of the Sharpshooters was the abandonment of a large hospital to the Confederates. While Lee demanded the injured be treated humanely as prisoners of war, the hospital, containing a number of Sharpshooters and others, took fire during the Glendale battle.

The following morning, Company H found itself resting adjacent to the Sixty-first New York near Malvern Hill. But their rest was broken by fierce combat. During a surprise Confederate assault, Captain Hastings volunteered Company H to Colonel Francis Barlow, the New Yorkers' commanding officer. Again, the company went into action utilizing its basic tactics of rapid concentrated fire against Confederate advances. Confederate forces found they were unable to force the New Yorkers into a retreat and lost a considerable number of their men. Hastings described Company H's role in the battle at Malvern Hill as frantic but effective: "We had to double-quick which caused at least a third of the men, fatigued as they were, to fall out so that I suppose not more than twenty-five of them went into action at first. These behaved nobly. They stood under a terrific fire of musketry in an open field within fifty paces of the edge of the woods in which lay concealed an enemy far outnumbering our own force." Hastings had a good view of the regiments at Malverton. Writing, "the 61st N.Y. and 81st Penn we held back until their fire ceased, and our ammunition being all spent retired about a hundred yards to the left edge of a wood facing the enemy's position. There we remained prepared if attacked to meet them with our bayonets."[65] But the attack did not occur, and the men of Company H were able to get through the night to retreat with the Sixty-first New York toward Harrison's Landing.

Colonel Barlow was so impressed by the firepower and discipline of the Sharpshooters during the battle that he placed Hastings in command of part of the New Yorkers in addition to his command over the Sharpshooters. In a report to divisional command written after Malvern Hill, Barlow wrote that Company H performed nobly and pointed out that Peet was mortally wounded.[66]

Malvern Hill was a showcase battle for the Sharpshooters. Arrayed behind wheat stacks in front of the Union lines, the Sharpshooters kept a steady rate of fire during the day, continually holding off one Confederate assault after another. The Sharpshooters maintained a fast rate of accurate fire and barely gave any ground, even when, in the middle of the battle, Lee augmented the numbers of Confederate troops to break the Union lines. But holding the line against the Confederates was no easy task.[67]

The only thing missing from the Sharpshooters' performance at Malvern Hill was their commander. Throughout the day, Berdan was nowhere to be seen near the front lines. According to a Lieutenant Seaton, Berdan had ordered the Sharpshooters to fan out in front of the lines and then disappeared from the battlefield, leaving them leaderless, at least of field-grade officers, since the deputy, Lieutenant Colonel Ripley, was seriously injured. Another officer recalled that he encountered Berdan two miles behind the front lines searching for food to bring forward. Given this pattern of Berdan's behavior that repeated itself over and over again, the junior officers and noncommissioned officers took matters into their own hands and held the line.[68]

Ironically, Malvern Hill could have been considered a complete Union victory, since Lee's forces were stymied. The Confederacy lost over one thousand more men than the Union. The Army of the Potomac retained the high ground throughout the battle. McClellan was in a position to regain the offensive from his position on the high ground. And if any regiment could claim the laurels of success, it was the First U.S. Volunteers. Placed in the front of the Union lines, firing rapidly down the slope into the oncoming Confederate ranks, the Sharpshooters ensured the Union frontline remained intact. Confederate forces paid a high price at Malvern Hill, over six thousand men, causing one Confederate commander to opine, "The battle wasn't war, it was murder."[69] The Confederate attacks never punctured the Sharpshooters' line. But the Sharpshooters paid a heavy price as well, losing over a tenth of their remaining strength. Colonel Berdan was not among them, avoiding combat once more. According to a number of the men, Berdan was several thousand yards behind the Union lines, making excuses such as the need to procure fresh meat for the men or tend to the wounded.

If Berdan knew that his men and a number of generals, including his brigade and divisional commander, were appalled at his conduct, he did not show it. Berdan made no attempt to refrain from his showmanship after the Peninsula campaign either, writing to newspapers and exaggerating his role on the battlefield. In writing an official report, Berdan recorded that at Gaines Mill, the Sharpshooters repulsed the enemy with great loss. He also reported he personally reconnoitered the battlefield and confronted a frantic retreat of twelve thousand Union soldiers clogging a bridge. When he approached these men, he drew his pistol and "threatened to shoot the first officer or man who passed me." Firing his pistol into the air, he then forced the men into line without regard to rank or regiment. At Malvern Hill, he claimed to have been responsible for keeping the Sharpshooters aligned during battle. Assuming Berdan's claims are dubious is not a great leap since he also expressed his regrets for not remembering the names of the officers and men he corralled at Gaines Mill. Additionally telling is the brigade commander General Morrell's comment on Berdan: "Colonel Berdan was not in the fight at Gaines Mill. What occurred far to the rear near the bridge I do not know of my own knowledge, but I have every reason to believe this [Berdan's] statement is highly exaggerated."[70]

Malvern Hill exhausted the Confederate army, and Lee did not have the resources to deliver a "knock out blow." McClellan had more soldiers under his command and the advantage of naval support, but he lacked aggression to reclaim the offensive. Only when prodded by the administration did McClellan respond with a proposal to attack Lee and move once again toward Richmond. By this time, it was too late and McClellan's capabilities had faded in Lincoln's estimation.

Malvern Hill also exhausted Company H. Its numbers fell below twenty men, which Hastings described as scattered. One of its two lieutenants was believed dead or certainly lost for good as a prisoner of Lee's army. Winthrop was weakened from dysentery and unable to effectively command. Hastings found himself without a company but did not desire to return to Berdan, so while the company rested, he served as an aide-de-camp to General Caldwell. He noted to Lillie Blake that as of July 6, twenty-eight men were all that were left for his company. He also wrote, "Our regiment has been badly cut up in the late battles and marches. The colonel is quite sick, the Lt Col (Ripley) wounded badly, Capt Drew (the best officer we have) killed. Lt Col Ripley covered himself with glory successively leading three regiments into action."[71]

Hastings believed the retreat from Richmond was no fault of McClellan's. This was likely a common belief in the Army of the Potomac, and McClellan certainly fostered it as well. Hastings wrote, "The failure to properly reinforce McClellan is also beyond doubt. There are some who think he made his base at the James immediately after the Battle of Williamsburg. . . . But it must be remembered that all his arrangements previously had been made while the York and Pamunkey were open. . . . He had a right to expect that Halleck would hold Beauregard in the west and Jackson in the Shenandoah." At the same time Hastings recognized Jackson's abilities. What Hastings did not understand at the time was that McClellan's detractors included the president. His letter aimed criticism at McDowell, Halleck, and the War Department: "The campaign thus far has vindicated McClellan and convicted the War Department."[72]

McClellan could not convince the administration he had the wherewithal to regain the offensive, in part, because of his continued belief in being outnumbered, but also because he drew no immediate plan for a counterstroke against Lee. As a result, Lincoln and Stanton ordered the Army of the Potomac to evacuate the Peninsula and return to the Washington area. The remaining men of the Sharpshooters were evacuated off the Peninsula with the rest of the Army of the Potomac, but not before they were reviewed by General McClellan, who commented, "It is too bad, there are few left, but I think enough to fight again."[73] Lee's offensive against McClellan had been so successful that it emboldened the Confederate leadership to seek the offensive with a move toward Washington, DC.

NOTES

1. Kenneth Katta, "Conflicts in Command: An Analysis of Leadership in the Berdan Sharpshooters in the Civil War," *Military Collector and Historian* 53, no. 2 (2001), 54. See also Roy Marcot, *Civil War Chief of Sharpshooters Hiram Berdan: Military Commander and Firearms Inventor* (Irvine, CA: Northwood Heritage, 1989), 21.
2. Wiley Sword, *Sharpshooter: Hiram Berdan, His Famous Sharpshooters, and Their Sharps Rifles* (Lincoln, RI: Andrew Mowbray, 1988), 9; Marcot, *Civil War Chief of Sharpshooters*, 17–19.
3. Robert Bruce, *Lincoln and the Tools of War* (Indianapolis: Bobbs-Merrill, 1956), 109.
4. Hinton Rowan, *Compendium of the Impending Crisis of the South* (New York: A.B. Burdick, 1864), 69.
5. Bruce, *Lincoln and the Tools of War*, 111.
6. Theodore Ropp, *War in the Modern World* (Durham, NC: Duke University Press, 1959), 181–184. Ropp argues that tactical innovations during the war occurred at the field instead of at the command level. Berdan's Sharpshooters' creation provides evidence for Ropp's argument.
7. Richard Pindell, "A Most Dangerous Set of Men," *Civil War Times Illustrated* 32 (July 1993), 42.
8. John Hay, "Life in the Whitehouse in the Time of Lincoln," *Century* 41 (January 1890), 34. This story is also found in John Hay, *Addresses of John Hay* (New York: Century, 1906), 328; Marcot, *Civil War Chief of Sharpshooters*, 26.
9. "Colonel Berdan's Sharp Shooting Organization," *New York Times*, July 20, 1861, 8.
10. *Scientific American*, October 3, 1863, 211.
11. Charles Stevens, *Berdan's United States Sharpshooters in the Army of the Potomac*, reprint ed. (Dayton, OH: Morningside Books, 1995), 3.
12. See, for example, Pindell, "A Most Dangerous Set of Men," 42–44, William F. Fox, *Regimental Losses in the American Civil War, 1861–1865*, reprint ed. (Northridge, CA: Morningside Books, 1974), 14–15; Brent Nosworthy, *The Bloody Crucible of Courage: Fighting Methods and Combat Experience of the Civil War* (New York: Carroll and Graf, 2003), 190–193.
13. Berdan wrote, "My reasons for selecting the uniform are that the men composing the regiment will not consent to wear the common U.S. uniform; and

as they are skirmishers, they should not be conspicuously dressed. The green will harmonize with the leaves of summer while the grey overcoat will accord with surrounding objects in fall and winter." Adjutant General's Correspondence (BO 462), Box 33, Fldr 12, New York State Archives, Albany, in *Military Collector and Historian* 53, no. 2 (2001). See also Rudolf Karl Aschmann, *Memoirs of a Swiss Officer in the American Civil War (Three Years in the Army of the Potomac or a Swiss Company of Sharpshooters in the North American War)*, ed. Heinz K. Meier, trans. Hedwig D. Rappolt (Bern, Switzerland: Herbert Lang, 1972), 30.

14. Fox, *Regimental Losses*, 418. See also Stephen Sears, *To the Gates of Richmond: The Peninsula Campaign* (New York: Houghton Mifflin, 1992), 50; Ernest B. Ferguson, *Chancellorsville, 1863: The Souls of the Brave* (New York: Vintage Books, 1993), 151–154; and Edwin B. Coddington, *The Gettysburg Campaign; a Study in Command* (New York: Touchstone, 1984), 352–353.

15. Frederick Tomlinson Peet, *My Personal Experiences in the Civil War* (New York: F. T. Peet, 1905), 62; see also George Brinton McClellan, *My Own Story: The War for the Union, the Soldiers Who Fought It, the Commanders Who Directed It, and His Relation to It and Them* (New York: Webster and Co., 1887), 400.

16. Peet, *My Personal Experiences*, 62.

17. Peet, *My Personal Experiences*, 65.

18. Stevens, *Berdan's United States Sharpshooters*, 20.

19. Winthrop, letter to his mother, undated (YALE).

20. Gerald Linderman, *Embattled Courage: The Experience of Combat in the American Civil War* (New York: Free Press, 1987), 192.

21. Peet, *My Personal Experiences*, 36.

22. Stevens, *Berdan's United States Sharpshooters*, 33.

23. Stevens, *Berdan's United States Sharpshooters*, 24.

24. Stevens, *Berdan's United States Sharpshooters*, 24.

25. Sword, *Sharpshooter*, 13; Aschmann, *Memoirs of a Swiss Officer*, 37.

26. Stevens, *Berdan's United States Sharpshooters*, 16.

27. See, for example, George W. Adams, *Doctors in Blue: The Medical History of the Union Army in the Civil War* (Baton Rouge: Louisiana State University Press, 1952), 3.

28. Stevens, *Berdan's United States Sharpshooters*, 8–9.

29. OR, ser. 1, vol. 11, ch. 13, pt. 2, p. 216 (Report of Brigadier General Smith, September 27, 1861); Margaret Leech, *Reveille in Washington* (New York: Harper Brothers, 1941), 116; Shelby Foote, *The Civil War, a Narrative: Fort Sumter to Perryville* (New York: Random House, 1958), 103–104. Russell H. Beatie, *Army of the Potomac: McClellan Takes Command* (New York: Da Capo, 2002), 25–26.

30. Francis A. Lord, *They Fought for the Union* (Harrisburg, PA: Stackpole, 1960), 33.

31. Kevin Dougherty, *The Peninsula Campaign of 1862: A Military Analysis* (Columbus: University of Mississippi Press, 2005), 60.

32. Ethan S. Rafuse, *McClellan's War: The Failure of Moderation in the Struggle for the Union* (Bloomington: Indiana University Press, 2005), 205; also James M. McPherson, *Battle Cry of Freedom: The Civil War Era* (New York: Oxford University Press, 1988), 424.

33. Peet, *My Personal Experiences*, 58.

34. For a description of the Confederate defenses, see Foote, *The Civil War*, 401; see also Bruce Catton, *Bruce Catton's Civil War: Three Volumes in One*, vol. 1, *Mr. Lincoln's Army* (New York: Fairfax Press, 1984), 66–68.
35. Stevens, *Berdan's United States Sharpshooters*, 41.
36. Stevens, *Berdan's United States Sharpshooters*, 41.
37. Lillie Devereux Blake (1835–1913), Winthrop's cousin, was an author, lecturer, and a leader in the women's suffrage movement. During her youth she resided in New Haven and moved to Philadelphia in 1855. Widowed in 1859, she obtained employment as the Washington correspondent for the New York *Evening Post*. She served as a war correspondent at the outbreak of war. Although it is not clear how Hastings and Blake knew each other, Hastings' correspondence evidences a friendship if not a past romance between the two, which probably began at Yale.
38. George Hastings, letter to Lillian Devereux Blake, April 12, 1862 (Missouri Historical Society).
39. William Winthrop, letter to his family, April 30, 1862 (YALE).
40. William Winthrop, letter to his family, May 3, 1862 (YALE).
41. Winthrop, letter to his family, May 3, 1862.
42. OR, ser. 1, vol. 11, ch. 13, pt. 1, p. 301.
43. OR, ser. 1, vol. 11, ch. 13, pt. 1, p. 302.
44. William Y. W. Ripley, *Vermont Rifleman in the War for the Union, 1861–1865 : A History of Company F, First United States Sharp Shooters* (Rutland, VT: Tuttle and Co., 1883), 23.
45. William Winthrop, letter to his family, May 4, 1862 (YALE).
46. Fitz-John Porter, OR (ser. 1, vol. 9, pt. 1, p. 286), May 5.
47. OR, ser. 1, vol. 11, ch. 13, pt. 1, p. 301.
48. OR, ser. 1, vol. 11, ch. 13, pt. 1, p. 312.
49. Winthrop, letter to his family, May 4, 1862.
50. Stevens, *Berdan's United States Sharpshooters*, 77.
51. J. Smith Brown, letter, May 6, 1862, in R. L. Murray, *Letters from Berdan's Sharpshooters* (Wolcott, NY: Benedum Books, 2005), 30.
52. William Winthrop, letter to his family, May 9, 1862 (YALE).
53. William Winthrop, letter to his family, May 16, 1862 (YALE).
54. Foote, *The Civil War*, 417.
55. David D. Eicher, *The Longest Night: A Military History of the Civil War* (New York: Simon and Schuster, 2001), 275.
56. J. Smith Brown, letter, May 27, 1862, in R. L. Murray, *Letters from Berdan's Sharpshooters*, 46.
57. R. L. Murray, *Berdan's Sharpshooters in Combat: The Peninsula Campaign and Gettysburg* (New York: Benedum, 2006), 26.
58. OR, ser. 1, vol. 9, pt. 1, p. 701 (Berdan, May).
59. Foote, *The Civil War*, 444; McPherson, *Battle Cry of Freedom*, 461.
60. George Hastings, letter to Lillian Devereux Blake, July 6, 1862 (MHS).
61. William Winthrop, letter to his family, dated June 6, 1862 (YALE).
62. Hastings, letter to Lillian Devereux Blake, July 6, 1862.
63. Alice Winthrop, Pension File Records, Medical History of Colonel Winthrop (hereafter, AWPF).

64. Hastings, letter to Lillian Devereux Blake, July 6, 1862. Hastings wrote these same facts in an official dispatch. OR, ser. 1, vol. 11, ch. 13, pt. 2, pp. 279–280 (Report of George Hastings from camp at Harrison's Landing, July 5, 1862).

65. Hastings, letter to Lillian Devereux Blake, July 6, 1862; see also Brian K. Burton, *Extraordinary Circumstances: The Seven Days Battles* (Bloomington: Indiana University Press, 2001), 352–353.

66. OR, ser. 1, vol. 11, ch. 13, pt. 1, p. 722.

67. Sears, *To the Gates of Richmond*, 325. Sears writes, "The ground north and west of Malvern Hill was planted in wheat, partly harvested and standing in shocks, and behind every shock there seemed to be one of Hiram Berdan's sharpshooters." See also Burton, *Extraordinary Circumstances*, 324–333; and Eicher, *The Longest Night*, 295–296. Interestingly, Burton did not seem to write on Berdan's complete absence from the Malvern Hill Battle.

68. Sword, *Sharpshooter*, 18.

69. Sears, *To the Gates of Richmond*, 335.

70. OR, ser. 1, vol. 11, ch. 13, pt. 3, p. 279.

71. Hastings, letter to Lillian Devereux Blake, July 6, 1862; see also Stephen R. Taaffe, *Commanding the Army of the Potomac* (Lawrence: University Press of Kansas, 2006), 25–26.

72. Hastings, letter to Lillian Devereux Blake, July 6, 1862.

73. Stevens, *Berdan's United States Sharpshooters*, 157.

7

From Second Manassas to Fredericksburg: "I Had Some Pretty Close Escapes"

> Winthrop, Weston, and six Sharpshooters were the last to leave the field which we did being wounded. Had we remained two minutes longer, we must have been made prisoners.
>
> —George Hastings to Lillie Devereux Blake

With the Army of the Potomac safe but hemmed in at Harrison's Landing, Lincoln and Stanton sought a strategic change in the direction of the war. Part of this change involved the appointment of Major General John Pope, a commander Winthrop found overly egotistical. Pope attempted to abandon the law of war restraints which McClellan had earlier embraced. But Pope's arrogant leadership caused dissension within his new command, almost from the start. This change influenced Winthrop in two fundamental ways: as a line officer, he was at the heart of the change, and as a scholar, he later analyzed it in light of professionalizing both the army and the practice of military law.

On assuming command, Pope issued three controversial orders which threatened the civilian population with loss of property or life should anyone assist the rebellion. The orders did not provide for military trials and enabled commanders to summarily order execution of suspected offenders. Winthrop believed Pope's approach to total lawless warfare immoral. Winthrop was not opposed to total war as an illegality, but even in the case of total war, the principles underlying the laws of war still applied. Yet, put in context, Pope's orders were part of an evolution into total war, an evolution that Winthrop was to encounter firsthand almost immediately after Pope took command. This too shaped his theories on the law of war and its relationship to strategy.

The Sharpshooters regiment may have served as a microcosm of Pope's forces. Its leader, Colonel Berdan, continued to be detested by almost all of the ranks. One of the Sharpshooters' junior officers, Lieutenant Karl Aschmann recollected in 1865 that by the evacuation off the Peninsula, "Berdan was not well liked by the rank and file and often made a fool of himself with his clumsy demeanor."[1] On July 4, 1862, five company officers wrote to their brigade commander, General Butterfield, complaining of "Berdan's dishonesty and cowardice." The officers specifically claimed, "The Colonel has not the confidence of any subscribing officers . . . he has proven himself neither a soldier, officer, nor gentleman." As proof of their allegations against Berdan, the letter concluded, "In every case of action wherever this command has taken part, he has been found absent from the field. But always out of danger . . . he abandoned his command to the gallant Lieutenant Colonel Ripley [at Malvern Hill] who fell wounded."[2]

The letter was signed by Captains Weston,[3] Austin, and Giroux and Lieutenants Gibbs and Beebe. Absent from these signatures were the names Trepp, Hastings, and Winthrop. Inexplicably, several days later the five officers withdrew their letter, asking General Morrell, the divisional commander, to ignore their earlier complaint as unfounded. Yet on July 13, Fitz-John Porter, the corps commander, condemned Berdan as incompetent. From July through August, Berdan unsuccessfully attempted to obtain a long furlough and this may be part of the reason for Porter's dislike of Berdan.[4]

This was not to be the end of Berdan's troubled command. On June 1, 1863, the deputy commander of the regiment, Caspar Trepp, wrote directly to Stanton about Berdan's malfeasance. He also provided a copy of his letter to Winthrop, who by then had transferred to the Judge Advocate General's Department. Trepp began his letter with a specific allegation against Berdan, writing, "Since the formation of the regiment, its commanding officer, Col. Hiram Berdan, has, in many instances and in various ways, been guilty of conduct unbecoming an officer and a gentleman." Trepp's evidence to support his allegation included purchasing fraud beginning with the regiment's formation, flight from battle, lying in official reports, and malingering.[5]

The Army of the Potomac was strung out across the Peninsula in its attempt to return to northern Virginia through mid-August. The Sharpshooters journey to Washington first took them south to Williamsburg and then Yorktown, concluding their march at Fort Monroe. The travel down the Peninsula began on August 14 and ended on August 18; four days to traverse in retreat what took four months to conquer. From Fort

Monroe, the Sharpshooters boarded vessels and sailed to Aquia Creek. After disembarking, they marched through Fredericksburg, where four months later they would fight yet another horrific battle. Only some of the Sharpshooters were permitted to spend time in Fredericksburg as the town was ordered off limits to the majority of forces transiting through the area. General Butterfield, the Sharpshooters brigade commander, forbade foraging on private property as well, though Lieutenant Aschmann and a number of others discovered Butterfield's staff was engaged in the very activity. But in August, Lieutenant Smith Brown recorded the town as quiet and abandoned by men. He also wrote of two women who serenaded the Sharpshooters with a tribute to the Confederate General Beauregard.[6]

George Hastings commented to Lillie Blake, "The army has suffered badly . . . but the enemy must also be badly crippled." For Hastings, and likely for most of the soldiers, a sense of realism about war had set in. His correspondence to Lillie Blake must have mirrored that of many Sharpshooters. "I have heard you say you would like to see a great battle. I hope to God I may never see another . . . if my duty again calls me into a fight, I shall go cheerfully, coolly, and without a thought of fear or danger, for I have solved to my satisfaction the problem that used to disturb me, 'whether I was a coward or not,'" he wrote. "I have seen enough carnage to know that there is no music in a grave and I can see no beauty in mangled bodies and gaping ghastly wounds." But battle was soon to come to Winthrop and the Sharpshooters.[7]

In late August, Robert E. Lee executed a maneuver that defied military convention. He split his army into two corps, sending them on separate northern invasion routes toward Washington. A corps under the command of Thomas Jackson, numbering roughly twenty-four thousand men, advanced north first. On August 27, Jackson's corps maneuvered behind the Army of Virginia and pillaged Pope's supply depot near Manassas, temporarily disabling the Union army's main supply line in the process.[8] This event caused Pope to issue a number of frantic orders for his corps commanders to converge on Manassas. Pope planned to encircle Jackson's men and annihilate them. But the Union cavalry could not locate Jackson's corps until late the following day and captured Confederates provided false information as to Jackson's whereabouts. Worse news was to follow. Behind Jackson's corps was another Confederate corps numbering thirty thousand and commanded by James Longstreet. Now, the Union army would be confronted by two corps led by three of the superior commanders of the war: Lee, Jackson, and Longstreet. Adding to the Union confusion, Pope never seemed sure as to Longstreet's actual whereabouts.[9] Writing a letter to Lillie Blake a week after the battle, George Hastings summed up his opinions of Pope's attempts to outmaneuver Jackson's corps as "feeble."[10]

During the night of August 28, Pope assembled what forces he had for an assault on Jackson's corps he intended to occur the following day. However, at no point before the Army of Virginia made contact with Jackson's corps on August 28 did Pope bring more than thirty-two thousand men onto the field. Pope had another thirty thousand men in two corps under the command of Irwin McDowell and Franz Sigel in the local area, and the two Union commanders attempted to link forces, but this was a slow process which did not conclude until the following day. McDowell's corps had exchanged fire with Jackson's but the results were inconclusive. At the same time, Jackson knew that Longstreet's larger corps was in the vicinity as well. Pope did not worry about Longstreet's corps, because he had been notified, wrongly, that Longstreet's corps was held in check at a gap in the Manassas Mountains.[11] As a result, Pope had an incomplete understanding about the forces opposing him as well as those at his disposition. He could find some solace in the fact that the size of his army was increasing as units from the Army of the Potomac were arriving in his theater. But these units were not effectively integrated into his command as late as the following morning.[12]

In the late morning on August 29, Pope's forces made a series of disjointed attacks against Jackson's corps but made little headway. The Union attacks were ill coordinated and piecemeal, depriving Pope of his advantage in numbers of men over Jackson. Both sides suffered heavy casualties. At midday, Longstreet's corps joined Jackson. However, this fact was initially unknown to Pope. Instead, Pope ordered a detached corps from the Army of the Potomac, under the command of Major General Fitz-John Porter, to advance to the battle and attack Jackson. This corps contained the Sharpshooters regiment. But Pope's orders were unclear as to where Porter was supposed to attack, and advice Porter received from McDowell proved contrary to Pope's intent. In addition to Pope's unclear orders to Porter, there were other problems with the disposition of Porter's corps. Porter could not obey Pope's orders as Longstreet's larger force blocked his advance. As a result of this inability, Porter's corps remained ineffectively stationary for a number of critical hours during August 29. Porter's perceived act of disobedience, coupled with a number of insulting remarks he made against Pope, were the genesis for later criminal charges and court-martial.[13]

During the night of August 29, Pope informed his corps commanders of his intention to attack Jackson the following day. By this time, Pope had almost his entire available force ready for a general assault. He could have arrayed one hundred thousand men against Lee's entire force, but he remained ignorant of Lee's and Longstreet's whereabouts.[14] Pope still did not know the position and extent of Longstreet's corps, and he chose to ignore Porter who had voiced concerns over Longstreet's strength. Pope considered Porter as untrustworthy and lethargic, a McClellan crony, and responsible for the army's overall poor performance on the 29th.[15] By this time, Pope may have already considered charging Porter under the Articles of War for dereliction of duty or treason. Pope certainly looked at Porter as a scapegoat for anything that went wrong in the battle. Despite his views on Porter, Pope believed be needed every regiment available in the fight. At 3 a.m., he shifted Porter's corps, including the Sharpshooters, northward to a position where they could be used to full effect against Jackson. As a result, Porter's corps, and in it the Sharpshooters, had little rest over a three-day period.

When the attack on Jackson's lines occurred, a sizeable part of the Union army, including Porter's corps, exposed its flanks to Longstreet's soldiers. As he would do more than once during the war, Longstreet took advantage of a Union commander's blunder and sent his army crashing into the Union flank. Historian James McPherson describes what occurred next: "Once Longstreet's men went into action they hit the surprised northerners like a giant hammer. Until the sunset a furious contest raged all along the line. The bluecoats fell back to Henry House Hill. . . . Here they made a twilight stand that brought the rebel juggernaut to a halt."[16] In one paragraph, McPherson captures the overall devastation the Army of Virginia and its supporting units suffered on August 30. Porter's corps did not retreat pell-mell, nor were they initially overwhelmed. Their attack was disciplined, but they were under strength in comparison to the Confederate forces opposite. What Winthrop and the Sharpshooters experienced was horrific in its own right, and the regiment found itself in a significantly weakened state.

In the morning hours of August 30, the First U.S. Sharpshooters were ordered to advance against Longstreet's lines outside of Groveton. Berdan insisted to the brigade commander, General Butterfield, such an attack would be unreasonable and result in extremely high casualties. Initially Berdan's arguments won the brigade commander over, and Berdan established a strong defensive position. However, as the day wore on, the division commander was instructed by Porter to advance against Longstreet. Porter appreciated that his corps was up against some of the more battle-tested Confederates. Earlier, after surveying his forces, Porter had requested reinforcements from Pope but none came, and the advance was ordered to commence as planned. In the lead were Porter's most battle-tested troops, the Sharpshooters.[17]

It seemed to Lieutenant J. Smith Brown that the Sharpshooters were ordered to cross a field "about 2000 feet wide and it ran up a bare knoll, this hill was encircled with woods nearly. In the woods on the right, and on the summit of this hill, and on the left, the rebels had batteries, also large forces of infantry. Across the face of the hill, at an acute angle with our road, striking it upon our right was a deep railroad cut, and large banks of blasted stone."[18] In essence, the Sharpshooters were ordered to advance across terrain that gave the enemy complete exposure to their movements.

Brown also recorded that prior to their advance, the Sharpshooters had already lost a number of men as a result of enemy shelling from their batteries and rifle fire from an apparently exposed flank. Even worse, the Sharpshooters could see the Confederate infantry take their positions on the crest of the hill they were expected to assault.

At 2:30 p.m., the Sharpshooters, along with a green New York regiment and the seasoned Sixteenth Michigan, clambered over a fence and crossed a treeless field along the Groveton-Sudley road, all the while facing Confederate artillery firing case shot and canister. The Sharpshooters' advance did not occur in close order, but rather by individual packets of men who moved to the cover of a schoolhouse. Although the Sharpshooters advanced through an intense cannonade, they held their own until at a given moment, they opened fire on the Confederate lines. In less than forty minutes, the regiment fired off its supply of forty rounds of ammunition per man, killing a number of Confederate artillery troops. Company H was in the lead of this advance, and according to Captain Hastings, Winthrop was the first officer in the front of the regiment rallying the troops forward.[19] The Sharpshooters succeeded in pushing the Confederates opposite them into a brief retreat that was long enough to get other regiments into the fight.[20] But reinforcements did not come and the Sharpshooters paid dearly, and the ground they gained was only temporarily held, for a number of reasons.

First, the Sharpshooters had no protection on their flanks, and as they advanced, Confederate artillery raked through their ranks from three directions. There have been allegations that Colonel Berdan placed his regiment in the wrong area, which led to this situation.[21] But in his thorough treatise on Second Manassas, national park historian John J. Hennessy does not mention any detrimental moves by Berdan. Likewise, Lieutenant Connington, Lieutenant Aschmann, and Lieutenant Brown, three vocal officers who despised Berdan, did not criticize him for the placement of the Sharpshooters. Still, the firing from three sides devastated the Sharpshooters ranks. Lieutenant Brown had lived through every action the Sharpshooters experienced on the Peninsula, and wrote of Second Manassas, "The canister, grape, and shrapnel [came] thicker than I ever saw before and I have seen something in this line. The enemy fired pieces of railroad iron. Piles of stone lay all around and when a shot would strike one of those heaps, the stones would fly off on tangents, each as destructive as a new shot." Brown also noted that the New Yorkers charged the stone wall with heavy losses, recording, "every man that obtained a foothold was instantly shot dead, and the rebels threw big stones down on the wounded."[22] Lieutenant Aschmann echoed Brown's memory of the battle writing, "Our line took the shape of an obtuse angle whose sides met at the right wing of the regiment. This soon became calamitous for our company since the enemy was now able to rake the entire length of our regiment."[23]

Second, the Sharpshooters faced numbers far greater than their own. "We had to fight at three to one odds, and the results you know, were a perfect slaughter and defeat," Winthrop's peer Lieutenant Connington penned to his sister. "We got within fifty feet of their battle line when we had to stop. We had not been there ten minutes before four of the best men I had were shot, all of which have since died."[24]

Third, despite the heavy losses and withering fire, the Sharpshooters advanced into a position where they fired into the Confederate lines with some effect. However, having exhausted their supply of ammunition and with no reinforcements to hold the ground that the Sharpshooters had taken, they were only in a position to undertake an orderly retreat. Their expected reinforcements failed to make headway. They did not flee the battlefield as some other regiments had done. Lieutenant Aschmann recollected, "Suddenly panic seemed to overcome the army and everything turned into a complete rout. Even the artillery was deserted."[25]

Lieutenant Brown also wrote of how other regiments streamed off the battlefield into Centerville. His final statement was most telling: "Fifty thousand men left the field without firing a gun: the most extraordinary, the most shameful proceeding I ever witnessed."[26] Hastings summed up the position of Company H: "Winthrop, Weston, and six Sharpshooters were the last to leave the field which we did being wounded. Had we remained two minutes longer, we must have been made prisoners."[27] That the Sharpshooters did not flee the field is a testament to their high level of discipline and training, but it also meant they were under enemy fire for longer than might otherwise have occurred.

Fourth, the disunity in command from Pope's headquarters on down caused the Army of Virginia to fail, and it also added to the casualty count. Pope's behavior during the battle was problematic, such that he issued contradictory orders and his assessment of the opposing forces was frequently so wrong as to ruin any chance for his battle plans to be well coordinated in their execution. Two decades after the war, McClellan recollected that "after Pope's campaign, it was not safe for McDowell to visit the camps of his troops as the men declared they would kill him."[28] McClellan's statement might have been self-serving, but there was truth to it. Assessing the high command's performance three months after Second Manassas, Connington placed the blame for the defeat squarely on McDowell.[29] And Hastings conveyed, "The confidence in the Army in McClellan is but very little impaired, but they have none in Pope, and detest McDowell."[30] This was a sentiment shared by many in Union uniform. Now, the Sharpshooters had two commanding officers to despise, McDowell and Berdan, although it is possible many despised Pope as well, since McClellan remained popular with them.

The Sharpshooters went into battle with 290 men, but emerged with only 225. Even Colonel Berdan did not escape unscathed as he was wounded by a piece of shrapnel.[31] Any analysis of the Sharpshooters performance on August 30 has to be one of localized success in a day otherwise surrounded by the failure of the greater army of which it was a part. This failure rested not only on Pope, but also some of his subordinate commanders. The Sharpshooters succeeded in pushing the Confederates opposite them into a brief retreat, which was long enough to get other regiments into the fight.[32] But they did not have enough men to make anything more than a temporary difference, and the regiments which followed them into battle were not enough in numbers to add to the temporary successes.

Porter's corps was decimated outside of the small hamlet of Groveton. Of its 6,000 men, 2,151 were killed or injured. Pope had fed all of his corps piecemeal, first against Jackson and then Longstreet, and lost the battle. Berdan's men were in the forefront of this fight, but this time, their superior firepower and tactics did not protect the regiment against the high rate of loss the rest of the Fifth Corps suffered. The following day, Pope ordered the Army of Virginia and the other units under his command to retreat to the Washington, DC, area defenses near Centerville. The retreat, in some places, degenerated into a rout. Two events occurred, however, that kept Lee from taking Washington, DC, and ending the war in a Confederate victory. The first was a stand by two Union divisions outside Chantilly that bought the rest of the army time to regroup. Although Chantilly has been looked on as an inconsequential battle resulting in the deaths of two colorful Union generals, it was an important strategic event, even if the battle ended with a tactical Confederate victory. The second was the fact that once inside the capital defenses, the remainder of the Army of the Potomac and the Army of Virginia still outnumbered the Confederates. Instead of assaulting the city, Lee decided to invade the north.[33]

The Battle of Second Manassas, as it came to be called, cost the Union more than quantifiable numbers. Lee had gained a moral ascendancy, and the administration had to replace Pope, turning once more to McClellan. Squabbling within the Union command structure grew worse as McClellan blamed the administration for the loss, while Lincoln believed McClellan intentionally stalled the transfer of units from the Army of the Potomac to Pope's command.[34] Pope came to blame Porter for the Union defeat that occurred the following day and issued formal charges against the corps commander. Unfortunately for Porter, he left behind a number of correspondences deriding Pope, which later resulted in a court-martial conviction. It would take Porter twenty-five years and the helpful testimony of Longstreet to overturn the conviction. Pope was relieved of command and sent to Minnesota to oversee a small force of soldiers campaigning against the Sioux who had risen against the settlers.

What Winthrop felt at the time about Second Manassas, Berdan's wound, Pope's charges against Porter, or Pope's dismissal is unknown. Two decades after Porter's dismissal and subsequent court-martial, Winthrop used the case in his legal scholarship on matters of court-martial jurisdiction and composition and the nature of military orders. Piecing his scholarship together, it becomes clear that Winthrop later felt a great deal of sympathy for Porter and believed the general suffered an injustice. However, it is difficult to know what Winthrop thought about Porter and Pope in the immediate aftermath of the disaster at Second Manassas, since there is no available record of his opinions. But, if his views on command mirrored the rest of the army, there was one positive note. Lincoln placed McClellan in command of the Army of Virginia and the Army of the Potomac once more. Though Lincoln expressed grave doubts as to McClellan's commitment to vigorously prosecuting the war, the "little Napoleon's" popularity with the Army of the Potomac had not yet diminished.

On September 12, Winthrop and the Sharpshooters left the capital defenses with the rest of Porter's battered corps and marched into Maryland. This time they were at the rear of the Army of the Potomac. Despite the knowledge of more fighting ahead, there was some good news which likely buoyed the Sharpshooters' morale. Colonel Berdan did not accompany their movement north as he was temporarily invalided from his wound at Second Manassas. In fact, Berdan would be absent from the Sharpshooters until late December 1862, allegedly recovering his strength, procuring more arms for the regiment, and recruiting new troops. Winthrop and his peers roundly believed Berdan exaggerated the extent of his wound.[35]

The Sharpshooters reached South Mountain in the Maryland Appalachians on September 15. As the regiment approached their destination, snipers concealed in a farmhouse fired on the Sharpshooters. Winthrop was the first to enter the house in search of the guilty party. "One of the adventures in the mountains was the discovery by Capt Winthrop about breakfast time of a small house full of a sallow-faced woman and several children, no doubt one of the 'first families.'[36] They all protested that there was no man in the place, but Winthrop with drawn sword went around pricking the beds and piles of dirty clothing, and at last discovered the proprietor crouched in the furthest corner under the bed," Hastings recorded. "They brought him to me, but he would furnish no information, however as to the enemy, and Winthrop's gallant storming of the cottage resulted only in a good breakfast for a half dozen of us."[37]

Although McClellan held the Sharpshooters in reserve during the ensuing battle at Antietam on September 17, none of the men were out of the range of Confederate artillery fire and two were killed. More American soldiers were killed at Antietam on 1862 than at Normandy on June 14, 1944, or Iwo Jima on February 19, 1945. The battle was fought to a draw, but as McClellan forces outnumbered Confederates, Lee opted to retreat into Virginia.[38]

For Winthrop, Lee's retreat did not mean an end to action, and in fact, intense combat was to shortly occur. Although McClellan opted to not renew the battle, by the morning of September 19, it was clear to him that Lee's army was in full but orderly retreat into Virginia. The Confederates crossed the Potomac at an area where it shallows known as Blackford's Ford, or alternatively Boteler's Ford. What was unclear to McClellan was the number of forces Lee left to cover this retreat. Lee had in fact left a forty-four-gun artillery battery and two infantry brigades, under the command of Brigadier General William Pendleton, to guard the Confederate army's crossing over the Potomac.

McClellan ordered Porter to use his corps in a limited foray against Lee's retreating army to ensure that Lee did not reverse course and reinvade Maryland. In the forefront of this movement were the Sharpshooters and three other regiments. Along with the Fifth New York Regiment and the Fourth Michigan Regiment, the Sharpshooters tailed Lee's army to the Potomac. Although the Southerners had already crossed the river and traversed several miles from it by the time the Sharpshooters arrived at the Potomac, the Confederate covering force remained on the opposite bank to slow any Union advance down.[39]

Porter ordered the three regiments to cross the river and seize the enemy's artillery, but this was a daunting task. Running parallel to the river on the opposite bank was a road, and above this road were cliffs which had been sheared of vegetation. On these cliffs, Pendleton arrayed his cannon guns in a crescent, with the longest range guns at the wings, so as to concentrate their fire at the shallow area. In the early afternoon, Union and Confederate artillery began to duel with each other across the river.

At five o'clock in the afternoon, the New Yorkers and several Sharpshooters including Winthrop, five hundred men in all, waded across the Potomac under enemy cannon and rifle fire. They were protected by the Michigan regiment and a number of Porter's artillery, though some of the cannon were directed at Shepherdstown across the river. Additionally, a number of other Sharpshooters took cover in a dry canal and fired away at Pendleton's artillery. When the advancing Sharpshooters found themselves within accurate rifle range and had a clear view of the enemy, they opened fire on the artillery positions and eventually captured a number of the Confederate guns.[40]

Winthrop led the advance against the Confederate positions and was the first Union soldier to cross the river into Virginia. Although his action was noted in official dispatches, he remained quiet in his letters as to his role in the Antietam campaign. Perhaps it is indicative of his character to have not boasted of his battle prowess. To date Winthrop had been disgusted with the effrontery of Berdan, and his letters describing his own role in combat were generally humble. But Lieutenant Aschmann recorded a general description of the engagement writing that "part of our skirmish line supported by a rifle regiment plunged into the river with a hurrah, waded across braving the enemy marksmen and took up positions on the opposite bank. The operation cost us twelve men."[41] If Aschmann's numbers are correct, the Sharpshooters involved in the operation suffered a 20 percent casualty rate.

Winthrop's leadership was noteworthy to his contemporaries as well. The acting regimental commander, Captain Isler, later specifically mentioned Winthrop to Major General Morrell as well as to Major General Porter, writing, "My men behaved well. Of those who especially distinguished themselves I have to mention First Lieutenant Nash, whose company constituted the larger part of the body of skirmishers and who was most instrumental in urging the men to attempt the crossing, and Lieut. (now Capt.) W.W. Winthrop, who in leading the line was the first to set foot on Virginia soil. As to the exact list of killed and wounded, I beg leave to refer you to the documents already sent."[42] Isler was not alone in noticing William in the lead. Lieutenant J. Smith Brown corroborated Captain Isler's report on Winthrop in a letter home to his family.[43] Yet, Charles Stevens omitted Winthrop's role in his Sharpshooters history.

This was not the only action Winthrop and the surviving Sharpshooters saw during the campaign. General Porter believed that the Sharpshooters and New Yorkers were not enough to hold onto the Confederate positions in case of a counterattack. On the morning of September 20, he added a number of regulars, plus a new regiment, the 118th Pennsylvania, to reinforce the Union position. Once this was accomplished, the Sharpshooters retired back across the river to serve as a reserve force and provide covering fire if the need arose. Porter assumed the Pennsylvanians and the New Yorkers were enough to hold the opposite bank since Lee appeared to continue the Confederate retreat into Virginia. But Lee's retreat halted in response to the previous day's action at Blackford's Ford. Pendleton had gotten word to Jackson that he too needed reinforcements. Instead of a division, Jackson sent in his entire corps. Jackson believed the Army of the Potomac intended to cross the river in force and vigorously pursue Lee. Acting on this belief, he rushed a number of other available units to the area and soon outnumbered the Union forces six to one.[44]

With the tables turned, Porter ordered a withdrawal from the far shore, but it had to be a fighting withdrawal as Jackson's men overwhelmed the Union forces on the Virginia side of the Potomac. The Sharpshooters provided cover for the New Yorkers to cross back over the Potomac. But the commander of the Pennsylvanians refused to order a retreat without first seeing orders in writing. This was a new regiment whose men had not participated in any combat prior to September 20. They witnessed the battle at Antietam two days earlier as the Sharpshooters had, but unlike the Sharpshooters, they had only recently formed and completed their short training. Within a few minutes of Jackson's assault, the Pennsylvanians found themselves in disorder. Their commanding officer was seriously injured and a number of their officers and men were killed. Indeed, of the 737 men in the 118th Pennsylvania, 63 were killed, 101 wounded, and 105 captured or missing, most within the first few minutes of Jackson's assault. However, these numbers could have been worse. Again, the Sharpshooters went into action, this time to cover the 118th for a retreat across the river.[45]

During this action, Winthrop crossed over the river once more under enemy fire to help guide the survivors of the Pennsylvania regiment to safety. With a characteristic modesty toward his military exploits, he did not mention this fact in any surviving correspondence. But General Morrell, a divisional commander, witnessed Winthrop's bravery and had him promoted to the rank of captain.[46]

The Battle of Shepherdstown ended as a Union defeat and likely sealed Porter's fate before his court-martial. Had Porter's corps defeated Jackson, the administration might have forgiven him. But with McClellan increasingly out of favor and Porter's outspoken criticism of Pope and the administration, Porter had few defenders in a position to help him. By the close of the year, he would be stripped of command, found guilty, cashiered from the army, and prohibited from government employment. Whatever Winthrop thought of this at the time is not available, but within the decade, he reviewed Porter's case and advised it be reversed. Porter personally commended the Sharpshooters during a review of them after Antietam and before his court-martial. And there was a change in temporary command of the regiment. Captain Isler was permanently invalided from the regiment as a result of severe illness, and Lieutenant Colonel Caspar Trepp returned to command as a result of Berdan's continued absence.[47]

After Antietam, the ideological force underlying the war changed from a war to preserve the Union to a war to end slavery. This was a welcome change for Winthrop, but it caused political upheaval in the Army of the Potomac's politically charged command. It was the response of this command which brought Winthrop to increasingly view McClellan as a military failure and a liability to the Union.

When Lincoln issued the Emancipation Proclamation, a number of officers from McClellan down disapproved and voiced their opinions as such.[48] Winthrop did not fall in the category of soldiers angry over the proclamation. Since he saw the war as the only means of destroying slavery, the Emancipation Proclamation was a welcome change. Although he had a lingering sense of loyalty and appreciation for McClellan, he had a greater loyalty to the memory of Theodore and the cause which led the brothers to join. As in the case of many soldiers who remained in the war, over time Winthrop's view of McClellan increasingly became negative. In 1864, McClellan ran for the presidency against Lincoln. Ironically, the votes of his former soldiers overwhelmingly went to Lincoln.[49] By that election, Winthrop found only revulsion for his former commander.

On December 12, 1862, the first Union regiments of the Army of the Potomac crossed the Rappahannock into Fredericksburg. Individual soldiers pillaged through private property, looting and destroying the town. A number of men defaced the interiors of houses. The pillage escalated beyond simple thievery into wanton destruction as Union soldiers sought to gain some measure of revenge against Southerners in general. General Marsena Patrick, who earlier weighed against Pope's license to loot, arrested officers caught with stolen goods.[50]

Winthrop deplored both the looting and Fredericksburg's destruction. "The town was pitiful, many articles of value had been removed from the houses but the streets were strewn with old papers, crockery, and broken furniture. The houses open and bare, many riddled with bullets as well as with grape, canister and spherical case (for the enemy's guns fired little else)," he wrote to his mother. "A portion of the town was also burnt by our shells, covering the crossing on the 11th."[51]

Winthrop's observations denoted something worse than a case of debauchery. What occurred in Fredericksburg was a violation of the laws and customs of war, and it was symptomatic that the discipline and morale of the Army of the Potomac were severely degraded on the eve of battle.

On December 13, part of the Army of the Potomac, including the Sharpshooters, assaulted entrenched Confederate positions outside of the town at Marye's Heights as well as at Prospect Hill. These troops had to traverse a mile of open ground once outside of the town to reach the entrenched Confederate positions at Marye's Heights. During this assault, they also had to cross a drainage canal all the while taking concentrated rifle and artillery fire. For the Union soldiers assaulting Longstreet's position at Marye's Heights, the battle was an unmitigated disaster. Attacking in waves, Confederate artillery and protected infantry raked regiment after regiment. The Army of the Potomac lost 12,000 men while Lee's army of northern Virginia lost 5,300. It was a singularly lopsided battle, and it came close to destroying the remaining morale of the Union army.[52]

Writing home, Winthrop conveyed his impressions of the Fredericksburg battle: "Our men marched forward in Caroline Street, on which two lines of battle formed for a mile or more, then before charging, they were marched at right angles to the back street where they were formed again." Although initially held in reserve, the Sharpshooters took enemy fire and found the need to seek cover as real as ever. Winthrop commented that the Sharpshooters were placed into one position, awaiting an order to charge, only to be relocated to another position. "Every approach was commanded by the [Confederate] fire. You can see thus the rashness of marching men into the very face of a position strong by both nature and fortification." Though he lauded the Sharpshooters, he recognized the difficulties and death faced by other units, writing that "of the corps, the 9th had the worst. Of ours, only Griffin's division was much engaged though the 3rd, Humphrey's had some fights."[53]

Winthrop alluded to an earlier letter, now missing or lost to history, of the lead-up to the battle: "As I wrote yesterday, our regiment was used on outpost duty mostly at night and shares the anxiety suggested by such a position, though by good luck we were not attacked." This meant that the regiment had not slept in at least two days prior to entering Fredericksburg. Though tired, the Sharpshooters were only one of many regiments suffering from sleep deprivation. During the battle, Winthrop rose from company commander to a command position, controlling the movements of four companies. He informed his family that Casper Trepp placed a great deal of faith in his abilities to command. In the afternoon, the Sharpshooters were assigned the task of defending a pullout of field artillery and wounded soldiers. Winthrop led the Sharpshooters' firing line in this operation. Under continual enemy fire, the task was anything but safe. Winthrop recorded, "I had some pretty close escapes, but my concern was the constant anticipation of our being driven in, in which case very few of us would have escaped." As the evening set in the carnage around Marye's Heights became apparent to all levels of command, including Winthrop. That night, the Sharpshooters were ordered to hold the line, "at all hazards, and delay the enemy to the last minute."[54]

Winthrop also noted that many of the houses were turned into makeshift hospitals and stained with blood. He did not view the destruction of Fredericksburg at the time of the letter, as a breach against the laws of war, but he did reflect much of the suffering might have been unnecessary. Fredericksburg was a costly operational defeat, but not necessarily a strategic one. The Army of the Potomac remained in a position of numeric strength.

It was too large to be defeated by Lee, but too poorly led to destroy the Confederate army. Winthrop saw this, writing, "We still of course hold Falmouth with strong pickets and artillery and infantry." Despite all of the carnage and death, Winthrop managed to end his letter on a hopeful note, as well as a concern for his family to keep warm through the winter.[55] This was to be one of his last letters for some time, though Hastings in writing to Lillie Blake later provided ample criticism of Burnside.

On December 31, the Sharpshooters engaged in combat with the First South Carolina Cavalry regiment along the Rappahannock. Burnside had sent out an advance unit composed of the Sharpshooters, a cavalry regiment, an artillery battery, and three infantry regiments. As this advance force moved up the Rappahannock River, it encountered the Confederate cavalry which fired a series of volleys, and then fled.[56] Although the Sharpshooters appeared to get the better of the cavalry, both sides suffered a small number of casualties. Shot through the chest, Winthrop was injured severely enough to be invalided out of the line.[57]

Winthrop had three options if he wanted to remain in the army. He could seek permanent service in another regiment if it came with a promotion and he had sufficiently healed. He could also have been sent into the Veteran Reserve Corps, a unit composed of invalided soldiers used to suppress civil unrest or be maintained in case of emergency. Or he could find a temporary staff position in a unit larger than a regiment until he found assignment to a staff position, such as the Judge Advocate General's Department. He took the third option and became temporarily assigned as aide-de-camp to Brigadier General Joseph J. Bartlett, while at the same time he applied for assignment as a judge advocate.

From March 10 through April 14, 1863, Winthrop served as aide-de-camp to General Bartlett, then in command of the Second Brigade under the command of the Sixth Army Corp's First Division. In turn, the Sixth Corps was commanded by Major General John Sedgwick, while the First Division was commanded by General William Brooks. Although the record of Winthrop's month-long service as aide is sparse, he was remembered by one contemporary, Captain H. Seymour Hall, who wrote in 1894, "Another good piece of fortune happened to me on the staff of General Bartlett of Captain W. W. Winthrop as additional aide de camp, and his taking quarters in the tent with me, so that during the winter I had thus the pleasure of being intimately associated with him."[58] Hall also noted that he had read all of Theodore Winthrop's works. Interestingly, Hall became acquainted with Colonel Emory Upton, a professional officer Winthrop later took issue with over the Constitution's placement of the military in a role subservient to the elected government. Hall and Winthrop must have maintained some correspondence because he further related in 1864, he and Winthrop dined together in Washington City.[59]

Hall and Winthrop shared other values. Hall later "commanded colored soldiers" at the Crater, and at the end of the war was brevetted brigadier general. He was injured and had one arm amputated during this battle, but he remained in uniform through 1866. He was awarded the Medal of Honor for his bravery during the Petersburg siege. After the war, Hall married and settled in Missouri and Kansas. He served as the Republican Party Chairman in Lawrence, Kansas, and taught at the university. One commonality between Hall and Winthrop was their desire to fight for justice and equality. Hall later argued that the colored soldiers had not received their due accolades and that if they had been supported better, they would have succeeded at the Crater. He supported the continued use of black volunteers in the postwar army, believing them the equal of their white counterparts. Hall outlived Winthrop and died in 1908.[60]

Winthrop may have known General Bartlett prior to the aide-de-camp posting, and the posting occurred at a time when Berdan was clearly looking to prosecute officers who challenged his inept command. Both Winthrop and Bartlett had grown up in the Tioga County region, and Bartlett was a lawyer practicing in New York prior to the war. Moreover, Bartlett was anything other than an inept commander. His reputation for personal bravery—he fought in every major engagement the Army of the Potomac took part in during the war—was unsurpassed. However, little has been written about Bartlett by contemporary historians. After the war, he served as United States ambassador to Sweden and a deputy commissioner of pensions in the first Grover Cleveland presidency.

Even though Winthrop left the regiment, he remained interested in the Sharpshooters in particular, because Berdan returned to the regiment shortly after Fredericksburg. No sooner did Berdan return than problems in the command began to arise once more. Berdan attempted to reassert control over the Sharpshooters officers, targeting his attention specifically at both his second and third in command, Lieutenant Colonel Caspar Trepp and Major George Hastings. Both had risen in prominence though the condition of the regiment was battle worn and not to the visual standards of newer regiments. Still, the regiment earned battle honors second to none, and a number of Sharpshooters had been named in official dispatches. Berdan's jealousy was piqued to the point that he accused Trepp of the very cowardice he had likely been guilty of. Lieutenant Aschmann recorded in 1865, "For awhile now, there had been such dissension between Colonel Berdan and Lieutenant Colonel Trepp which was of such virulent nature that first the colonel took action against Trepp for dereliction of duty and later Trepp did the same against Berdan."[61] Aschmann did not record that Berdan also took action against Hastings, alleging Hastings acted with cowardice before the enemy and was generally insubordinate.

The genesis of Trepp's and Hastings' courts-martial began when Berdan ordered Trepp and Hastings to drill in the manual of arms under the supervision of a lieutenant. Both Trepp and Hastings interpreted Berdan's order as a deliberate plan to publicly humiliate them. However, they complied with the order and drilled. Afterward, both officers were overheard in a private conversation loudly disparaging Berdan. Additionally, Trepp tendered his resignation in a lengthy and accusatory letter to Berdan. Instead of accepting Trepp's resignation, Berdan had Trepp arrested and confined to quarters on January 25, 1863. Two days later, Berdan charged Trepp under the Articles of War specifically for cowardice in the face of the enemy. The charge was capital in nature, and Trepp faced a potential death sentence if found guilty. However, the evidence against him was nonexistent. Berdan could not produce any witnesses to prove his case against Trepp. On the other hand, there was a great deal of evidence that Berdan was guilty of cowardice.

On February 25, 1863, Trepp was brought to trial. Trepp was defended by Colonel Strong Vincent, a lawyer who enlisted at the outbreak of the war but rose in rank. Colonel Vincent later commanded the division defending "Little Round Top" at Gettysburg but was mortally wounded at the battle. A superb officer, Vincent was partly responsible for saving a vital Union flank during Gettysburg and was posthumously promoted to brigadier general.

It appears Berdan's testimony was the only evidence presented against Trepp. On the other hand, a number of documents and witness statements supported Trepp, who was acquitted after very short deliberation. Although Captain Winthrop was recovering at this time and serving as an aide-de-camp, he provided Trepp a deposition damning Berdan. Hastings recorded the result of Trepp's trial, writing, "Hallelujah, Lt Col Trepp is honorably acquitted, released from arrest and in command of the regiment." In a hopeful prediction, he added, "Trepp will upset all the nonsensical arrangements which Berdan has made, abolish the grand staff, and have all Berdan's aides, sycophants,[62] and relatives sent back to their companies."[63]

Hastings was never prosecuted in a court-martial. After Trepp's acquittal, General Whipple "dissolved the charges" against Hastings. Moreover, General Whipple sought to have Berdan prosecuted first before Hastings. Hastings relayed to Lillie Blake, "Oh, how chap fallen [Berdan] looked! He is now under arrest, in the brigade commanded by Colonel Potter. The trial commences today. He must inevitably be convicted. The testimony will be tremendous, and I will probably not be tried at all." Hastings concluded with a tirade against Berdan, "You should see how wretched, mean, and malignant our old enemy looks."[64]

Berdan's court-martial was more complex than Trepp's. It had its roots predating Berdan's allegations against Trepp. On October 6, 1862, formal charges were brought against Colonel Berdan by Captain Benjamin Giroux, then serving as a company commander in the regiment. Giroux charged that Berdan was guilty of misbehavior and cowardice before the enemy at the battles of Yorktown, Hanover, Mechanicsville, and Gaines Mill, by abandoning his post. Giroux also accused Berdan of conduct unbecoming an officer and a gentleman on a number of occasions, including threatening enlisted personnel with his sword. Additionally, Giroux alleged Berdan committed fraud against the government. As in the case of Berdan's later charges against Trepp, Giroux's charges against Berdan were capital in nature. However, unlike Berdan's charges against Trepp, Giroux's charges against Berdan had to be reviewed by the commanding general of the Army of the Potomac, and this took four months. (Regimental commanders enjoyed an extra layer of protection from prosecution. The commanding general of the Army of the Potomac—or other theater army—had to approve of the charges.) As a result, Berdan was not formally charged until early February 1863. By that time, Lieutenant Colonel Trepp filed counter-charges against Berdan, and Giroux's original charges were merged with Trepp's. Finally, a third officer filed charges against Berdan alleging the same criminal conduct as the other two.

Colonel Berdan was brought to trial on March 10, 1863, two months before the Battle of Chancellorsville. He too was acquitted on all charges. However, there was ample evidence Berdan intimidated some of the witnesses from testifying. Even the divisional commander, Brigadier General Amiel Whipple, who had replaced Morell, felt Berdan's acquittal a travesty. As a professional officer who had graduated West Point in 1841, served as a topographical engineer, and remained in uniform through to the Civil War, Whipple understood the legal definition of desertion, cowardice, and conduct unbecoming an officer. He published his opinion on the court-martial through his adjutant general stating, "The reviewing officer regards the evidence in the forgoing trial of Colonel Berdan in a different light from that in which it is viewed by the court. The substance of the specifications is clearly proved."[65] Whipple did not let the matter rest, writing a week later, "A commanding officer is expected to be with his troops, especially on the field of battle, and during an engagement. A proof of absence from his command at such a period is prima facie evidence of his misbehavior, or at least of neglect of duty."[66] Finally, in early April, Whipple became aware of the extent to which Berdan intimidated witnesses and wrote, Berdan "shows a limitable ignorance of military affairs in supposing that by the course pursued, he could circumvent the acts of his superior and arrest trial by general court-martial, legally convened."[67] It may have been the case General Whipple sought to prosecute Berdan again, but this did not occur. General Whipple was killed at Chancellorsville, shortly after Berdan's acquittal.

Colonel Berdan ensured his acquittal was well publicized through the regiment as well as the other regiments in the brigade. Lieutenant Colonel Trepp did not remain quiet on the subject and convinced General Whipple to publish the court-martial proceedings, including the evidence brought against each officer. This ensured the rank and file knew of Berdan's guilt despite the acquittal. Lieutenant Aschmann formed the opinion shared by many in the regiment, including Winthrop, that although both Berdan and Trepp were found not guilty, "Trepp however came off more brilliantly than his superior."[68]

Perhaps in an attempt to avoid bringing to the fore bitter memories, Charles Stevens brushed aside the episode of the courts-martial with the following statement: "Officers in camp would find fault, often amongst themselves almost to an open quarrel; prevented only by the fear of the consequences under the strict rules of the regulations. As it was, arrests were made and courts-martial summoned." The Sharpshooters' historian did not name Trepp, Winthrop, or Hastings as victims of Berdan's malice; instead, with a neutral tone, he continued, "Nor did Berdan himself escape; on the contrary, a long list of charges and specifications were preferred against him." Stevens later noted Berdan was acquitted on all charges, but he avoided any mention of Berdan's low reputation among the officers in the Sharpshooters, or the anger from higher command at Berdan's acquittal. Nor did Stevens note accusations that Berdan had tampered with witness testimony. Stevens concluded his commentary by saying, "The enlisted men, they that handled the weapons that did the fighting were silent lookers on, wondering why their officers quarreled so. Was this setting a proper example?"[69] Winthrop's writing is silent regarding Hastings and Trepp's arrest and treatment from Berdan. But it may be surmised that the process leading to Trepp's acquittal and Hastings' exoneration did not offend him to the point of resigning his commission or lobbying for an overhaul of the Articles of War. Instead, he placed great faith in the Articles of War and the army's disciplinary system in the years ahead, arguing for improvements, but not for its evisceration.

NOTES

1. Rudolf Karl Aschmann, *Memoirs of a Swiss Officer in the American Civil War (Three Years in the Army of the Potomac or a Swiss Company of Sharpshooters in the North American War)*, ed. Heinz K. Meier, trans. Hedwig D. Rappolt (Bern, Switzerland: Herbert Lang, 1972), 37.

2. Letter to General Butterfield, July 4, 1862, in Roy M. Marcot, *U.S. Sharpshooters: Berdan's Civil War Elite* (Mechanicsburg, PA: Stackpole Book, 2007), 52.

3. Roswell Weston was a lieutenant at the time this particular letter was drafted. There is no available explanation for his signature bearing the rank of captain.

4. Marcot, *U.S. Sharpshooters*, 52. Charles Stevens does not note this even in his book, *Berdan's United States Sharpshooters in the Army of the Potomac*, reprint ed. (Dayton, OH: Morningside Books, 1995).

5. Caspar Trepp, letter to Edwin Stanton, June 1, 1863 (Caspar Trepp Papers, NYHS).

6. Aschmann, *Memoirs of a Swiss Officer*, 84; J. Smith Brown, letter, August 30, 1862, in R. L. Murray, *Letters from Berdan's Sharpshooters* (Wolcott, NY: Benedum Books, 2005), 101. Brown's itinerary is confirmed by Charles Stevens. Charles Stevens, *Berdan's United States Sharpshooters*, 174–175.

7. George Hastings, letter to Lillie Devereux Blake, July 6, 1862 (MHS).

8. John J. Hennessy, *Return to Bull Run: The Campaign and Battle of Second Manassas* (Norman: Oklahoma University Press, 1999), 136; Shelby Foote, *The Civil War a Narrative: Fort Sumter to Perryville* (New York: Random House, 1958), 618–619; Thomas Buell, *The Warrior Generals: Combat Leadership in the Civil War* (New York: Three Rivers Press, 1997), 101.

9. Hennessy, *Return to Bull Run*, 161.

10. George Hastings, letter to Lillie Devereux Blake, September 5, 1862 (MHS).

11. Foote, *The Civil War*, 623; Hennessy, *Return to Bull Run*, 197.

12. Stephen R. Taaffe, *Commanding the Army of the Potomac* (Lawrence: University Press of Kansas, 2006), 32–34.

13. Hennessy, *Return to Bull Run* 233; Foote, *The Civil War*, 635; Buell, *The Warrior Generals*, 102; Maurice Matloff, ed., *American Military History* (Washington, DC: Office of the Chief of Military History, United States Army, 1969), 226.

14. Paul D. Casdorph, *Lee and Jackson* (New York: Paragon, 1992), 309.

15. Foote, *The Civil War*, 635.

16. James M. McPherson, *Battle Cry of Freedom: The Civil War Era* (New York: Oxford University Press, 1988), 531.

17. Hennessy, *Return to Bull Run*, 336.

18. J. Smith Brown, letter to unknown party, August 30, 1862, in R. L. Murray, *Berdan's Sharpshooters in Combat: The Peninsula Campaign and Gettysburg* (New York: Benedum, 2006), 49.

19. Hastings, letter to Lillie Devereux Blake, September 5, 1862.

20. Hennessy, *Return to Bull Run*, 336.

21. See, for example, Wiley Sword, *Sharpshooter: Hiram Berdan, His Famous Sharpshooters, and Their Sharps Rifles* (Lincoln, RI: Andrew Mowbray, 1988), 18. Sword argues that Berdan placed his regiment in an area designated for another regiment, which ironically caused the Sharpshooters to be closer to the Confederates than intended. However, in none of the Official Records of the War does this allegation arise.

22. Sword, *Sharpshooters*, 18.

23. Aschmann, *Memoirs of a Swiss Officer*, 87.

24. Lieutenant Connington, letter to his sister, Celia, May 25, 1862 (MIH).

25. Aschmann, *Memoirs of a Swiss Officer*, 88.

26. Brown, letter to unknown party, August 30, 1862.

27. Hastings, letter to Lillie Devereux Blake, September 5, 1862.

28. George B. McClellan, *My Own Story: The War for the Union, the Soldiers Who Fought It, the Civilians Who Directed It, and His Relations to It and Them* (New York: Webster and Co., 1887), 71.

29. Connington, letter to Celia, May 25, 1862.

30. Hastings, letter to Lillie Devereux Blake, September 5, 1862.

31. Stevens, *Berdan's United States Sharpshooters*, 185. See also Bruce Catton, *Bruce Catton's Civil War: Three Volumes in One*, vol. 2, *Glory Road* (New York: Fairfax Press, 1984), 329.

32. Hennessy, *Return to Bull Run*,, 336

33. Herman Hattaway and Archer Jones, *A Military History of the Civil War: How the North Won* (Urbana: University of Illinois Press, 1991), 229–231.

34. Foote, *The Civil War*, 640; John F. Marszalek, *Commander of All Lincoln's Armies: A Life of General Henry W. Halleck* (Cambridge, MA: Harvard University Press, 2004).

35. Stevens, *Berdan's United States Sharpshooters*, 192. During his absence, Berdan fathered a child with his wife that undoubtedly added to the belief among the Sharpshooters officers that Berdan was a "coward and liar." Accusations of his cowardice and dishonesty anonymously appeared in an upstate New York newspaper, the *Pen-Yan*, in October 1862. It appears, however, based on the content of the editorial, that it was written prior to the Maryland campaign and was apparently sent on September 12. It derided Berdan's dishonest attempts to heroize himself in the press, as well as detailing a number of aspersions to his character from senior officers.

36. A "first family" refers to Confederate sympathizers who Lee hoped would secede from the Union and force Maryland into the Confederacy.

37. Stevens, *Berdan's United States Sharpshooters*, 192.

38. McPherson, *Battle Cry of Freedom*, 544; Taaffe, *Commanding the Army of the Potomac*, 42–44.

39. Peter S. Carmichael, "We Don't Know What on Earth to Do with Him: William Pendleton and the Affair at Shepherdstown, September 19, 1862," in *The Antietam Campaign*, ed. Gary W. Gallagher, 266–268 (Chapel Hill: University of North Carolina Press, 1999); Mark A. Snell, "Baptism of Fire, the 118th 'Corn Exchange' Pennsylvania Infantry at the Battle of Shepherdstown," *Civil War Regiments* 6 (2000), 125.

40. Carmichael, "William Pendleton and the Affair at Shepherdstown," 269.

41. Aschmann, *Memoirs of a Swiss Officer*, 93. Peter Carmichael writes that the Sharpshooters lost only four men. However, there is no reason to doubt Aschmann's recollections of the event, and it may be the case Aschmann compiled losses from both days of fighting while Carmichael only counted Spetember 19. See Carmichael, "William Pendleton and the Affair at Shepherdstown," 269.

42. OR, ser. 1, vol. 19, pt. 1 (Antietam—Serial 27), pp. 344–345.

43. J. Smith Brown, letter to his family, n.d., in Murray, *Letters from Berdan's Sharpshooters*, 111.

44. Burke Davis, *They Called Him Stonewall: A Life of Lieutenant General T.J. Jackson, CSA*, reprint ed. (Short Hill, NJ: Burford Books, 1999), 341; Casdorph, *Lee and Jackson*, 336.

45. Samuel P. Bates, *History of the Pennsylvania Volunteers: 1861–1865* (Harrisburg: Pennsylvania State Legislature, 1870), 1311; also Snell, "Baptism of Fire," 125.

46. Aschmann, *Memoirs of a Swiss Officer*, 94.

47. Aschmann, *Memoirs of a Swiss Officer*, 95. Lieutenant Aschmann did not consider Isler a competent officer, referring to him as incompetent (p. 41).

48. McPherson, *Battle Cry of Freedom*, 559. McPherson notes that while most of McClellan's friends advised him to submit to the president's authority, Fitz-John Porter denounced the Emancipation Proclamation as the "absurd proclamation of a political coward"; Taaffe, *Commanding the Army of the Potomac*, 42–44.

49. Soldiers voting from the field voted for Lincoln 119,754 to 34,291 for McClellan. By 1864, most soldiers realized McClellan was a detriment to the war. Benjamin P. Thomas and Harold Hyman, *Stanton: The Life and Times of Lincoln's Secretary of War* (New York: Alfred Knopf, 1962), 334.

50. William A. Blair, "Barbarians at Fredericksburg's Gate: The Impact of the Union Army on Civilians," in *The Fredericksburg Campaign, Decision on the Rappahannock*, ed. Gary W. Gallagher, 155 (Chapel Hill: University of North Carolina Press, 1995); William Marvel, *Burnside* (Chapel Hill: University of North Carolina Press, 1991), 179.

51. William Winthrop, letter to his family, December18, 1862 (YALE).

52. Matloff, *American Military History*, 232; McPherson, *Battle Cry of Freedom*, 571–573.

53. Winthrop, letter to his family, December 18, 1862.

54. Winthrop, letter to his family, December 18, 1862.

55. Winthrop, letter to his family, December 18, 1862.

56. OR, ser. 1, vol. 31, ch. 23, p. 781.

57. Winthrop's medical record notes the wound, and later in the late 1890s, an attending surgeon, Major General Leonard Wood, surmised Winthrop's heart condition was related to the bullet.

58. General H. Seymour Hall, "Fredericksburg and Chancellorsville," in *War Talks in Kansas: A Series of Papers Read before the Kansas Commandery of the Military Order of the Loyal Legion of the United States* (Kansas City, MO: Franklin Hudson Publishing, 1906), 196. Hall related that shortly after Winthrop's appointment, he was transferred "for duty in the office of the Judge Advocate General, Joseph Holt." However, Hall wrote one error in his recollections, at the time of his essay Winthrop was assigned as deputy judge advocate general, but Hall listed him as an instructor at the United States Military Academy.

59. Hall, "Fredericksburg and Chancellorsville," 217.

60. Hall, "Fredericksburg and Chancellorsville," 248–249; Obituary, *the Lawrence Daily Gazette*, July 4, 1908, p. 2.

61. Aschmann, *Memoirs of a Swiss Officer*, 107.

62. Allegations continually followed Berdan, specifically that he had a number of soldiers and other retainers receiving pay for positions which they did not hold, and work which they did not perform.

63. Aschmann, *Memoirs of a Swiss Officer*, 107.

64. George Hastings, letter to Lillie Devereux Blake, March 4, 1863 (MHS).

65. George Hastings, letter to Lillian Devereux Blake, July 6, 1862 (MHS).

66. Hastings, letter to Lillian Devereux Blake, July 6, 1862.

67. Hastings, letter to Lillian Devereux Blake, July 6, 1862.

68. Aschmann, *Memoirs of a Swiss Officer*, 107.

69. Stevens, *Berdan's United States Sharpshooters*, 25.

8

Civil War Judge Advocate

> I think Winthrop could have such a position if he should apply for it, though he is so useful here that the War Department would not like to spare him.
>
> —Major George Hastings to Lillie Devereux Blake

On May 18, 1863, William Winthrop was promoted to the rank of brevet major of volunteers and assigned to the Judge Advocate General's Department. His initial duty placed on him two responsibilities. He was assigned to the headquarters of the judge advocate general in Washington, DC, and he was also appointed as judge advocate to the department of the Susquehanna. This geographic department was created on June 9, 1863, in response to Lee's invasion through Maryland and into Pennsylvania and was formally disbanded on December 1, 1864. As a departmental judge advocate, Winthrop advised the department commander, Major General Darius Couch, on courts-martial and the enforcement of military discipline in the department.

Winthrop was promoted to the permanent rank of major on December 12, 1864. It was common for an officer to remain attached to one regiment but serve in another, and this may account for some of the biographical sketches on Winthrop listing him as joining the Judge Advocate General's Department in 1864. He remained listed on the First United States Sharpshooters rolls until the expiration of his service on September 19, 1864. A review of General Joseph Holt's correspondence as well as the various records of the judge advocate general firmly place Winthrop in the Judge

Advocate General's Department in May 1863. He remained a judge advocate for the duration of his military career, retiring in 1895.[1]

When Winthrop transferred from the line to the Judge Advocate's Department, he did not completely divorce himself from the Sharpshooters. Instead, he remained in contact with his peers, including Caspar Trepp, the officer he most admired. Indeed, one of his first legal opinions as a judge advocate related to Colonel Berdan, the Sharpshooters' commander. After Winthrop left, a number of Sharpshooters alleged Berdan acted with cowardice and abandoned his post at the Battle of Chancellorsville. Berdan had once again positioned himself to the rear of the regiment, but as he had already successfully withstood cowardice charges stemming from his conduct on the Peninsula, there was confusion as to how to deal with Berdan. Lieutenant Colonel Trepp considered charging Colonel Berdan once more and sought Winthrop's advice.

On May 11, 1863, Winthrop advised Trepp not to personally charge Berdan. Instead, Winthrop suggested Trepp collect statements from the other officers and then send the statements to Secretary of War Stanton.[2] "Do not prefer charges against the party to whom you allude. Instead of this, make up an account of his proceedings in full at the late battle, formally written and signed by all the officers cognizant of the fact," Winthrop specifically recommended to Trepp. Trepp followed Winthrop's advice and sent a written account directly to Stanton. The account was signed by several officers and endorsed by Winthrop. In the three-page document, Trepp cataloged a number of grievances against Berdan, including his cowardice dating to the Peninsula campaign.[3]

Trepp's other ally and Winthrop's close friend, Major George Hastings, had been severely wounded at Chancellorsville and was recuperating in New York. He too would leave the Sharpshooters and become a volunteer judge advocate. Trepp was unable to leave the regiment and served honorably until his death at the November 1863 Battle of Mine Run. Berdan remained with the regiment only through the July 1863 Battle of Gettysburg, where he once more showed misjudgment in his control over the Sharpshooters.[4] Although Berdan technically had a year remaining on his service obligation, he was granted permission to leave the regiment for good after Gettysburg.[5]

However much in his new position Winthrop became involved in the adjudication and review of courts-martial, criminal prosecution was only one focus area for him. More than any conflict in American history, the Civil War brought to the fore the intersection of civil rights guaranteed by the Constitution (and considered an inalienable birthright) and the same Constitution's grant of authority to the executive branch to lead a nation through its greatest dangers. Whatever criticisms opponents of the Lincoln administration publicly enunciated, the administration was generally commanded by its staunch belief in the rule of law. That Lincoln, Stanton, and Seward, among the other cabinet chiefs, were gifted lawyers is well-known. What has not been articulated is how talented and important the individual officers of the Judge Advocate General's Department were to the administration in guiding the army through this intersection. Although Winthrop did not command this department, his Civil War service in it was important in preserving the rule of law and confidence in it in many areas ranging from the prosecution of civilians in military trials, to curtailing the excesses of commanders such as General Sherman.

The term *judge advocate* requires clarification because prior to World War II, in a specific sense it only applied to officers who were permanently assigned to the judge advocate general's staff. Moreover, before 1917 only a few officers served as permanent judge advocates assigned to the judge advocate general's staff. A far larger number of line officers, perhaps numbering well into the hundreds, served as temporary or ad hoc judge advocates assigned to specific regiments, brigades, divisions, and geographic commands. In many instances, an ad hoc judge advocate was appointed to oversee a single court-martial. Indeed, it was not until late 1862 where a designated army numbering well over one hundred thousand soldiers, such as the Army of the Potomac, could be said to have a staff officer assigned permanently as its judge advocate. Although permanent judge advocates adjudicated courts-martial from time to time, the bulk of courts-martial were overseen by ad hoc judge advocates.[6] Ad hoc judge advocates were appointed to their temporary staff positions by general officers, the secretary of war, or the president.[7]

In the nineteenth century, a judge advocate was not merely a prosecutor. A judge advocate served as a legal advisor to a board of officers, who in turn fulfilled the role of a jury. However, the judge advocate's duties went further than his mere presence in the court-martial. These duties included preparing, perfecting, and serving charges against an accused (the military term for defendant); summoning witnesses; and ensuring the accused was able to present favorable evidence in his defense. Because most of the individuals prosecuted were undefended, the judge advocate also filled the role of protecting the accused's rights. Winthrop later wrote that a judge advocate was a "minister of justice" whose duties included "the protection of the innocent, as much as the prosecution of the guilty."[8] Winthrop was not the first to consider a judge advocate as "a minister of justice," and the term had been used well prior to Winthrop's service. But it must be noted that in cases where an accused went undefended, the judge advocate did not serve as a defense counsel in any traditional sense since he could not zealously serve both sides equally in an adversarial proceeding.

On the eve of the Mexican-American War, Captain William De Hart (himself a line officer serving as an ad hoc judge advocate) wrote, "A judge advocate is also counsel for the prisoner and has a duty to prevent, in many instances, the perpetration of injustice." De Hart's purpose in writing his text, in his own words, was "the observation of such irregularities which the author in his capacity as the acting Judge Advocate of the Army was frequently called to notice has been the leading cause." De Hart's 1846 treatise, *Observations on Military Law and the Constitution and Practice of Courts-Martial*, was reprinted in 1862 and again in 1863. In 1863, Captain Henry Coppee, also a Mexican-American War veteran, stated in his treatise *Field Manual of Courts-Martial* that judge advocates serving on courts-martial had, as part of "their duties, to ensure for the accused that the case is fairly conducted."[9] The extent to which these works were used by Civil War officers is unknown, and as a result it is difficult to surmise what impact they made.

Additionally, the term *court-martial* necessitates a brief explanation. At the time of the Civil War, there were four classes of court-martial, and these operated under the 1806 Articles of War.[10] Under the most severe of these, the general courts-martial could adjudge a sentence of death, if the nature of the charge warranted it. Moreover, regardless of the severity of the charge, all officers accused of violating an article of war or another punitive regulation were prosecuted in general courts-martial.[11] Only a commanding general of an army or a geographic division had the authority to convene general courts-martial. A general court-martial required a minimum of five officers in addition to the judge advocate to establish jurisdiction, though the 1806 Articles of War noted thirteen officers constituted an appropriate maximum ceiling. Officers assigned to the court functioned in a manner similar to the American jury, though there were some differences. In the absence of a formal judge, the serving officers had to decide, with the advice of the judge advocate, whether to consider evidence which had been objected to. Additionally, officers serving on courts-martial could ask questions of witnesses, as well as have evidence produced that neither the judge advocate nor the accused had brought before the court. Thus, in addition to sitting as a trial court, it also served as a court of inquiry.

The Judge Advocate General's Department (and after 1864, the Bureau of Military Justice) reviewed all general courts-martial resulting in conviction for sufficiency of evidence and legality of procedure. For most of the nineteenth century, and indeed well into the twentieth century, the judge advocate general reviewed results of courts-martial conducted in the manner described above. In essence, the Judge Advocate General's Department served as an appellate authority in addition to its other duties. It was not until over a half century after Winthrop's death that a court of military appeals was established.

Regimental, garrison, and field officer courts-martial constituted the lesser (or as nineteenth-century legal commentators titled them, "inferior") trials. The lesser courts-martial required only a regimental or garrison commander—usually at the rank of colonel—and their maximum sentences were capped at confinement of one month and forfeiture of one month's pay. Because these lesser courts did not possess the sentencing authority to discharge or dismiss enlisted men, the presence of a judge advocate was not deemed necessary. Instead, these courts consisted of three officers serving in the same regiment or garrison as the accused. The junior officer had the additional duty of serving as "recorder." Coppee described this duty as "the preparation of trial, conducting the prosecution, and keeping the record . . . he merely conducts the case with the aid and concurrence of the other members." During the Civil War and after, judge advocates assigned to designated armies and geographic divisions reviewed all lesser court-martial convictions, or assigned an ad hoc judge advocate to do so.[12]

In 1863, Congress legislated a significant jurisdictional expansion of military law to cover violent crime felonies. As a result, the numbers of courts-martial of all types increased beyond traditional expectations. The purpose behind this expansion, as later explained by Winthrop, was to protect citizens from the "violence of soldiers and to ensure order and discipline among soldiers." It is difficult to ascertain the actual increased numbers of courts-martial resulting from the jurisdictional expansion, but additional courts enabled a commensurate expansion in the numbers of judge advocates.[13]

The Judge Advocate General's Department Winthrop entered had an inconsistent history. The office of the judge advocate (prior to the Civil War, the title did not include the additional word *general*) dated to George Washington's Continental Army, though the British Articles of War mandated a judge advocate general serve with the king's army. The Continental Army was modeled in several respects after the British Army, and the adoption of the judge advocate position was one example of this mimicry. During the Revolutionary War with Great Britain, the judge advocate's office was first led by Lieutenant Colonel William Tudor. Prior to the Revolution, Tudor attended Harvard and then studied law under the guidance of John Adams. Tudor's appointment as judge advocate of the army was legislated by the Continental Congress in 1775. Tudor was brevetted to colonel as part of this legislation. The Continental Congress also enacted the first American Articles of War, though these were based on the British model. (One year later, in 1776 the articles were redone, but were largely similar to the earlier law.)[14]

Colonel Tudor's duties were to enforce the Articles of War and oversee the administration of military justice. In essence, Tudor's role was to ensure the Continental Army's morale and discipline remained intact.

George Washington and William Tudor both understood that the enforcement of military discipline was a two-edged proposition. If the Articles of War were laxly applied, then the army's discipline degraded. The methods of eighteenth-century conventional warfare required strict soldier discipline. If the Articles of War were applied too strictly or arbitrarily, then the army's morale would erode. Enforcing the articles presented a delicate balance since the Continental Army was composed entirely of volunteers who ostensibly fought for personal liberty.[15]

Tudor began a tradition of oversight which remains through the present day. That is, the judge advocate as a staff officer does not order trials but advises on their necessity and is charged with regulating their fairness. These three men also began a tradition which lasted through the nineteenth century, though vestiges remain to the present. They served as line officers in addition to their judge advocate duties. Additionally, during the period 1771 to 1812, a number of different lawyers served as judge advocates of various armies. This list includes John Marshall, Caleb Strong, and John Taylor. Each of these men were prominent jurists in the early antebellum period, and in the case of Marshall, perhaps the most influential jurist in American history.

While judge advocates served without criticism in the War of 1812, in 1821, Congress discontinued the office of the judge advocate entirely. However, as the prosecution of courts-martial did not end, these had to be administered by line officers who were temporarily appointed judge advocates on an ad hoc basis.[16]

Although a number of officers served as ad hoc territorial judge advocates between 1821 and 1849, the army did not have a full-time judge advocate dedicated to the administration of military justice. As a result, courts-martial were conducted without centralized oversight and often with uneven results. Since the decisions of courts-martial were not considered open to judicial review, the fate of convicted soldiers rested with their commanding generals, the secretary of war, and the president. This is not to suggest that officers appointed as temporary judge advocates were incompetent or that no guidance existed for the operation of military law.

To the contrary, a number of legal treatises were published prior to the Civil War in addition to De Hart's and Coppee's which provided guidance to ad hoc judge advocates. In 1809, Isaac Maltby, a Yale-educated brigadier general in the Massachusetts militia during the 1812 war, published a comprehensive overview of courts-martial and military law titled *A Treatise on Courts-Martial and Military Law*. In 1833, another officer, Major Alfred Mordecai, the assistant chief of fortifications, wrote *A Digest of Laws Relating to the Military Establishment*. Like De Hart and Coppee, neither Mordecai nor Maltby provided analysis for enforcing the laws of war, but all four described in sufficient detail the processes involved in courts-martial as well as the general duties of appointed judge advocates. Additionally, De Hart, Maltby, Coppee, and Mordecai did not utilize foreign law or international law in their texts. Winthrop would be the first to do so. One theme common to De Hart, Maltby, and Mordecai was a view that not enough officers, as a general rule, possessed the legal education requisite for judge advocate duties.

De Hart summed up the army's shortcomings on competency in military law in 1846, writing, "There is now, for the army, no established military law department and the consequence is, that it frequently happens that officers without experience, or the necessary qualifications . . . that the person officiating as judge advocate is frequently less fitted to advise the court, than any individual making part of it."[17] Additionally, for the reasons De Hart pointed to, the Mexican-American War showed significant shortcomings in the adjudication of courts-martial and other military inquiry processes, resulting in one significant improvement. In 1849, Congress once again legislated the existence of the Judge Advocate's Department.[18]

The decision to provide a full-time judge advocate influenced the Supreme Court in its 1857 decision *Dynes v. Hoover*, the seminal nineteenth-century case on military law, to reaffirm that courts-martial were only reviewable for jurisdictional grounds.[19] *Dynes* was a case arising not from an army court-martial, but a naval court operating under Naval Articles of War. However, navy court-martial procedure was sufficiently similar to the army's so that in pre–Civil War treatises on military law, authors tended to comment on naval law as persuasive examples. From 1849 to the present, the army—and consequently the other service branches—has maintained a judge advocate general, though the roles of the office have considerably expanded since that time.[20]

Major John Fitzgerald Lee remained judge advocate of the army when the Civil War began and he received a promotion to the permanent grade of major. But early on he became unpopular with Lincoln's cabinet for his opposition to prosecuting civilians in military commissions. Lee was not alone in his opposition to using military courts to enforce civilian laws. A number of congressmen and judges viewed the legality of civilian trials in military courts with skepticism. Even in occupied areas where the civil government ceased to function, Lee believed such courts were unconstitutional. To a section of the public, the military judicial process smacked of martial law. Lee opted to resign from the army rather than become involved in the prosecution of civilians. He had advised the secretary of war that military commissions were unconstitutional and only grudgingly reversed his position. As a Virginian, he also may have believed South Carolina's secession to be constitutional but did not argue this point. According to General

Pope, Major John F. Lee's Southern sympathies were "too strong to justify the government in retaining him in a position of trust and confidence."[21] Perhaps Pope's claim was correct, but Winthrop sought Lee's help in drafting *Military Law and Precedents* in the 1890s.[22]

The unique constitutional challenges were not only related to questions involving the prosecution of civilians in military courts. Rather the challenges involved the broader issue of military authority over citizens. From the very beginning of South Carolina's secession, the army had to protect its individual soldiers and private property important to the war effort against attacks from private citizens. On May 25, 1861, Union soldiers arrested John Merryman, a Maryland state legislator and militia officer. He was accused of destroying railroad bridges and impeding Union access into the city. After his arrest, he appealed via a writ of habeas corpus which was brought to no less a judge than Roger Taney, the chief justice of the Supreme Court and author of the infamous *Dred Scott* decision. Taney did not sit in decision of Merryman in his capacity as a Supreme Court justice. Instead, he reviewed the case as part of his additional duty as a judge for the United States Circuit Court for the District of Maryland. In essence, Taney's authority extended no further than a United States District Court judge and his ruling was appealable to a higher court.[23]

Not surprisingly, Taney ruled against the administration's actions and disagreed with the contention Lincoln had the authority to suspend the writ of habeas corpus or that his authority as commander in chief extended to a power where he could override the citizenry's due process of law rights.[24] Framing the issue with a criticism of Lincoln, Taney wrote, "I understand that the president not only claims the right to suspend the writ of habeas corpus himself, at his discretion, but to delegate that discretionary power to a military officer, and to leave it to him to determine whether he will or will not obey judicial process that may be served upon him."[25] Taney not only reviewed constitutional precedent to support his ruling, but he also brought into the case British law and legal history dating to the Magna Charta, as well as the deceased Justice Story's observations on law and liberty. He concluded his opinion with an ominous warning for future deprivations of civil liberties.[26]

Lincoln ignored Taney's ruling. He could politically do so since Congress was out of session at the time of the arrest, and Taney's ruling was from a single federal judge, instead of the Supreme Court. Lincoln also permitted the blockade of Southern ports, seizure of mails, and arrests of more citizens believed disloyal. When Congress went into special session on July 4, Lincoln addressed them with a largely rhetorical question, "Are all the laws, but one, to go unexecuted, and the government itself go to pieces, lest that one be violated?" Lincoln repeatedly permitted the army to disregard Taney's ruling before Congress voted to suspend habeas corpus in 1863. It was this act of Congress which brought the government more in line with Taney's Merryman opinion.[27]

Winthrop later utilized the Merryman case to show that because civilians were not amenable to court-martial jurisdiction in time of peace, court-martial jurisdiction did not extend to civilians during a period of war either. Instead, the military's authority to prosecute civilians extended into another forum, the military commission.[28] In making his arguments, Winthrop pointed out that military jurisdiction over soldiers was based on military law, that is, the Articles of War. Military jurisdiction over civilians was founded in martial law. Winthrop and his peers generally accepted the Duke of Wellington's earlier observation that martial law was the law of a commander in a war zone. However, Winthrop never argued that martial law could be imposed without limits. To the contrary, as a corollary to his views on martial law, Winthrop stated that while military trials of civilians were a completely separate forum from courts-martial, the two types of trials had to be substantially similar. He did not believe it lawful to prosecute civilians, or even enemy combatants, in a forum of lesser rights than found in a court-martial. To Winthrop, the test for efficacy of military commissions was whether United States soldiers were accorded similar treatment in terms of trial structure, procedure, and rights.[29]

In spite of Winthrop's support for the administration and his Republican loyalties, he did not take issue with Taney's reasoning. Having earlier in his life been thoroughly appalled with the *Dred Scott* decision, Winthrop wrote that Taney held true to the rulings of Chief Justice John Marshall in that only Congress, with the concurrence of the executive, could suspend due process rights in periods of national crisis where the country's survival was threatened. In other words, Winthrop argued the efficacy of martial law was only sound when Congress granted the right of the executive to enact it over limited periods and geographic areas.[30]

In early July 1862, General Henry Halleck pushed for the creation of a judge advocate general to supersede the position of judge advocate. At a minimum, Halleck argued for the position to have the rank of colonel, though he sought a general's rank for the position. Stanton wanted Joseph Holt, a former political ally that he served alongside of in the Buchanan administration. Congress found Halleck's and Stanton's arguments compelling to a point, and on July 17, 1862, created the position of judge advocate with the accompanying rank of colonel. Congress also legislated that each field army, such as the Army of the Potomac and the Army of the Ohio, be provided a permanent judge advocate for its staff.[31]

Holt had briefly served as secretary of war in the Buchanan administration, but he advocated a tougher position against secession than the president's other cabinet officers with the exception of Stanton. Lincoln ultimately sided with Stanton and nominated Joseph Holt to head the department. Lincoln had met with Holt prior to the bombardment on Fort Sumter and appreciated the secretary of war's candor. With the rapid concurrence of Congress, Holt became the judge advocate of the army. Lincoln found Holt a talented patriot, and perhaps found a kinship with Holt's Kentucky roots. Holt had been the Kentucky Commonwealth's attorney earlier in his career. Lincoln was willing to overlook the fact that Holt had fashioned himself as a Jacksonian Democrat and briefly owned slaves, because he was also a staunch unionist. It did not appear to Lincoln that Holt harbored any political ambitions that might undermine the administration, and as the war expanded, Holt became an ardent abolitionist.[32]

Additionally important was the experience Holt brought to the position. As a former commissioner of patents and postmaster general, Holt was intimately familiar with the bureaucratic machinery of government. He also worked in the arena of international law with both jobs. When the war broke, Holt maintained his allegiance to the Union, and Lincoln appointed him as a special commissioner to look into over six thousand civilian monetary claims against the government in John Fremont's military department. Most of these claims were not for damages, but rather government purchases that went unpaid, such as $481,939.17 to James B. Eads. Holt was partially responsible for uncovering Fremont's largess and became a thorn in that general's side.[33] However, Holt's tenure as judge advocate general was not universally welcomed.

No sooner had Holt reentered the War Department than he was besieged by old Democrat acquaintances, some of whom did not support the war. A number of surviving correspondences questioned his wisdom in siding with Lincoln. There were also pro-Union Democrats who hoped Holt would run for Congress and maintain a patriotic Democratic presence in government. Throughout his wartime tenure as judge advocate, he was charged with not only maintaining the discipline of the army but also advising on the pressing issues of the day. These issues, many constitutional in nature, included the jurisdiction of military authority, as well as the administration of martial law over civilians. But other salient issues arose such as the law of neutrality and the constitutionality of conscription. The United States had not fought a "total war" since its existence, and arguably King Philip's War was the only prior time government officials in North America universally believed the survival of the sitting government was at stake.

Holt was not without his detractors. Some Democrats considered him a turncoat. His professional relationship with Stanton was a source of difficulty since Stanton could be divisive and at times turned on the generals in the field. Holt's role in the Emancipation Proclamation was but one area of contention with former allies. He supported the president's authority to issue the proclamation, fully cognizant of how the declaration of slavery's demise affected not only the strategic direction of the war but also the war's effect on the army. He had to answer statements from former allies such as, "His proclamation has paralyzed our armies, you must stop him."[34] Another issue that immediately created enemies was the Fitz-John Porter court-martial. However, it was Holt's prosecution of Clement Vallandigham before the Supreme Court that generated the greatest number of critics. Finally, Holt's unquestioned support of Lincoln in the 1864 election was criticized by McClellan supporters, who wrote editorials disparaging him as "a man . . . who will stoop to such depths of infamy and curry favor with the despot."[35]

Thirty-three judge advocates were appointed under the 1862 legislation. Seven of these judge advocates were assigned to Washington, DC, and the others were sent to the geographic departments and field armies. Over the course of the war, their number included John Bolles, who in 1864 left the army to become the solicitor general of the navy; William McKee Dunn, who served as a Whig and then Republican Indiana Congressman through 1862; De Witt Clinton, the son of a former New York governor and Fusion Party presidential candidate against James Madison; John Chipman Gray, later the foremost authority of western property law; and Henry Bingham who, along with Holt, prosecuted the Lincoln assassination conspirators, served in Congress for eighteen years, and then became ambassador to Japan. (Bingham had served in Congress prior to the war as well.)

Judge advocates generally tended to come from one of two different backgrounds. A small number, such as Bingham and Dunn, served in Congress or possessed other political experience. With the exception of Holt, these men were uniformly Republicans. The larger number of judge advocates, who Winthrop worked closely alongside of, began their military careers as volunteer line officers. Eliphalet Whittlesey, Lucien Eaton, Norman Lieber, Thomas Barr, Henry Burnett, and William Winthrop each began their military tenure in this manner. However, as in the case of the former congressmen, all had loyalty to the Republican Party and many had political connections to gain their position. Interestingly, not all of the judge advocates sought to become staff officers and initially preferred the line.

As an example, Burnett was third in command of a regiment in the Army of the Cumberland, when the judge advocate to that army, Major Madison Cutts,[36] was court-martialed. General Burnside then ordered Burnett (who had been educated as a lawyer prior to the war) to the staff. Burnett later characterized his appointment as a judge advocate as "an accident" and one he, at the time of the appointment, "regarded at the time as a personal misfortune." His first duties included the prosecution of Cutts, as well as a detail to the commission prosecuting "members of the Knights of the Golden Circle, and sons of liberty."[37] Thus, Burnett went from commanding infantry to prosecuting civilians accused of undermining the Union to the point of treason. Although he initially considered his appointment a misfortune, he later sought to make a career in the Judge Advocate General's Department.

There has never been a full published study on the backgrounds and political ideologies of the thirty-three men assigned to the department, but it appears to be the case that some of them shared Winthrop's set of political and socially progressive beliefs. Moreover, their quality as lawyers was above the norm in the United States. For instance, Lucien Eaton, who had been educated at Harvard Law, gained a minor degree of prominence after the war for advocating the admission of women to the bar. Eaton also served as the first editor of the *American Law Review*, the preeminent late nineteenth-century journal. Likewise, Eliphalet Whittlesey attended Yale's law school, graduating in 1842, and went on to serve in the Freedman's Bureau after the war.[38] That Winthrop stood out among his contemporaries evidences the esteem and confidence Holt and Stanton placed in his abilities.

Winthrop could have been assigned to one of the fielded armies or geographic divisions, but opted to stay in Washington, DC. Indeed, in regard to serving as a judge advocate to one of the fielded armies, Hastings shed some light on Winthrop's status in the department. "I think Winthrop could have such a position if he should apply for it, though he is so useful here that the War Department would not like to spare him," Hastings observed.[39]

The 1862 legislation did not boost the Judge Advocate's Department to a size where it could accomplish all of its necessary functions. From September 1, 1862, to November 1, 1863, the department reviewed 17,357 court-martial records and published 2,490 legal opinions. One of the unfortunate elements in many courts-martial which added to the department's workload was the underlying reasons a number of courts-martial were brought in the first place. Some officers charged their contemporaries as a method of personal vendetta, while other officers charged and counter-charged each other with gross allegations, which in reality were nothing more than a form of libel. In many instances, a lack of legal knowledge by ad hoc judge advocates and officer-preferring charges caused judge advocates to recommend convictions overturned from otherwise legitimate courts. Moreover, more than two-thirds of the 13,535 civilian arrests during the war occurred in this period, which also generated investigations and legal reviews.[40]

It is impossible to lump all ad hoc judge advocates into a single category of competency, and the records available at the National Archives display diversity in legal talent from the intelligent and diligent to the outright incompetent. However, one commonality that most ad hoc judge advocates shared appears to have been an understanding that they were responsible for not only the adjudication of courts-martial but also an understanding of the laws of war, as well as military and civilian relations. And yet, very few ad hoc judge advocates had the requisite legal training to qualify for their duties.

By the end of 1862, the number of courts-martial requiring review was a tremendous workload for the assigned judge advocates, and it was for this reason Stanton and Holt urged Lincoln to further expand the size of the department. In late 1863, Stanton reported to Lincoln, "The machinery of the Judge Advocate remains as when the Army consisted of some thirteen thousand men." Stanton also noted that many of the investigations, reports, and courts-martial records were "long and elaborate, involving an examination of complicated masses of fact and of difficult legal questions."[41] These legal opinions consisted of a variety of issues, including the status of runaway slaves found in Union lines as well as the authority of general officers over Southern civilians. Most of the complicated legal issues involved in the Civil War were not solved through rash, quick decisions. Stanton often provided personal direction to the individual judge advocates, though this tended to detract from his all-pressing duties as the secretary of war. For instance, in September 1862 Stanton ordered Major L. C. Turner to "proceed to Fort Lafayette to examine and report on the cases of prisoners . . . and to discharge such as he may deem proper."[42]

Major Turner, who later became a friend to Winthrop and ally to Holt, had, in fact, spent much of 1862 at Camp Chase reviewing over six hundred military commission results, as well as all general courts-martial in the Department of the Ohio. Turner was already well-known to the administration at the time Stanton assigned him the duties described above. In late September, President Lincoln ordered him to investigate reported statements of disloyalty made by a major on McClellan's staff.[43]

Turner was not alone in being assigned such diverse duties. At one point Winthrop was ordered to investigate the treatment of Union prisoners of war in Alabama and recommend as to whether to prosecute Confederates for abuses committed against the prisoners of war. As the war enlarged, Stanton could not afford to micromanage the Judge Advocate General's Corps, and this provided Holt as well as the other judge advocates a greater degree of autonomy. And yet, there were other sources of authority which influenced the role of the individual judge advocates.

On its own, Congress investigated Confederate atrocities such as the Fort Pillow massacre as well as conditions in Richmond's Libby Prison, making determinations of war crimes. It also subpoenaed several general officers throughout the war, who in turn looked to Holt for guidance. For Winthrop, these investigations provided a strategic insight into the war he might not have otherwise gained as an infantry officer. The investigations also enabled him to witness in close proximity how a constitutional republic such as the United States could fight a war without devolving into a dictatorship. Both of these experiences later proved critical to the formulation of his treatises *Military Law* and *Military Law and Precedents*.

Winthrop joined the Judge Advocate General's Department at a time that a number of Civil War historians have posited as transitory between a "soft war" and a "hard war." That is, after the devastation of Antietam and the defining of the war as a crusade to end slavery by the Emancipation Proclamation in late 1862 and the appointment of Ulysses Grant as commanding general of the Union armies in early 1864, the war transitioned from one fought with the limited aim of restoring the Union to one of near total war. How this transition affected the enforcement of discipline and the system of courts-martial is a question not fully studied. Yet, some measure of that transition may be taken from the experiences of Winthrop at the Judge Advocate General's Department.

After 1864, the composition of the army changed in two fundamental ways. The addition of black troops into the army was one factor which increased its potency and reliability. In contrast, draftees and volunteers after 1864 who were induced by increased bonuses likely served as a counterweight to the army's effectiveness. Desertion rates increased after the 1863 Conscription Acts, and the problem of bounty jumpers—men who collected a cash inducement to enlist and then avoided service—escalated. So too did the numbers of Northern civilians who disrupted the government's attempt to increase the size of the army through conscription. One of Winthrop's ongoing tasks at the Bureau of Military Justice was to stop the comptroller general from paying bounties to individuals who had already deserted from one regiment and attempted to join another. At one point, Winthrop complained directly to Stanton and drafted a model law for the secretary to consider forwarding to Congress.[44]

From 1861 through 1867 the Union army carried out 267 executions as part of a court-martial sentence. (It may be the case that there were more executions in the field than the courts-martial records indicate.) Between 1868 and 1913, the army executed three men as a result of a court-martial sentence. Thus while the numbers of courts-martial sentences carried out during the Civil War may seem low in comparison to the size of the army and the number of overall courts, sentences of death could, and did, occur. The low numbers may have had something to do with the system of appeals. On December 24, 1861, Congress placed division commanders as the final appellate authority to commute sentences. On July 27, 1862, this responsibility was placed with the commander in chief. Even when, in 1863, Congress legislated the appellate authority to corps commanders, the president could—and often did—override capital sentences.[45]

Winthrop had a role in drafting *The Report of the Judge Advocate General on the Order of American Knights Alias, "The Sons of Liberty," a Western Conspiracy in the Aid of the Southern Rebellion,* in which Holt claimed Democrats in the western states were plotting the overthrow of the Union by inducing desertions, obstructing enlistments, and arming the Confederacy. The report named a number of individuals including Vallandigham and Lambdin Milligan, both prosecuted for aiding the Confederacy.[46]

He also took part in the legal saga of Clement Vallandigham, drafting Holt's brief to the Supreme Court. The issues surrounding Vallandigham are important to understanding Winthrop's views on civil liberties in wartime. Vallandigham, a former Ohio congressman, supported Stephen Douglas in the 1860 election. Like most "peace Democrats," Vallandigham did not approach all war as a moral wrong, but rather, a war to end slavery as evil. He belonged to a class of Northern Democrats who espoused a particularly virulent strain of racism, even by mid-nineteenth-century standards.[47] Clearly his racial and political beliefs ran completely counter to Winthrop's and those of his fellow judge advocates.

Vallandigham was an ardent supporter of states' rights, believed in the constitutionality of secession, and opined slavery was a legally defensible institution. His criticisms of Lincoln included allegations that the president intentionally misled citizens as to the purposes of the war, and he accused Lincoln of desiring a tyranny. After a number of inflammatory speeches, General Ambrose Burnside (commanding the Department of the Ohio after his resignation from the Army of the Potomac) had Vallandigham arrested and tried before a military commission on May 6, 1863. Vallandigham appealed via a writ of habeas corpus to the federal court. But his appeal went to an unsympathetic federal judge who sided with Burnside and found the government's actions legal.[48]

Winthrop believed that constitutionally guaranteed freedoms of speech and assembly existed in wartime as they did in peace. But the line between where the exercise of these freedoms crossed into a prosecutable offense had to do with fomenting treason against the United States. While he tolerated peace Democrats as evidence of democratic virtue, Winthrop believed Vallandigham encouraged desertion and undermined the war effort. He also believed the government acted properly in issuing an arrest warrant and prosecuting Vallandigham in a military court. Interestingly, for many years after the Civil War, mainstream historians considered the Copperheads as a political nuisance whose dangers Lincoln and Stanton inflated. Some of these historians felt Lincoln was understandably worried at the political opposition but also overestimated the strength of the opposition. Recently, a study has argued otherwise; the Copperheads constituted a short-lived, but very real internal threat to Lincoln and the prosecution of the war.[49]

Winthrop's postwar academic approach to the Vallandigham case was typical of his retrospective presentation of other controversial prosecutions he supported, such as the Johnson impeachment proceedings and the trial of Mary Surratt. He presented the Vallandigham case in his *Military Law and Precedents* treatise as a means for stating its procedural correctness. For instance, he pointed out Vallandigham's refusal to enter a plea resulting in the commission entering a plea of not guilty as evidence of the military tribunal's adherence to procedure.[50] Likewise, while most military commissions were composed of five members and a nonvoting judge advocate, Vallandigham's was composed of seven officers. In practical statistical terms, this made a finding of guilty more difficult, though Vallandigham was found guilty.[51] However, Winthrop reserved his greatest salvo in arguing the legitimacy of the Vallandigham prosecution over the subject matter jurisdiction.

Winthrop argued that Vallandigham was guilty of hostile and disloyal acts and had uttered "declarations calculated to excite opposition to the federal government or sympathy with the enemy." Moreover, he found Lincoln's expulsion of Vallandigham into Confederate lines a perfectly justifiable decision.[52] Winthrop's views coincided with Lincoln's, namely, that Vallandigham knowingly prevented the raising of troops, encouraged desertion, and damaged the Union army.[53] Winthrop never commented on Vallandigham's activities after expulsion into Confederate lines, but it is worth noting that after the expulsion, the peace Democrat met with Confederate officials, who apparently desired his presence in their country less than Lincoln wanted him in the United States. Vallandigham traveled through the blockade to Canada, and reentered the United States. He challenged the government's actions, but the Supreme Court sided with Lincoln, mainly through its nondecision in *ex parte Vallandigham.*

On June 20, 1864, Congress elevated the rank of the judge advocate to brigadier general of cavalry and created a deputy position of assistant judge advocate with the rank of colonel.[54] From this time to the present, the judge advocate of the army was properly referred to as the judge advocate general. And it can be fairly stated that Holt became the United States' first judge advocate general since independence. Congress also established a Bureau of Military Justice, whose role was to oversee courts-martial as well as advise the president and secretary of war on matters of military law. Moreover, the Bureau of Military Justice was made a part of the War Department. Thus while the judge advocates assigned to the bureau were supervised by the judge advocate general, the secretary of war enjoyed administrative control over it, as opposed to the commanding general of the army.[55]

The Bureau of Military Justice was relegated to a set number of judge advocates, and it was by no means assured that Winthrop on his own could gain a position in the bureau. It was easier to attach to one of the geographic army or department commands as a staff officer. For an army numbering roughly one million men, there were open judge advocate positions in the field. Although thirty-three judge advocates officially served in the various departments and the Bureau of Military Justice as appointees, there were also volunteer judge advocates attached to the various staffs as well. The field judge advocates were typically selected by the various commanders, and not the judge advocate general, though both Stanton and Holt had to approve of the selections.[56]

Winthrop had a direct role in the June 20, 1864, law. When Winthrop arrived in Washington, DC, Holt had him draft the initial recommended legislation for Stanton to forward to Lincoln and then on to Congress. However, Winthrop's proposal to Holt and Stanton had the Bureau of Military Justice staffed with two assistant judge advocates at the rank of colonel. Holt assured Winthrop that if there were two colonels assigned to the bureau, one would be him. But the law passed by Congress only had one colonel to head the bureau.[57]

Despite the numbers of courts-martial records and continuance of legal analysis on matters as weighty as the Vallandigham case, Winthrop's tenure in the Judge Advocate General's Department was by no means assured in the summer of 1864. Even with the legislation further expanding the Judge Advocate General's Department, Winthrop could not be sure he would retain a position. Writing to Theodore Weston in June 1864, Winthrop conveyed his desire to remain on active duty as a judge advocate.[58] He expressed his appreciation and admiration for General Joseph Holt, but he had a number of worries for the country, his family, and himself. Like George Hastings, Winthrop commented on the abilities of the various Union generals. Winthrop found Ulysses Grant as the best commander in the Union. This opinion seems to have been the consensus in the Bureau of Military Justice. He also expressed confidence that the assistant secretary of war, Charles Dana, felt the same. (At some point prior to writing Weston, Winthrop discussed issues arising from General David Hunter's activities in the Shenandoah Valley with Dana. However, the purpose of this discussion is no longer known.)

Winthrop remained intensely interested with the strategic political direction of the war as well. He was relieved Congress ended the legality of purchasing substitutes for military service, writing, "The final passage of the enrollment bill abolishing commutation, now rendered nearly certain gives us great encouragement. Things looked bleak here for several days, while it was supposed that the House would refuse to rescind the commutation privilege. Such refusal being regarded as a practical abandonment of the war among those who had the figures, or in other words, the War Department."[59]

Although Winthrop did not approve of commutation or substitution, he was willing to lend Theodore Weston "any funds of mine may have." Winthrop worried for Theodore though he expressed encouragement Theodore would be exempted from service as he had a family to support. Winthrop did not explain his concern for Theodore, but he did mention that he had not heard from Theodore's brother Roswell in some time. Perhaps at the time of Winthrop's letter he did not know that Roswell Weston had been cashiered following a court-martial conviction. On the other hand, having experienced the horrors of war at the front, Winthrop may have simply wanted to spare Theodore the risks of service.

Winthrop's 1864 appointment to the Bureau of Military Justice occurred with Theodore Dwight Woolsey's intervention, just as his initial appointment as judge advocate. Sponsorship into the Judge Advocate General's Department was not unusual. For instance, Norman Lieber's appointment occurred at the behest of Massachusetts Senator Charles Sumner and General Halleck. Another judge advocate, Ralston Skinner, was Salmon Chase's nephew. As Lincoln's treasury secretary, Chase certainly had enough influence to pull Skinner onto the staff. Advancement within the department often required additional political pull. Winthrop recognized as much, hinting, "If the bill had provided as it should have done, for two working majors, I should have been appointed, I think without the need of the slightest political influence."[60] Woolsey had regular contact with Francis Lieber and General Halleck, and his circle of associates included Stanton. There were judge advocates senior in grade to Winthrop, and he was not surprised he was not appointed as assistant judge advocate general, stating, "The bill providing for one assistant, a colonel—he much needs to be appointed on political pressure."[61]

Although the size of the office eventually grew through legislation, the workload of the staff did not level off. From November 1, 1863, to March 1, 1865, the Bureau of Military Justice reviewed 33,869 court-martial records and published 9,340 legal opinions. These legal opinions included issues as complex as the Milligan case and international law matters arising from Confederate operations in Canada. Early on, Winthrop must have impressed Holt because he increasingly turned to Winthrop for assistance. Notably, Holt entrusted Winthrop to begin compiling courts-martial and federal court results as well as opinions from the judge advocate general dating back to Colonel Tudor. Winthrop saw the need for a compilation to be published and provided to the departments and armies so that commanders could make uniform and consistent decisions in regards to the administration of military justice, civil relations, and procurement.

This compilation of opinions and cases, titled the *Digest of Opinions*, was not published until early 1865, and as a result it made little impact during the war. However, it was widely used by the army during Reconstruction, and a number of federal courts incorporated it as an authoritative source. Of greatest importance was that the compilation constituted the first standardized legal guidance for fielded judge advocates and commanders. Holt and the secretary of war both praised the *Digest* and considered it invaluable which must have given Winthrop some measure of professional satisfaction.

And yet, there were personal disappointments for Winthrop. In July 1864, Winthrop informed Theodore Weston that one William McKee Dunn was expected to arrive in Washington, but he did not intend to be hospitable to him; "'Dunn,' has not yet appeared here. . . . His being here will not interfere with me particularly, as I shall continue to be independent, and shall not write him often to dine." In the same letter to Weston, Winthrop again expressed anxiety at not using political connections to secure his own appointment, writing in almost duplicate, reflecting his angst, "If the bill had provided as it should have done for two working majors, I should have been appointed, I think, without the slightest need of political influence; as to the assistant, Colonel Dunn was appointed on political pressure."[62] As William had drafted the original legislation proposal, he would have been in a position to know that he was close to being promoted to the regular grade of colonel and having a secure position in the Judge Advocate General's Department. Or he could have left with an honorable discharge on October 1, 1864, having fulfilled three years of duty. But he did not do so, living up to his brother's earlier statement, "Will and I want to see this to the end."

Winthrop's comments regarding the political nature of the appointment of an assistant were accurate. Dunn had been named assistant judge advocate, and it caused Winthrop some personal grief. On July 1, 1864, President Lincoln was presented with a petition to nominate Dunn as the assistant judge advocate. The petition bore over seventy signatures from Republican congressmen as well as Indiana state legislators. Lauding Dunn's congressional service, the petition also highlighted his military experience as a judge advocate to the Missouri Department: "Mr. Dunn while in Congress was an active and influential member of the Military Committee and being a lawyer of superior qualifications, combines the military and judicial knowledge requisite of the position . . . he has served with rare ability and eminent success. This position would therefore be not only fitting, but as we believe conducive to the interests of the service." The petition's signatories included congressmen such as Amasa Cobb, from Wisconsin then serving as a colonel; Nathaniel Smithers, an "Unconditional Unionist Party," member from Delaware; Thomas D. Elliot of Massachusetts, who later headed the chairmanship overseeing the Freedman's Bureau; and all four of the Indiana Republican congressmen.[63] Winthrop did not have political backing of this strength, and his surnamed family political connections were unlikely to be accorded any deferential treatment by the administration. Nor did Winthrop seek any help from Robert Charles Winthrop, perhaps indicating a break from that part of the family.

Despite a sixteen-year age difference between Colonel Dunn and Winthrop, the two men traversed some of the same paths in their lives, including a connection to Daniel Webster and schooling at Yale. Like Winthrop, Dunn's political affiliation had initially been with the Whigs, and in the later 1850s, he became a Republican. Winthrop did not leave to posterity the reasons for his initial dissatisfaction of having to work alongside Colonel Dunn. Winthrop's misgivings do not appear to have lasted. When Dunn retired as the judge advocate general, he sought to have Winthrop replace him and was unhappy with the choice of another judge advocate, Major David Swaim. Moreover, when in 1882 Winthrop was transferred to the Division of the Pacific, Dunn and his wife vacationed with the Winthrops in the Yosemite area. At some point a friendship beyond a professional relationship between the two rivals grew and lasted through to Dunn's death in 1887.

Like Brigadier General Joseph Holt, Dunn had prewar political experience and also possessed strong evidence of an intellect. Born in Hanover, Indiana, his father was a territorial judge and military veteran of the War of 1812. Dunn graduated from Indiana State College with a degree in mathematics at the age of eighteen. The school offered him a mathematics professorship. Instead, he accepted an offer to teach at Hanover College, a Presbyterian school closer to his father's residence, and in line with his religious beliefs. Moreover, Hanover's trustees first decided to send him to Yale to further his education. In 1835, Dunn traveled to New Haven, "armed with letters of introduction," where he not only attended school but also, according to his biography, "had access to the best homes in the city, and formed many intimate friendships."[64] Whether he became friends with Francis Bayard Winthrop is absent from the historical record, but it is likely the two met since Francis was intimately involved in the social surroundings of Yale, and Theodore Dwight Woolsey served there as a professor of Greek languages during this time. There is no surviving correspondence linking Dunn and Woolsey. On the other hand, there is no evidence Dunn helped Winthrop into the Judge Advocate General's

Corps. At the time Winthrop transferred into the corps, Dunn was finishing his lame duck session as a defeated congressman and had yet to enter the corps. Still, given the overlapping experiences of the two men, it is likely they knew of each other sometime prior to 1861.

After returning to Indiana in 1836, Dunn taught mathematics at Hanover College, as well as natural philosophy and chemistry.[65] He might have spent his life teaching at the school, but the following summer a tornado destroyed the campus. The college did not possess enough funds to continue paying its entire faculty. As a newer hire, Dunn was likely to be asked to leave until the school became solvent. Before this could occur, he resigned his professorship to spare Hanover's administrators any embarrassment. As an alternative means of income, he studied to become a lawyer under the tutelage of a circuit judge.[66] He did remain as a trustee to the school through much of his life.

By 1840, Dunn was a licensed attorney and the following year a named partner in a Madison, Indiana, law firm. In 1848, he successfully ran for the state legislature as a Whig, where he championed free public education for all Indiana residents. In 1850, he served as a state delegate to its Constitutional Convention. Although Indiana was a free state, its residents did not want to see free Africans enter into their borders and attempted to pass a provision making it a criminal act to knowingly bring Africans into the state. Dunn vigorously opposed this amendment and managed to politically survive.[67] He was elected as a representative to Congress in 1858 as a Republican, and again in 1860, but suffered defeat in 1862. While in Congress, he served as the chairman on the House Committee on Patents. He also verbally accosted Congressman Rust of Arkansas, a Southern Democrat who had labeled all Republicans as "treasonable." Rust demanded satisfaction and challenged Dunn to a duel, which Dunn accepted. The duel never occurred, in part because a number of ministers intervened and the two men exchanged apologies instead. Additionally, Rust did not seem to know that at the time of the challenge, Dunn was an accomplished shot and found out this fact during a meeting with one of the ministers. After the outbreak of war, he had a brief stint in the Army of the Potomac, serving for one month as a volunteer aide-de-camp to McClellan in June 1861.[68]

Among the reasons Dunn lost the 1862 election was his support for enlisting volunteer Africans, as well as the declining fortunes of the Union army. He also supported the Emancipation Proclamation, and the concept of fighting a war to free slaves was unpopular in his southern Indiana district. On March 13, 1863, four months after his election defeat, he secured a position as a judge advocate with the rank of major attached to the Department of the Missouri. There, he provided advice to General John Schofield. To Dunn's credit, when the Indiana state governor offered

Dunn a colonelcy and a number of other friends attempted to obtain command with the rank of general over regular forces, he declined these offers, believing he did not possess the competence to command forces in battle.[69] So many others did not decline similar offers and showed their ineptness at command. Their number included Nathaniel P. Banks, John A. McClernand, and Benjamin F. Butler, and Union soldiers suffered through any number of unwise decisions and brash egos.

Colonel Dunn was not the only Dunn family member to wear the Union uniform. His nineteen-year-old son, William, was commissioned as a lieutenant and saw action at Vicksburg, in the Wilderness Campaign, as well as in front of Petersburg. Like Winthrop, the younger Dunn was promoted to captain for gallantry. The younger Dunn had the distinction of escorting General Lee to the Appomattox Court House on April 9, 1865. General Grant had selected Captain Dunn for this task on the basis of his heroism in battle.[70] After the war, Captain Dunn left the army for the private practice of law, but in 1897 he returned to the army as a judge advocate of volunteers and served under Norman Lieber during the Spanish-American War.

As judge advocate assigned to the Department of the Missouri during the war, Dunn presided over a number of trials of captured guerrillas. These guerrillas included members of Quantrill's raiders. He also advised General Schofield that the army did not possess the jurisdiction to court-martial civilians who either contracted with the army or accompanied it where civilian courts remained viable.[71] On June 22, 1864, Dunn was promoted to lieutenant colonel and assigned as assistant judge advocate of the army. This rank and position placed him as Holt's deputy, and when Holt retired in 1875, Dunn succeeded him as the judge advocate general with the rank of brigadier general.[72] How long Winthrop's dislike of Dunn lasted is unknown, but it was likely short-lived. The two shared similar views on the enforcement of the laws of war, as well as the importance of continuing the war through to the defeat of the rebellion. By 1864, Dunn also had changed his view from supporting a war of reconciliation to fighting a war to end slavery and obtain unconditional surrender. Winthrop may have also realized that Dunn thought very highly of his legal talents and often sought his advice.

In addition to ensuring the regularity of courts-martial, Winthrop provided advice to the various commands on law-of-war issues. In one instance, he was assigned the task of investigating the proper disposition of a case where one Confederate prisoner of war held at Camp Chase, Ohio, murdered another prisoner of war. Winthrop advised that military courts were not the proper venue for trials of prisoners of war where one prisoner was a victim of another, as long as local prosecutors and judges were able to fairly adjudicate the case.[73] Even after 1865, a number of other law-of-war issues arose requiring guidance. These included investigations into the murder of Union prisoners of war by Confederate guards. In one instance, a Union officer, Captain Hanchett, had been killed in Cahaba, Alabama, by enlisted guards under the orders of one Lieutenant Colonel Jones, CSA. The facts underlying the death of Hanchett were of interest to the War Department. A number of Union prisoners were held at Cahaba, and there were reports of prisoner mistreatment. Orders to execute Hanchett had been issued through Jones' adjutant to an enlisted guard, Private P. B. Vaughn. Union forces captured Vaughn, but the officers eluded the military. Winthrop advised the secretary of war that until the responsible officers were captured, the War Department should avoid prosecuting Vaughn. Although Winthrop did not, in his opinion, specifically state the principle of command responsibility, his legal reasoning latched on to that theory of liability then becoming universally accepted. That is, the greatest liability for a war crime rested with the commanding officer who ordered the crime committed or was in a position to stop it and did not do so.

This theory of liability had its origins in the fifteenth-century case of Peter von Hagenbach, a Burgundian Duke in command over the town of Breisach, whose soldiers committed a number of heinous atrocities, even for that period. When captured by the Archduke of Austria, he was prosecuted in front of an ad hoc tribunal consisting of judges of different nationalities. In that case, he was sentenced to death for the conduct of his subordinates. In 1945, United States forces under the command of Douglas MacArthur prosecuted a Japanese general who, it was alleged, willfully permitted Manila razed and the civilian population massacred.

The Bureau of Military Justice also extensively dealt with military jurisdiction over civilians. The use of military courts to try civilians during the war created reams of trial records, often with complex legal issues. The level of work had grown to a breaking point for the bureau. For instance, between 1861 and 1863, Camp Chase, a prisoner of war camp, adjudicated over six hundred military tribunals of civilians. Although most of these tribunals were adjudicated and reviewed by the judge advocate assigned to the particular district, many of their records made their way into the bureau for review. Major Levi Turner, the judge advocate assigned to the Ohio District, sifted through the cases and where he saw fit, recommended reversals, usually for evidentiary weaknesses, but on occasion for want of jurisdiction.

As the Union armies occupied Southern areas, military commanders set up courts under the authority of their provost marshals. As in the case of general courts-martial, civilian convictions were supposed to be forwarded to the bureau for review and recommendation. This did not always occur, but there is a record of some cases catching the bureau's attention. In particular, trials of recently freed slaves were a focus for the bureau. In one case, Winthrop wrote to Holt that instances of former slaves engaging in self-defense to stop recapture could hardly constitute murder.[74]

Winthrop reviewed one such case where a recently freed slave named John Glover was accused of murdering a white overseer and had been convicted and sentenced to be hanged. Sherman approved the sentence, writing, "The evidence by no means warrants the sentence, there can be no doubt the prisoner discharged a pistol at George Redman." Winthrop found Sherman's analysis brief and legally deficient. Redman had captured two African American girls, one of them Glover's daughter, and this was in violation to the emancipation law issued by Lincoln over a year earlier. Writing, "Redman was retaining the two girls in violation of the emancipation proclamation and he declared his intention to keep them . . . and swore to shoot any man who came after them," Winthrop found the conviction unsupported by the facts. Instead, he found the rescue "a lawful and justifiable act," and as to Glover's possession of a pistol during the rescue, Winthrop opined, "It can scarcely be imputed to him as a crime that he took with him a weapon of defense."[75]

Notwithstanding the reams of court-martial records, there were other important constitutionally pressing issues for the Bureau of Military Justice which involved the conduct of Union generals. On April 14, 1865, Sherman entered into peace negotiations with General Joseph E. Johnston in North Carolina. Although Sherman notified Grant and Stanton of his initial parley with Johnston, he did not share with either superior that Johnston had offered to negotiate surrender terms for the entire Confederate army. Although Sherman did not agree to Johnston's specific offer of peace terms, he counter-offered terms that had the effect of a general amnesty. This offer clearly exceeded the authority of a general, an army's commanding general. Truces were a commanding general's prerogative, but armistices and treaties were the province of the elected executive and the United States Senate. Grant had the authority to take Lee's surrender at Appomattox because Lincoln had granted that authority. Sherman had no such grant of authority and was rebuked by Grant, Halleck, and Stanton. Sherman was willing to let Grant's admonition serve as guidance, and the friendship between the two generals was too solid for Sherman to indulge in personal pettiness. But Sherman broke off any cordial relations with the others, Stanton and Halleck. Stanton added fuel to Sherman's anger by branding him a despot while newspapers questioned Sherman's loyalty to the Union.

The War Department was not alone in criticism of Sherman's actions. Francis Lieber opposed Sherman's armistice, writing, "It will be the death of our cause." A number of newspapers condemned Sherman's actions. In the end, the termination of hostilities with Johnston was conducted along the same lines as that of Lee and Grant. But an angry Sherman made it clear that his respect for Stanton and the War Department was no longer the case, and later he overtly snubbed Stanton.[76]

The Bureau of Military Justice's role in Stanton's rebuking of Sherman was passive. Holt corresponded with Stanton, assuring the secretary that Sherman had overstepped his authority. Dunn, Winthrop, John Bolles, and Levi Turner, the judge advocates attached to the bureau, were involved in Holt advising Stanton as to what action to take toward Sherman. In the end, an informal censure tantamount to a scolding was decided on. But Sherman carried a lifetime grudge over the matter toward Stanton and refused to see that he overstepped his authority. Winthrop, too, kept a memory of the incident and highlighted it in *Military Law and Precedents* as an example of a military commander unlawfully violating the authority of the elected executive.[77]

The voided surrender agreement between Sherman and Johnston unintentionally served another purpose. Lee had surrendered to Grant, but there remained two other Confederate armies fighting against Union armies. Johnston's army was one of these. Since the Confederate government had taken flight and not surrendered, the United States was still technically at war with the South. On April 26, Johnston formally surrendered, but by then Lincoln had been assassinated. As a result, the assassination was, under the law of war, considered a war crime. It was not the only civilian act considered a war crime either. Another civilian, more prominent than the assassins, faced a military trial for aiding escaped prisoners.

Winthrop's duties at the Bureau of Military Justice extended beyond drafting legislation and reviewing court-martial records. He served as a judge advocate to general courts-martial as well as military commissions, and it was in this later category where he participated in one of the potentially more controversial trials of the war which likely crossed into the realm of unconstitutionality.

On April 26, 1865, as the war concluded, Holt selected Winthrop to prosecute Benjamin G. Harris, a Maryland congressman who harbored and aided two escaped Confederate prisoners of war. Holt's appointment of Winthrop as judge advocate was approved by the adjutant general on May 1, 1865. The same orders appointed General John G. Foster president of the court, and Major General John G. Parke, brevet Major General Orlando Wilcox, brevet Brigadier Generals G. H. Sharp and Joseph A. Haskin, and three colonels as members.[78] Initially Harris did not want to be represented by counsel, but in the course of the trial, Harris employed P. W. Craine, a retired Maryland judge.

As noted above, on April 26, 1865, the Union technically remained in a state of war. Harris had not taken an oath of loyalty during the war, and he had made a number of disloyal statements against the Union dating to 1861. On May 1, 1865, Harris was charged with two specifications of violating the fifty-sixth Article of War. Winthrop had earlier drafted charges against Harris and forwarded these to Holt for review. Holt's response, "The facts set forth make out a prima facie case of violation of the 56th Article of War for which the party may be tried by General Court-Martial charges and specification enclosed," gave Winthrop confidence in the efficacy of the charges.[79]

In essence, Winthrop had to prove that Harris provided the escaped prisoners housing, food, and money. The Confederate prisoners, Sergeant Chapman and Private Read, testified that Harris had assisted them, and moreover, that he encouraged them to continue south to rejoin their army to "make war against the United States." According to Chapman, Harris expressed support for Lincoln's assassination, called Grant "a damned rascal," and stated Jefferson Davis was "a good man, a great man, a gentleman." Winthrop also called Harris' captor, Sergeant Reuben R. Stewart, to testify that Harris referred to Lincoln and other republicans as "black republicans" during his arrest.[80]

Harris objected to Chapman's and Read's testimony as they were "enemies of the United States testifying against a United States citizen." In response, Winthrop notified the court he intended to call witnesses testifying to Harris' past statements supporting secession. In an attempt to create a factual defense, Harris claimed Chapman and Read told him they had been paroled and were in need of lodging, and as he took pity on their impoverished condition, he loaned them money. He also testified that he sent them to a friend's residence precisely because he did not want his otherwise lawful acts misconstrued as treason. His friend, Aloysius Fenwick, attempted to corroborate his claims, but Winthrop cross-examined Fenwick, proving bias.[81]

During the trial Harris sought two delays. The first delay was to secure a defense counsel and the second to enable Fenwick to testify. Winthrop did not object to either delay, but he objected to Harris' attempt to introduce muster rolls from Chapman's regiment to prove neither prisoner was in the Confederate army. The muster rolls were problematic. Chapman and Read were captured in the summer of 1864, and the rolls were not drafted until Lee's surrender. Moreover, the regiment had 260 men assigned to it, but the rolls only listed forty-two. Despite Winthrop's objection, the court permitted the muster rolls into evidence.

Harris' closing arguments consisted of an attack on the jurisdiction of the court as well as the credibility of Chapman and Read as Confederates. He also noted that even if the facts were true, he assumed Chapman and

Read had been paroled and he only secured them lodging in a barn, not a house as listed in the first specification of the charge.[82] Winthrop dissected Harris' arguments, and his closing argument is perhaps the best evidence of his superb courtroom acumen.

Winthrop began his arguments by addressing each of Harris' objections. Referencing John O'Brien's 1846 *A Treatise on American Military Laws, and Practice of Courts Martial* and S. V. Benet's 1864 *A Treatise on Military Law and the Practice of Courts-Martial*, Winthrop addressed the nature of the Articles of War and military jurisdiction over civilians in wartime. To Harris' objection that the trial had no constitutional jurisdiction, Winthrop sarcastically replied, "It is thus seen that if these articles of war are unconstitutional, the men who made them and who at the same time made the Constitution were unaware of that fact."[83] Winthrop then rebutted Harris' assertion that Chapman and Read were unreliable witnesses by placing their testimony alongside Harris' past statements of support for the Confederacy. Although Winthrop proved Chapman and Read had not been paroled, he pointed out that even had they been, it would have made no difference as to Harris' guilt. In making his point, Winthrop used an unusual source of law, an act of King George III, as well as a British case, *Rex v. Martin*. In doing so, he told the court, "I need here hardly remind the court that the common law, where not modified by state legislation is as much a part of the law of this country as it is of Great Britain."[84] When he closed his argument, Winthrop reminded the court that Harris had taken an oath to defend the Constitution as a congressman, and as a result, Harris was guilty "of a far greater crime then in relieving, harboring, encouraging the public enemy and inciting them to continue the war."[85]

The court found Harris guilty of violating the fifty-sixth Article of War by encouraging the escaped prisoners to continue to fight against the United States and furnishing them with the means to do so. Harris was sentenced to "forever be disqualified from holding office and imprisonment for three years." General Holt recommended the decision and sentence be upheld, claiming, "The proceedings were conducted in accordance with the law and court-martial regulations."[86] However, President Andrew Johnson pardoned Harris, and the congressman returned to private life, though not before fulfilling his final term in the House of Representatives.[87]

Winthrop's opinion on Johnson's action is not recorded in any surviving correspondence, but it is likely he did not approve of releasing Harris from prison, and Harris' later acts likely reinforced Winthrop's views as to Harris' guilt. In a speech to the House of Representatives opposing Reconstruction, Harris attacked the administration and the military disciplinary system. He fashioned himself an "old-line democrat who believes in the doctrine of secession." But he did not rest with his political statements and called courts-martial "instruments of tyranny." With the same invective, Harris attacked "Negro equality, Mormonism, and, strong-minded Massachusetts women." But perhaps his greatest offense to Winthrop was defending Mary Surratt and comparing John Wilkes Booth favorably to John Brown.[88]

What Winthrop did not know, or at least did not have possession of, was ample direct evidence of Harris' intent to see the Union lose the war. Harris' wife, Martha Elizabeth Harris, kept a diary detailing their hopes for a Confederate victory. On July 4, 1861, she recorded sardonically, "We are not a free people, we are under the control of a miserable, bloodthirsty government, one who would be too happy to see us thrust upon a pike." After the Battle of Antietam, she recorded, "Bad news from the army." And on April 11, 1865 she wrote, "Terrible news from the Army, Lee has surrendered to Grant, I fear that there is no longer hope for the south. To think that Lincolns' should be sitting in Jeff Davis' reception chairs in Richmond!! Oh, it is too sad to contemplate." Although she did not attend her husband's trial, she left unsurprisingly strongly worded views on its "injustice," and she personally attacked Winthrop as "a miserable puppy belonging to the federal government."[89]

The trial of Harris by military commission was not, at the time of its hearing, publicly controversial most likely as it was overshadowed by other events such as the end of hostilities and Lincoln's assassination. Holt advised Stanton that the trial was fair. "The prisoner was assisted by four able counsel, and the trial appears to have been a thorough investigation, and the prisoner granted unusual indulgence," he concluded.[90] As of May 1865, Holt's reputation for legal acumen in the Union government appeared unimpeachable.

Moreover, Harris was an unapologetic Confederate sympathizer. From his deathbed in 1893, he wrote to the president of the Maryland Confederate Soldiers Home that he declined an invitation to give a public address due to his failing health. He added, however, "You are right in saying I was a friend of you all when your souls were tried, and I now truly grieve that the cause was lost." He also heaped abuse on Lincoln in writing, "Is it not sad that men of the greatest minds and most highly talented men in the north should be its greatest villians." But, the military commission did not have to guess on how Harris viewed the Union's leaders. In 1864 Harris had traveled to the Democrat Convention in Chicago and publicly denounced McClellan as a "despot and tyrant," claiming McClellan's promise to continue the war treason. He also lauded Vallandigham as a hero.[91] Few citizens were likely to argue for Harris. And yet, the fact that the army, an agency of the executive branch of government, prosecuted a United States Constitution, Article I "elected representative of the people," was a significant undertaking.

The trial was covered by a few newspapers. For instance, on May 8, 1865, the *Philadelphia Inquirer* reported Harris was a "Rebel member of Congress," and Major Winthrop, the judge advocate. One day later, according to the Inquirer, Winthrop presented evidence that Harris had opined to the escaped prisoners, that it was "too late to kill Lincoln, since he had already been assassinated."[92] This point is important for understanding Winthrop's views on a connection between the Confederate government and Lincoln assassination.

At the same time, the *Baltimore Sun* covered the trial, generally showing Winthrop in a favorable light. For instance, that paper reported Winthrop did not object to Harris' jurisdictional objection to the commission or to Harris' request to reopen the commission after the close of evidence, so that he could present more evidence to the court members. Winthrop also did not object to the defense counsel cross-examination of witnesses although military practice would have allowed him to do so.[93]

The trial became a rarely noted event in historical works on the Civil War. Winthrop used it as a footnote in his first treatise, *Military Law*, to show that military commissions were on the whole conducted in a fair manner. He had advised the court to permit Harris unusual latitude to introduce new testimony two days after the commission had closed the hearing for deliberations and took this as proof of his own fairness. Yet while the vigor in which a congressman was prosecuted before a military trial instead of a federal court evidenced Winthrop's mindset on the authority of the executive branch in wartime during the Civil War, it did not appear to ever enter into his scholarship the possibility that the Harris trial came closer to giving the appearance of a military trial than perhaps any other action during the war.[94]

In his treatises, Winthrop also utilized the case to show that Harris' sentence of disqualification from further government office was not unique in the context of the Civil War and that it was an authorized sentence.[95] In *Military Law and Precedents*, Winthrop stated, "In the leading case of B. G. Harris, a member of Congress from Maryland, the relieving by the accused, with money, of two soldiers of the army of our enemy, at large under their parole as prisoners of war, and unlawfully within our lines, was considered by the court to be, as charged, an offence under Article 45, and the conviction and sentence of the accused accordingly, were duly approved."[96]

In his publications, Winthrop never noted that Andrew Johnson gave Harris a full pardon, enabling Harris to resume political life shortly after the sentence. On the other hand, Winthrop was not the only judge advocate to support the military trial and conviction either. In none of the succeeding treatises on military law did any criticism appear. In 1915 as the army prepared for a possible war against Germany, the judge advocate general, Major General George B. Davis, opined that Harris' prosecution was proper.[97] Over time, the story of Harris' trial and imprisonment has been forgotten to the point that in historic works detailing the end of the Civil War, Reconstruction, and even the trials of the Lincoln assassins, the case is not mentioned. And yet, there is a clear tie to the zeal in which the assassin conspirators were prosecuted as well as that of the radical Republican approach to Reconstruction, with the willingness to prosecute a congressman in a military trial.

NOTES

1. See, for example, United States House of Representatives, *Executive Journal* (Washington: Government Printing Office, 1865), 68–69. On December 12, President Abraham Lincoln promoted the following line officers as majors in the Judge Advocate General's Department: DeWitt Clinton, Eliphalet Whittlesey, John C. Gray, Seth Farrington, E. L. Joy, William Winthrop, Henry Bingham, James McElroy, H. B. Burnham, and Francis E. Wolcott. All of these men had served as line officers attached to volunteer regiments. As an example of a biographical sketch in error, see Lieutenant Colonel William R. Hagan, "Overlooked Textbooks Jettison Some Durable Military Legends," *Military Law Review* 113 (1986), 170–171. Hagen states that Winthrop fought at Gettysburg and became a judge advocate in 1864.

2. Sharpshooters' historian Marcot lists Trepp corresponding with a judge advocate named H. H. Winthrope at the Bureau of Military Justice. However, there was no one with this name in the Judge Advocate General's Department with that name. It is likely that had Marcot compared the signatures in the letter to Trepp with that of William Woolsey Winthrop, he would have understood that the signature was Winthrop's.

3. William Winthrop, letter to Caspar Trepp, May 11, 1863 (Caspar Trepp Papers, NYHS); Roy Marcot, *Civil War Chief of Sharpshooters Hiram Berdan: Military Commander and Firearms Inventor* (Irvine, CA: Northwood Heritage, 1989), 88; Caspar Trepp, letter to Edwin Stanton, June 1, 1863 (Caspar Trepp Papers, NYHS).

4. Berdan's behavior at Gettysburg differed from previous battles. Under the eye of General Daniel Sickles, Berdan led his regiment on a foray near the Confederate lines. This proved costly and the maneuver did not have a discernible effect on the Confederates.

5. Marcot, *Civil War Chief of Sharpshooters*, 88.

6. In the nineteenth century, ad hoc appointed judge advocates were referred to as temporary, special, and appointed without statute. For the purpose of consistency, the term *ad hoc* is used.

7. William Winthrop, *Military Law and Precedents*, 2nd ed. (Washington, DC: GPO, 1920), 180–183; William De Hart, *Observations on Military Law and the Constitution and Practice of Courts-Martial* (New York: D. Appleton and Co., 1846), 323;

Henry Coppee, *Field Manual of Courts-Martial: Containing the Forms of Proceeding, of All Kinds of Courts-Martial and an Explanation of the Duties of All Persons Connected with Military Tribunals* (New York: J.B. Lippincott, 1863), 56–58.

8. Winthrop, *Military Law and Precedents*, 180–183.

9. De Hart, *Observations on Military Law and the Constitution*, 82; Coppee, *Field Manual of Courts-Martial*, 57.

10. Winthrop, *Military Law and Precedents*, 976–985; Stephen A. Lamb, "The Court-Martial Panel Selection Process: A Critical Analysis," *Military Law Review* 137 (Summer 1992), 117.

11. In fact, only a general court-martial could impose dismissal from the service (a punishment for officers only), forfeiture of more than three months of pay, or incarceration exceeding three months. See, for example, B. Kevin Bennett, "The Jacksonville Mutiny," *Military Law Review* 134 (1991), 157.

12. Coppee, *Field Manual of Courts-Martial*, 41. In advocating junior officers volunteer for recorder duties, Coppee added, "Regimental courts are good schools in which young officers may, while acting as recorders, learn the duties of judge advocates."

13. Act of March 3, 1863, ch. 75, § 30, 12 Stat. 731, 736; Winthrop, *Military Law and Precedents*, 667.

14. George J. Stansfield, "A History of the Judge Advocate General's Department, United States Army," *Military Affairs* 9 (1945), 219–220; William McKee Dunn, *A Sketch of the History and Duties of the Judge Advocate General's Department*, (Washington, DC: GPO, 1878), 1; Jonathan Lurie, *Arming Military Justice: The Origins of the United States Court of Military Appeals* (Princeton, NJ: Princeton University Press, 1992), 3–6; Winthrop, *Military Law and Precedents*, 21; Thomas H. Green and William F. Frachter, "History of the Judge Advocate General's Department," *Army Lawyer* (June 1975), 16; L. D. Ingersoll, *A History of the War Department of the United States with Biographical Sketches of the Secretaries* (New York: Francis B. Mohun, 1879), 146–147.

15. Dunn, *A Sketch of the History and Duties of the Judge Advocate General's Department*, 2–3; Ingersoll, *History of the War Department of the United States*, 147.

16. See, for example, Richard Kohn, "The Constitution and National Security: The Intent of the Framers," in *The United States Military under the Constitution of the United States: 1789–1989*, ed. Richard Kohn, 88–90 (Baton Rouge: LSU Press, 1991); also, Dunn, *A Sketch of the History and Duties of the Judge Advocate General's Department*, 2–3; and, Ingersoll, *History of the War Department of the United States*, 147.

17. De Hart, *Observations on Military Law and the Constitution*, 97

18. Isaac Maltby, *A Treatise on Courts-Martial and Military Law* (Boston: Thomas B. Wait and Co., 1809); Alfred Mordecai, *A Digest of Laws Relating to the Military Establishment of the United States* (Philadelphia: Thomas and Homans, 1833); Dunn, *A Sketch of the History and Duties of the Judge Advocate General's Department*, 4.

19. 61 U.S. (20 How.), 65 (1857). The concluding language of *Dynes* is as follows:

> With the sentences of courts martial which have been convened regularly, and have proceeded legally, and by which punishments are directed, not forbidden by law, or which are according to the laws and customs of the sea, civil courts have nothing to do, nor are they in any way alterable by them. If it were otherwise, the civil courts would

> virtually administer the rules and articles of war, irrespective of those to whom that duty and obligation has been confided by the laws of the United States, from whose decisions no appeal or jurisdiction of any kind has been given to the civil magistrate or civil courts. But we repeat, if a court martial has no jurisdiction over the subject-matter of the charge it has been convened to try, or shall inflict a punishment forbidden by the law, though its sentence shall be approved by the officers having a revisory power of it, civil courts may, on an action by a party aggrieved by it, inquire into the want of the court's jurisdiction, and give him redress.

See also, for example, Jonathan Lurie, *Military Justice in America: The United States Court of Criminal Appeal in the Armed Forces, 1775–1890* (Lawrence: University Press of Kansas, 2001), 1–20.

20. Lurie, *Military Justice in America*, 34–38.

21. John Pope, *The Military Memoirs of General John Pope*, ed. Peter Cozzens and Robert Girardi (Chapel Hill: University of North Carolina Press, 1998), 190.

22. Winthrop, *Military Law and Precedents*, 181. In the section on the history and role of the judge advocate, Winthrop turned to Lee. He credited Lee for assisting him in verifying Lee never deputized any officers to serve as ad hoc or temporary judge advocates.

23. James S. Simon, *Lincoln and Chief Justice Taney: Slavery, Secession, and the President's War Powers* (New York: Simon and Schuster, 2006), 186–187.

24. William Marvel, *Mr. Lincoln Goes to War* (New York: Houghton Mifflin, 2006), 69–70.

25. 17 F. Cas. 144 (1861). Taney's criticism included the following admonition against the president: "The great importance which the framers of the constitution attached to the privilege of the writ of habeas corpus, to protect the liberty of the citizen, is proved by the fact, that its suspension, except in cases of invasion or rebellion, is first in the list of prohibited powers; and even in these cases the power is denied, and its exercise prohibited, unless the public safety shall require it."

26. 17 F. Cas. 144 (1861). The conclusion went as follows:

> These great and fundamental laws, which congress itself could not suspend, have been disregarded and suspended, like the writ of habeas corpus, by a military order, supported by force of arms. Such is the case now before me, and I can only say that if the authority which the constitution has confided to the judiciary department and judicial officers, may thus, upon any pretext or under any circumstances, be usurped by the military power, at its discretion, the people of the United States are no longer living under a government of laws, but every citizen holds life, liberty and property at the will and pleasure of the army officer in whose military district he may happen to be found.

27. Marvel, *Mr. Lincoln Goes to War*, 71–72.

28. Winthrop, *Military Law and Precedents*, 105.

29. Winthrop, *Military Law and Precedents*, 833–846. Winthrop's test for efficacy was later embodied in the 1949 Geneva Convention principles which mandate that captured soldiers (prisoners of war) are entitled to be prosecuted by the same procedures and courts which prosecute the captor state's soldiers. See, for example, Article 84, Third Geneva Convention (1949). The article states, "A pris-

oner of war shall be tried only by a military court, unless the existing laws of the Detaining Power expressly permit the civil courts to try a member of the armed forces of the Detaining Power in respect of the particular offence alleged to have been committed by the prisoner of war."

30. Winthrop, *Military Law and Precedents*, 829–831.

31. William F. Fratcher, "History of the Judge Advocate General's Corps," *United States Army, Military Law Review* 4 (1959), 95–97. See also Pope, *The Military Memoirs of General John Pope*, 190; and Dunn, *A Sketch of the History and Duties of the Judge Advocate General's Department*, 4; also, Ingersoll, *History of the War Department of the United States*, 148.

32. Marvel, *Mr. Lincoln Goes to War*, 12–14; Green and Frachter, "History of the Judge Advocate General's Department," 14; David D. Eicher, *The Longest Night: A Military History of the Civil War* (New York: Simon and Schuster, 2001), 35.

33. John Fullerton, letter to Joseph Holt, April 22, 1862 (PJH, box 34).

34. Hugh Campbell, letter to Joseph Holt, September 26, 1862 (PJH, box 34).

35. "A Letter from Oswego, New York" (PJH, LOC, box 45).

36. Madison Cutts does not appear in the *Army Lawyer*'s history of the judge advocate, nor is he noted in any of the other published histories of the Judge Advocate General's Department. Cutts was court-martialed for looking at a woman undressing in a hotel, found guilty of conduct unbecoming an officer, and sentenced to a dismissal. However, Lincoln reinstated him into the line, and he later earned a Medal of Honor for bravery during the wilderness battles. Interestingly, Cutts was also a Harvard Law–educated attorney prior to the war.

37. Henry Burnett, *Some Incidents in the Trial of President Lincoln's Assassins: The Controversy between President Johnson and Judge Holt, Printed for the Commandery of the State of New York* (New York: D. Appleton and Co., 1891), 1; also, *Records of Living Officers in the United States Army* (Philadelphia: L.R. Hammersly and Co., 1884), 15–16.

38. *The Bench and Bar of Saint Louis, Kansas City, Jefferson City, and Other Missouri Cities* (St. Louis: American Biographical, 1884), 90; also, *Directory of the Living Graduates of Yale University* (New Haven: Yale University Press, 1908), 1.

39. George Hastings, letter to Lillie Devereux Blake, July 30, 1863 (MHS). Butler's request for Winthrop to be assigned to his command occurred both in late 1863 and on March 22, 1864. In March 1864, Butler requested both Addison Hosmer and Winthrop. Joseph Holt, letter to Benjamin Butler, March 22, 1864 (NA RG 153.2.1, folder 7).

40. Edwin Stanton, letter to Abraham Lincoln, 1863 (Papers of Edwin Stanton, LOC); William McKee Dunn, *A Sketch of the History and Duties of the Judge Advocate General's Department* (Washington, DC: GPO), 1877), 5; Shelby Foote, *The Civil War: A Narrative; Fredericksburg to Meridian* (New York: Random House, 1958), 631.

41. Stanton, letter to Abraham Lincoln, 1863.

42. Edwin Stanton, letter to Major Levi C. Turner, September 8, 1862 (PES, LOC).

43. Major Turner investigated a Major John Key who stated to Turner after Antietam that the reason McClellan did not "bag the rebel army," was "that is not the game. The object is that we should tire the rebels out and ourselves; that was the

only way the Union could be preserved, we come together fraternally and slavery be saved." See, for example, Arthur Brooks Lapsley, ed., *The Writings of Abraham Lincoln* (New York: Lamb Publishing, 1906), 148–149.

44. William Winthrop, letter to Stanton, June 26, 1865 (NA RG 153.2.1, folder 14). For the the increase of desertion and "bounty jumpers," see Ella Lonn, *Desertion during the Civil War* (Lincoln: University of Nebraska Press, 1998), 140–141. For the service of "colored" troops and their strong contribution to the war effort, see, for example, Dudley T. Cornish, *The Sable Arm: Black Troops in the Union Army, 1861–1865* (Lawrence: University Press of Kansas, 1987), 261–291.

45. Robert I. Alotta, "Military Executions in the Union Army: 1861–1866" (Ph.D. diss., Temple University, 1984).

46. Joseph Holt, *Report of the Judge Advocate General on the Order of American Knights, Alias, "The Sons of Liberty," a Western Conspiracy in the Aid of the Southern Rebellion* (Washington, DC: Daily Chronicle Printing, 1864); also Hastings, letter to Lillie Devereux Blake, July 30, 1863.

47. Jennifer Weber, *Copperheads: The Rise and Fall of Lincoln's Opposition Opponents in the North* (Oxford: Oxford University Press, 2006), 6–7; also, Foote, *The Civil War, a Narrative: Fredericksburg to Meridian*, 631–632.

48. James McPherson, *Battle Cry of Freedom: The Civil War Era* (New York: Oxford University Press, 1988), 591–598; Weber, *Copperheads*, 94–100.

49. Weber, *Copperheads*, 10–12.

50. Winthrop, *Military Law and Precedents*, 238; Foote, *The Civil War, a Narrative: Fredericksburg to Meridian*, 633.

51. Winthrop, *Military Law and Precedents*, 836; Foote, *The Civil War, a Narrative: Fredericksburg to Meridian*, 633.

52. Winthrop, *Military Law and Precedents*, 840–846.

53. McPherson, *Battle Cry of Freedom*, 598.

54. Dunn, *A Sketch of the History and Duties of the Judge Advocate General's Department*, 6; Frachter, "History of the Judge Advocate General's Corps," 97.

55. Ingersoll, *History of the War Department of the United States*, 147; Lieutenant Colonel J. W. Clous, "The Judge Advocate General's Department," in *The Army of the United States, Historical Sketches of Staff and Line with Portraits of Generals in Chief*, 34 (New York: Maynard, Merrill, 1896). Clous was a judge advocate who rose to the position of judge advocate general in the early twentieth century. See also Dunn, *A Sketch of the History and Duties of the Judge Advocate General's Department*, 5; and George S. Prugh, "Colonel William Winthrop: The Tradition of the Military Lawyer," *American Bar Association Journal* 42, no. 2 (May 1956), 127.

56. Dunn, *A Sketch of the History and Duties of the Judge Advocate General's Department*, 5.

57. Prugh, "Colonel William Winthrop," 127.

58. Theodore Weston was William's brother-in-law through his marriage to Elizabeth.

59. William Winthrop, letter to Theodore Weston, June 30, 1864 (YALE).

60. Winthrop, letter to Theodore Weston, June 30, 1864.

61. For Norman Lieber's initial commission and appointment into the Judge Advocate's Department, see letter from Charles Sumner to Francis Lieber, dated June 1861, in *The Selected Letters of Charles Sumner*, vol. 2, ed. Beverly P. Wilson

(Boston: Northeastern University, 1990), 71. Sumner wrote to Francis Lieber after securing for Norman Lieber a commission, "I hoped that you would read the official list of appointments containing the name of your son. Give him my benediction." For Ralston Skinner's appointment and family ties, see Albert B. Hart, "Salmon Chase," in *American Statesmen*, ed. John T. Morse, 24 (Boston: Houghton Mifflin, 1899). Chase served as a judge advocate between 1862 and March 1865; also see Winthrop, letter to Theodore Weston, June 30, 1864.

62. Winthrop, letter to Theodore Weston, June 30, 1864.

63. Petition recommending W. McKee Dunn, July 1, 1864 (William McKee Dunn File LOC).

64. William Wesley Woolen, *William McKee Dunn, Brigadier General U.S.A., a Memoir: With Extracts from His Speeches, Decisions, and Correspondence* (New York: Knickerbocker Press, 1888), 25–26; *Biographical History of the American Congress: 1774–1996* (Alexandria, VA: CQ Staff Directories, 1996), 971.

65. William Alfred Millis, *History of Hanover College: From 1827 to 1927* (Hanover, IN: Hanover College, 1927), 203; A. Y. Moore, *History of Hanover College* (Indianapolis: Hollenbeck Press, 1900), 50–51.

66. Woolen, *William McKee Dunn*, 28; Millis, *History of Hanover* College, 58–59.

67. Woolen, *William McKee Dunn*, 74–75.

68. See Woolen, *William McKee Dunn*, 56; *Biographical History of the American Congress*, 971.

69. Woolen, *William McKee Dunn*, 58.

70. National Park Service Pamphlet, *Appomattox* (2000), 1; Woolen, *William McKee Dunn*, 135.

71. Woolen, *William McKee Dunn*, 60–61.

72. *Biographical History of the American Congress*, 971.

73. OR, ser. 2, vol. 8, p. 638. Winthrop advised the secretary of war, "In cases of this character of homicide of one rebel prisoner by another at one of our prison camps this Bureau has expressed and still adheres to the opinion that such crime is not one that can properly be taken cognizance of by a U.S. military court. If the local criminal tribunal should desire to pass upon this or any other criminal case, the post commandant would properly respond to a formal request to that effect placing the accused party in the hands of the civil authorities for trial."

74. Opinion of Major Winthrop, May 1864 (PJH).

75. Case of John J. Glover, June 6, 1864 (PJH).

76. William T. Sherman, *Memoirs*, reprint ed. (New York: Library of America, 1990), 866; Benjamin P. Thomas and Harold Hyman, *Stanton: The Life and Times of Lincoln's Secretary of War* (New York: Alfred Knopf, 1962), 406–410; John F. Marszalek, *Sherman: A Soldier's Passion for Order* (New York: Vintage Civil War Library, 1994), 341–350. In Sherman's memoirs, he admitted he intentionally declined Stanton's hand when the secretary offered it during the army's march through the capital.

77. Winthrop, *Military Law and Precedents*, 401.

78. See 39th Congress, 1st Session, House of Representatives, Executive Document No. 14, *The Honorable Benjamin G. Harris; Letter from the secretary of war in Answer to Resolution of the House of Representatives of December 20, transmitting Records and Testimony of the Court-Martial in the Trial of the Hon B.G. Harris* (Washington,

DC: Government Printing Office, 1865) (hereafter Exec. Doc. 14). This document was prepared by the Bureau of Military Justice and it appears to be the only surviving complete record of the transcript of trial.

79. Joseph Holt, letter to William Winthrop, April 29, 1865 (NA RG 153.2.1 Folder 11).

80. Exec. Doc. 14, p. 17.

81. Exec. Doc. 14, p. 22.

82. Exec. Doc. 14, pp. 30–34.

83. Exec. Doc. 14, p. 35.

84. Exec. Doc. 14, p. 37. In *Rex v. Martin* (1 Russell and Ryland 196), it was held that in certain circumstances, "fraud does not vitiate consent."

85. Exec. Doc. 14, p. 32–34.

86. Exec. Doc. 14, pp. 47–48.

87. General Court Martial Order (GCMO 260), dated, June 1, 1865; also J. Thomas Scharf, *A History of Maryland from the Earliest Period to the Present Day*, vol. 3 (Baltimore: John B. Piet, 1879), 658–659; Robert A. Campbell, *The Rebellion Register* (Kalamazo, MI: R.A. Campbell, 1866), 157; William Winthrop, *Military Law* 1 (Washington, DC: W.H. Morrison, 1886), 401. Harris had been censured by the House of Representatives on April 9, 1864, for stating in his defense of another congressman, "The South asked you to let them live in peace. But no; you said you would bring them into subjugagtion. That is not done yet; and God almighty grant that it never may be. I hope that you will never subjugate the south." *Journal of the House of Representatives, The Congressional Globe*, 37th Cong., 2nd Sess., April 9, 1864, 506.

88. Benjamin G. Harris, "The Rights of the States," June 14, 1866, reprinted in Harris Papers (MDHS) and Congressional Globe Office, June 14, 1866.

89. Diary of Elizabeth Harris; dated entries as noted (MDHS).

90. Joseph Holt, letter to Edwin Stanton, May 13, 1865 (NA RG 153.2.1 Folder 11).

91. Benjamin G. Harris, letter to General Bradley J. Johnson, June 4, 1893 (MDHS).

92. *Philadelphia Inquirer*, May 8, 1865; *Philadelphia Inquirer*, May 9, 1865.

93. *Baltimore Sun*, May 19, 1865; *Baltimore Sun*, May 20, 1865.

94. Winthrop, *Military Law* 1, 401.

95. Winthrop, *Military Law and Precedents*, 633.

96. Winthrop, *Military Law and Precedents*, 631.

97. George B. Davis, *A Treatise on the Military Law of the Untied States, Together with the Practice and Procedure of Courts-Martial and Other Military Tribunals* (New York: John Wiley and Sons, 1915), 131.

9

Professionalizing a "Constitutional Army" in a Time of Uncertainty: 1865–1895

An excellent digest of these opinions was prepared by major W. Winthrop of the United States Army, in 1868, and published by the authority of the Secretary of War.

—Supreme Court Justice Stephen J. Field

William Winthrop decided to remain on active duty after the Civil War, but like most officers he likely had only a partial idea as to what the army's postwar role entailed, or his place in that institution. In fact, the army had four roles in the thirty years of Winthrop's remaining service, and only one of these was the conventional function of defending the United States against a foreign enemy. This conventional function appeared to the government as the least important of the four, and the general public considered it the least likely to occur. The other three functions involved Reconstruction, the suppression of labor and social unrest when police forces and militia proved unequal to the task, and the enforcement of treaties with Indian tribes. The Civil War legacy cast a wide influence over Army operations in each of these areas to the point that more than one officer questioned the nature of civilian control over the military. Others, such as Winthrop, sought to maintain a constitutional army. That is, they believed that the army best served the United States when it existed completely as a reflection of the constitutional constraints which governed it.

It was during this time of postwar uncertainty when Winthrop first researched and then, in 1886, published his influential treatise *Military Law.* Although there were a number of reasons Winthrop embarked on his research, there were two underlying causes for it. He sought to reinforce the army's constitutional place while it professionalized, and he also wanted to modernize (and at the same time defend) the criminal law component of military law. His other major literary contribution occurred over a decade prior to publishing *Military Law*, but it was not a publication in which his name would be carried on a title page. In 1873 he penned the first draft of a new set of Articles of War for General Holt to forward to the secretary of war, and then to President Grant.[1]

The legislated 1874 Articles of War differed little from Winthrop's draft. Congress enacted the Articles of War the following year, and these remained in effect until 1916. However, the 1874 articles were not substantially modified until 1920. As a result, Winthrop's work on the 1874 articles impacted the army through World War I. The 1874 articles were not a radical departure from their predecessor, the 1806 articles, but a new series of articles was necessary as legislation and the experience of the Civil War and Reconstruction had significantly altered the practice of military law since 1806 in the sense that it affected a larger part of the population than at any time prior to 1942 (and arguably more than in World War II). For reasons discussed later in this chapter, Winthrop's success in drafting the 1874 articles, and the army's benefit from the new articles, is that the new laws were not affected in any great detail by foreign, particularly Prussian, influences.

However, it was in the publication of *Military Law* that Winthrop made his most significant contribution to the army prior to 1895. In the two decades after Appomattox, he saw a significant need for army modernization through reforms in military law, as well as providing education to the army's leadership. At the same time, Winthrop sought to professionalize the army without changing its constitutional nature. In sum, although he believed the "constitutional army" was sacrosanct, it could evolve to rival any other force in the world. He also saw a need for professionalizing the Judge Advocate General's Department. His views on the necessity for professionalizing the army as a whole came from a number of sources including the inconsistency in courts-martial adjudication, his perception of a professionalism deficit in some of his judge advocate peers, his experiences in the military prosecution of civilians, and his view that the rise of a "Prussian" school of military thought in the officer ranks necessitated a moderating influence.

This last influence—the rise of a Prussian school—was fostered, though not necessarily led, by General William Sherman. While Winthrop admired much in Sherman, there were many points of Sherman's conduct and views on law that Winthrop quietly took exception to and addressed in his scholarship. Winthrop's impact and contribution to professionalizing the army occurred in two distinct, but related areas: the military law governing the army and the practice of military law in the army. This chapter describes the first area.

That the army's conventional role against a foreign power was seen as unnecessary by many in government is unsurprising. Prior to the 1890s, the closest the United States came to war with a foreign country was against France. As of 1865, thirty-five thousand French soldiers were in Mexico propping up Napoleon III's puppet government.[2]

There were political pressures in the United States pushing for military intervention in Mexico. Some of these pressures came from within the military establishment. In May 1865, the influential *Army-Navy Journal* headlined, "Maximilian's presence in Mexico is a menace and prospective danger."[3] The Monroe Doctrine remained the central feature of United States foreign policy, and Republicans and Democrats alike believed the French invasion an opportunistic act, occurring during the height of the Civil War when the United States could not oppose the French maneuver. However, an internal anti-monarchal insurgency ended French control over Mexico before American military intervention was felt necessary. The demise of Maximilian and erosion of French control in Mexico may have accelerated because of the actions of the United States government. At the very end of the Civil War, President Johnson sent a sizeable force under the command of General Philip Sheridan to the Texas-Mexican border. This force did not cross into Mexico, and it never came into contact with the French Army, but its presence had an effect.[4]

The army's demonstration on the Mexican border did, however, catch Napoleon III by surprise. He clearly did not contemplate the possibility of a war against the United States. Once confronted with this prospect, he sought a diplomatic exit from Mexico. The United States Navy could have easily sealed off eastern Mexico to the French, and without reinforcements, Sheridan's forces would have annihilated the thirty-five thousand French soldiers. At any rate, in 1865, French Army reinforcements would have likely faced complete destruction in North America. But this is all conjecture. In addition to Sheridan's border demonstration, the United States supplied opposition Mexican forces with surplus arms. In 1866, the French Army evacuated Mexico and the following year, Maximilian was deposed, tried by a military court, and executed by a newly restored Mexican government.[5]

Winthrop viewed the fate of Maximilian as a matter of justice, and it is likely most of his judge advocate contemporaries believed similarly. He opined that the international law norm of "retaliation," served as the lawful basis for Maximilian's trial and sentence. Maximilian had decreed "all Juarists were to be treated as bandits." In other words, Maximilian declared Mexican nationals fighting against the French-backed puppet government were not entitled to prisoner of war status. Thus, according to Winthrop, on capture, Maximilian could be treated in kind. This is not to state that Winthrop believed retaliation "in kind" was always permissible. To the contrary, he argued any resort to "means of measures repudiated by civilized warfare," were impermissible derogations of law.[6]

Aside from the possibility of a war in Mexico, the army existed in large measure as a constabulary force. War with a European state was remote, and the interests of Japan and the United States had yet to collide. Foreign policy remained, at its core, one of isolationism except in the arena of trade. The Monroe Doctrine was one exception to this isolation, and it eventually placed the United States and Spain on a collision course. But this collision did not occur until the eve of the twentieth century. This is not to suggest the army was less than gainfully employed. To the contrary, it policed the South, it fought Indians, and it also fired weapons at citizens and residents. But its continued existence fell into doubt on more than one occasion. It faced hostility from Southern politicians and Northern machine Democrats.[7]

Part of the army's difficulties rested with its civilian leadership. Twelve men served as secretary of war between 1866 and 1891. Most of these men were appointed as part of the spoils system and did not express an enormous interest in the welfare or effectiveness of the army. Only three of the secretaries had prior military experience. One of the men appointed by Ulysses Grant, William W. Belknap, was impeached for corruption directly related to army contracts. In 1878, Secretary George W. McCrary, while giving a speech, stated the most pressing issues facing the nation were fair and open elections in the South, labor strife, and "stable, equal, and honest dollars." He did not mention the role of the army in his speech, even in the context of labor strife which he alluded to. In 1890, Secretary of War Redfield Proctor declared that a war with a European enemy was unlikely.[8]

On some level, the army's morale suffered because its unconventional missions were often contrary to the beliefs of its own soldiers. Its morale and efficiency were also reduced by the soldiers' perception—and quite often the reality—of a faulty system of military justice. Yet, societal neglect of the army was also a root cause of diminished morale precisely because the needs of its soldiers were seldom addressed. The army's infantry weaponry remained inferior in quality to modern European armies, and on occasion its arms were inferior even in comparison to its Indian opponents. The U.S. Army lagged behind Prussia and France in artillery as well. The quality of post life, medical care, and sustenance varied from posting to posting, but as in the case of its weaponry, the quality tended to be poor.[9]

William A. Ganoe, one of the first historians to study the post–Civil War army, labeled the postwar period, the "dark ages of the army."[10] Ganoe posited that in the years between Appomattox and the establishment of the School of Application for Cavalry and Infantry at Fort Leavenworth in 1881, the army's officer corps suffered a dearth of professionalism. To Ganoe, the army as a whole was hardly reliable in contrast to the Army of the Potomac in 1865 or its European counterparts. The overarching feature of these so-called dark ages was the military's isolation from society and its neglect by the government. But it was also during this time when the seeds of a modern professional army were first planted. Ganoe argued these dark ages gave way to an era of modernization, when officers internally professionalized the army beginning in the mid-1870s, though he also acknowledged that the effects of the internal professionalization were not felt until early in the twentieth century.[11]

Ganoe's thesis remains largely accepted by most American military historians, though a number have expanded on it. Notably, Samuel P. Huntington, in his classic *The Soldier and the State: The Theory and Politics of Civil-Military Relations,* concluded that the army's organizational successes in 1917 and 1942 were rooted in its isolation from society in the years 1865 to 1899. That is, without intrusive bureaucratic interference, the army was able to model its organizational structure and culture as its leaders thought best.[12]

Huntington and Ganoe theorized that the army's internal professionalizing occurred much in the same way other American occupations such as law, medicine, accounting, and engineering professionalized. These occupations internally addressed the needs of quality standards and proof of expertise in an age mostly devoid of government regulation. Like law, medicine, accounting, and engineering, the military profession erected midlevel schools, created peer-reviewed journals, and shared occupational information from within. This also occurred in part through clubs and societies. Moreover, the industrial equivalent of midlevel managers, the military's company-grade officers, analyzed the militaries of other nations, especially—for reasons discussed in this chapter—Germany. A select few of them then published their observations and analysis for their peers to study. This is not to state that military men and industrialists worked in close association, because the two groups did not. Nor did the professionalizing of the army occur across a broad spectrum of individual officers. Indeed, there is a historic consensus that while Sherman sparked an interest in military modernization, the professionalizing occurred at the hands of a small number of mostly junior officers.[13]

This consensus has merit. General Sherman encouraged officers to publish military literature in the new professional journals. These journals included the *Journal of the Military Service Institution of the United States* (1878), the *United Service Journal* (1878), the *Cavalry Journal* (1888), and the *Journal of the United States Artillery* (1892).[14] Another shift toward professionalism occurred with the establishment of professional schools, beginning with the cavalry and infantry school at Fort Leavenworth, but also including the artillery school at Fort Monroe. The artillery school was actually established prior to the Civil War, but it had fallen into disuse and its prior role was oriented solely toward improving artillery tactics. By 1900, most career officers had attended a professional school for their line duties. Winthrop influenced authorship in these journals, and his own work was taught in the service schools.

One area devoid of historic analysis is how the Judge Advocate General's Department contributed to the professionalization of the army during this period. The small numbers of judge advocates serving in this period weighed against the department mimicking the line by establishing its own school, professional journal, and a supporting professional society. However, behind the volumes of military publications and development of professional schools of the line were a number of judge advocates contributing to the professionalizing process.

While Winthrop was the foremost judge advocate in contributing to professionalizing the officer corps, he was not alone. Others such as William Dunn, Norman Lieber, John W. Clous, Asa Bird Gardner, and George Davis authored articles in professional journals advocating the importance of the judge advocate to the military. They also provided legal education and perspective on the means by which to maintain a capable army. Moreover, these judge advocates also assisted the line and other staffs in their respective professionalizing processes. For instance, Lieber and Gardner coauthored a history of the adjutant general with General James Fry.[15]

To fully gauge Winthrop's contributions to army modernization, an understanding of the army's "state of being" during the years 1865 to 1895 is essential. It is not enough to state, however accurate, that Winthrop's *Military Law, Military Law and Precedents*, and his earlier *Digest of Opinions* were taught as standard texts at the intermediate service schools, and as a result two generations of officers attended lectures and finished assignments where his writing was utilized. However factual this last statement is, it does not begin to show the part Winthrop played in forming the modern military and how he reinforced its constitutional place through a scholarly process.

When the Civil War ended, the nation found itself with an armed force far larger than the founding fathers imagined. The American liberal tendency of aversion to standing armies remained a salient political feature. As a result, Congress sought a vast reduction in the army's size. In June 1865, the army numbered over one million soldiers. By January 1866, the army had mustered out 800,936 soldiers. In November

1865, roughly 19,000 United States soldiers occupied the South. In 1866, Congress legislatively reduced the size of the regular army to forty-five infantry regiments, ten cavalry regiments, and five artillery regiments. By the end of that year, owing to requirements on the frontier, Congress added four cavalry regiments, but it reduced the army to a total ceiling of 54,000 men.[16] In 1867, the army's numbers reached 56,815, but this was its peak number for decades. In 1869, Congress lowered the army's numbers to 37,313. Five years later, Congress further reduced the army to 25,000 men. These numbers were problematic; the army's functions in national defense, Indian warfare, and internal stability required far more than 25,000 men.[17]

Many in Congress remained wedded to the idea that the militia system, which had served the Union in the Civil War, remained capable of expanding the army to confront external threats. Several congressmen who achieved high rank through this system, such as John Logan and Benjamin Butler, were particularly loyal to it. Moreover, as the likelihood of a foreign invasion was very low, there existed no "clarion call" for expansion. And yet the seeds of imperial expansion had begun to grow after 1865. The industrial revolution steadily increased American interests overseas. Some military men recognized this prior to 1897, but most politicians did not acknowledge a relationship between international economics and interests. Moreover, a continued adherence to the Monroe Doctrine meant the United States had to at least maintain a sufficient armed force capable of keeping European armies out of the Caribbean. Though this was primarily a naval issue, it did have implications for the army and militia.

Despite its isolation from society, the army was to some extent a demographic mirror of the nation as a whole. The nation entered into a new era of mass immigration, industrialization, and internal unrest. Its political leaders increasingly found their ideologies primarily centered on the limited role of government in promoting economic growth. This postwar period, often referred to as the "Gilded Age," was characterized by unparalleled demographic and economic changes in which most of the elected political leaders and their appointed jurists felt the best approach was that of laissez-faire, or "hands off." Government regulation of wages and working conditions was mostly nonexistent, and its oversight of immigration loose. It was also perhaps the most politically corrupt period in American history, and while Grant's appointment of Belknap evidenced that corruption crept into the War Department, his activities were not the only evidence of corruption.[18]

This so-called Gilded Age was a time of the economic monopoly in the industrial North and the railroad trusts of the Midwest and West. Unregulated gold and currency speculation contributed to economic instability as well. Rapid industrialization and the rise of the city contributed to unstable social conditions. So too did a dramatic increase in immigration. Not only were the numbers of immigrants unparalleled in American history, the majority of immigrants came from nontraditional locations: Eastern, Southern, and Central Europe, and China. The peoples from these regions did not speak English as a native tongue, nor did the majority of them immediately embrace traditional American religious and social culture. This latter point had an impact on army recruiting. A number of soldiers did not speak English fluently, and at times, up to 50 percent of the enlisted forces were immigrants. On occasion, reliance on foreign soldiers proved detrimental to the efficiency and even survival of whole units. During the 1876 campaign against the Sioux Indians, Custer relied on a messenger who spoke primarily Italian.[19]

Adding to the public disinterest in the army was a belief among some of the laissez-faire adherents that war had become a historic relic as corporation interests interlocked the interests of all modern countries. Late nineteenth-century proponents of this idea included the eminent political scientists John Fiske and William Graham Sumner in the United States, and their British counterpart, Herbert Spencer.

Spencer had another argument against states resorting to war. He professed that armed conflicts deprived modern states of their full pool of young men, thereby reducing the numbers of the "superior civilized races." To Spencer's adherents, war caused a diminution in the populations of civilized races to the benefit of the weaker and less advanced peoples. It was a eugenics-based argument against war, and it had some popularity in the United States. Interestingly, these same men professed a creed of "Social Darwinism" and saw the need for the government to maintain an indigenous police force capable of suppressing insurrection against free markets. In the United States, Social Darwinism did not always translate into imperialism, but there were enough shared beliefs between Social Darwinists and pro-expansionists to establish intellectual links between the two groups.[20] What these men and their receptive audiences failed to grasp was the relationship between laissez-faire policies, declining social conditions of the industrial working classes, mass immigration, and the rise of political movements such as labor anarchy and communism. They also failed to understand that economic expansion created international tensions that could lead to war.

As a result of its laissez-faire approach, Congress in the Gilded Age rarely concerned itself with the state of the country's armed forces. There were notable exceptions such as the Endecott Board in 1885, which reviewed the state of coastal defenses against attack, as well as one effort by Congress to reorganize the army in a joint committee led by Senator

Ambrose Burnside. Congress also, from time to time, had an interest in Indian affairs. But for the most part Congress expressed its disinterest in the army by ignoring the institution to the point that between 1865 and 1893, soldiers did not receive a single pay raise.[21] This had significant repercussions on the army's reliability.

In tandem with the army's reduction in numbers came a reduction in the ranks of its officers. During the Civil War, it was not uncommon for a captain to be brevetted to the rank of colonel. Brevet ranks were by their nature temporary. At the conclusion of hostilities, officers holding a brevet rank were reduced to their permanent rank. (The Judge Advocate General's Department was no different. Winthrop had been brevetted colonel and by 1867 was reduced to the rank of major.) Consequently, it was not uncommon to see a brigadier general reduced to major or even captain. Moreover, the source of an individual's commission had a direct bearing on whether the officer could remain on active duty and at what grade. The ability to successfully remain on active duty at a higher grade heavily favored United States Military Academy graduates. Civil War volunteers had to apply to remain on active duty. As the regular army shrunk, the opportunity to command a regiment shrunk with it. Regimental command was almost a prerequisite for promotion into the general officer ranks. Assignments to command regiments occurred partly for political reasons and partly on the basis of seniority. Political influence was often tenuous because old antagonisms between senior officers dating to the Civil War remained and were augmented by new ones.[22]

Fitz-John Porter's case continued to interest a number of general officers and colonels (as well as congressmen) who felt Pope and McDowell lied to justify their poor performance at Second Manassas. Likewise, Pope and McDowell sought to preserve the findings of the original court, and any officer expressing support for Porter was unlikely to fare well under their respective commands.[23] A biographer of General Sheridan once pointed out that General Joseph Hooker despised every other general officer in the postwar army. It is quite likely this feeling was reciprocated. General Halleck was disliked and distrusted by many of his contemporaries, though they must have appreciated his intellect. Other officers must have felt disbelief that McDowell could remain a commissioned general officer after his repeated bungling. General Thomas and General Schofield, two very successful and astute commanders, had difficulty in getting along with each other. Their disputes were fueled by supporters who wrote editorials and gave speeches deriding the commands of each other's champion. These antagonisms were only a fraction of the existing infighting between general officers, and in many cases the generals themselves vocally denounced their peers. The behaviors of the generals must have influenced the conduct of mid- and junior-grade officers as well. The officer ranks in the decade after the Civil War were hardly characterized by an esprit de corps the profession of arms usually embodies.[24]

The antagonisms did not go away for a number of years. In 1884, the army's commanders were many of the same commanders serving since the end of the Civil War. Thomas, Meade, and Halleck were dead by this time, and McDowell had retired, but only Pope immediately benefited in rank advancement as a result. General William Sherman remained the commanding general, and Philip Sheridan had been promoted to the permanent grade of lieutenant general. But Sheridan would be the last general to hold this rank until the American entry into World War I in 1917. Behind Sheridan were three major generals: Winfield S. Hancock, John Pope, and John Schofield. There were also five brigadier generals, all distinguished Civil War veterans. This number included O. O. Howard, Alfred Terry, Christopher Augur, Nelson A. Miles, and Ranald MacKenzie.[25] In order to advance beyond the rank of colonel, one of these men had to retire or die. And it was not until 1882 where Congress set a mandatory retirement age at sixty-four years of age.[26]

At times advancement from brigadier general to major general caused dissension in the army. When this occurred, the affected generals often turned to their judge advocates to champion their personal cause. For instance, when General Hancock died in 1886, disagreement between O. O. Howard and Alfred Terry ensued as to who had seniority. The argument may have had its genesis as early as 1875.

Major Thomas Barr, then serving under General Terry in St. Paul, wrote to General Joseph Holt, "General Terry has submitted to me, as a personal matter of concern the question of what his real rank is in the grade of brigadier general. After consideration of the facts and the law bearing upon them, I have become convinced that, instead of ranking below General Howard, his real status is next above that officer."[27] Barr's reasoning was that while Howard was brevetted to the rank of brigadier general before Terry, Terry's actual regular promotion to brigadier general predated Howard's. Ten years after Barr's letter was written, both generals believed they were entitled to promotion to major general based on their seniority. This issue brings to light the relationship between individual judge advocates and commanders. Through a number of correspondences between judge advocates and General Holt, it became apparent some of the commanders had their favorite judge advocates: Sheridan took a liking to Lieber; Schofield to Winthrop; McDowell to Gardner; Grant to Holt; and so on.

But even promotion to the rank of colonel was problematic. Promotion through the rank of captain was internal to specific regiments so that it was not uncommon for a lieutenant to remain in that rank for over a decade. According to historian Robert M. Utley, it took a lieutenant an average of twenty-four to twenty-six years to make major, and over thirty to make colonel. As one indicator of the age of the army's officers in 1895, of the 2,100 officers on active duty, 279 were Civil War veterans. It was not until 1890 that the promotion system switched to being based on seniority within each combat arm, rather than by regiment. As an example of the lack of progress, Emory Upton, one of the military's leading minds, was brevetted major general in March 1865. Within a year, he was reduced to lieutenant colonel and remained in that rank until 1880. Neither his scholarship nor importance to stimulating the military's evolution into a modern force brought him promotion. Only time accomplished this.[28]

The system of commissioning officers did not guarantee the best candidates, but in the postwar years, the Department of War did try to provide some diversity of background to the officer corps. Roughly half of the regular officers obtained their commission by successfully graduating from the service academy. Some officers who were commissioned from civilian life during the Civil War were permitted to retain their commissions, though often they were reduced to the company grades. There were some exceptions such as Colonel Nelson Miles, who enlisted as a private during the Civil War and rose to the brevetted rank of general, only to be reduced to lieutenant colonel, and William R. Shafter, who enlisted during the war, rose to the brevetted rank of brigadier general, stayed in the army after the war, and was reduced to major. In 1897, Shafter was once more a general officer, this time in command of all forces in the Cuban invasion during the Spanish-American War.[29]

After 1865, some enlisted men were commissioned from the ranks after successfully passing a field examination. There were a number of foreign-born officers who obtained direct commissions as well, though by the 1880s their numbers dwindled. Most, if not all, of the foreign-born officers previously served in a Continental European army. However, there is little evidence this brought the army any benefit in the development of professionalism. It may have been the case that the bottom-rung officers of the German, French, and Austrian armies became the bottom rung of the United States Army.[30]

At times, officers reverted to the Civil War practice of substituting the Articles of War for dueling. Frequent allegations of cowardice and misconduct resulted in unwarranted courts-martial. When, according to Schofield's most recent biographer, Schofield recommended Fitz-John Porter's conviction be reversed, Pope exacted personal revenge by prosecuting Schofield's younger brother in a baseless court-martial. The younger Schofield was acquitted and continued on in his career, but the episode evidenced the need for reform in both officer training and the court-martial process. Robert Utley's statement, "As officers aged without advancement, their initiative, energy, and impulse for self-improvement diminished . . . they bickered incessantly over petty issues," was certainly true of many officers in the post–Civil War army. His observation that "these officers preferred court-martial charges on the slightest provocation and consequently had to spend a preposterous share of their time on court-martial duty," is equally correct. Winthrop understood these cultural impediments to professionalism, and—though analyzed in greater detail in the following chapter—sought to reform the court-martial process as early as 1865. For instance, in reviewing a court-martial, he conveyed to Stanton that too many junior officers sought advancement by preferring courts-martial charges against their superiors.[31]

The changing organization of the army also had an impact on its efficiency and morale. When the Civil War ended, the army was divided into five territorial divisions overseeing nineteen departments. The five territorial divisions consisted of the Atlantic, commanded by Major General Meade; the Mississippi, commanded by Lieutenant General Sherman; the Gulf, commanded by Major General Philip Sheridan; the Tennessee, commanded by Major General Thomas; and the Pacific, commanded by Major General Halleck. These divisions and their departments were purely territorial in nature, and the roles of the army differed in each according to the character of the territory. For instance, the Division of the Mississippi encompassed the Departments of the Ohio, the Missouri, and the Arkansas. The army's primary role in this division was the enforcement of the government's Indian policy. The Division of the Gulf, the Division of the Tennessee, and the Division of the Atlantic each contained departments wherein the army's primary role was to support Reconstruction programs, though the Gulf Division had Indian enforcement missions as well.

In 1879, the army was reorganized into three territorial divisions: the Atlantic, the Pacific, and the Missouri. In turn, these three divisions were further subdivided into eight departments and eleven districts.[32] The effect of these changes on the Judge Advocate General's Department was nominal, except in regard to its manning. Fewer geographic divisions translated into fewer fielded judge advocates. However, the roles and responsibilities of the individual judge advocates remained as before. Judge advocates did not attend most courts-martial, although in the more serious cases there were exceptions. Line officers fulfilled the role of "acting judge advocates" in regimental and garrison courts, while judge advocates reviewed the testimony, evidence, and findings for fairness and regularity. Every year when the judge advocate general filed a report to the secretary of war, a number of acting judge advocates—captains chosen as departmental judge advocates—reported on the number and types of cases tried.

In understanding the evolution of the army out of its dark ages, as well as the development of the Judge Advocate General's Department (and Winthrop's contributions to both the Judge Advocate General's Department and the army), it is worthwhile to review, albeit briefly, the three unconventional missions independently, beginning with Reconstruction—since it was a salient feature of the Johnson and Grant administrations—and then turn to Indian policy and domestic policing. The most conventional function, the defense of the nation against foreign enemies, requires treatment as well, and it is in that context where the influence of Prussia is analyzed for its effects on not only the line of the army but also the Judge Advocate General's Department. Judge advocates played a role in each of these functions, and until 1876, the Bureau of Military Justice remained at the center of advising commanders on the laws and regulations involved in each function. Moreover, in terms of Reconstruction, the Constitution was uniquely at the center of the army's operations in a manner never paralleled.

By the time Winthrop published *Military Law,* Reconstruction had run its course so that the treatise had nominal value to army operations in the South. It may be for this reason that he did not cover the army's role in Reconstruction in great detail until 1895. In *Military Law and Precedents,* Winthrop argued that the lessons of Reconstruction, and much of the legal framework developed during its course, was important for future military operations. He felt that a new Civil War was a remote possibility though not one necessarily based on sectionalism. Like many army officers, he believed that communism presented a potential peril. And by 1895, he was convinced that the military would be called on, from time to time, to police civilians during insurrection. Thus he wrote, "To complete the general subject under consideration [jurisdiction over civilians], it will be proper to give some account of the military government administered during the Reconstruction period of 1867–1870." Additionally, Winthrop would, in the last year of his life, argue that much of the legal guidance on the Reconstruction program contained in *Military Law and Precedents* was applicable to the army administration of the Philippines and Cuba.[33]

In a generic sense, the aim of Reconstruction was to restore the Southern states into the Union while cementing civil rights laws into place. However, there were multiple views even within the Republican Party as to the status of former Confederates or newly freed slaves. Just as many antislavery adherents had stressed that they did not advocate racial equality, a number of prominent Republicans and certainly pro-Union Democrats did not support racial equality laws. (It does appear, though, through more than anecdotal evidence that Winthrop supported colorblind laws and later opposed the segregationist "Black Codes.") White

Southern politicians and former Confederate officials also raised the specter of the government forcing equality through intermarriage. Individuals such as Winthrop's nemesis, Congressman Harris, argued that "the negro must be kept subordinate to the white man."[34]

The biggest overt Southern threat to Reconstruction's success, notwithstanding a deep substratum of racism, was the formation of the Ku Klux Klan. Founded as a social club in 1866, this organization spread terror by murdering blacks and white Republicans. By the time Grant became president, the Ku Klux Klan had entered into the political and social fabric of every Southern state. At least one-tenth of the black members of state constitutional conventions became victims of the Klan. The Klan murdered three white Republicans in the Georgia legislature. Teachers who educated black children were assaulted. Challenging the Klan's growing power was extremely difficult since it was decentralized without a true organizational structure, and its membership stretched across economic class lines.[35]

In some areas, local federal authorities found it impossible to defeat the Klan, even with the use of militia, so that in 1870, Congress legislated an act specifically targeting the Klan's activities. Known as the Force Act, the new law criminalized conspiracies designed to deny citizens voting rights. The following year, Congressman Benjamin Butler spearheaded the creation of a second law designed to destroy the Ku Klux Klan. Section 3 of the Ku Klux Klan Act authorized the president to employ the army "to suppress insurrection, domestic violence, or combinations." The act empowered the army to protect federal marshals, but it did not create military jurisdiction to try civilians. By the time of the act, the Reconstruction commissions had come to a virtual end so that suspected Klansmen were prosecuted in federal court.[36]

In October 1871, Grant announced that the Klan's lawlessness in South Carolina required military occupation of several counties, and he suspended habeas corpus to citizens arrested by the army. Hundreds of blacks and white Republicans fell victim to assaults and the destruction of their private property. Soldiers under the direction of federal authorities arrested thousands of men, and the government prosecuted several hundred, though mainly in civilian trials. By 1872, the Klan's power had significantly diminished, though the prevalent racism did not and would not for well over a century.[37]

Although Winthrop only briefly touched on the use of the army in suppressing the Klan, he supported Grant's authority to use the army in this manner. Winthrop labeled the Klan "an unlawful combination" and endorsed the use of the army to destroy it. He also found that Grant's action against the Klan "virtually initiated martial law," but constitutionally did so. By analogy, Winthrop was not opposed to the use of the army in very limited circumstances to destroy an organized conspiracy designed to overthrow the government or shred the Constitution.[38]

The primary judicial enforcement mechanism in Reconstruction was the continued use of the military commission. By 1865 the use of military commissions had become so common that many officers assumed these trials would continue indefinitely. There was a widespread belief that military jurisdiction over civilians was essential to protect citizens. For instance, in response to the New Orleans riots, the *Army-Navy Journal* called for military commissions to try the riot's perpetrators and place New Orleans under military jurisdiction.[39] Commissions continued to function in areas under army occupation because commanders felt it necessary to maintain order, and with the emergence of such antiblack groups, there was a belief that Southern white–dominated courts would not conduct trials fairly. However, one difference between the Civil War commissions and those conducted during Reconstruction is that the latter ceased prosecuting law-of-war violations and instead prosecuted offenses under state and local laws.[40]

Winthrop did not endorse the widespread use of commissions in his advice to Stanton and Holt. However, he assisted in the drafting of charges against Lincoln's assassins, and he supported Holt in defending himself against public charges that he knowingly used perjured evidence in the trial of Mary Surratt and the other conspirators. Later, when President Andrew Johnson publicly attempted to dismiss Stanton and denounced Holt, Winthrop aided Holt in defending himself as well. Although these issues, along with Johnson's impeachment, were clearly a political crisis which would determine whether Reconstruction would survive, Winthrop's role was as a quiet, staunch ally to Holt. But he did not depart from his ideological principles in doing so.[41]

As early as June 1865 he advised Holt that a military trial of an individual who exulted on the news of Lincoln's assassination was not proper. Ten days after providing that advice to Holt, Winthrop notified Stanton that "the robbery of a discharged soldier which occurred in Baltimore was not an offence prosecutable under the law of war and must be referred to a civil court." However, he supported commissions trials that occurred under congressional scrutiny and oversight when these occurred on American soil.[42]

Winthrop began his analysis of trials by military commission with a constitutional and statutory overview. As in the case of the Civil War military trials, he separated courts-martial from commissions as a matter of jurisdiction. That is, the jurisdiction of a court-martial prosecuted within the sovereign boundaries of the United States was statutorily restricted "almost exclusively to members of the military force." In overseas theaters of war, Winthrop noted, courts-martial possessed jurisdiction over civilians. He also buttressed his guidance by providing a brief history of the use of military commissions from the Revolutionary War to General Winfield Scott's use of them in Mexico in 1847.[43]

Similar to his review of Civil War military trials over civilians, Winthrop succinctly presented the Reconstruction military trials over civilians as legal in both statute and custom. As in the case of the Civil War trials, he insisted that the procedure and rights afforded in courts-martial be present in commissions as well. He noted that "trials by military commission under the Reconstruction laws were in all not much over two hundred in number."[44] However, Winthrop may have been wrong in this estimation, though he noted that commissions tried under the Reconstruction Laws frequently had multiple defendants. According to historian Mark Neely, a total of 1,435 commissions were adjudicated.[45]

In his presentation on the jurisdiction of commissions, Winthrop supported Attorney General Hoar, who favored the continued use of military trials over civilian trials.[46] The Reconstruction military trials themselves were not so controversial at the time to the point of congressional dissension. Unlike the Vallandigham and Surratt cases, trials conducted under the Reconstruction laws tended to involve common-law offenses rather than law-of-war violations. For instance, in Texas between October 1868 and September 1869 there were fifty-nine cases tried before a military commission resulting in twenty-one convictions and thirty-eight acquittals.[47] Most underlying offenses in these cases were murder and assault. The number of acquittals is important to note, for it shows that commissions could acquit, but it also evidences a military judicial commitment to enforcing the rule of law.

Winthrop's position on the constitutional use of military commissions was not without its critics, even during his own lifetime. One legal scholar accused him of complacency in the face of unconstitutionality and wrote, "Justice will not be evenly administered by any body of men who are dependent on the power which institutes the prosecution and is interested in the result."[48] Winthrop did not respond to this accusation in *Military Law and Precedents*, and there is no surviving account indicating whether he knew of this criticism.

At no point did Winthrop find that the use of commissions was unconstitutional or of questionable morality, though while at the Bureau of Military Justice he pointed out procedural deficiencies in reviewing several records. Nor was he alone in defending military jurisdiction over civilians during Reconstruction. Dr. Francis Lieber favored the continued use of commissions in the South, particularly in cases which relied on African American witnesses, or if the defendant was African American.[49] His son, Major G. Norman Lieber, provided to the Bureau of Military Justice, as well as to his father, his own observations of the need to continue the use of military tribunals. "Most of the local courts are in bad hands whose political views necessarily color their judicial actions," Major Lieber recorded in July 1867. He elaborated on the need to continue military courts writing, "Many of the officers in these courts were in the rebel armies . . . the condition of affairs in the county parishes of Louisiana and Texas where military authority is not suspended is even now far from satisfactory. It is cut-throat."[50]

Nor were Major Lieber and Winthrop the only judge advocates to express the need to continue the use of commissions. Major Thomas Barr, the judge advocate assigned to the Department of the Mississippi, wrote to Holt in June 1869, stating, "Murders in this state are now averaging fully ten a month, incredible as it may appear. There ought to be several military commissions in session here all of the time, with more soldiers to sustain them."[51] By the time Barr was transferred back to the Bureau of Military Justice, he left with an indelible impression of Southern whites: "I hope to leave here Thursday or Friday next with the records and would like to feel assured that I will never meet these people again. The record of their lawlessness is sickening and their falsity is appalling."[52]

Although perhaps odd in the early twenty-first century, judge advocates, and many commanders who received their advice, were convinced that the army was the only institution both capable and willing to provide a fair and open judicial system to the citizenry in the South. In looking at the background of the judge advocates—mainly pro-Republican—their beliefs in the efficacy of the commissions are completely understandable. Their commitment to civil rights and justice for the newly freed slaves was clearly evident. Yet, the instrument in which they sought to guarantee those rights had fundamental constitutional flaws to it; namely, the right to a trial by a jury of one's peers, as well as trial in a court independent of executive suasion. As in the case of the Civil War military trials of civilians, Winthrop advocated the narrow use of commissions, but only when the commissions fundamentally mirrored courts-martial.[53]

There were other arenas outside of the military trials of civilians which Winthrop found important to note in *Military Law and Precedents*. He primarily focused on the responsibility of commanders to ensure that the right to vote was preserved and that commanders maintained the authority to remove civil officers and policemen from office. Even controls over the manufacture of liquor could, in Winthrop's view, fall under the authority of a military commander.[54]

Two decades before the publication of *Military Law and Precedents*, Winthrop's scholarship made an impact on judicially interpreted constitutional limitations to military authority, although in the civil law arena. Judicial review over the establishment of military courts to adjudicate civil law disputes provided a fertile ground for shaping the extent of military authority over civilians, and this continued into the Reconstruction period since many of the determinations during the war did not reach the appellate courts until after the cessation of hostilities. For instance, no Union general was more controversial than Benjamin Butler during his tenure as commander of the Department of the Gulf. That he was despised for a heavy-handed administration over the New Orleans population is well-known. And yet, he neither sought to rule by decree nor permit the establishment of a corrupt civil court system. He found it necessary to replace civil courts with provost courts, granting jurisdiction to these provost courts over tort and contract disputes.[55]

In an 1874 case, *Mechanics and Traders Bank v. Union Bank*, the Supreme Court determined the jurisdictional reach of provost courts. The issue specifically had to do with the repayment of notes in Confederate specie after Union forces seized control of the area. One of Butler's provost courts issued a verdict adverse to a party so that the party suffered a pecuniary loss amounting to over one hundred thousand dollars. The case found its way to the Supreme Court.

The majority found that General Butler had the right to order jurisdiction over civil matters, if he found that the civil courts could not competently exercise their jurisdiction. The court found that normally provost courts only had jurisdiction over minor offenses but there was no constitutional prohibition against expanding the scope to include serious offenses and civil matters. The majority further held that Butler was given this authority both by the president as well as the Louisiana Supreme Court. Justice Field, writing a dissent, opined provost courts were by their nature limited to minor offenses which undermined the peace and order of an area. In writing his dissent, Justice Field noted that he relied on "Major Winthrop's *Digest of Opinions*," calling it "excellent." Utilizing the *Digest*, Field concluded that a military commander did not have the authority to settle civil matters between private parties.[56]

Reconstruction formally ended with the ascension of Rutherford Hayes to the presidency as a result of de facto compromises resulting from a severely contested election. While the program did not instantaneously end, there is a historic consensus that with the reentry of all of the Southern states into the Union, the ability and interest of the Republican Party to ensure the civil rights of blacks diminished. Reconstruction required a long-term commitment from the legislative and executive branches along with a willingness to maintain a large military presence in the South in order to have a chance at success. In the end, Reconstruction failed, not because of military force, but because of the lack of it.[57]

In 1866, the majority of the Indian tribes remaining free from federal authority were seminomadic. However, they were fast becoming hemmed in by white migration. Military historian Robert Utley opined that many of these remaining tribes had a long history of warfare, but because of their decentralized and democratic power structures, treaties were only as reliable as the individuals who entered into them.[58] The corollary to this was the fact that treaties entered into by the government were only as reliable as the government was willing to enforce. The culture of the Plains Indians and the often duplicitous nature of government officers made many treaties meaningless.

It has been estimated that the army fought approximately 950 engagements against Indian tribes and tribal alliances between 1865 and 1898.[59] Most of these were small scale but a few, such as the Fetterman Massacre and Custer's "last stand," had significant repercussions on Indian policy. Between 1870 and 1890, most of the twenty-five thousand active duty soldiers served on the frontier enforcing the government's Indian policy. Enforcement of the government's Indian policy was not relegated to fighting Indians.[60] At times, the army was used to prevent white encroachment and treaty violations. As in the case of the Civil War, but perhaps even more so, these soldiers often suffered through detrimental living conditions and a capricious disciplinary system which seemed far removed from the safety of courthouses.

Winthrop did not serve in any Indian campaigns, nor was he stationed in areas likely to place him in proximity with warring tribes. However, earlier in his life he came into contact with the Minnesota Sioux, and he viewed the Indians he met as men of equality. Likewise, his brother, Theodore, never evidenced any animus toward the Indians, instead conveying his experiences with them in a positive, albeit adventurous light. Like a number of eastern intellectuals, Winthrop sympathized with the plight of Indians, blaming conflicts chiefly on white greed and bureaucratic incompetence. He was, in all likelihood, an assimilationist who believed in "Christianizing the tribes." Winthrop's position was consistent with a number of other senior officers and government officials such as General O. O. Howard and members of Ulysses Grant's cabinet such as Ely Parker, the head of the Bureau of Indian Affairs. Moreover, true to Winthrop's beliefs on the rights of Indians, he objected to a congressional draft of the 1874 Articles of War in that it did not provide a means to prosecute white murderers of Indians where civil courts were unable or unwilling to do so.[61]

Although Winthrop seldom discussed the state of the army in his legal treatise, it is worth noting that desertion plagued the frontier army at an unprecedented rate. Often in debt, soldiers simply abandoned their posts to seek employment elsewhere. Service on the frontier did not possess the glamour or rewards portrayed in the era's "dime store novels" or other media. By the time Winthrop authored *Military Law* in 1886, the

Indian wars were largely over. By the time *Military Law and Precedents* was published in 1895, the frontier had, for all practical purposes, closed. The "Ghost Dance" and Wounded Knee massacre had occurred five years earlier, and no further significant campaigning involving the regular army against Indians took place. Still, as in the case of his Reconstruction overview, Winthrop believed that the Indian wars offered significant lessons for the reform and enforcement of military law.

The nature of fighting Indians was different from conventional warfare in many respects. Indian warfare took place on a small scale in comparison to the Civil War and European campaigns. No single battle between the army and its Indian adversaries involved the numbers of troops at Gettysburg or Petersburg. And the law of war was designed to be binding to sovereign states which warred with each other, not with insurrection or rebellion. Nonetheless, Winthrop believed the law of war applied to Indian conflicts as much as it did conventional warfare between states. Winthrop did not advocate for Indian rights such as return of tribal lands, but he did seek to protect Indians who resided on reservations or in designated Indian Territory. Toward these Indians, he advocated equality before the law. For Indians in a state of hostility with the government, he argued the law of war governed military operations.

As to protecting the "peaceful" Indians residing on reservations, Winthrop opined that the army's responsibility was to ensure their protection from trespassers. He advised commanders that the army had the right to arrest and deport whites who encroached on Indian Territory and he especially reinforced his argument that army officers had a duty to remove alcohol salesmen from reservations. Although he did not write his views on the causes of conflicts with Indians until the last year of his life, when he did so, he placed the bulk of the blame on white greed and not on the Indians.

In one example of breaking from his own ancestry, Winthrop noted that the use of men unlikely to follow the laws of war, was in and of itself, a law-of-war violation, "such as occurred early in our own history."[62] One need only look to the conduct of the Puritan commanders in the Pequot War and in King Philip's War to remember that the use of Indian allies resulted in Indians committing atrocities against other Indians, which often would have been considered a violation of the laws of war, even by the standards of the 1670s. As a result, Winthrop was leery of using Indian warriors as allies, though he certainly supported incorporating Indians into the regular army as scouts or in special regiments subject to the Articles of War.

Several post–Civil War campaigns were directed by a strategy of fighting that was intended to annihilate a tribe's ability to wage war by forcing its relocation to a controlled environment. The most successful army campaigns were those conducted against the Indians' ability to survive in the winter seasons. Although officers commanding campaigns were aware of General Order 100, the conventional law of war was often not applied against Indian adversaries, despite its application to all conflicts. For instance, on October 21, 1869, General Philip Sheridan suggested the army conduct a surprise attack on the Piegan Indian winter camps. What resulted was a winter attack led by Major Eugene M. Baker ending in the massacre of fifty-three women and children. Many Americans, including Winthrop, were disgusted by Baker's conduct in the raid. However, Sheridan and Sherman endorsed Baker's actions.[63]

The Modoc War of 1872 provides an interesting case study, and one in which Winthrop was involved through his position in the Bureau of Military Justice and later commented on, albeit mainly in footnotes. (Later, as the judge advocate assigned to the Pacific Division, Winthrop became involved in an Indian migration resulting from that war's decade-old effects.) The war had its roots in the white settlement of northern California in the 1850s. During that decade, a brief conflict broke between the settlers and Modocs in which both sides killed noncombatants. In 1864, the Modocs agreed to cede their land to the army and reside on a reservation as neighbors to the Klamath tribe. However, by late 1871, the Klamaths saw the Modocs as competitors and mistreated them to the point that most of the Modocs left the reservation to find a peaceful area. The Modocs did not intend to make war on white settlers. Rather they wanted to escape from an oppressive environment, but the lands they chose were also claimed by settlers, and this led to violence between the Indians and settlers. A series of discussions between settlers and the Modoc chieftains, led by Captain Jack and Bureau of Indian Affairs agents, failed to solve any of the Modocs' grievances.[64]

Inevitably, the army was called to remove the Modocs back to the reservation lands, and just as inevitably the Modocs refused. Operating from a stronghold in the Lassen area lava beds, the Modocs were able to resist the army units sent against them. In April 1873, Captain Jack agreed to meet with a peace commission led by General E. R. S. Canby. On April 11, Canby along with six others entered into Captain Jack's shelter for negotiations. While the men were conducting negotiations under a flag of truce, the Modocs ambushed the government's representatives, killing Canby and one other commissioner. After more skirmishing, the army defeated Captain Jack and the Modocs under his command. But this victory occurred only with the help of Indians who turned against Captain Jack. Winthrop later observed, in *Military Law*, that the truce violation was "a gross instance of a breach of the laws of war."[65] The Modocs who assisted the army were equally culpable under the law of war as they had taken part in Canby's killing.

There were internal pressures in the army to annihilate the Modocs for taking arms against the government. Instead of massacring the Modocs, the commander of the Pacific Division, General Schofield, determined to prosecute them before a military trial.[66] Unsurprisingly, judge advocates—and in particular the Bureau of Military Justice—opposed any punishment or other actions without a trial as well.

On July 5, 1873, six Modocs, including Captain Jack, were brought to trial. Each of the six faced four specifications contained in two charges. The charges were "murder in violation of the laws of war" and "assault with intent to kill in violation of the laws of war." During the trial, Captain Jack testified in his defense, but his statements were an admission of guilt. He explained that his reason for killing Canby was a fear that Canby might do the same to him. He did not perceive that killing Canby under a flag of truce violated any law. He also called witnesses in his own defense, though none appears to have been helpful in the sense that none provided exculpatory or even mitigating evidence. In all, it appears that Captain Jack had no understanding of the trial or his rights. When asked why he did not request a lawyer, he allegedly responded, "I do not know of any lawyer who understands this affair. They could not do me any good. Everyone is against me. Even the Modocs have turned against me. I have but few friends. I am alone." In the end, all six accused were convicted and four, including Captain Jack, were sentenced to death.[67]

Following the rules of military trials, the accused Indians were permitted to speak in their own defense. In theory, each Indian was entitled to representation by a defense counsel if one volunteered to appear. However, the defense was flawed from the start in the sense that the defendants did not appear to understand the functions of the commission.

The fundamental flaws in the Modoc trials were not that they were conducted against Indians, but rather that the commission rules and procedures inherently made for a trial that was tilted toward the prosecution in comparison to a federal criminal trial. This was no different than the military trials of Mary Surratt or Clement Vallandigham. In the case of the Modoc trials, the attorney general opined that the army's jurisdictional authority to prosecute in a military commission extended beyond the customary limitation of only permitting trials during active hostilities.

Military trials could acquit, and often did so. This fact alone did not make the commissions fair by any constitutional standard. And yet, in comparison to courts-martial and nineteenth-century criminal trials, the commissions may not have been any less fair. After all, state and federal criminal trials were adjudicated before all-white male juries, and usually these juries were composed of the middle and upper classes. And in cases of "notorious persons" tried by commission of criminal court, where the accused's guilt was assumed (often because it visibly abounded), a fair trial was unlikely to occur.

To be sure, the trials of Indians were only as fair as the officers sitting on the panel and the judge advocates and War Department officials involved in the quasi-appellate process. Although not studied in great detail, judge advocates involved in these trials were not always passive in their opinions about the fairness and conditions of the prosecutions. For example, during the prosecution of Modoc Indians involved in the killing of General Canby, Major Herbert Curtis notified General Holt that in his opinion, "while the country supposes there is an abundance of proof, there is in truth scarcely any . . . everybody thinks, everybody knows."[68] Curtis was adamant to Holt that his advice to the commission was ignored. However, "Barncho" and "Sloluck," two of the six Modocs, were not sentenced to death, and it appears Curtis advised the commission to make such a sentence. Curtis later wrote to Winthrop, "I would have liked to have said a word about lenity toward Barncho and Sloluck. . . . I regard [them] as common soldiers who obeyed orders."[69] Echoing his concerns to Holt, Curtis also noted to Winthrop that Barncho and Sloluck "took no interest in the trial and I doubt if they ever understood it."[70]

To Curtis, it was repugnant that the commission had to decide critical issues of life or death on an appalling lack of evidence. He was certain of Captain Jack's guilt as well as that of another Indian named "Curly-headed Jack." But he could not be sure as to the guilt of the other defendants. In the end, Curtis predicted, "I shall be certain to be demarked for throwing away the case by those who believe (as I did before coming here) that the testimony was abound."[71] Curtis believed the trial had another fundamental flaw. The Modoc witnesses, in his estimation, "were utterly ignorant of the nature of their oath . . . or punishments." In other words, some of the Modocs—presumably those testifying against their brethren—provided false testimony to curry favor with the army or Indian Bureau agents.[72]

Holt shared Curtis' views with the Bureau of Military Justice during their review of the Modoc trials. If Winthrop concluded that the Modoc or Sioux Indian trials were procedurally unfair, he did not record it in either *Military Law* or *Military Law and Precedents*. He supported the use of military trials against Indians just as he did against Southerners in the Reconstruction trials. And yet, he quietly criticized bringing the Modocs before a military commission for another reason.

He advised Holt that the prosecution of the Modocs in a military trial was jurisdictionally defective in that the trial occurred after the Modocs surrendered. Instead, Winthrop argued a civil trial was the appropriate venue. In *Military Law and Precedents*, Winthrop noted that the jurisdiction of a military commission was not only geographically limited to a theater of war, it was limited by time as well. The jurisdiction of military commissions ended when an opposing force surrendered or a pact, treaty, or agreement concluded between the warring sides. Captain Jack and his partners were tried in a military court after peace was reestablished between the army and the Modocs. Winthrop disagreed with Attorney General George H. Williams' statement that "doubtless the war with the Modocs is practically ended, unless some of them should escape and renew hostilities. But it is the right of the United States, as there was no agreement for peace, to determine for themselves whether or not anything more ought to be done for the protection of the country, or the punishment of crimes growing out of the war."[73] He considered Williams' views wrongly exceptional to the rule and argued against convening commissions outside of the jurisdictional limitations set by custom and statute. However, Holt apparently did not agree with Winthrop's assessment, and he recommended the findings and sentences be upheld.

It would be absurd to believe that prejudices did not enter into the trial equation. Officers empanelled on commissions, judge advocates, witnesses testifying both for and against the Indians could not help but to be encumbered by whatever stereotypes they deeply held. But Winthrop sought to counter these prejudices, reminding officers that witnesses, regardless of their race, were as trustworthy as Christian whites. He wrote that Indians—as well as persons of other races—"were fully competent as witnesses, equally with white persons."[74] He also noted that Christianity was not a predicate for truthfulness, reminding officers that there were a number of faiths in the United States, and each enjoyed equal constitutional rights. His observation on the laws of equality did not only apply to trials by military commission. Rather, Winthrop intended equality before the law as a universal application in all military courts, and his views were a considerable departure from the nativist elements which crept into United States courts in the nineteenth and twentieth centuries.[75]

The question of when a war began and when it ended had a direct relevancy to conflicts with Indians, and for that matter, with other non-Western opponents. Limitations on military jurisdiction over civilians and adversary combatants included geography (the theater of war), time, and the absence of competent civil courts. In terms of the time limitation, military jurisdiction was confined to the duration of hostilities. That is, the beginning and ending of a conflict were the confining times as to when an adversary could be held and tried in a military court. In his analysis of the Articles of War in *Military Law and Precedents*, Winthrop pointed out that while modern states often declared war, Indian warfare began differently. However, Winthrop opined that the jurisdictional phrase *in time of war* applied to all Indian campaigns "while soldiers were away from their garrison posts." This was an important feature of the fifty-eighth Article of War because it incorporated common-law offenses into military jurisdiction. As a result, when a soldier committed rape or murder against Indians, a court-martial maintained jurisdiction over the soldier instead of a civil court.[76] At the same time, Winthrop supported military jurisdiction over civilians who accompanied the army into Indian Territory as well as whites who independently encroached on it. The corollary to this rule was that Indians were amenable to military jurisdiction only when the same conditions applied to soldiers and civilians accompanying them.

Finally, Winthrop did not believe in the subjugation of Indians or violations of their basic rights to live in peace—albeit in a geographically contained area. He did not fall into the Sherman-Sheridan school of thought which embraced a strategy of annihilation. Writing, "It remains to remark that the relations of the military with the friendly Indians should be distinguished by a particular and scrupulous justice, humanity, and discretion," he clearly intended a trust between Indians and soldiers. He also conveyed that failures to uphold honor and trust with the Indian tribes led to hostilities. Perhaps as a tribute to a fallen general, Winthrop placed into *Military Law and Precedents* Canby's position that offenses committed by soldiers against Indians were more serious than ordinary crimes committed against civilians.[77]

Notwithstanding the Civil War and Reconstruction, there were a number of other violent acts of insurrection against state governments and commercial interests which plagued late eighteenth-century and nineteenth-century America.[78] Between 1865 and 1914 a number of labor strikes resulted in public violence. Anti-immigrant movements mirroring the worst excesses of the Klan were directed against Chinese immigrants in Wyoming, Washington, and California. And there remained a very real possibility that the Klan, or a similar organization, would terrorize Southern blacks once more.[79]

As in the case of Reconstruction, Winthrop saw that the army's role in ensuring domestic stability was fraught with peril. He fully recognized that the president's use of the military to suppress insurrection had a constitutional basis. He pointed out that Article I, Section 8 of the Constitution granted to Congress the responsibility over the state militias when it became necessary to enforce law, suppress insurrection, and repel invasion. However, he further advised commanders that the Constitution's framers intended state governments as primarily responsible to respond to internal crisis. The eighth section was crafted, in part, in response to Shay's Rebellion, but it had applicability in a number of instances after the

Constitution's ratification. Article IV, Section 4 of the Constitution placed a responsibility on the federal government to guarantee every state a republican form of government.

There were other legal mandates for using the military in suppressing domestic disorders. In 1792, Congress drafted an act which gave the president the authority to call the militia of one state into federal service to suppress an insurrection in another state. The act did not confer unlimited executive power. To the contrary, there were a number of checks on the president, including judicial oversight. Yet, historically when the president ordered the army to police a domestic disturbance, the order was usually sustained by the courts and Congress. In 1794, presidential authority to suppress insurrection was tested and generally accepted in the so-called Whiskey Rebellion. In 1832, Andrew Jackson threatened to use military force to prevent South Carolina from seceding. And in 1861 Abraham Lincoln called into service the state militias for a period of ninety days to defeat the Southern insurrection, though it took more than ninety days and the available militia to do so. Likewise, during the Civil War draft riots, state militias fired on mobs of rioters. The army, as a result, not only had become an instrument to fight conventional warfare but it had a policing role as well. It may seem odd from a twenty-first-century vantage point that Winthrop spent any time on the subject of domestic policing by the army, but Winthrop wrote his two treatises in a time of continued unrest, and like many officers, he assumed that insurrection and riot control would remain a fundamental army mission.

Public violence exceeding the scope of the 1863 draft riots occurred in a number of urban and industrial areas between 1865 and 1900. Generally, this violence was in response to two separate issues: Southern antipathy to Reconstruction as well as Northern demonstrations against poor working conditions and diminished standards of living. In the West, these demonstrations often took on the added element of violence directed against a small but growing Chinese minority. Although the state militias were the primary means of suppressing industrial violence, the army was used in many instances where the state law enforcement apparatus proved ineffective.[80]

In 1877, the United States was paralyzed by a labor strike against the railways. On July 21, 1877, in Pittsburgh, a number of Pennsylvania state militia units battled with strikers, and at the end of the day, twenty-four strikers were found dead. Hayes did not want the army to become a strike-breaking tool for corporations. And yet, by the end of the strike, the general public often saw the army as siding with capital over labor. Winthrop supported the use of the military to protect federal properties and ensure mail delivery continued. He did not side with business interests, such as was the case with General Nelson A. Miles. Indeed, it is likely the case Winthrop found Miles' political commentary in an 1894 *North American Review* article too political. In his article, Miles called Eugene Debs a "dictator," espoused military intervention in strikes, and encouraged citizens to "take sides either for anarchy, mob violence, and universal chaos under the red flag of socialism on the one hand . . . or side with the established government, the supremacy of the law . . . on the other." Yet, like Miles, Winthrop recognized there was an occasional need for the army to enforce the law and ensure public safety. There were a number of other instances where the army was called to preserve order and protect classes of persons against criminal activities, and Winthrop generally supported the use of the army in such cases.[81]

In the 1880s, the army was ordered to protect Chinese immigrants in Rock Springs, Wyoming, as a result of anti-Chinese rioting which resulted in the massacre of more than twenty Chinese miners. The perpetrators of the riot were mainly white immigrants who believed that Chinese laborers reduced wages. In response to the territorial governor's appeals, President Grover Cleveland ordered several companies of infantry to protect the Chinese in Wyoming. Winthrop approved of this action, as he did when the army was used to protect Chinese immigrants in Washington from similar threats. His support for the army's protection of Chinese immigrants was primarily rooted in the 1868 Burlingame Treaty signed between the United States and China, but there was a humanitarian aspect as well. He believed that exclusionary laws and bigotry undermined the constitutional aspiration of equal treatment under the law. His uncle, the former Ohio governor George Hoadly, argued to the Supreme Court in 1893 that the treaty trumped congressional legislation excluding Chinese immigration.[82]

Winthrop cautioned military commanders that under the Articles of War ultimately they were responsible for the acts of subordinates. The failure to vigorously control soldiers assigned to a commander could result in a dereliction of duty. As a result, soldiers deployed against domestic disorders were tightly bound by regulations, and unruly mobs had to be given a chance to disband before the army could resort to using force. Winthrop was so concerned with the use of the army to contain mobs of civilians that he provided tactical guidance, even in the decision to use force. He noted that innocent civilians were often present in labor demonstrations, and as a result the minimum use of force should always be used: "In the first stage of an insurrection, lawless mobs are frequently commingled with great crowds of comparatively innocent people, drawn there by curiosity and excitement."[83]

Perhaps as a lingering anger over Canby's belief that the Bureau of Indian Affairs had authority over a military operation, Winthrop reminded officers placed in charge of military operations that they were only subject to the orders of the president and superior officers. He argued that claims by other agencies of authority over military operations were without any constitutional basis. And, in *Military Law and Precedents*, Winthrop took credit for influencing general officers in drafting orders to their subordinates which reinforced this point.[84]

Winthrop's superb historic scholarship was evident in his commentaries on the use of military force to quash social insurrection. He took exception to Attorney General Caleb Cushing's view that there had to be "a state of domestic war," for a president to use military force against civilians. Cushing's opinion made it impossible for the military to conduct any operations on sovereign United States soil absent a foreign invasion or civil war fought over secession. Instead, Winthrop argued, "domestic violence, considerably less pronounced than the Dorr Rebellion, for example, will, it is considered, justify an appeal for military aid, by the authorities of a state, under the Constitution."[85]

Winthrop's allusion to the Dorr Rebellion is a telling sign of his views on insurrection. In 1841, a large number of Rhode Island citizens were frustrated at restrictive voting laws which excluded nonlandowners from voting. Rhode Island's voting law predated the Revolution, and its continuation accrued to the benefit of a landowning political class. Led by Thomas Dorr, the group established a separate state government and drafted a separate constitution. Their constitution had overwhelming popular support, but failed to be ratified in the original legislature. The Rhode Island government responded by calling up the militia, though this did not succeed in putting down Dorr's rebellion since many serving in the militia were denied the vote under the old state constitution and sympathized with Dorr. President John Tyler decided not to supply federal troops to aid the Rhode Island government despite the Rhode Island governor's request to do so. Although Dorr's movement ultimately crumbled and he fled an arrest warrant, the issue had ramifications over how a state government could control a political movement. To Winthrop the use of federal forces in the Dorr Rebellion would have been permissible, even though in hindsight it proved unnecessary.[86]

Dorr did not rebel against the federal government or the Constitution. Rather, his followers sought to overthrow a state government which, by the standards of 1895, could have been reasonably considered as something less than a representative government. But the Rhode Island government was the legally constituted government despite its self-protection through oppressive laws. It is likely Winthrop's position on the Dorr Rebellion was not a defense of the deceased Whig Party although the Rhode Island state government was primarily Whig at the time of the rebellion and its actions were defended before the Supreme Court in a seminal case, *Luther v. Borden*, by Daniel Webster. Rather, Winthrop viewed the army as having to side with a constitutionally established government over mob violence and insurrection under any circumstance, and at the time of the insurrection, the Rhode Island state government was not viewed as unconstitutional.

On June 16, 1878, Congress enacted the Posse Comitatus Act, which prohibited the unrestricted use of the federal military to act in a law enforcement capacity.[87] The passage of this act could be considered the final end to Reconstruction, but there were a number of reasons for the congressional action. Southern Democrats railed against the use of military to arrest white citizens and enforce civil rights during Reconstruction. Enough Southerners believed that the army helped Republican Rutherford Hayes "steal the election" from the Democrat candidate, Samuel Tilden, in the 1876 election. Pro-labor Northern politicians were angry at the army's role in strikebreaking. A residual anger in the Irish immigrant community over the army's suppression of mobs in the Civil War draft riots may have also fueled animus toward the army's use against citizens.[88]

Winthrop did not support the Posse Comitatus legislation, writing that it "evolved as it was out of a temporary political antagonism on the question of the extent of the authority of the President to employ the military to preserve elections in the States."[89] This statement was not only a continued defense of Reconstruction, it was also a criticism of what he considered an irrational response from congressional Democrats. His criticism of the act was that it hampered the army's ability to preserve order in the western territories. He acknowledged that the army could still be used to suppress "lawless combinations," but that soldiers were no longer to effectuate arrests of individuals at the behest of the United States marshal, even when an arrest warrant was lawfully presented. He termed this restriction as an embarrassment to the army.

Winthrop was not alone in his criticism of the act. Writing after Winthrop's death, Norman Lieber questioned the wisdom of the act, writing, "Is the government so impotent that it must wait for the crime to be committed, its instrumentalities obstructed, its properties destroyed, before it can act?" Lieber's point was identical to Winthrop's in that often the mere presence of the army prevented disorder and crime, and the act stripped the government of this option.[90]

Finally, Winthrop noted that the while Constitution did not expressly authorize the use of the army in its terms, other statutes enable the army to perform a variety of domestic enforcement missions such as preventing persons from entering Indian reservations and removing white trespassers, enforcing the abolishment of peonage in New Mexico, assisting in extraditions, and enforcing quarantine laws.

The Franco-Prussian War of 1870 significantly altered the balance of power in Europe and later consequently affected United States foreign and military policy. A German confederation led by Prussia decisively defeated the French Army in a quick war. Although the war barely involved the United States, its outcome influenced the United States Army and in some manner it had the potential to affect United States military law as well. Winthrop believed that the influence of this conflict threatened the army's traditional subservient role, and because of Winthrop's strong views on this matter, the subject of Prussia's rise requires explanation.

At the time of the war, few officers expected a quick, decisive Prussian victory. After the war, the Prussian Army, and in particular its General Staff, was at the center of American military studies. Winthrop recognized that the German Army possessed a number of traits worthy of emulation. He admired the Prussian Army's discipline and the intelligence of its officers. He studied the Prussian military successes as closely as any other professional officer. But the fundamental place of the German Army in their government was something Winthrop could not agree to. As in the case of Winthrop's study on Reconstruction, Winthrop's contributions to developing a constitutional army requires detailed analysis on the rise of a Prussian (and then German) school of military thought in the United States.

From the end of the Thirty Years' War to 1870, it was generally accepted France possessed the dominant military in the world. Even though France was defeated in 1814 and again in 1815, American and European military theorists and generals looked to the French Army as a model for emulation. After all, it took the combined forces of Russia, Austria, Britain, and Prussia, along with a number of smaller states, to finally defeat Napoleon in 1815.

By 1870, Prussia possessed the best army the world. It could quickly mobilize six hundred thousand highly trained and disciplined reserves, expanding its standing army from two hundred thousand to eight hundred thousand. Prussia did not have the largest army (Russia did, and France possessed a standing army of slightly larger size, though Prussia's reserve system put the numbers of overall soldiers in its advantage). Nor did Prussia as a country have an industry suited for a long war. But no other country possessed a General Staff as professionally suited or well prepared for war as that in Prussia.

Located in Prussia's political center was its army, which had geared for a war with France since the fall of Napoleon. Coupled with the army was Prussia's superbly shrewd chancellor, Otto von Bismarck. His plotting enabled a war with France, where Napoleon III appeared as the aggressor. Moreover, despite the Prussian victories over Austria and Denmark, the French had no reliable allies. Bismarck's exceptional statesmanship abilities resulted in Austria's, Britain's, and Russia's neutrality, and Italy's nominal support to France. Ninety years earlier, the French Navy enabled the creation of the United States. In 1870, no American politician vociferously campaigned to support France against Prussia.[91]

After 1870, the Prussian General Staff was the envy of the world's armies, including the United States. Greek, Rumanian, and Turkish officers came to Berlin to study at the German military school, the *Kiegsakademie*, and the other European army leaders began to realize how far their forces slipped in comparison to Prussia. Perhaps the British Army command did not feel threatened as the Royal Navy remained the strongest combat arm in the world, but Prussia's lopsided victory cast an influence over Europe. And yet, the Prussian (now German) General Staff was uniquely German. That is, it was an undemocratic, anti-Republican institution. Led by Helmuth von Moltke, the General Staff was a political force unto itself. It could do more than influence Germany's foreign policy; it could—in the absence of Bismarck—make it. Indeed, von Moltke's successor, Alfred Graf von Waldersee, engineered Bismarck's dismissal by Kaiser Wilhelm.[92]

The *Army-Navy Journal* editorial staff showed is prescience of the Prussian General Staff as early as September 1, 1866, when it reported on the General Staff's school. Writing, "We have singled out the school for two reasons—one is that it is perfectly favorable to adopt at once."[93] Although for reasons noted below, the Prussian General Staff model was, in many ways, incompatible with the constitutional framework of the nation—Winthrop certainly believed so—its activities were noted and often accurately analyzed by the *Journal*. In April 1867, the *Army-Navy Journal* writers surmised that as von Moltke's General Staff was clearly planning for a war with France, one would likely come by the end of the decade.[94]

Problematic to Prussia's military ascendancy was its General Staff's view on international law and politics. Leading Prussian officers viewed matters of international law and diplomacy as solely within the purview of the monarch. Their job was to prepare for a war, and fight one if it came. Alfred von Schleiffen and Helmuth von Moltke the Younger fell into this category, but both failed to understand that diplomacy in war by commanding generals is important. Most of the Prussian commanders fell into the elder von Moltke school of thought. Von Moltke was not a proponent of international law. Deriding Germany's foremost international law scholar and contemporary of Francis Lieber, Johann Bluntschli, von Moltke wrote, "International agreements could not have the force of domestic law" and "Everlasting peace is a dream and not even a beautiful dream, and war a link in God's ordering of the world."[95] To the elder von

Moltke, the law of war was a nicety, often made impossible to follow by strategic considerations.

One of von Moltke's protégés, Colmar Freiherr von der Goltz, seconded Moltke, arguing that "the idea of making war impossible by any means of courts of arbitration has not led to any practical results because the power to enforce the decisions of such courts, to cause their general and unrequisitioned recognition is found wanting."[96] As evidence of the importance of German military thought, the *Journal of the United States Artillery* reprinted von der Goltz's writings on this subject. Von der Goltz looked at Napoleon's inability to secure Russia after the seizure of Moscow and the French population's uprising after their armies were defeated at Sedan and Metz as an example of the need to occupy an enemy's state and impose harsh measures. Perhaps foreshadowing the German Army's conduct in Belgium and France in 1914 through 1918, von der Goltz did not stop with his initial criticism of international law, concluding that "the destruction of an enemy's army may not be enough to secure peace."[97] As a testament to this thinking, the older von Moltke's second successor, Alfred Graf von Schlieffen, planned for an aggressive war with France in which the German invasion would deliberately invade two neutral countries, Belgium and the Netherlands, and order them to succumb to German rule.[98]

The 1870 Franco-Prussian War altered United States military thought, though not universally. General Sheridan believed little could be learned from the Prussian Army. General Pope believed that the United States would not fight a war against a modern European army for many decades, if ever, and therefore any emulation was wasteful. General Sherman felt otherwise. So too did an emerging energetic military thinker and a favorite of Sherman's, General Emory Upton. With the exception of Sherman, Upton had the most profound intellectual influence on army leadership between the Civil War and World War I.[99]

Although Winthrop disagreed with Upton's approach to military reform, he never openly confronted Upton. And there were areas in which Winthrop agreed with Upton. For instance, Upton espoused an increased level of professional military education, testing for promotion, and a larger army. He wanted an officer corps based on a meritocracy rather than seniority or favoritism. Winthrop embraced these very positions. However, it was in the arena of civil-military relations where Winthrop's ideology ran counter to Upton's. Upton and his followers sought a constitutional realignment and a Prussianization of the army. Upton failed to realize that the political powers vested in the Prussian Army by its monarch were intolerable in the United States.[100]

In 1876, Sherman sent Upton on a global trip to research the armies of Asia, believing the United States could gain insight into unconventional warfare through the British experience in India. Although the purpose of Upton's mission was centered on unconventional warfare, his journey took him through Europe where he became enamored with the German military organization. In a short time, Upton believed the United States military required a drastic reorganization, which in turn required a displacement of civilian oversight as dictated in the Constitution. After his tour, he authored *The Armies of Europe and Asia*, in which he concluded that the United States military organization was, in comparison to its European counterparts, "worthless."[101]

It was from the German Army that Upton argued the United States Army had the most to learn. He advocated some structural adaptations such as altering officer assignments between the line and the staff so that officers who advanced through the military were familiar with all aspects of it. He also argued for schools of instruction for all ranks, and testing as a prerequisite for officer promotion to the higher grades. Upton advanced the idea that officer formal schooling had to concentrate on the "art of war, and in the higher branches of their profession."[102] Each of Upton's arguments for the internal professionalization of the army was obtainable. However, Upton also advocated an army free from legislative control, and he sought to reduce the secretary of war's authority.

Upton provided detailed analysis of the professional officer educational structures of the British, French, and German armies. He found that in each there were commonalities, one of which was that each military educational system taught some aspect of military law. He also provided information on the disciplinary systems of each. He did not dissect the various military codes, and provided little commentary. He found the British Indian Army code successful in its standardization of punishments.[103] Upton barely described the disciplinary system of the German Army, though he was thoroughly enamored of that army on the whole. It is likely he wanted the United States Army to adopt the German disciplinary system given his admiration for the German Army.[104]

In drawing lessons from his investigations, Upton concluded that among other education subjects, young officers ought to be required to master "military law and the proceedings and practice of courts-martial." Upton also joined the number of officers critical of the system of garrison courts-martial that resulted in unequal and often arbitrary punishments so that one outpost might imprison a man who was drunk on duty, while another court might only issue a reprimand.[105] On this last point Winthrop and Upton were in agreement.

Upton's greatest work—one that he would not see published in his own lifetime as a result of his suicide in 1881—was *The Military Policy of the United States*, an intellectual attack on the militia as well as the various secretaries of war. Although the *Military Policy* was a critical work which focused on domestic military affairs from the time of the Continental Army to 1862, it clearly was written with the purpose of arguing for Prussian reforms. For instance, Upton disparaged the militia system and advocated for an expansible army. Upton's basic arguments against the state militias were that as an institution these units were hardly disciplined or trained for modern warfare and that militia commanders had conflicting political loyalties. He criticized the importance of Congress in military affairs and would have its constitutional role of oversight thoroughly diminished. To Upton, the congressional oversight of the army during the Civil War was a hindrance to effectiveness. It overly politicized officers and forced professionals such as McClellan into battles and campaigns before the army was ready. And he sought the creation of a general staff mirrored on the Prussian model.[106]

Interestingly, Upton sympathized with Fitz-John Porter and McClellan. He felt that both were treated unfairly, and in *Military Policy*, Upton evidenced hostility toward Stanton. Writing, "Stanton should have given all of his attention to exclusively organizing, recruiting, and supplying our armies, he first blindly gave to revising the plans of military commanders," Upton argued that no secretary of war should have the authority to oversee the movement and allocation of forces.[107] That the secretary of war served as a further check against unconstitutional despotism did not enter into Upton's arguments. This was another area that Winthrop and Upton diverged on, and one only need look back to Winthrop's writings on Reconstruction to see how the two men differed.

There were a number of reasons Upton and his followers did not succeed in "Prussianizing" the military. Among these reasons was the resistance from senior officers who believed in the sanctity of the constitutional framework governing the military. For instance, General Schofield, Winthrop's mentor, sought to structurally reform the army by concentrating legal authority in the commanding general over the staff bureaus. He did not advocate increasing power over the secretary of war, and believed that the commanding general primarily had only an advisory responsibility to the president and the secretary.

In at least one fundamental respect, Schofield was anti-Prussian. He did not glorify war, believing it an evil for which the United States had to prepare. In an era of jingoism, Schofield was not a proponent of imperial expansion. He argued, unlike von Moltke, that the so-called "natural law of survival of the fittest . . . is not a law of Christianity nor of civilization, nor wisdom. It is the law of greed and cruelty, which generally works to the destruction of its devotees." It does not appear that Schofield and Upton regularly corresponded or that the two publicly challenged each other's views. It might also have been the case that Upton would have made a larger impact in military reform if not for his early death and

Schofield's longevity. While Upton committed suicide, Schofield went on to replace Sheridan as commanding general of the army.[108]

A third reason Upton failed had to do with the Constitution itself. Congress would never willingly abrogate its authority over the army or lose its "power of the purse." The country as a whole would not tolerate the army's supremacy in American politics, particularly not when the army conducted almost all of its operations in the sovereign United States or on the periphery of it. Even within the army, constitutionalists such as Winthrop and Schofield would have vigorously fought against Upton's vision of constitutional realignment had it been considered by any administration.

There is nothing Uptonian in either *Military Law* or *Military Law and Precedents*. The fact that the law as Winthrop advocated it was taught in the intermediate service schools and the United States Military Academy meant that officers understood their position relative to the Constitution and were restrained by it.

Winthrop did not ignore the evidence of Prussian military success, and he did not, unlike General Pope or General Sheridan, minimize Prussian prowess. Indeed, Winthrop provided to the army an insight into the German military justice system by translating the Prussian military code into English. Published in 1873, the *Military Penal Code for the German Empire*, or *Militärstrafgesetz-buch*, was a compilation of military justice rules. These rules were not entirely new to the German Empire; they were in fact in use in the Prussian Army for the previous fifty years. In his translation, Winthrop did not advocate adopting any of the German Army code's provisions. He found much of it unconstitutional and therefore unsuitable to the army. But the publication provided to American military commanders insight into the internal disciplinary system of the Prussian Army, and as a result, the work served as "intelligence" in understanding German military operations.

Winthrop's analytical comments in his translation on the German Army generally echoed admiration for the Prussian Army insofar as Winthrop spoke to the effectiveness of the German Army. He briefly analyzed the structure of the Prussian Army, providing contrast to the United States military. He noted that as Germany had a twelve-year compulsory service, its army had a very large force in contrast to the United States. The German Army had three component parts, and a serviceman would serve in all three. A serviceman first was obligated to serve three years in the standing army followed by four in the reserves, and then five in the *Landwehr*. Each of these classes of person was subject to the military code for military offenses. Reserves and *Landwehr* were part of the *Beurlaubtenstand*, or persons on military leave. Thus, a refusal to drill would subject a *Landwehr* soldier to the jurisdiction of the German court-martial. So too would the murder of one reserve by another, even when the murder occurred while both reserves were not in uniform. Winthrop noted, "The existence of this class numbering upwards of a half million civilians but always soldiers, subject to the jurisdiction of military courts, and awaiting only the rappel of war to hasten to the colors, is a striking and spirited feature of that military system which we saw so brilliantly illustrated in 1866 and again in 1870."[109]

Just as Winthrop did not completely disagree with everything Upton advocated, there were features of the German code Winthrop approved of. Like the Articles of War, the German Code had a law-of-war element to it. The destruction or theft of civilian property in time of war was considered a military offense and carried with it a five-year sentence. Likewise, when plunder was committed in conjunction with murder or bodily harm to an innocent party, the offense carried the possibility of the death penalty.[110] In this sense, the German code compared favorably to General Order 100. On the other hand, the German Army conducted few prosecutions for law-of-war violations in the 1870 war, and the German Army conducted summary executions of French citizens suspected of offenses against its soldiers. Additionally, the starvation of Paris was not universally accepted as comporting with the laws and customs of war.

One area which Winthrop translated but did not provide commentary to was the applicability of the German Military code to enemy prisoners of war. International law permitted the captor government to institute disciplinary systems for prisoners but was largely silent as to whose disciplinary system was applicable, the captor's or the captive's. Likewise, the code mandated its jurisdiction over civilians in occupied areas, where the alleged crime was committed against German troops. This included efforts to free prisoners of war or knowingly giving false information to a German officer. Such crimes could be sentenced by death. There was no counterpart to this set of rules in the Article of War. The German code was harsh.

The German code developed, in part, out of the franc-tireurs experiences of the 1870 war. In the early part of the war as German forces crossed into France, French citizens began a guerrilla war against the Germans. The franc-tireurs originated from rifle and hunting clubs, and once the war broke, they operated as irregular forces, killing German soldiers and disrupting lines of communication.[111] (In his law of war section in *Military Law and Precedents,* Winthrop comparatively wrote of irregular Confederate forces and the franc-tireurs.) The German code applied to these individuals when captured. Interestingly, the German code's jurisdiction extended to foreign officers attached to the German Army in time of war, even when those officers were observers.[112]

It is not surprising that Winthrop approved of the law of war provisions written into the German military code. To Winthrop, the law of war, as a part of international law, codified behavior required of all soldiers, regardless of on which side soldiers fought. On the whole, however, Winthrop did not advocate adopting the German code because it placed complete authority in the sovereign without any legislative oversight. The German code was austere and undemocratic; it did not embody the rights of citizens found even in the Articles of War.

In ascertaining Winthrop's contributions to the preservation and strengthening of the "constitutional army," it needs to be reiterated that his three treatises were well-read. It is impossible to quantify the numbers of officers and officer-candidates who parsed through *Military Law, Abridgement of Military Law,* and *Military Law and Precedents,* but given that the first two works were mandatory texts in both the professional military education centers and the United States Military Academy, it stands to reason that a sizeable majority of the officers serving from the late nineteenth century into the early twentieth century were familiar with Winthrop's work. Aside from the later plaudits and recognitions from civilian judges and scholars, it is clear that he quietly influenced army and civilian leadership.

Anecdotally, there is the failure of Upton's ambitious goals to realign the army's constitutional position, although his more pragmatic suggestions were incorporated into Secretary of War Elihu Root's reforms beginning in 1903. Yet, no commanding general of the army from Schofield, through Leonard Wood and John Pershing, to George C. Marshall ever advocated Upton's more radical ideas. And it is clear that Winthrop had direct contact with Schofield, Wood, and Pershing, and they read his treatises during the course of their careers.

NOTES

1. George Prugh, "Colonel William Winthrop: The Tradition of the Military Lawyer," *American Bar Association Journal* 42, no. 2 (May 1956), 128.

2. Philip Sheridan, *Personal Memoirs of Philip Sheridan*, vol. 2 (New York: Jenkins and McCowan, 1888), 210. Sheridan wrote in his memoirs that Grant looked at Maximilian's invasion of Mexico as part of the Southern rebellion and believed the Confederacy encouraged Napoleon III to establish a puppet government in Mexico.

3. *Army-Navy Journal*, May 13, 1865, 610.

4. Sheridan, *Personal Memoirs*, 210.

5. William Winthrop, *Military Law and Precedents*, 2nd ed. (Washington, DC: GPO, 1920), 798.

6. Winthrop, *Military Law and Precedents,* 798. Winthrop pointed out that Maximilian's trial consisted of a panel of one lieutenant colonel and six captains.

However, he defended the composition of this court as several American generals such as David Swaim and Fitz-John Porter were prosecuted before a panel of officers junior in grade to the accused. *Military Law and Precedents*, 73.

7. William A. Ganoe, *The History of the United States Army* (New York: D. Appleton and Co., 1924), 306.

8. George W. McCrary, *The Political Issues of Our Time: A Speech by Hon, G.W. McCrary, Secretary of War* (Washington, DC: National Republican Publishing Co., 1878). For Redfield Proctor's quote see Russell Weigley, *Towards an American Army: Military Thought from Washington to Marshall*, reprint ed. (Westport, CT: Greenwood Press, 1974), 139.

9. For the quality of life in the West, see Don Rickey, *Forty Miles a Day on Beans and Hay* (Norman: University of Oklahoma Press, 1963), 116–136. For the quality of the army's weaponry, see Perry D. Jamieson, *Crossing the Deadly Ground: United States Army Tactics, 1865–1899* (Tuscaloosa: University of Alabama Press, 1994), 30–34; also, Weigley, *Towards an American Army*, 228. For the general attitudes of officers regarding fighting against Indians as well as the inferiority of the army's weaponry, see Allan R. Millet and Peter Maslowski, *For the Common Defense: A Military History of the United States* (New York: Free Press, 1994), 253–245. The health of individual soldiers also affected the efficiency and readiness of the army. According to Edward M. Coffman, the army suffered a high rate of venereal disease, smallpox, and other detriments. See Edward M. Coffman, *The Old Army: A Portrait of the American Army in Peacetime, 1784–1898* (New York: Oxford University Press, 1986), 385–389.

10. Ganoe, *History of the American Army*, 306.

11. Ronald J. Barr, *The Progressive Army: United States Army Command and Administration, 1870–1914* (New York: St. Martin's Press, 1998), 3.

12. Samuel P. Huntington, *The Soldier and the State: The Theory and Politics of Civil-Military Relations* (Boston: Harvard University Press, 1959), 229. See also Carol Reardon, *Soldiers and Scholars: The U.S. Army and the Uses of Military History, 1865–1920* (Lawrence: University Press of Kansas, 1990), 2; Paul C. Koistinen, *Mobilizing for Modern War: The Political Economy of American Warfare, 1865–1919* (Lawrence: University Press of Kansas 1997), 5.

13. Weigley, *Towards an American Army*, 230.

14. Russell Weigley, *History of the United States Army* (Bloomington: Indiana University Press, 1984), 274.

15. James Fry, *A Sketch of the Adjutant General's Department, U.S. Army, from 1775 to 1875* (Washington, DC: GPO, 1875). Fry notes that both Norman Lieber and Asa Gardner were assistant authors.

16. Ganoe, *The History of the United States Army*, 302; also, Huntington, *The Soldier and the State*, 154–155.

17. Coffman, *The Old Army*, 218–222.

18. For an overview of War Department corruption, see, for example, Edward S. Cooper, *William Worth Belknap: An American Disgrace* (New York: Farleigh Dickinson, 2003).

19. Koistinen, *Mobilizing for Modern War*, 59; Robert Utley, *Frontier Regulars: The United States Army and the Indians, 1866–1891* (New York: MacMillan, 1973), 267.

20. See Gaston Bodart, *Losses of Life in Modern Wars* (Oxford: Claredon Press, 1916), 163; also, Huntington, *The Soldier and the State*, 222–225.

21. Coffman, *The Old Army*, 347.

22. See, for example, Robert Wooster, *The Military and United States Indian Policy: 1865–1903* (New Haven: Yale University Press, 1998), 62. Wooster aptly noted, "In an army troubled by low pay, infrequent promotions, and inadequate training, jealous officers often magnified petty quarrels into major controversies."

23. Utley, *Frontier Regulars*, 226–227; Wooster, *The Military and United States Indian Policy*, 62. One of Winthrop's fellow officers, General August Kautz, recorded in his diary that as late as 1885, Pope approached some of his subordinates at the Presidio to proofread an article on Fitz-John Porter and Second Manassas that Pope wrote for the *Century* magazine. Since Winthrop was serving as the judge advocate at the Presidio during this time, Pope might have approached him as well.

24. Richard O'Connor, *Sheridan* (Indianapolis: Bobbs-Merrill, 1953), 320–322.

25. *Records of Living Officer of the United States Army* (Philadelphia: L.R. Hamersly and Co., 1884), 5–7.

26. Weigley, *History of the United States Army*, 291.

27. Thomas Barr, letter to Joseph Holt, November 27, 1875 (PJH, box 70).

28. Weigley, *History of the United States Army*, 291; Rickey, *Forty Miles a Day on Beans and Hay*, 77; Barr, *The Progressive Army*, 6; Utley, *Frontier Regulars*, 20. Utley writes that the promotion system badly damaged the officer corps.

29. For an overview of Shafter's career, see, for example, Paul H. Carlson, *"Pecos Bill": A Military Biography of William R. Shafter* (College Station: Texas A&M University Press, 1989).

30. Utley, *Frontier Regulars*, 15.

31. Utley, *Frontier Regulars*, 21; William Winthrop, letter to Edwin Stanton, June 20, 1865 (NA RG 153.2.1, folder 14).

32. Weigley, *History of the United States Army*, 267.

33. Winthrop, *Military Law and Precedents*, 846.

34. Benjamin G. Harris, "The Rights of the States," June 14, 1866, reprinted in Harris Papers (MDHS) and Congressional Globe Office, June 14, 1866.

35. Eric Foner, *Reconstruction: America's Unfinished Revolution, 1863–1877* (New York: Harper and Row, 1988), 425–431; also, Eric Foner, *A Short History of Reconstruction* (New York: Harper and Row, 1990), 146.

36. Winthrop, *Military Law and Precedents*, 827–830; See also, Foner, *Reconstruction*, 452.

37. Foner, *Reconstruction*, 431; Coffman, *The Old Army*, 235–238.

38. Winthrop, *Military Law and Precedents*, 827.

39. *Army-Navy Journal*, October 6, 1866, 108.

40. James E. Sefton, *The United States Army and Reconstruction, 1865–1877* (Baton Rouge: LSU Press, 1967), 31.

41. Winthrop helped author Holt's defense against slander, the "Vindication of Judge Advocate General Holt from the foul slanders of traitors, confessed perjurers and suborners, acting in the interest of Jefferson Davis." William Winthrop, letter to Joseph Holt, August 6, 1866 (PJH, box 53); William Winthrop, letter to

Joseph Holt, August 18, 1866 (PJH, box 53). On August 5, 1867, Stanton directed Winthrop to take the entire record of the conspiracy case, including all personal notes, to President Johnson. Winthrop notified Holt he complied with Stanton's order and described his meeting with President Johnson as follows: "After turning over the sheets for some little time in my presence, the President said he would retain them and dismissed me. He has them still, at least they have not been sent back to the office." For the first time, Winthrop ascribed ill motives to Johnson, writing, "I have little doubt the President has directly authorized the statement which has appeared in the papers—that he was not advised of the recommendation at the time of the proceedings." Winthrop also advised Holt that a colonel in the White House informed him of Johnson's malfeasance. William Winthrop, letter to Joseph Holt, August 12, 1867 (PJH, box 57).

42. William Winthrop, letter to Joseph Holt, June 20, 1865 (NA RG 153.2.1, folder 12); William Winthrop, letter to Edwin Stanton, June 30, 1865 (NA RG 153.2.1, folder 12).

43. Winthrop, *Military Law and Precedents*, 822–823.

44. Winthrop, *Military Law* 2, 91.

45. Mark Neely, *The Fate of Liberty: Abraham Lincoln and Civil Liberties* (New York: Oxford University Press, 1991), 176–177.

46. Winthrop, *Military Law and Precedents*, 822.

47. Sefton, *The United States Army and Reconstruction*, 44.

48. J. J. Clarke Hare, *American Constitutional Law*, vol. 2 (Boston: Little Brown and Co., 1889), 983.

49. Francis Lieber, letter to Joseph Holt, June 1866 (PJH, box 54).

50. Guido Norman Lieber, letter to Joseph Holt, July 11, 1867 (PJH, box 56).

51. Thomas Barr, letter to Joseph Holt, June 25, 1869 (PJH, box 61).

52. Thomas Barr, letter to Joseph Holt, July 17, 1869 (PJH, box 61).

53. Winthrop, *Military Law and Precedents*, 855–862.

54. Winthrop, *Military Law and Precedents*, 855–862.

55. 89 U.S. (22 Wall) 276 (1874).

56. *Mechanics and Traders Bank v. Union Bank*, 89 U.S. 276, 308 (1874). Winthrop later adopted another dissent of Justice Field in formulating his analysis of the reach of the laws and customs of war. Field was a pro-Union Democrat who supported the war, but not the expansion of executive authority. He did not endorse McClellan's candidacy or overtures for peace with the South that would deprive the North of its ability to enforce the Emancipation Proclamation. Field was also a perpetual lesser candidate in the Democrat Party Conventions for the presidency after the war as the Democrats lacked a large number of viable alternatives. He was never on the ticket for election, however.

57. Weigley, *History of the United States Army*, 261.

58. Utley, *Frontier Regulars*, 7–8.

59. Weigley, *History of the United States Army*, 267.

60. Weigley, *History of the United States Army*, 267.

61. Bureau of Military Justice, letter to Secretary of War Belknap, April 16, 1874, in the *Congressional Record* for 1874, 24–25.

62. Winthrop, *Military Law and Precedents*, 784; also, *Military Law and Precedents*, 869.

63. Paul A. Hutton, *Phil Sheridan and His Army* (Lincoln: University of Nebraska Press, 1985), 189.

64. Utley, *Frontier Regulars*, 206–210. Canby mistakenly believed that the orders of the Division of the Pacific were channeled through the Bureau of Indian Affairs agent. In fact, the agent possessed no authority to issue Canby orders.

65. William Winthrop, *Military Law*, vol. 2 (Washington, DC: W.H. Morrison, 1886), 14.

66. Utley, *Frontier Regulars*, 206–212; also, Arthur Quinn, *Hell with the Fire Out: A History of the Modoc War* (New York: Faber and Faber, 1997), 173–174. Sherman wanted to "exterminate" the Modocs in revenge for Canby's murder. However, Schofield, who commanded the military division, opted for a military trial.

67. See generally, *Proceedings of a Military Commission Convened at Fort Klamath, Oregon, for the Trial of Modoc Indians* (Washington, DC: War Department, 1873); also, A. B. Meacham, *Wigwam and Warpath, of the Royal Chief in Chains* (Boston: John P. Dale and Co., 1875), 607–630.

68. Herbert Curtis, letter to Joseph Holt, July 1, 1873 (PJH box 66).

69. Herbert Curtis, letter to William Winthrop, in Francis S. Landrum, *Guardhouse, Gallows, and Graves: The Trial and Execution of Indian Prisoners of the Modoc Indian War by the United States Army, 1873* (Klamath Falls, OR: Klamath County Museum, 1988), 59.

70. Curtis, letter to William Winthrop.

71. Curtis, letter to Joseph Holt, July 1, 1873.

72. Herbert Curtis, letter to Joseph Holt, July 10, 1873 (PJH, box 66).

73. William Winthrop, letter to Joseph Holt, June 12, 1873 (NA RG 153.2.1, folder 24); Winthrop, *Military Law* 2, 68; also, *Military Law and Precedents*, 837.

74. Winthrop, *Military Law and Precedents*, 337. In *Military Law*, Winthrop recorded that witnesses were to be sworn according to their beliefs. For instance, he wrote, "Jews are sworn by the five books of Moses"; *Military Law*, 400.

75. Winthrop, *Military Law and Precedents*, 876.

76. Winthrop, *Military Law and Precedents*, 670.

77. Winthrop, *Military Law and Precedents*, 876.

78. Jerry M. Cooper, "Federal Military Intervention in Domestic Disorders," in *The United States Military under the Constitution of the United States*, ed. Richard Kohn, 120–122 (New York: NYU Press, 1991).

79. Lawrence Friedman, *A History of American Law* (New York: Simon and Schuster, 2005), 381–389.

80. Maurice Matloff, ed., *American Military History* (Washington, DC: Office of the Chief of Military History, United States Army, 1969), 285.

81. Nelson A. Miles, "The Lesson of the Recent Strikes," *North American Review* 159 (1894), 180–188; also, Robert Cherny, *American Politics in the Gilded Age* (Wheeling, IL: Harlan Davidson, 1997), 63; Walter Millis, *Arms and Men: A Study in American Military History* (New York: G.P. Putnam's Sons, 1956), 143; Koistinen, *Mobilizing for Modern War*, 58–59.

82. Winthrop, *Military Law* 2, 109; Winthrop, *Military Law and Precedents*, 865; *Chinese Exclusion Cases*, 130 U.S. 581 (1893). Winthrop considered the Burlingame Treaty required the United States government to protect Chinese immigrants and laborers.

83. Winthrop, *Military Law and Precedents*, 865. .

84. Winthrop, *Military Law and Precedents*, 864.

85. Winthrop, *Military Law and Precedents*, 864. The Dorr Rebellion resulted in a significant Supreme Court decision, *Luther v. Borden*, in which the court found that the Constitution guaranteed to each state a republican form of government.

86. Melvin Urofsky, *A March of Liberty: A Constitutional History of the United States* (New York: Alfred Knopf, 1988), 332–333; also, Robert Remini, *Daniel Webster: The Man and His Life* (New York: W.W. Norton, 1997), 640–641.

87. Army Appropriations Act, ch. 263, § 15, 20 stat. 145, 152 (1878).

88. H. W. C. Furman, "Restrictions upon Use of the Army Imposed by the Posse Comitatus Act," *Military Law Review* 7 (1960), 92–96; Millis, *Arms and Men*, 143.

89. Winthrop, *Military Law and Precedents*, 867.

90. Norman Lieber, *The Use of the Army in the Aid of Civil Power* (Washington, DC: GPO, 1898), 45–46.

91. Adrian Bucholz, *Moltke, Schlieffen, and Prussian War Gaming* (New York: St. Martin's Press, 1991), 46. J. F. C. Fuller, *A Military History of the Western World: From the Seven Days Battle to the Battle of Leyte Gulf* (New York: Funk and Wagnalls, 1956), 96–97. Fuller concluded that Bismark sought to reduce Austrian influence in Germany without creating a permanent enemy. The peace terms with Austria were generous.

92. Walter Goerlitz, *History of the Prussian General Staff: 1657–1945* (New York: Praeger, 1954), 100.

93. *Army-Navy Journal*, September 1, 1866, 28.

94. *Army-Navy Journal*, April 27, 1867.

95. Von Moltke's correspondence to Bluntschli is found in Goerlitz, *History of the Prussian General Staff*, 100, and, G. A. Simcox, "Natural Religion," *Nineteenth Century* 12 (1882), 410. Simcox's translation of von Moltke's full statement is, "I fully appreciate the philanthropic efforts being made to soften the evils of war. But perpetual peace is a dream, and not even a good dream. War is a God established element of order. It is a means for the development of man's noblest virtues—courage, renunciation, faithfulness to duty, and the spirit of sacrifice. The soldier gives his life. Without war, the world would stagnate and lose itself in materialism."

96. Colmar Freiherr von der Goltz, "Principles of War," *Journal of the United States Artillery* 6 (1896), 33.

97. von der Goltz, *Journal of the United States Artillery*, 33.

98. Goerlitz, *History of the Prussian General Staff*, 100.

99. Hutton, *Sheridan*, 201–202; Millis, *Arms and Men*, 138–140; Don Alberts, *Brandy Station to Manila Bay: A Biography of General Wesley Merritt* (Austin, TX: Presidial Press, 1980), 264.

100. Weigley, *History of the United States Army*, 280–281; Barr, *The Progressive Army*, 14.

101. Peter S. Michie, *The Life and Letters of Emory Upton* (New York: D. Appleton and Co., 1885), 379; also, Steven F. Ambrose, "Emory Upton and the Armies of Europe and Asia," *Military Affairs* 28, no. 1 (Spring 1964), 27. Upton specifically wrote, "Since arriving in Europe, I have discovered our military organization is so worthless that I now feel that a thousand pages would not suffice to show it up."

102. Michie, *The Life and Letters of Emory Upton*, 386–387.
103. Emory Upton, *The Armies of Europe and Asia: Embracing Official Reports on the Armies of Japan, China, India, Persia, Italy, Russia, Austria, Germany, France, and England* (New York: D. Appleton, 1878), 61.
104. Upton, *The Armies of Europe and Asia*, 224.
105. Upton, *The Armies of Europe and Asia*, 356–359.
106. Millis, *Arms and Men*, 140.
107. Emory Upton, *The Military Policy of the United States* (Washington, DC: GPO, 1916), 405.
108. Russell F. Weigley, "The Military Thought of John M. Schofield," *Military Affairs* 23 (1959), 77–84.
109. William Winthrop, *Military Penal Code for the German Empire*, or *Militär-strafgesetz-buch* (Washington, DC: Army Department, 1873), 6.
110. Winthrop, *Military Penal Code for the German Empire*, 40–43. Articles 127 through 133 provide the different layers of offenses related to the law of war.
111. See, for example, Geoffrey Wawro, *The Franco Prussian War: The German Conquest of France in 1870–1871* (Cambridge: Cambridge University Press, 2003), 237–238.
112. Winthrop, *Military Penal Code for the German Empire*, 50: Article 157.

10

Professionalizing the Practice of Military Law: Winthrop's Influence Cemented

> My literary work is the only means by which I can add to my reputation or record as an officer, or perform satisfactory service of a valuable and pertinent character.
>
> —Major William Winthrop to Secretary of War William Endicott

In writing *Military Law* and *Military Law and Precedents*, Winthrop sought to professionalize the practice of military law alongside of maintaining and modernizing a "constitutional army." To Winthrop, professionalizing the practice of military law required three related successes. Internally the Judge Advocate General's Department had to be professionalized, which in turn would improve the standards of ad hoc judge advocates; and the part of military law which involved courts-martial and criminal jurisdiction had to be both improved without changing its fundamental purpose and defended.

There were a number of influences both internal and external to the Judge Advocate General's Department which shaped Winthrop's work. His personal experiences as an officer during the Civil War, Reconstruction, and the Gilded Age, were, in his own words, the reason he embarked on writing *Military Law*. However, changes in the American practice of law as well as the development of new jurisprudential philosophies such as the codification movement and a reemergence of emphasizing the common law also played a role in the approach, format, and stylizing of his treatises. Additionally, he viewed his research as a defense against what he perceived as unwarranted external attacks on the military disciplinary system as well as a defense against retrenchment and a refusal to modify any military practice and procedure.

The Articles of War, and for that matter other aspects of the military disciplinary system, had come under attack in Congress and from within the military, as well as from civilian lawyers. For instance, one R. McKinlay, a representative in the Illinois legislature, criticized the 1874 Articles of War, arguing, "Nothing short of a definite and carefully digested code of punishments for each and every military offense,"[1] could make the military law fair. He also argued (in an argument with which Winthrop did not disagree) that a cause of desertions and low morale was in the inequality of the military's administration of courts-martial.

In Winthrop's view, a court-martial was an "instrumentality of the executive," designed to reinforce discipline, and it was, by necessity, without formal judicial oversight in the form of appellate review. However, he also believed that although it was a separate system, subjected to the executive alone, it had to mirror the due process requirements in civilian courts, but without changing its fundamental structure or character.[2]

A number of officers did not believe in a harsh, unyielding disciplinary system and some argued for fundamental change. For instance, General James Fry opined that the military required an appellate court because of a lack of fair review by an independent authority. Fry believed that the court-martial had to evolve into something more than an executive instrument. At the same time, General Schofield admonished "the discipline which makes the soldiers of a free country reliable in battle is not to be gained by harsh or tyrannical treatment. On the contrary, such treatment is far more likely to destroy than to make an army."[3]

On the other hand, Generals Sherman and Sheridan argued that civilian influences had already crept into the military disciplinary system, rendering it weaker than intended. In typical forceful commentary, Sherman wrote,

> It will be a grave error if, by negligence, we permit the military law to become emasculated by allowing lawyers to inject into it principles derived from their practice in the civil courts, which belong to a totally different system of jurisprudence. . . . The object of the civil law is to secure to every human being in a community all of the liberty, security, and happiness possible, consistent with the safety of all. The object of military law is to govern armies composed of strong men so as to be capable of exercising the largest measure of force at the will of the nation.[4]

Sherman's view was not unique. Civil War veteran and Indian fighter Major General John Gibbon in 1880 decried the 1874 revision to the Articles of War. He began his general criticism with the statement, "Wars, notoriously always introduce loose notions into a country, and the military service does not escape the general demoralization." Gibbon continued with a specific attack on the revision stating, "Since the close of the Civil War, the revisions are matter of notoriety in the army." These views had their counterparts in foreign armies as well. In 1862, the French Marshal Auguste Marmont wrote that military justice "is not established, in an absolute manner, upon moral principles: its foundation is necessity." And, as noted in the prior chapter, a number of younger military theorists subscribed to the view of a stringent military justice system.[5]

In effect, Winthrop selected a middle ground in which the military maintained a separate system, but one in which fairness was judged by a continuing comparison—where possible—to the civilian practice of law. However, he did not lose sight of the general consensus in the military's leadership that, in his own words, "any radical remodeling would divest this time honored body of law of its historical associations and interest would be greatly depreceated."[6] Sherman likely did not agree with many of Winthrop's conclusions or his use of "comparative law" to ensure due process existed in the military courts-martial system. And yet, the fact that Winthrop took a historic common-law approach must have blunted some potential criticism from officers who believed, as Sherman did, in a retrenched military disciplinary system.

Opinions and criticism of the military justice system did not exist only at the highest echelon of command, or within the Judge Advocate General's Department either. In 1873, General Irwin McDowell after visiting Canada reported, "In the manner of enforcing discipline, we are much behind the British service . . . much of this difference between us, in the latter particular, is due to their system and our wont of one."[7] McDowell's assessment of the British system of discipline was inaccurate. That system suffered from the same, if not more severe, problems as the United States Army. At the same time as McDowell provided his views, Captain Frank Baldwin, serving as the acting judge advocate for the Department of the Columbia, argued the United States should employ the same disciplinary systems as the continental armies.[8] Opposite of McDowell and Sherman were a few judge advocates, including General Joseph Holt and Winthrop, but Norman Lieber and David Swaim criticized parts of the Articles of War and courts-martial practice.[9]

Winthrop believed that courts-martial served as a barometer for the efficiency and morale of the army. He argued that an unfair system contributed to the degradation of the army and actually caused more men to desert before their term of service was legally concluded. There was a good reason for Winthrop's belief in the relationship between a fair system of military justice and morale. Courts-martial were administered irregularly, and often for baseless reasons. Moreover, the sentences in each department often differed wildly from one another despite the similarity of offenses. In one geographic department it was possible for a deserter to be prosecuted in a general court-martial. In another department, the regimental court might be used, or none at all.

In 1872, Winthrop drafted General Holt's report to the secretary of war and included the statement, "The most serious defect in the administration of justice, and a positive injury to the service is the inequality of sentences adjudged by different courts for identical offenses."[10] Neither Holt nor Winthrop called for a sentencing structure that divested the court-martial of its charge in sentencing and the creation of sentencing guidelines. Yet, both men understood that the military courts-martial system was vulnerable to favoritism and despotic abuse, and the Bureau of Military Justice could not possibly discover and rectify all errors.[11]

Winthrop's later critics, notably World War I–era judge advocates Samuel T. Ansell and Edmund F. Morgan, a Yale law professor, viewed him as archaic and unresponsive to a modern and fair practice of law. Captain William Birkhimer, a contemporary of Winthrop's toward the end of Winthrop's career, also criticized Winthrop, albeit for a different reason. Birkhimer's criticism was chiefly that *Military Law* and *Military Law and Precedents* relied on hundreds of courts-martial records and general orders, many of which were drafted by Winthrop and located in the Judge Advocate General's Department, making them not readily available to the public. In essence, Birkhimer accused Winthrop of drafting general orders and courts-martial record reviews as part of his official duties and then presenting these as legal authority. Birkhimer was also a formalist interested only in the strict reading of rules, in an era where such scholars as Oliver Wendell Holmes Jr. stressed that law was a historic study and had to be liberally approached as such. As evidence of his retrenched view of military law, Birkhimer opined that William De Hart remained a superior source of law. Interestingly, De Hart had argued that American court-martial practice should be free from foreign influences and Birkhimer followed suit, claiming that the United States had little to learn from foreign military laws, even in a comparative legal analysis.[12]

Professionalizing the Judge Advocate General's Department in the post–Civil War period posed significant difficulties, in part, because Congress altered the Department's composition on several occasions. The act of July 28, 1866, organized the War Department staff into ten administrative departments and technical bureaus, including the Judge Advocate General's Department. The department possessed administrative oversight into not only courts-martial, but all legal matters affecting the army's geographic divisions and departments. Within the Judge Advocate General's Department, the subsidiary Bureau of Military Justice remained responsible for reviewing courts-martial records and providing advice to the secretary of war as well as the commanding general. Beginning in 1874, a judge advocate was assigned to the United States Military Academy at West Point, and the duties there included both instruction as well as the typical duties found in the geographic divisions.[13]

In its 1866 legislation, Congress authorized the continued existence of the judge advocate general and assistant judge advocate, but only provided for the temporary retention of "not more than ten judge advocates." Congress lowered the number of temporary authorizations to eight in 1869. In 1874, Congress abolished the assistant judge advocate general position and froze the accession of new judge advocates until the number of judge advocates was attrited to four.[14] As a result, the second-ranking judge advocate in Washington, DC, served as a non-statutory de facto deputy to the judge advocate general. The law did not create a line of succession in the event the judge advocate general was unable to serve or a vacancy occurred. In 1881, this had an unfortunate consequence for Winthrop. He was General Dunn's de facto deputy. But Winthrop did not possess any statutory authority so that when Dunn retired, Winthrop only served as an acting judge advocate general until a replacement was appointed.

In its act of July 5, 1884, Congress legislated the Judge Advocate General's Department to consist of one judge advocate general with the rank of brigadier general, one assistant judge advocate with the rank of colonel, three judge advocates with the rank of lieutenant colonel, and three judge advocates with the rank of major. The act also terminated the Bureau of Military Justice, combining its duties with the Judge Advocate General's Headquarters. This had the effect of consolidating review of courts-martial into a single appeal stage. And, for the first time, Congress sanctioned the temporary detailing of line officers with the rank of captain to the judge advocate position for the various departments. In effect, Congress legislated a century-old practice which had existed as a matter of custom.[15]

The stagnation in career advancement affecting the army as a whole held true in the Judge Advocate General's Department in 1884. At its head was General David Swaim, but his selection was a classic Gilded Age appointment and would, for reasons later noted, prove to be a bane to the department. Indeed, Swaim's conduct as judge advocate general was one of the three specific influences that gave Winthrop impetus to professionalize the practice of military law.[16] This is not to suggest that Swaim was devoid of all morality. To the contrary, prior to the Civil War, he was a member of an Ohio abolitionist group, and he generally acted in the interests of racial equality under the law. Prior to 1882, Winthrop had supervised Swaim when the two were assigned to the Bureau of Military Justice.

Second in seniority to Swaim was Norman G. Lieber, who was appointed as assistant judge advocate. Lieber saw action in the Peninsula Campaign as an infantry officer. He became a judge advocate in November 1862 and served that capacity in New Orleans and in the Red River Expedition of 1864 under General Nathaniel Banks. Lieber remained on active duty after the war, first as the judge advocate to the Gulf Division, followed by the Department of the Dakota, and later as an instructor at the United States Military Academy. In 1884, he was transferred to the Bureau of Military Justice just before it was consolidated into the Judge Advocate General's Department. In terms of seniority, Lieber ranked just ahead of Winthrop, and this fact, along with his posting, made him the assistant judge advocate when that position was statutorily restored.

In addition to Swaim, Lieber, and Winthrop, there were five other judge advocates of note between 1868 and 1884: Majors Horace Burnham, Thomas Barr, Herbert Curtis, Henry Goodfellow, and Asa B. Gardner. (In 1872, Gardner was appointed a judge advocate after De Witt Clinton died.) All of these staff officers fought in the Union army during the Civil War. Herbert Curtis served as an infantry officer at Antietam, while Henry Goodfellow also saw action at Yorktown, Malvern Hill, Fredericksburg, Chancellorsville, and Gettysburg. Goodfellow served in the British Army during the Crimean War as well. During the war, Gardner was awarded a Medal of Honor for his regiment's valor at Chambersburg and later became well-known for his prosecution of a black military cadet at the academy as well as his service on the Schofield Board of Inquiry into Fitz-John Porter. Though the Medal of Honor was later rescinded, it made him unique among his fellow judge advocates. He also became the most controversial of all judge advocates in the late nineteenth century and—for reasons later noted—earned Schofield's enmity.[17]

The 1866 act also cemented the other staff departments that were already in existence and would remain so through World War II. These staff departments included the adjutant general, who was responsible for conveying orders to the geographic divisions and departments. The adjutant general's duties had the most immediate impact on the judge advocates, in some part because a number of courts-martial charges involved the lawfulness of orders. There was some crossover in responsibilities between the adjutant general and judge advocate, but it does not appear to have resulted in tension between the two offices. However, the actions of the various adjutant generals may have had an indirect influence in the practice of military law in that the promulgation of military-wide regulations ordered the behavior of soldiers. The 1866 act also legislated the inspector general, responsible for inspecting all aspects of the army, which also had a nominal influence in the practice of military law; the Quartermaster's Corps; the Subsistence Department; the Medical

Corps; the Paymaster; the Corps of Engineers; the Signal Corps; and the Ordnance Bureau. Although the geographic divisions and departments changed a number of times between 1865 and 1897, the staff departments remained largely stable.[18] However, the independence of the staff departments occasionally caused contention between the commanding general and the department heads.

Prior to Swaim's leapfrog promotion, Winthrop occasionally took on the mantle of acting judge advocate general such as when General Dunn went on leave. Even prior to Dunn's promotion, there were occasions when both Holt and Dunn were out of the capital, leaving Winthrop the senior judge advocate. Only once, however, was Winthrop's tenure as the acting judge advocate general officially ordered. When Dunn retired on January 22, 1881, Winthrop assumed the position of acting judge advocate general. He remained in the position until February 18 of that year when President Hayes nominated Swaim. On February 2, the adjutant general issued an order which read, "the President directs that Major Winthrop, Judge Advocate, be assigned to act as Judge Advocate General until a Judge Advocate General shall have been appointed and entered upon duty." Clearly, it was intended Winthrop would not rise to the top position at that time. During his occasional tenures as acting judge advocate general, Winthrop performed diverse legal duties, which included engaging the Justice Department to press a railroad corporation to fulfill its contractual duties or face a suit in United States District Court, as well as advising on issues such as foreign military officers' inspection of United States soldiers and United States–Canadian military relations.[19]

Winthrop's regular duties at the Bureau of Military Justice were the same as during the Civil War. Occasionally, he investigated matters assigned to him from Holt or Dunn. In April 1870, he was ordered to investigate an allegation from a civilian in Philadelphia who claimed an officer had seduced his wife, taken her to Idaho, and "ruined her." Whether the allegation was founded and the officer court-martialed is unknown.[20] But in the mainstay of his work, Winthrop reviewed results of trials and recommended to Holt and then Dunn whether a conviction or sentence should be modified, sustained, or disapproved. Conveying court-martial records to the Bureau of Military Justice was undoubtedly an imperfect process. However, one of Winthrop's sources of angst was the number of these records which arrived with critical information missing. This had been a problem in the Civil War, leading to a number of convictions being overturned by the president. It was also a source of friction between the geographic division judge advocates and the bureau.

One instance might have been the origin of a dispute between Barr and Winthrop which did not abate until Winthrop's retirement in 1895. Following Winthrop's advice in late 1874, Holt chastised Barr for a number of imperfect court-martial records. Defending himself while assigned to the Department of the Dakota, Barr sought to shift the blame back onto the Bureau of Military Justice, writing, "I cannot express to you how much I am annoyed by the contents of your official communication of the 23d. Blame should not attach to me for intentional loss."[21] The following month, Winthrop advised Barr to recuse himself from a case in which he prejudged the veracity of witnesses, likely to the detriment of the accused. Again writing to Holt, Barr conveyed in an accusatory tone that he saw no need to withdraw from the case.[22]

Winthrop was not relegated to the nation's capital while assigned to the Bureau of Military Justice, and he did not merely conduct appellate-level reviews of courts-martial. Nor was he simply a law commentator. He was a practitioner who brought his idealism and principles into the practice of law. Like the other judge advocates, his duties took him on assignments away from headquarters.

In 1870, Winthrop was sent to the United States Military Academy to serve as judge advocate in a court-martial of the academy's first black cadet, James Webster Smith. Although the case has languished in obscurity for most of the twentieth century, it was an important case when it went to trial. Part of the reason Cadet Smith's court-martial has been largely forgotten is the shoddy scholarship of some military historians writing on the history of the academy.[23] The *New York Times* reported the case on its front page three times, alongside news as important as the 1870 Franco-Prussian War. Smith was accused of criminal conduct and any hope of instilling an egalitarian environment at the academy rested with the outcome of the case, in part, because it was the first case of its kind.

Cadet Smith was born into slavery on a South Carolina plantation. His father became a prosperous carpenter after emancipation. In his youth, Smith was educated in a Freedman's Bureau school. He was, by all records, intelligent and articulate, and in his early teens he was brought to Hartford, Connecticut, by a white benefactor named David Clark. In early 1870, Smith attended Howard University. However, a unique opportunity presented itself shortly after his course of study began at Howard. A vacancy occurred at the academy, and the year prior a Republican congressman had forwarded Smith's nomination.[24]

At first Cadet Smith performed relatively well despite ostracism from his mainly Northern classmates. Frederick Grant, the president's son, was a classmate though not an ally to the cause of promoting blacks into the officer ranks. Indeed, it has been well argued that Cadet Fred Grant participated in Smith's downfall.[25] A few of the academy's administrators supported Smith in the sense that his fellow cadets' efforts to isolate him were monitored. But Smith encountered difficulties which the faculty could not protect him from unless it placed him isolation. For instance, the night Smith arrived at the academy, he and another black cadet were attacked in their sleep when other cadets dumped the contents of a slops bucket on them.[26]

Smith passed his experiences to Clark, who in turn publicized the accounts to the *Hartford Currant*. On July 2, 1870, the *Currant* published Clark's account of Smith's ostracism and the cadet hazing against him at the academy. One professor retorted that Smith was "malicious, vindictive, and untruthful." It also seems the case that Colonel Emory Upton, then serving as the academy's commandant, did not approve of Smith's presence. Many cadets and faculty officers opined Smith lied about his mistreatment. Yet, Smith's claims of abuse were later corroborated by another black cadet, Henry Ossian Flipper. Smith's public allegations set off a series of arguments over the propriety of a black cadet between Colonel Thomas G. Pitcher, the superintendent, and other faculty on one side, and General O. O. Howard and Senators Charles Sumner and Benjamin Butler on the other. Howard, Butler, and Sumner saw it as their duty to integrate the academy, and Butler possessed antipathy toward the academy dating to before the Civil War.[27]

In response to the demands of Congress, as well as growing newspaper interest in the matter, the academy held a court of inquiry to investigate Smith's allegations of mistreatment. On July 21 the inquiry concluded that most of Smith's claims were unfounded, and it recommended Smith face a court-martial. The court-martial never convened as Secretary of War Belknap reduced Smith's liability to a formal reprimand. However, one month later Smith was involved in an altercation with another cadet named J. Wilson. It is likely the other cadet stuck the first blow, and Smith responded by assaulting the other cadet with a water dipper. A third cadet formally reported that Smith had "acted in a disrespectful manner" during an evening drill. To back his claim, the cadet brought three other witnesses to testify against Smith. Emory Upton preferred charges against Smith, alleging assault as well as making false official statements in denying his disrespect.[28]

This time Secretary Belknap ordered a court-martial. There was nothing out of the ordinary in a cadet facing court-martial for offenses such as this. Indeed, the experience of the army in the Civil War revealed the propensity of some officers to use the court-martial as a means for revenge or engineering an individual's personal advancement. But Smith's court-martial captured the interest of newspapers in a way routine courts-martial did not. To ensure a fair trial, General Joseph Holt appointed Winthrop as judge advocate. The role of the judge advocate had not changed since the Civil War, and Winthrop found himself acting as legal advisor to the board of officers, prosecutor for the government, and representative of the interests of the accused. This last role occurred in conformity with the duties of a judge advocate since Smith declined all counsel. Also present on the court was its president, General O. O. Howard, as well as General Thomas C. Devin, a cavalry veteran of Gettysburg and a number of other Army of the Potomac campaigns, and three other senior officers.[29]

It is understandable to see why Smith thought his trial would result in an injustice as even the *New York Times* initially presented the case in a biased tenor. Prejudging the case as Wilson being the victim and Smith the aggressor, it reported on its front page, "Cadet Wilson has the sympathy of the entire corps. He is a much smaller person than his antagonist and has always enjoyed a good reputation of being a good, quiet, well-behaved fellow." In opposition to this glowing characterization, the *Times* stated, "Smith is the exact opposite, his obstinate manner and many inconsistencies have brought him into disrepute."[30]

On October 21, 1870, the court-martial convened and heard the testimony of several witnesses swearing Smith acted in a disrespectful manner to senior cadets and claiming that he assaulted the other cadet with the water dipper without any provocation. Testifying in his own defense, Smith admitted to assaulting the other cadet, but only as a matter of self-defense. He denied any act of disrespect to senior cadets while on drill. He also took exception to the date of the assault offense listed on the charge sheet. He delivered an eloquent closing argument, stating, "I am here seeking an honorable acquittal, not on technicalities but on the unimpeachable strength of a sound cause that justice shall be done me and the cadet boys."[31] Winthrop did not, in his closing argument, concentrate on the conflicting testimony between the cadets, but he did use Smith's testimony against him. Smith, in fact, admitted to assaulting the other cadet with the water dipper and did not back away from the fight. Winthrop used this admission to establish guilt.[32] Smith's admitted conduct presented a conundrum occasionally faced by cadets and officers alike. The law on self-defense required Smith to back away from the fight unless becoming involved in it was a matter of last resort. On the other hand, had Smith followed the law, his fellow cadets would have branded him a coward, which in and of itself would have been a violation of a "custom of the service." In *Military Law* and *Military Law and Precedents*, Winthrop pointed out that the law always trumped a custom of the service. Although Winthrop used a number of examples in *Military Law and Precedents* to show how a custom of the service conflicted with law, he did not use Smith's conduct as such. Winthrop's argument accorded with his position on the law trumping custom.

The case concluded in three days, but it took an unusually long period for the court to publish its verdict and sentence since the secretary of war had to approve the findings and sentence before its release. On

October 26, the court closed and found Smith only guilty of the assault, but the public was unaware of the result until November 14, 1870. Disregarding the testimony of the white cadets, the court did not find Smith guilty of any false statements. It also sentenced Smith the very light punishment of having to walk post from two o'clock p.m. until retreat for six consecutive Saturdays.[33]

After the court-martial, Clark criticized the selection of Howard and Winthrop to the case. The criticism was not personally directed at the two officers, but rather Clark claimed that they were selected for political reasons, so that in the event Smith was convicted and dismissed, the public would have perceived the trial was fair. Clark also alleged that President Grant engaged in what would be today termed as "unlawful command influence" by leaning on Howard to convict and dismiss Smith. However, Howard denied Clark's allegations, and there is nothing in the available records to support Clark's claims. Indeed, it is the case that Holt, acting on the advice of Winthrop, advised the secretary of war and President Grant to remit Smith's sentence.[34]

Smith was permitted to remain at the academy for the duration of his education. He faced another court-martial, this time spearheaded by then Lieutenant Asa Gardner. However, unlike his first trial, the *New York Times* supported Smith. Writing, "The charges are, in military ambiguity, conduct unbecoming an officer and a gentleman and insubordinate conduct," the *Times* went on to ridicule the timing of the trial, arguing "this alleged offense occurred on 28 November, the very afternoon that the official order of the War Department was published to the cadet corps at evening parade, acquitting Wilson of the charges entertained at his court." And the paper damned Smith's fellow cadets who had arrayed against him, claiming, "With one or two honorable exceptions, the entire corps of cadets cherish the most bitter hatred against the color of Smith."[35]

Smith was convicted of inattention in the ranks and sentenced to a dismissal from the academy, but once more on the advice of the Bureau of Military Justice, the secretary of war reduced the sentence so that Smith was held back for one year. But he struggled academically after his second court-martial. Even the arrival of Henry Ossian Flipper did not reverse Smith's slide in class standing. By the summer of 1874, Smith was dropped from the academy and returned to civilian life in South Carolina.[36] He then wrote a series of articles criticizing the academy and relating his personal experiences while a cadet. He never criticized the judge advocate from his first trial or named Winthrop in his articles. Perhaps he would have eventually done so, but as he died of tuberculosis in 1876, Smith did not finish his quest for personal justice. On the other hand, it may be the case Smith felt his original court-martial result was fair, and that the board of officers did not exercise any racism against him. After all, the court-martial under Winthrop's guidance took the word of a black cadet over the sworn testimony of several white cadets. He later complained that he did not have counsel at the second trial, writing in 1874, "I had no counsel at this trial as I knew it would be useless, considering the one-sided condition of affairs."[37]

Smith's fellow cadet Henry Flipper met an equal and, perhaps, even more unkind fate. He was commissioned into the officer ranks, only to be sent west and ostracized from his fellow officers. Ultimately, he too was court-martialed on specious grounds. Monies that Flipper had been placed in charge of were stolen or lost, and he was accused of embezzlement. He was found guilty of conduct unbecoming an officer but not embezzlement, though his sentence consisted of a dismissal from the service. Lieutenant Flipper left the service in disgrace and spent the rest of his life unsuccessfully trying to reverse his conviction and sentence. In 1982, the Department of the Army posthumously upgraded Flipper's discharge to honorable, and in 1999 President William Clinton issued a pardon.[38]

The second half of the nineteenth century proved almost impossible for black cadets to graduate, let alone have a successful military career. Racism was a "clarion call," and enough white officers and cadets stooped to low enough levels to ensure only a trickle of black officer aspirants could succeed. In 1880, an equally repugnant injustice was not stopped with the court-martial of Cadet Johnson Chestnut Whittaker. In that case, Major Asa Bird Gardner spearheaded a conviction resulting in expulsion from the academy despite specious evidence behind the charges against the cadet. Gardner's conduct in the case may not have been the initial reason behind Winthrop's slight regard for his fellow judge advocate, or Gardner's mentor Major Thomas Barr, but it certainly contributed to Winthrop's disdain for both, whom he saw as conniving and unethical.[39]

On April 6, 1880, Cadet Whittaker was assaulted by "unknown persons" and discovered bound and unconscious on the floor. His feet and ears were cut as well. Not surprisingly, some of the faculty suspected that Whittaker staged the incident to avoid failing an exam for the second time. General Schofield, then serving as the superintendent, convened a court of inquiry to determine whether Whittaker was assaulted or staged the incident. The findings of the court of inquiry were examined by Major Barr who, in turn, recommended the prosecution of Whittaker. The central reason for Barr's advice had to do with a letter of warning Whittaker claimed he received prior to the assault.[40] Barr surmised that the letter matched Whittaker's handwriting. The case had such a high level of interest that President Hayes appointed a defense counsel for Whittaker.

At trial, Gardner engaged in racial stereotyping which would be so objectionable today as to warrant a new trial if not a dismissal of charges with prejudice to the government. At the time of the trial Gardner's conduct was, to many including Winthrop, clearly objectionable and offensive, depriving Whittaker of a fair trial. For instance, Gardner argued that "Negroes are noted for their ability to sham and feign." Gardner also introduced questionable "expert" testimony matching the warning letter with Whittaker's other writing. The evidence was persuasive enough to the court-martial to convict Whittaker of the charges of conduct unbecoming an officer as well as conduct to the prejudice of good order and discipline.[41] However, President Chester Arthur and Attorney General Brewster determined the handwriting expert's testimony was neither fair nor accurate. Swaim, who by this time was promoted as judge advocate general, bolstered their belief. On March 22, 1882, President Arthur ordered Whittaker released from arrest and voided the trial. Although Whittaker was exonerated, he did not return to West Point.[42]

General David Swaim excoriated Gardner's performance in the Whittaker case. The judge advocate general did not conclude his criticism with Gardner; he also blasted Schofield for permitting the case to go forward.[43] Winthrop agreed with Swaim's assessment on Gardner. As a professional, he had long looked at Gardner as an undesirable officer with a lack of professionalism; an arrogant showboat. But he did not, for reasons discussed in the following chapters, agree with Swaim's assessment on Schofield.

It was not until the publication of *Military Law* in 1886 that Winthrop found a means to criticize Gardner's performance in the case. The specific issue addressed the use of handwriting experts. He suggested that Gardner had handpicked the few correspondences of Whittaker's which favorably showed a comparison to the warning note, while ignoring the reams of other correspondence which did not. He also called the government's expert evidence in Whittaker's case "fanciful, unsubstantial, and of slight value."[44] Given Winthrop's views on racial equality before the law, just as it was unlikely he conducted the Cadet Smith court-martial unfairly, it was equally likely that Gardner's race baiting offended his beliefs. Yet, in *Military Law and Precedents*, Winthrop acknowledged the special status of the case and opined, "There were, however, special circumstances in this case which doubtless availed to induce the authorities to give to the accused (a colored person), the full benefit as to the application of law in his defense."[45]

Did Winthrop change his position on Whittaker's innocence, racial equality in military law, or colored persons serving as commissioned officers in the intervening nine years? In the context of the whole 1895 treatise, the answer is clearly no, because he also noted that the prosecutor's use of otherwise inadmissible evidence, rendered "one of the most laborious and extended investigations by courts-martial ever held in this country . . . to naught."[46] Thus Winthrop placed the blame squarely on Gardner and remained objective as to Whittaker's conduct. Interestingly, however, at the same time he argued that the strict common-law prohibition against introducing expert testimony on handwriting should terminate as state jurisdictions had adopted a more liberal admissibility standard, and that a court-martial "composed of educated and intelligent officers of the army" may be safely trusted to depart from the strict common-law rule "where other sufficient means are wanting."[47]

While Winthrop felt the Whittaker court-martial proved a need to professionalize the practice of military law, there were other reasons as well. Officers were unaware as to the extent of their authority. Although there was any number of times in a year that an officer overstepped the limits of his authority, a few examples stand out. In one instance, Winthrop had to advise the secretary of war and General Holt on a case of a captain who, on his own volition, went into Manitoba, Canada, to arrest deserters. The captain, one J. Granville Gates, left "on personal business from Fort Pembina" in the Dakota Territory and learned of a deserter in Manitoba.[48] Without the permission of the Canadian government and in civilian attire, he arrested the deserter and conveyed him back to Fort Pembina. Once at the fort, Gates apparently obtained the permission of the post adjutant and the post's acting judge advocate to return to Canada and arrest other deserters. Gates traveled as far as Hudson Bay and arrested another civilian he believed to be a deserter. On their way out of Canada, Gates was stopped by a Canadian policeman, but Gates assured the officer that he had permission to enter into Canada to arrest deserters. Gates also apparently thought after consulting the *Digest* that his actions were legal. Problematic to the deserters' arrests, aside from the violation of Canadian sovereignty, was the governor general of Manitoba's response. He protested to the United States Consul at Winnipeg, according to Gates, informing the consul that incursions into crown territory for whatever reasons would not be tolerated.

It was not unusual for officers to search for deserters and return them to the jurisdiction of the army. But in this case, the fact that an officer crossed into the territory of a foreign country was a patently illegal act. In their own defense, Gates and the adjutant stated that the apprehension of deserters in Canadian Territory was a normal occurrence. To Gates, the fact that the army assisted British Army officers in apprehending British deserters in the Dakota Territory evidenced the legality of his act. Moreover, Gates was under the impression that his superiors endorsed his conduct. Seeking help, Gates contacted Holt directly, perhaps not realizing Holt had retired three months earlier. Gates inquired whether his conduct was illegal and if so, could Holt "spare a moment to point out the best line of defense in case of trial."[49]

Instead of Holt privately reading the letter, Bureau of Military Justice personnel opened it and conveyed it to Winthrop. Winthrop resealed the letter after reading it and contacted Gates on his own. Apprising Holt of his actions, Winthrop assured Holt that he provided basic legal advice to Gates, including collecting all exculpatory and extenuating evidence in the event of a court-martial. Winthrop also informed Holt that the bureau had not as yet heard of the case. He conveyed his impressions as to the need for increased law education as well.[50] It does not appear that Gates was prosecuted in a court-martial after all. But the fact that Gates and the acting judge advocate erroneously interpreted the *Digest* rankled Winthrop. Gates' conduct further enforced Winthrop's belief that the officer corps needed a service-wide legal reference, and the *Digest* fell short of providing this. While Gate's conduct was not a primary reason Winthrop authored *Military Law*, the issue added to his view that training in the military law was essential for officers. While the matter quietly died, the Gates case showed that the conduct of a single officer could affect foreign relations with the British Empire. And it may have been for this reason that Winthrop later wrote that a superior officer's order to a subordinate to cross into Mexico or Canada for the purpose of arresting deserters was an unlawful order.[51]

While the Cadet Smith and Cadet Whittaker cases reinforced Winthrop's belief that military law had to enforce equality because without the strong arm of that body of law, too many officers would seek to deny equal justice to black soldiers, there was another case which convinced Winthrop that the practice of military law needed to professionalize commensurate, if not to a greater degree, to the civilian practice of law. The case directly involved David G. Swaim, judge advocate general, and its importance to Winthrop cannot be understated.

Swaim had served as line officer in the Union army during the Civil War, though usually as James G. Garfield's aide-de-camp or adjutant in the western theater of the war. He served as an ad hoc judge advocate for the Fourth Military District at Vicksburg, where he oversaw a number of military commissions. According to one historic source, Swaim drafted the government's brief for *ex Parte McCardle*.[52]

In 1881, Swaim entered into a business relationship with the firm of Bateman and Company through a loan to a third-party partner in the firm. As a result of the loan, Swaim was given an account which covered stock and bond purchases, as well as personal checking. He also received a five thousand dollar "due bill," which Swaim considered as a corporate debt, owed by Bateman. In 1884, Swaim attempted to cash out his account and obtain a return on his due bill. The firm claimed Swaim's investment and due bill were worth less than one hundred dollars, and Swaim responded by bringing suit through an unconventional means. He assigned the due bill to a construction company, of which he was also a shareholder, for the purpose of the company bringing suit against Bateman. This meant the construction firm paid for all of Swaim's legal expenses involved in the suit. While Swaim's assignment of the construction firm to represent him would unlikely be permitted in the twenty-first century, it was not illegal when Swaim transferred the debt.[53] Still, the transfer of funds to an unknowing third party for the purpose of shifting liabilities showed an ethical lapse in Swaim's conduct.

There were other problems with the transfer of the debt. Swaim commented to the *Army-Navy Journal* that his purpose in transferring the debt to the construction firm was to "avoid newspaper talk." This reason cut against him as much as it provided a possible exculpatory intent. And the week following Swaim's stated reasoning, the president of the construction firm contradicted Swaim, claiming the judge advocate general owed the firm $3,500 to $4,000.[54]

In response, Bateman brought the matter to Secretary of War Robert Todd Lincoln claiming to be a victim of Swaim's fraud. Bateman also claimed to have knowledge of other frauds involving Swaim. Two allegations in particular against Swaim struck at the heart of the military. Bateman accused Swaim of negotiating fraudulent army pay vouchers to the firm and pressuring a lieutenant colonel to pull his personal investment from the firm or face dismissal from the army. As an aside, if Bateman did in fact have truthful knowledge of fraudulent pay vouchers transferred to the firm, he knowingly benefited from this illegal act but was never prosecuted for taking part in it.[55]

Lincoln initially wanted the parties to settle their differences by arbitration, but both Bateman and Swaim took their claims to the public. Moreover, Swaim, in attempting to explain his position, appeared to Lincoln to have been untruthful about any of Bateman's allegations. As a result, President Chester Arthur ordered a court of inquiry, which in turn recommended court-martial.

In response to the court of inquiry's recommendation, Lincoln convened two separate courts-martial against Swaim. The first was to determine whether Swaim violated Article of War 61 (conduct unbecoming an officer and a gentleman) in his dealings toward Bateman. Four specifications were drafted under a single charge, including dishonesty toward Lincoln and the threat to dismiss an officer. A second charge against Swaim was brought up under Article 62 (neglect of duty), which involved the fraudulent pay accounts. The two sets of charges were split into separate courts-martial. Swaim could have resigned at this point, but he provided to the *Army-Navy Journal* his reason for remaining on active duty as confidence of his exoneration.[56]

Major Gardner was appointed judge advocate to the court-martial. Gardner's appointment was problematic for two reasons. He held a deep-seated resentment against Swaim over the Cadet Whittaker case, and his deportment during Swaim's court-martial was no better than it had been during the Fitz-John Porter court of inquiry.

The first court-martial panel consisted of a veritable "who's-who," of army officers, including Major General Schofield; Brigadier Generals Alfred Terry, Nelson Miles, William Rochester (the paymaster general), Samuel Holabird (the quartermaster general), Robert Murray (the surgeon general), and John Newton (the chief of engineers); and six colonels. After the court, Schofield and Miles consecutively became commanding generals of the army. Along with Schofield and Miles, each of the staff generals saw significant action in the line during the Civil War.

Swaim objected to Schofield, Terry, and Rochester. In the modern era, Swaim had a valid objection against both Rochester and Schofield. Rochester had testified in Swaim's court of inquiry, and Swaim excoriated Schofield during a legal review of the court-martial against Cadet Whittaker. Under Gardner's guidance, the court retained Schofield, but not Rochester.[57]

Despite Schofield's retention on the court, the result of trial was not a complete defeat for Swaim. The trial lacked excitement and even the *Army-Navy Journal* ceased placing the news in its headlines, writing, "The proceedings have not been exciting, the trial being occupied with the minute examination and cross examination of Bateman as to his transactions with General Swaim." As a result, evidence of Swaim's conduct ceased to be presented to the public eye. Swaim was found guilty of the lesser included offense of "conduct to the prejudice of good order and military discipline," in violation of the Article of War 62. As a result, the court did not sentence Swaim to a dismissal, and instead suspended him from rank, duty, and pay for three years. The second court-martial, with the same officer members, acquitted Swaim outright. However, Swaim's conviction and sentence from the first case did not conclude the matter.[58]

President Arthur, relying on the advice of the attorney general, found errors in the sentence and ordered the court to reconvene to sentence Swaim once more. This time, the court sentenced Swaim to a one-year suspension and reduction to the grade of judge advocate. Once more, President Arthur found error and reconvened the court. The error was legitimate since the second sentence carried a reduction in rank from brigadier general to major. The law did not at that time, as it does not today, empower a court-martial to reduce an officer's grade. Once more the court reconvened and sentenced Swaim on February 16, this time to a twelve-year suspension of rank, duty, and pay. At the time, the court-martial's ceiling was not limited by the original sentence.

Although Arthur expressed disgust at retaining Swaim as a "pensioner," he accepted the sentence.[59]

Two aspects of the Swaim trial stood out to Winthrop. Swaim's selection to the highest staff position and his lack of professionalism were not merely a personal matter. It reflected a need for professionalism among the judge advocates. The second aspect was the conduct of the prosecuting judge advocate. Winthrop already disliked Major Gardner before the trial. During the trial, Gardner's treatment of African American witnesses was appallingly unprofessional and often laced with prejudicial stereotypes. He also rudely treated prominent civilian defense counsel, accusing one of feigning a real illness to gain a delay.[60] So while Winthrop was disgusted with Swaim, he was equally critical of Gardner. However, unlike his approach to the Whittaker case, Winthrop was silent in *Military Law* as to Gardner's performance in Swaim's trial. He was not silent in his opinion of Swaim in a letter to General Holt, however, in which he excoriated both Swaim and Gardner.[61]

Just as Winthrop did not overtly display anger at having been passed over by Swaim for the top position, he did not publicly gloat over Swaim's court-martial. It may be the case that since he was already stationed in California, he was too distant from the court-martial to comment on it at the time it occurred. August Kautz, one of Winthrop's fellow officers at the Presidio, commented in his diary that the Swaim case was the foremost subject of discussion among officers stationed at the division headquarters. Kautz did not record Winthrop's opinions on Swaim, however, and it may be that Winthrop held his opinions to himself.

Winthrop's distance from the Bureau of Military Justice did not stop members of his family, including Laura Johnson, from publicly arguing Swaim's ascension to Judge Advocate General was flawed from the start. She wrote an editorial to the *New York Tribune* using the case to call for civil service reform. She also lashed into Swaim's selection, stating, "Swaim was put in by President Hayes at the close of his administration to please Garfield whose selection he was." She charged that Swaim's appointment was "a political bargain" and then unfavorably compared Swaim to his peers, claiming, "He was the youngest and last appointed of the judge advocates, and to give him the place above Lieber and Winthrop who stood at the head of the list were passed over, is an affront."[62]

Laura did not place Winthrop at the head of the eligible judge advocates, writing, "Lieber was the first appointed judge advocate and son of Prof. Lieber (of Columbia College) and an able man." Instead, Laura listed Winthrop as a second choice, writing, "Winthrop, educated as a lawyer at Yale and Harvard had been chief assistant in the Bureau of Military Justice for eighteen years and highest recommendations from Generals Holt and Dunn." Her summation, "To have passed over such men as these and appoint a man who has himself been brought to trial as chief judicial officer of the army is a disgrace to that body of men, as a rule so honorable and unimpeachable," echoed what Winthrop and his peers likely felt.[63] But he could not agree with the publication of the letter and on receiving notice from the editor, he asked for the letter not to be published. While he clearly appreciated his sister's support, he could not endorse bringing the army or Judge Advocate General's Department into further disrepute.[64] This incident stands as a testament to his loyalty to the army; he placed the good of the service over his own anger and desire for advancement.

Winthrop had a readily available outlet by which to keep the Swaim case at the forefront of military legal practice. He explained his reason for researching and writing *Military Law* to Secretary of War William C. Endicott as partly one in which he hoped the work would rebuild the damaged reputation of the Judge Advocate General's Department. Writing, "Especially in view of the embarrassing, and to me, humiliating state of my department of the Army consequent upon the trial and sentence of its official head, my literary work is the only means by which I can add to my reputation or record as an officer, or perform satisfactory service of a valuable and pertinent character." The statement indicated an overt personal ambition for the first time in his career, but it also, and more importantly, described that his work was in direct response to Swaim's connivance.[65]

In *Military Law,* Winthrop cited Swaim's court-martial five times. In no less than twenty cites did Winthrop reference Swaim in *Military Law and Precedents*. For instance, Winthrop used the case to explain that while commanders generally convene courts-martial, the president, as commander in chief, maintained the authority to do so in particular cases.[66] Likewise, the requirement of trial before members equal or superior in rank to the accused could give way in instances where the accused was of such high rank that it was impossible to find unbiased members otherwise fitting the rank requirement.[67] Winthrop commented that the validity of any charge is not negated simply because it was preferred against an accused by a competent civilian (though at Winthrop's time there were only two civilians fitting this description, the president and the secretary of war).

In his treatment on the nature of courts of inquiry, Winthrop used the Swaim case as an example of how such courts functioned. He noted that "a court of inquiry is neither a court-martial, nor a court of justice." Its limited scope was, in Winthrop's words, "to examine and inquire." In Swaim's court of inquiry, the officers determined there was enough evidence to warrant a court-martial prosecution. Winthrop did not limit his treatment of courts of inquiry to the Swaim case. He utilized the British spy Major John Andre's court of inquiry as well to serve as an example of how an inquiry functioned in investigating charges of spying. Placing Swaim's case alongside of Andre's may have been nothing more than an instance of using well-known examples for the purpose of education. Yet, one has to wonder whether Winthrop believed Swaim's conduct constituted a betrayal of the Judge Advocate General's Department to the point that it bordered on a personal treason.[68]

As to President Arthur's treatment of the court's sentence, Winthrop agreed with the president's actions, stating that where the president finds a sentence to violate law, he possesses the authority to order the court to reassess the sentence. In Swaim's case, the sentence of reduction to a lower rank had no basis in law. The fact that the court-martial panel committed a further error did not divest the president of the authority to resend the trial back to the court a third time.[69] Winthrop's commentary on Swaim may have served another purpose as well. President Arthur's decision to twice send the sentence back to the court drew congressional criticism over the fairness of the military court system. In arguing the lawfulness of Arthur's decisions, Winthrop may have helped to quiet criticism of the Articles of War.

Winthrop reserved his harshest criticism for Swaim in his analysis of the Article 61. Also known as conduct unbecoming an officer and a gentleman, there were hundreds of trials Winthrop could have used. However, while Winthrop listed hundreds of cases by their corresponding convening order number, he listed Swaim's case by name. Winthrop stated the offense of conduct unbecoming an officer and a gentleman "need not amount to a crime, it must offend so seriously against law, justice, morality, or decorum and at the same time must be of such a nature or committed under such circumstances as to bring dishonor or disrepute upon the military profession." To Winthrop, this was precisely the nature of Swaim's conduct. The judge advocate general's conduct might not have amounted to a crime in a civil court, but when committed by a general officer, it certainly brought disrepute on the officer as well as the service.[70]

When, in 1893, Swaim failed to have his sentence overturned by the Court of Claims, he appealed to the Supreme Court. Swaim had advanced a unique argument to the Court of Claims, arguing that since—in his opinion—the court-martial was not lawfully constituted, he was improperly deprived of full pay and allowances. The Court of Claims issued an adverse decision to Swaim, relying on the jurisdiction precedent established in *Dynes v. Hoover*. In 1897, the Supreme Court upheld the Court of Claim's decision.[71] Winthrop used both courts' decisions in *Military Law and Precedents* to detail the legality of the procedures and jurisdiction of courts-martial. Moreover, in upholding the Claims Court and the original verdict, the Supreme Court legitimized the possibility of having court members junior in rank to an accused.

While the Swaim court-martial and a variety of other personal experiences led Winthrop to research and write *Military Law*, his scholarly approach to the treatise mirrored a growing late nineteenth-century jurisprudential philosophy stressing the importance of the military common law and the influence that individual jurists had on it. Winthrop authored *Military Law* in a period in which the academic approach to law and the practice of law were both undergoing change.

In 1881, Oliver Wendell Holmes Jr., then a Harvard Law professor, published *The Common Law*. It was an instrumental work by a legal scholar whose background was similar to Winthrop's. Both men were born into privileged families. Both served in the Civil War, but where Winthrop remained in the regular army, Holmes attended Harvard Law and then went into private practice. Holmes later became a professor, served as a judge on the Massachusetts Supreme Judicial Court, and concluded an almost unparalleled career as a justice on the United States Supreme Court. It can be fairly argued that *The Common Law* propelled Holmes from a career of excellent legal scholarship to the nation's highest court.[72] Holmes' introductory statements in *The Common Law* could fairly characterize Winthrop's approach to the study of military law. Although Winthrop did not cite Holmes in either *Military Law* or *Military Law and Precedents*, it is worth noting that *The Common Law*'s fourth introductory sentence reads: "The life of the law has not been logic: it has been experience. The felt necessities of the time, the prevalent moral and political theories, intuitions of public policy, avowed or unconscious, even the prejudices which judges share with their fellow-men, have had a good deal more to do than the syllogism in determining the rules by which men should be governed."[73]

Whether Holmes' treatise influenced Winthrop is an unanswerable question, and the fact that Winthrop had a fifteen-year lead in legal practice and scholarship over Holmes may make the similarity in their approach to the law merely coincidental. And yet, there are many similarities between Winthrop's and Holmes' approach to the common law. This is partially the case in ascertaining the common law's influence in the purpose or reason of military criminal law. Perhaps their approach reflected nothing more than a shared jurisprudential philosophy then prevalent in post–Civil War legal circles.

Evidencing similarity in their approaches, Winthrop wrote, "While the military law has derived from the Common Law certain of the principles and doctrines illustrated in this code, it also has a *lex non scripta*, or unwritten common law of its own."[74] He pointed out that Congress accepted the underlying basis for the general common law as well as a more specific military common law in the 1874 Articles of War (as well as its predecessors) in that officers assigned to court-martial service had to rely on military custom when the codified law was silent on an issue.[75] To Winthrop, the unwritten military common law and general common law alike had applicability to courts-martial and military commissions of civilians during wartime.

Winthrop cautioned that while the military common law existed and served as a structural foundation of courts-martial, the prosecution always had the burden of proving a specific offense existed within that body of common law. Moreover, he pointed out that the means to do so was "to show a uniform known practice of longstanding, which is also certain and reasonable." That is, the prosecution could not simply make an argument that a non-enumerated common-law offense existed simply because the prosecution believed it should or because a single officer had been court-martialed for it in the past.

Finally, Winthrop noted that the military common law did not rest at the top of the hierarchy of military law. In instances where custom conflicted with an existing statute or the Constitution, the custom could not rise to the level of law. Indeed, Winthrop noted that "an illegal or unauthorized practice, however frequent or long continued, cannot constitute a legal usage."[76] He later used this very point in arguing the illegality of dueling, though he, like Holmes, recognized that the duel was at one point a quasi-judicial instrument to settle debts and assaults on personal honor. Winthrop also made this argument in prosecuting the court-martial of Cadet Smith who fought to defend his honor, but violated the statutory prohibition against assault.

There is only anecdotal evidence Winthrop and Holmes ever corresponded, but there are a number of interesting connections between the two men. John Chipman Gray, a Civil War judge advocate whom Winthrop, it may be recalled, met in prewar Boston, and Holmes were close friends in postwar Boston. Gray and Holmes taught at Harvard at the same time. However, no evidence exists to indicate Winthrop corresponded after the war with Gray either. During the war Gray served as a judge advocate to a field army, so that while Winthrop would have been familiar with his work, it is not necessarily the case the two exchanged correspondence during the war. Holmes, Gray, and Winthrop were also members of the American Bar Association. And prior to his judicial career, Holmes was a junior partner to George Shattuck, who attended Harvard Law at the same time as Winthrop.[77] In essence, there is more than one connection between Holmes and Winthrop, but no direct evidence of the two men ever conversing.

Winthrop did not cite Holmes in either *Military Law* or *Military Law and Precedents*. Instead, Winthrop not only incorporated the works of military legal scholars from prior generations such as De Hart and O'Brien, but he also included one of Professor Thomas M. Cooley's seminal treatises, *The General Principles of Constitutional Law in the United States*; Augustus Kautz's *Customs of the Service for Officers* and *Customs of the Service for Non-Commissioned Officers and Soldiers*; and the British military scholars William Hough's *Practice of Courts Martial and other Military Courts* and Charles M. Clode's, *The Military Forces of the Crown, Their Administration and Government*. Although these were not the only scholars Winthrop incorporated into his treatises, the diversity and standing of their works evidenced Winthrop's attempt at a complete defense of the character and practice of American military law.

Thomas Cooley was one of the noted constitutional law scholars of his time, and while he was later criticized as a champion of laissez-faire law, in 1869 as a judge on the Michigan Supreme Court he ordered the Detroit Board of Education to admit black children to schools previously restricted to white children. Also, while Cooley served as the dean of the University of Michigan Law School, the school did not pursue a discrimination policy in admissions (though it might also be noted that consistent with a late nineteenth-century-approach to race relations, Cooley did not take into account the prospect that blacks suffered discrimination in all aspects of life, making it unlikely many would have the requisite education for entry). During Winthrop's life Cooley was touted as a leading candidate for the Supreme Court, but his nomination was never forwarded to the Senate. Cooley did not object to a separate military disciplinary system as long as its jurisdiction remained confined to soldiers, and on rare instances, martial law.[78]

Winthrop's selection of Kautz on the one hand and Clode and Hough on the other is notable for two different reasons. Clode and Hough were British military law scholars and the extensive use of their work, along with other foreign authors, evidences Winthrop's view on the importance of not only comparative law, but also the widespread commonality of various aspects of military law. Moreover, on one of Winthrop's trips to Europe he met with Clode, and the two men discussed their armies' respective military codes. Winthrop wrote *Military Law* while he and Colonel Kautz were assigned at the Presidio, and two men explored the California coastline together. While there is no surviving correspondence between the two men, Kautz's diary records the two men dined together with their respective wives and on one occasion fished.[79]

In addition to Cooley, Winthrop also relied on a number of nonmilitary scholars, including Francis Wharton and Joel Prentiss Bishop, both of whom might well carry the mantle of the United States' leading criminal law scholars in the 1870s and 1880s.[80] Both Bishop and Wharton included brief statements on military law and the law of war in their scholarship. For instance, in his 1884 treatise, *Commentaries on Law, Embracing the Nature, Source, and History of Law; on International, Public and Private; Constitutional and Statutory Law*, Wharton opined that the Articles of War were a necessity to protect soldiers by providing legitimate belligerent status so that in the event of capture by an enemy state, the soldiers would be accorded full protections as prisoners of war.[81]

In his 1886 treatise, *Military Law*, Winthrop cited Wharton twenty-nine times and Bishop thirty times. He did not merely use Bishop and Wharton as footnotes to prove contemporary military practice as an equal to civil criminal law, but quoted their opinions on such matters as proof requirements for forgery, assault, and criminal intent, in an effort to provide greater knowledge where he perceived a gap existed. Winthrop also cited the works of a leading British scholar of criminal law, Joseph Chitty. In the late nineteenth century, the use of prominent English jurists was not unusual, and Chitty was noted as a leading jurisprudential scholar on both sides of the Atlantic. Chitty's oft-cited treatises covered commercial law, international law, and government, as well as criminal law. Winthrop cited Chitty's treatises on pleading and criminal law a combined thirty times.[82]

A brief mention of the biographies of Bishop and Wharton adds an additional context to Winthrop's use of both authors. Bishop wrote on the law before and after the Civil War. He was an abolitionist in the 1840s, and his views on the law were rooted in a specific late nineteenth-century Protestant morality. Bishop approved of the codification of criminal law, and he took a basic, though flexible, view that the difference between criminal law and tort liability was the intent of the defendant. That is, an act (*actus reus*) became a crime if the intent of the perpetrator (*mens rea*) was malicious or antisocial.[83] Interestingly, Francis Wharton's legal philosophy differed from Bishop's in that he did not emphasize intent as a defining separation between tort and criminal law. Instead, Wharton adopted the common-law belief that every person who caused a criminal harm was criminally responsible, except for a few rare exceptions such as insanity.[84]

Winthrop's use of Bishop, Wharton, and Chitty is one example of his reinforcing the argument that the substance of military law did not depart in great measure from the contemporary practice of international law, or the common-law underpinnings of each system. That is, the inclusion of the works of his famed contemporaries served as a defense to the system of military law. In another sense, Winthrop's treatise served as a bridge between adherence to the common law on one shore and the codification movement on the other. Finally, Winthrop's use of Chitty, Wharton, and Bishop was not isolated. The Supreme Court has cited their works into the twentieth and twenty-first centuries as well.[85]

Winthrop's discussion on the illegality of dueling is one example of his incorporation of the leading legal scholars into his work. In addition to proving that a military custom could not trump a statute, he turned to Wharton. Dueling was illegal under Article of War 26, but its historic roots as a means for settling disputes between officers were well cemented into military custom. Winthrop relied on Wharton's reasoning that dueling was a form of premeditated murder. Wharton had argued, "Cool and deliberate homicide in a duel is murder in the guilty party, and this, though the latter had received the provocation of a blow, or had been threatened with dishonor." The principle behind the common-law consideration of dueling as attempted murder had to do with the absence of "hot blood"—or in twenty-first-century parlance, "immediate anger."[86] That is, dueling constituted a deliberated cool act based on what both Wharton and Winthrop termed "a sense of conceited honor." Winthrop accepted Wharton's views as reflecting common law, and like Wharton considered persons taking on the role of "seconds"—or substitutes—as aiding and abetting in a murderous act.[87]

Although both *Military Law* and *Military Law and Precedents* incorporated a wide array of historic sources, events, and anecdotes throughout their texts, Winthrop's use of history in providing context to the various articles of war and courts-martial procedures was clearly designed as a defense of those articles and procedures. But he also intended his historic analysis to reinforce the importance of specific areas of military law in the hopes of creating a greater uniformity in its practice, particularly in courts-martial punishing. Military law was often viewed—then as even occasionally now—as a historic artifact retained for the purpose of instilling discipline with little regard to due process. The view was simplistic and erroneous. Yet Winthrop, like any scholar of military law, had to present the historic antecedents of the Articles of War and the practice of military law as proof of the law's durability and use. Winthrop included the constitutional basis for the law as well as its history, but he uniquely used its history in his defense of military law. That is, he was able to show that historically, military law and discipline were often practiced in a manner parallel to their nonmilitary counterparts.

Winthrop noted that the earliest military codes dated to the various ancient Greek and Roman armies, but he also acknowledged the dearth of available information as to the full extent of what the codes prohibited, how they punished, and how determinations were administered—by court or summary opinion. He was not alone in finding a lineage between the American military disciplinary system and those of the ancient armies. Winthrop and some of his contemporaries, as well as prior scholars including Blackstone, pointed out uniquely military offenses such as desertion, cowardice, and striking a superior were also found in these ancient codes.[88]

Like Holmes, Winthrop presented the ancient Germanic influence in the law as important. Winthrop presented the historic underpinnings of trial by courts-martial to the medieval courts of chivalry. In this, he was joined by Wharton and the British scholar Charles Clode. Winthrop also relied on the mid-nineteenth-century writings of the Habsburg military scholar Ignaz Ortwein von Molitor, who presented the origins of courts-martial based in chivalry courts and early Germanic trials.[89] He correctly noted that the first courts-martial were adjudicated under Germanic laws in the period between the Holy Roman Emperors Frederick III (1415–1493) and Maximilian II (1527–1576). He also noted the French *conseils de guerre* did not form until 1655, though prior to that military discipline was enforced in quasi-courts. Winthrop found it important that in both the Germanic and French courts-martial there was a customary requirement that the hearings were open to the public.[90] Winthrop did not elaborate on medieval custom, which tended to more harshly treat foot soldiers than knights, nor did he include some of the more prominent medieval court trials such as the case of Peter von Hagenbach, who was executed for the pillage and murder of noncombatants.[91]

However, it was not in the German or French law where the American court-martial owed its fundamental character, and Winthrop pointed this out. Instead, the American court-martial, unsurprisingly, was most similar to its British counterpart, though it also owed—for reasons Winthrop explained toward the end of his work—some of its character to the Swedish court-martial. In part, this was explained by Winthrop as a function of British officers serving in the Swedish Army as mercenaries during the Thirty Years' War.[92] He noted the British codes as well as Gustavus Adolphus' throughout his treatises.

The British courts-martial system originated in the "Kings Court of Chivalry," and although some of the Frankish customs were retained or reintroduced to British military law through the 1066 invasion, it was not until the reign of Edward I (1239–1307) that military courts adjudicated matters such as determining the status of prisoners of war, as well as crimes and offenses by English soldiers. Winthrop did not point out in any detail the full jurisdiction or rules of these courts other than to comment on their jurisdictional expansion into civil matters, and eventual curtailment by Henry VIII.[93]

Winthrop noted that the British Articles of War incorporated those established under the Swedish warrior king Gustavus Adolphus (1594–1632). He wrote that in some instances—he called them "identical quaint expressions"—there were vestiges of Adolphus' military code in the Articles of War. Winthrop's tribute to Adophus' influence was not mere pandering to a Protestant military code. Since the French Revolution, military historians have viewed Gustavus Adolphus as the brilliant commander and strategist of early modern Europe. His prowess in the Thirty Years' War was credited with saving the Protestant Reformation, though he was killed in November 1632 leading his men at the Battle of Lutzen. His army was composed of a higher caliber of soldiers than the era of mercenaries was accustomed to, and his approach to enforcing discipline was partly based on the concept of an open, rules-oriented trial, with an opportunity for advocacy for accused soldiers. Winthrop found Gustavus' code of 1621 so important, he included a translation in an annex section of *Military Law*.[94]

There were a number of specific offenses in the Articles of War which Winthrop believed were necessary to defend through the use of history. To Winthrop, the two most important were the Articles 61 and 62. The former article made punitive "conduct unbecoming an officer and a gentleman," while the latter article punished "conduct to the prejudice of good order and discipline." Only officers could be tried under the first article, while both soldiers and officers could be tried under the second. Neither article enumerated specific offenses. Both articles were the essence of *lex non scripta*, the common law of the military. Winthrop argued that both articles were important to maintain, but he did not rely in detail on ancient historic practice, only mentioning the code of the seventeenth-century British king James II. However, it seems fairly clear that the sixty-first article had its antecedents in the concept of chivalry, and it may be the case Winthrop could have strengthened his argument for its continued usage by expounding on this point.

Two decades prior to the publication of *Military Law*, Winthrop began providing advice to the executive branch on the parameters of both offenses. For example, in the closing days of the Civil War, Winthrop answered an inquiry from President Johnson regarding whether a convicted officer should be given clemency. The officer, a lieutenant Joseph Broadfoot, sought to have his sentence of cashiering removed, claiming it caused a hardship to his family. Winthrop conveyed to Johnson, "Broadfoot was tried and found guilty to the prejudice of good order and discipline in selling liquor to the enlisted men of the 1st and 8th Maryland volunteers. It was conclusively proved that he had sold at exorbitant prices whiskey to enlisted men for as much as ten dollars for a single carton full of the commodity." As to the sentence, he concluded, "A less punishment than dismissal could not have been well imposed for an officer offense so obnoxious to the character of an officer and there is no recommendation which can properly be made in the petitioner's favor."[95] Winthrop did not believe that all officer conduct merited a conviction. Eight days later, Winthrop advised the secretary of war that an officer who publicly criticized his quartermaster in obscene terms was not guilty of violating the sixty-first article.[96]

In 1881, General Swaim notified Congress that prosecutions under the article were abusive because the offenses alleged often failed to provide notice to the accused officer that an act constituted a crime. Swaim opined that the article itself violated the legal maxim that a court should declare law but not make law. He similarly attacked the sixty-second article, calling it the "Devil's article," for similar reasons. Swaim's moniker for Article 62 was not an original. Clode noted that the British counterpart to the sixty-second article had been referred to as such by British soldiers in 1869. However, unlike Swaim, but in concert with Winthrop, Clode believed in the utility of the article.[97]

One method Winthrop used to defend both articles, which no prior author had accomplished, was to collect well over four hundred examples of conduct that clearly violated military custom. By no means close to a complete list, these included an officer poisoning his wife, publicly committing indecent acts while in uniform, encouraging others to duel, "rendering oneself unfit for duty by excessive use of spirituous liquors," public drunkenness, assuming a rank superior to one's own, misconduct at target practice, and employing soldiers for nonmilitary purposes. His presentation of some of these offenses was counter to the Gilded Age spoils system practices. For instance, he found that an officer's payment of monies to a congressman so that the officer's son could gain an appointment to the Naval Academy constituted the act and effect required to prove an offense under the sixty-first article.[98]

While Winthrop defended most of the Articles of War on their individual historic basis, he made some exceptions. Notable in his criticism of these were the fifty-second and fifty-third articles of war. The former article recommended all officers "attend divine service," and prohibited indecent or irreverent conduct at the service. The later article prohibited "profane oaths or execrations." Winthrop acknowledged that the two articles originated in the British Articles of War of 1639 as well as Gustavus' code, but he found that both articles were "clumsy and antiquated, and having no material value or significance." Moreover, he commented that as the Constitution prohibited the government to establish a religion or prohibit the free exercise of a faith, the articles stood on tenuous legal ground. It was for these reasons that he recommended the articles be dropped from the code. He also opined that the fifty-third article's prohibition against the use of excessive profanity was obsolete and unenforceable.[99]

Having defended the Articles of War, Winthrop turned to the conduct of courts-martial prosecutions. The jurisdiction and procedure of courts-martial were painstakingly detailed in *Military Law* and *Military Law and Precedents* (though not here in this biography). The role of the judge advocate at trial, however, was one that had come under criticism both from within the army and from without. Winthrop recognized the often haphazard approach to courts-martial prosecution undermined the military disciplinary system and believed that it contributed to the high numbers of desertions.

Beginning in 1886 and culminating in 1895 with *Military Law and Precedents*, Winthrop focused some of his scholarship on professional ethics for judge advocates. In *Military Law* he provided a framework of professional ethics for judge advocates, which was little expanded in *Military Law and Precedents*. Winthrop was not the first commentator on military jurisprudence to define the role of the judge advocate. Maltby, O'Brien, De Hart, and Coppee preceded Winthrop in notating the dual demands on judge advocates, but Winthrop believed their treatises outdated and lacking in context.

Moreover, it is essential to recognize that Winthrop both practiced military law and wrote his treatises during a period of transforming the civilian practice of law. One of the changes in the practice of civilian law was the move toward a codification of professional ethics. His experiences, along with his observations of the conduct of Swaim, Gardner, and Barr, led to him to conclude that further explanation of the duties and ethical requirements of judge advocates was necessary. He initiated his analysis of judge advocate responsibilities with a brief overview of the history of judge advocates. Winthrop's approach to the law was generally historic and his treatment of judge advocates was no different. The position originated in the seventeenth-century British Army, where an officer was appointed as judge-martial (or marshal) to assist a general in determining the proper outcome of "doubtful cases." Winthrop also noted the German Army possessed a similar position, roughly titled as "advocate of the army."[100]

After a brief overview of the legislative histories involving the judge advocates, he detailed the statutory and military custom–based responsibilities of judge advocates. As in the case of his predecessors, Winthrop noted the other traditional roles of judge advocates included preparing and serving charges, summoning witnesses, and generally preparing a case for trial. Of the responsibility of preparing a case, he wrote, "The further duty is devolved upon the judge advocate of assuring himself, before going to trial, and that the proper evidence is available and is sufficient to establish the charge." He was highly critical of officers who did not effectively prepare cases for trial, and without naming any individual instances he wrote,

"In several instances, judge advocates have been severely censured in General Orders for proceeding with the prosecution without duly preparing their cases, or informing themselves whether the witnesses proposed to be called could establish the facts alleged in the specifications." Winthrop succinctly concluded that where a judge advocate believed a case could not be fairly adjudicated, he had a duty to inform the convening authority and ask for instructions. Implicit in this comment was the implied duty to advise the convening authority when a case developed shortcomings and whether these shortcomings could be overcome.[101]

Winthrop reasoned that the proper appointment of a line officer to a judge advocate rested on the officer's training and aptitude for the position. He noted that where a judge advocate errs, "all may go wrong." The level of law training available to officers was fairly consistent across the army, particularly for those commissioned after the United States Military Academy established its law department. To Winthrop, the more important question was an individual officer's fitness to ethically serve as a judge advocate. He noted that a determination of fitness was subjective (he called it relative), but that the best officers would have been educated in not only military law but also general criminal law, civil law, and the "general law of evidence." Indeed, Winthrop stressed mastery of the law of evidence as the most important of any body of law.[102]

But fitness meant more than competency in the law. He noted that because a judge advocate was not subject to be removed from the court, officers serving as judge advocates could not possess a bias in favor of the government or the accused to effectively serve and had a duty to ask to be excused before the court convened should they have such a bias. Winthrop noted instances where officers serving as temporary judge advocates prosecuted cases in which a dismissal against an accused officer automatically resulted in the promotion of the judge advocate to the dismissed officer's position. Winthrop deplored this practice, considering it not only unethical, but also in and of itself in the realm of conduct unbecoming an officer.[103]

In Winthrop's time, the judge advocate was, among his other roles, a prosecutor, defined as such by the Articles of War. To place the prosecutorial function in context, Winthrop pointed out that just as the United States military law differed from the British and French counterparts, the role of judge advocates somewhat differed as well. However, he did not seek to build confidence in the United States system by contrasting it with the British. Rather, he presented similarities between the systems to show the universality of the practice of military law. He pointed out that British Army courts-martial were composed of both a judge and prosecutor serving in their independent functions, through in that system, the judge and court president were often one and the same. Likewise, in the French *conseils de guerre*, the president of the court conducted the questioning of the witnesses, and the accused's defense counsel was permitted, "by courtesy," to add questions. Winthrop did not disparage these systems. To the contrary, Winthrop opined that the British and French military judicial systems were fair, but merely a product of their different sovereigns. It bears mention that Winthrop had firsthand knowledge of the French and British courts-martial process as he personally attended a number of courts in each country.[104]

One area of similarity, however, had to do with the independence of a judge advocate to prosecute a case as he felt best. In the British system, the judge advocate retained independence to exercise discretion on how a case should be tried once the convening authority ordered an accused to trial.[105] This was an identical practice of judge advocates in United States courts-martial. Equally important was the observation by a British military scholar that judge advocates had to administer military law according to their conscience and custom of the service. This was a theme which Winthrop used throughout his treatises as well when discussing the roles and responsibilities of judge advocates.[106]

To Winthrop, the judge advocate's independent authority to try a case was balanced by an equally fundamental duty to serve as a minister of justice.[107] He not only used past military law commentators to support his arguments that this duty of ensuring justice was as important, if not more, than that of prosecutors, but he also looked to British and state court precedent. Importantly, he found a commonality in the British and American courts to support the proposition that "the prosecuting officer, in presenting his case, is not at liberty to select those witnesses only whose testimony will conduce to a conviction, leaving the accused to offer the rest." He also argued that the "prosecuting officer represents the public interest which can never be promoted by the conviction of the innocent," and followed with the statement, "His object like that of the court should be simply justice, and he has no right to sacrifice this to any pride of professional success." But perhaps it was his conclusion that best represented a slap at Gardner when he wrote, "In the opinion of the author, this rule, though not followed by some others . . . is believed especially to commend itself to the adoption of court-martial practice.[108]

Winthrop's 1886 treatise had a direct effect on one specific, but critical change in the prosecutions of courts-martial. Until 1892, a judge advocate was permitted to sit in the closed-door deliberations of the court-martial while the accused soldier and his defense counsel—if any existed—were excluded. He noted that this function "was a feature of the proceedings of a military trial most open to criticism." At the same time he also argued that any unfairness existed more in appearance than in fact. As a result, he cautioned that because the requirements of strict justice made the practice open to question, the judge advocate had to "scrupulously avoid the office and animus of a prosecutor," when in the deliberations of the court.[109]

On the issue of the judge advocate present in court-martial deliberations, Winthrop did not stop with *Military Law*. Assisting Colonel Lieber, he argued to the secretary of war in 1886 that the judge advocate should not be permitted into the court-martial deliberations. The two men noted that the British courts-martial abandoned this system after it was concluded to be noxious to the demands of justice.[110] In 1892, Congress ended this practice, but there remained issues regarding the conduct of judge advocates in other closed-door sessions. In one case, a judge advocate attended the closed-door deliberations of the court, and while Winthrop wrote that "it was deemed best to disapprove the sentence as fatally irregular," he also noted that in his opinion, "the sentence is not invalidated in such a case."[111]

Winthrop's efforts to professionalize the practice of military law did not occur in a vacuum. There were a number of external sources which may have influenced the nature and style of Winthrop's work. It is essential to recognize that Winthrop wrote in a time when the civilian practice of criminal law was professionalizing, both from the bench and bar. Although Winthrop wrote during a time where the model rules of professional conduct had yet to be established, there was a growing concern about attorney conduct. The lack of a body of professional ethics rules had implications for the fair adjudication of the federal and state criminal justice systems. Without an appellate court, a review of the conduct of judge advocates impacting the results of courts-martial was subject only to the convening authority, the secretary of war, or the president. No judge advocate prior to Winthrop had provided a detailed professional ethics framework for both judge advocates and the reviewing authorities. When, in the 1886 *Military Law*, Winthrop provided such a framework, in more than one instance his views were ahead of the federal and state law.

Although the Constitution did not, in direct language, prohibit prosecutorial malfeasance, it left to the judicial arm of the government the responsibility that trials were conducted in a fair and impartial manner. In 1935, the Supreme Court decided in *Berger v. United States*, a civilian criminal case involving prosecutorial misconduct, that a prosecutor's malfeasance could render a criminal trial unconstitutionally defective.[112] The justices described the role of the prosecutor as a servant of the people whose duty was to justice, rather than to simply secure a conviction. They acknowledged that the prosecutor had a responsibility to strike hard blows. However, the Court also admonished prosecutors that these same blows may not be used to produce a wrongful conviction or to let "innocence suffer." To the Court, *Berger* represented the constitutional expectation that prosecutors would prosecute fairly, consistently, and within the ethical canons of their profession. The Court did not state any new tenet of law in this decision, and in comparison to some state jurisdictions, *Berger* was surprisingly late. Yet, the decision recognized that prosecutorial misconduct could deprive an accused of his Sixth Amendment right to a fair trial.

There were a number of state decisions predating *Berger* that clearly stated the very rules against misconduct *Berger* enunciated. The late nineteenth century saw a number of malfeasance- and misfeasance-based complaints against the conduct of prosecutors. For instance, in 1873, the Supreme Court of Michigan found that prosecutors engaged in misconduct when they improperly cross-examined a defendant with prejudicial, inadmissible, and possibly fictitious evidence.[113] The court dismissed the conviction of the defendant on these grounds. In 1903, the Idaho Supreme Court decided a similar issue with the same result as the Michigan court.[114] In 1891, the Nebraska Supreme Court held, "The state has guaranteed to every one a fair trial, and such trial cannot be had if the prosecution can resort to tricks to secure a conviction. If such practice was sanctioned it would result in many cases in the conviction of innocent persons."[115] In 1928, a New York Court of Appeals overturned a number of convictions of labor agitators after it determined a prosecutor's incendiary remarks deprived them of a fair trial.[116] Likewise, the California Supreme Court held in 1893 that it "is too much the habit of prosecuting officers to assume beforehand that a defendant is guilty, and then expect to have the established rules of evidence twisted, and all the features of a fair trial distorted, in order to secure a conviction. If a defendant cannot be fairly convicted, he should not be convicted at all; and to hold otherwise would be to provide ways and means for the conviction of the innocent."[117] Earlier, the California court admonished a prosecutor who used anti-Chinese commentary, referred to inadmissible evidence in his argument, and knowingly empanelled inebriated jurors. The court reminded prosecutors of their duty to ensure a fair and impartial trial.[118]

In 1886, the year *Military Law* was published, the newly formed American Bar Association adopted a resolution that "the law itself should be reduced, so far as its substantial principles are settled, to the form of a statute."[119] Not surprisingly, that same year the members of the American Bar Association elected Winthrop as a member. At the time, he was the first and only judge advocate to be accorded that distinction. None of Winthrop's contemporaries was ever accorded this distinction. From the time Winthrop was accepted into its membership until his death, the American Bar Association stressed the importance of uniformity of statutes. Winthrop stressed the principle of uniformity in courts-martial practice in terms of ensuring due process and correct procedure. However, it was through a new publishing medium which Winthrop found inspiration for structuring *Military Law*.[120]

In 1879, the West Publishing Corporation established a long-standing method of standardized case reporting with the publication of the *Reporter*. The West case reporting system enabled lawyers to find cases grouped within specific legal categories such as contracts, property, and torts, and created multiple subcategories. The cases were grouped according to jurisdiction. In order to save money and recognizing that some attorneys practiced in neighboring states, West grouped state case reporting in regional books. Within ten years, the "Reporter system" dominated the law press. Although there was no case Reporter system for courts-martial until the post–World War II establishment of the Court of Military Appeals, the 1865 *Digest of Opinions* and its progeny were structured in a manner similar to West's system. There is no evidence that the *Digest* had an influence in the development of the Reporter system, but it is interesting to note the similarities.

West also developed an approach to legal writing where a specific subject's general rules were presented in readable English, but heavily footnoted so that the reader could then select cases pertinent to a specific jurisdiction. Known as the Hornbook series, West's approach remains a staple of law students through the present day.[121] At least one nineteenth-century military officer published a Hornbook with West, but it was not Winthrop. In 1895, Captain Edwin F. Glenn, the acting judge advocate for the Department of the Dakotas, authored a treatise titled the *Handbook of International Law* through West Publishing. Interestingly, Glenn criticized the Prussian Army's siege of Paris in 1870–1871 as violating the laws of war. A quick comparison of the Hornbook series and *Military Law* and *Military Law and Precedents* shows that Winthrop's works are presented in a similar structure.

While Winthrop focused on a myriad of issues in addition to professional ethics, four appear to stand out: the role of defense counsel, the right to present a complete defense, prosecution of desertion, and inequality of courts-martial results. However, it was within the context of his approach to military law that these issues were discussed and dissected, and both the military practice of law and the Articles of War defended.

In addition to advocating the minister of justice role of judge advocates, Winthrop also sought to modernize the role of the defense counsel to make the court-martial a fairer process. The 1806 and 1870 Articles of War never granted an accused the right to a defense counsel, but rather held that the status of such counsel in courts was a privilege. Winthrop did not take exception to this basic premise because courts-martial were structured in a manner where the judge advocate was responsible for assuring the accused received a fair trial. Yet he did not object to defense counsel and indeed strongly supported courts-martial permitting their active presence at trial, so long as counsel conducted themselves in a respectful manner.[122] This had become the practice in British courts. And the actual rules were at variance with the practice of military law as enforced by the Bureau of Military Justice. In his 1865 *Digest of Opinions*, he wrote, "The accused is entitled to counsel as a right and this right the court cannot refuse to accede to him. Whenever it is refused, the proceedings should be refused."[123] While Winthrop's views might appear archaic in the twenty-first century, it was not until 1963 that the Supreme Court, in *Gideon v. Wainright*, found the right to a defense counsel an absolute constitutional right.[124]

As early as 1886, Winthrop urged courts-martial to permit an increased role for defense counsel. In writing that the old rule prohibiting defense counsel from cross-examining witnesses, "rendered their position embarrassing if not humiliating," Winthrop clearly found that the older court-martial exclusion of defense counsel failed to comport with standards of fairness. Defense counsel had been statutorily prohibited from addressing the court-martial, and Winthrop found this rule untenable. He acknowledged that courts-martial had long departed from enforcing the rule, but that in instances where an accused's counsel acted in a disrespectful manner, the court-martial had the rule to enforce at its discretion.[125]

Winthrop also conveyed that in a number of notable trials, defense counsel had rendered invaluable service to the court. The particular foreign instances Winthrop noted were the French courts-martial of Marshal Ney in 1815 and Marshal Bazaine in 1873. He also lauded the performance of defense counsel in the 1863 Fitz-John Porter court-martial along with a number of other courts. However, it was Reverdy Johnson's arguments in the assassination conspiracy trial which impressed Winthrop the most, though interestingly, the trial ended in a total defeat for the defendants, and this was the same Reverdy Johnson who represented Porter.[126]

The right to conduct a complete defense is a Sixth Amendment right, and while Winthrop did not reference this right, or use the term *complete defense*, he noted that "it is a principle to be scrupulously observed in a military trial that the accused, whatever his rank, is not only to be deprived of no right, but is to be accorded ever proper privilege—is in no manner to be embarrassed or placed at a disadvantage, but in every reasonable degree facilitated, in making his defense."[127]

Winthrop's view meant that no trial by court-martial could be lawfully conducted unless the accused was in full control of his faculties, and that his physical presentation to the court had to be accorded the same level of dignity as that of the prosecution. As a result, an accused could not be shackled before the court unless he posed a risk of escape or violence. Nor could an accused be dressed in a degrading manner, blocked from securing evidence, or stopped from cross-examining witnesses for the prosecution. Moreover, both Winthrop and Cooley posited that a court-martial result could not be lawful unless the accused soldier had full notice of the charges against him or was able to conduct a complete defense.[128]

At multiple times, in both *Military Law* and *Military Law and Precedents,* Winthrop reminded officers that the burden of proof always rested on the prosecution. Thus defenses such as obedience to orders (e.g., following a legal order which results in harm to a third party), compulsion by the enemy, and enforcing the requirements of military discipline could overcome any number of charges. However, he noted that in establishing a defense, an accused had to present some evidence of alibi or absence of criminal capacity or intent. Ignorance of fact, in Winthrop's time as in the present, was a defense uniquely presented in military courts. For example, it protected an infantryman if he accidentally killed a fellow soldier while in combat as long as the accident was reasonable.

Winthrop was not as concerned with the specific defense of alibi or ignorance of the fact as he was the category of defenses involving the accused's *mens rea,* or mental state. These defenses included ignorance of the law, drunkenness, or insanity. Winthrop was unwilling to excuse officers accused of offenses from using the ignorance of law defense, but he was willing to admit that some new enlisted soldiers might be unaware of the Articles of War, and therefore a violation of one of the articles might be excusable from constituting a crime. Nonetheless, he found that the ignorance of the law defense could be seldom used with any success. As for drunkenness, Winthrop found that the issue of whether an accused was drunk at the time of an offense was relevant to determining the "species or quality" of offense, but not whether some criminal liability accrued to an accused who was drunk at the time. As a result, criminal acts such as premeditated murder or burglary, might, when committed in a state of intoxication, be only properly classified as assault or trespass. To ensure a fair trial, he noted that when evidence supporting a defense of drunkenness was brought before a court-martial, the evidence could not be excluded and the court-martial instructed on the effect of drunkenness on the accused's mental state at the time of a criminal act.[129]

It was with the affirmative defense of insanity where Winthrop argued that military practice was equal to, and in some cases surpassed, the criminal law practice in the civilian courts. Insanity provided a unique defense to a soldier accused of any crime. Winthrop defined it as "a disease so perverting the reason or moral sense, or both, as to render a person not accountable for his acts." This was little different from either Bishop's or

Wharton's definition of insanity, and indeed Winthrop cited Bishop as well as other legal commentators in dealing with the subject. Foremost among these commentators was Simon Greenleaf, a Harvard law professor who taught during Winthrop's student tenure. Greenleaf's *Treatise on the Law of Evidence* noted that "just as the law in all its charity, always presumes men innocent until proven guilty, [it] also assumes that every person is of a sound mind until proven otherwise."[130] It is interesting that Winthrop did not address Holmes' view of insanity, and it can be fairly argued that Winthrop's position on the defense was more expansive and progressive than Holmes', who argued that "there is no doubt that in many cases a man may be insane, and yet perfectly capable of taking the precautions, and of being influenced by the motives, which the circumstances demand."[131]

Winthrop was familiar with a number of senior officers who lapsed into insanity during their tenure in uniform. General Ranald MacKenzie, a famed Indian fighter, succumbed to mental instability though he had not committed any offenses. August Kautz recorded in his diary that he and Winthrop discussed MacKenzie's departure from the army as it opened a possibility for Kautz's promotion to brigadier general.[132] A number of other soldiers showed signs of insanity while serving in remote outposts. And in a case in which Winthrop never agreed with the results, Daniel Sickles had been acquitted on the basis of temporary insanity prior to the Civil War.[133]

No statute mandated the quantum of insanity or proof required to establish a cognizable defense. Winthrop adopted a classic evidentiary quantum known as the Mc'Naghten test, which survives in evolved form into the present day. Although overlooked by any prior analysis of Winthrop's works, his use of the Mc'Naghten test is indicative of his comprehensive knowledge of civil and foreign law. The Mc'Naghten test stemmed from a British case where the delusional defendant, Mc'Naghten, murdered a British civil servant. The House of Lords codified the standard of insanity to cases where an individual did not, as a result of mental derangement, comprehend the nature of his acts or the wrongfulness of them.[134] Winthrop also used a number of state and federal cases to buttress his position on the Mc'Naghten rules.

Winthrop provided further guidance which was reflective of the psychology of his time in that he listed a number of manias, such as homicidal mania, kleptomania, pseudomania, and pyromania, which could divest an individual of criminal liability. However, Winthrop cautioned judge advocates that in order for insanity to constitute a defense, it had to be absolute. That is, individual eccentricities did not construe insanity, and Winthrop pointed out insanity was not a common defense in courts-martial. On the other hand, Winthrop was the first military law commentator to delve into the defense of insanity, and that he articulated the defense in a manner consistent with civilian criminal law evidenced his progressive understanding of changes in the law.

In a number of different writings, Winthrop noted that desertion had been an issue of concern to armies predating the formation of the United States Army, and over time, military law has dealt with deserters in a variety of often harsh ways. The act of desertion plagued United States forces in every conflict in its history, as well as during peacetime. But it was in the Civil War where deserters constituted a sizeable number of solders.

Desertion as a sole charge constituted roughly 43 percent of all enlisted trials during the Civil War and by far the majority of courts-martial tried during the conflict had a charge of desertion as part of the case. If one considers that the Union army prosecuted some eighty thousand men in general courts-martial, the number of prosecuted deserters was well over forty thousand. For an army which at times numbered over a half million, forty thousand desertions could hardly be absorbed without some operational detriment. In all, the Union army suffered over two hundred thousand desertions, and of these only eight thousand were caught and returned to the army. Not all deserters were prosecuted in a court-martial. Some men were given second chances and returned to the ranks with little punishment. Others were prosecuted, found guilty, and sentenced to death, though this sentence was almost always commuted to some form of hard labor or even a return to the ranks.[135]

Poor command decisions, inadequate training, incompetent commanders, and superior Confederate leadership at such battles as Fredericksburg and Chancellorsville were a cause of many desertions, though low pay and a general lack of adaption to military life were an endemic cause as well. But the effect of desertions on the Union forces has not been alleged to have caused defeats in battle. Certainly, the Union army could have fought more effectively and achieved a quicker victory if not for the desertions.

If desertions were a problem for effectiveness during the Civil War, the problem was an outright disaster for the army when it numbered twenty-five thousand men and was expected to accomplish more missions than it had available manpower. Historian Don Rickey, in his book, *Forty Miles a Day on Beans and Hay*, argued that desertion was by far the most prevalent serious military crime in the post–Civil War army. Roughly one-third of all men who enlisted in the army between 1867 and 1891 deserted. The roots of the problem were well-known to the army command. Living conditions were onerous, pay was spotty, and some officers and noncommissioned officers were so abusive as to cause soldiers to risk prison. There was a link between alcohol and desertion as well.[136] In one year alone, no soldier received pay for several months because Congress failed to pass an appropriations act. Moreover, some areas offered more lucrative jobs than soldiering. Even the unpredictable administration of military justice was a contributor to the desertion rate.[137] Some offenders were treated lightly while others spent considerable time in prison for committing the same crime.

The secretary of war in his annual report to Congress frequently addressed the problem of desertions. In 1870, Secretary of War Belknap reported that desertions increased as the soldiers' pay was reduced from sixteen dollars to thirteen dollars per month. The high rates of desertion were still being articulated in the 1890 report to the secretary of war.[138] In between these two reports, the army never had a year in which under 10 percent of its soldiers did not leave its ranks under illegal means. No modern European force suffered close to similar rates of desertion, including the French Army during the 1870–1871 disaster.

Some commanders, including the commanding general Sheridan, believed the Bureau of Military Justice treated desertion laxly and vented in the annual report, "The desertion of his comrades in danger is, and ever should be, construed as the basest and most heinous crime possible to a soldier, whereas of late years, under the benign influence of the Bureau of military Justice, it has grown to be considered as of little more concern than for a laborer to quit his employer without notice." Sherman and Sheridan, like the majority of officers in the line, wanted to prosecute and punish deserters harshly and wanted the widest jurisdiction to do so. Problematic to their desire was that the Articles of War were written in a manner which did not permit this to occur.[139]

Winthrop was in the minority of judge advocates in arguing that the statute of limitations affected the army's ability to prosecute many deserters. Simply, the 103rd article of war established a two-year statute of limitations. Indeed, only a select number of the Articles of War were not encumbered by a two-year statute of limitations. Winthrop had the weight of federal judicial rulings and the opinions of two attorneys general on his side.[140] Unfortunately, as Winthrop noted, one secretary of war and a number of commanders took exception to the statute of limitations and considered a deserter amenable to court-martial at any time. This led to courts-martial for desertion in some geographic divisions and a virtual immunity from prosecution of desertion in others, though it must be noted that soldiers who were immune from desertion in the mind of a geographic commander were often tried for the lesser offense of absence without authority, which Winthrop argued was exempt from the jurisdiction limitation by operation of the specific language.[141]

The issue of whether the statute of limitations barred trial for deserters after two years had passed was not simply a matter of lawyers and other interested parties nitpicking the strict language of the law. To Winthrop, the prosecution of deserters who were strangely immune under the specific language of the article struck at the heart of the fairness of the military disciplinary system. His logic was that desertion had a specific intent element to it which its lesser offense did not. The specific intent of a soldier to desert meant that at the time of the absence, the soldier intended to permanently leave the military service. Thus the crime was found in the mental state of the accused soldier and not merely the act of absenting the service without authorization. The two-year limitation applied to the intent and not the act. In this sense, Winthrop's views on desertion were similar to Holmes' and Bishop's views on the importance of intent. And yet, Winthrop did not bow to the idea that a customary practice had supremacy over a clearly written, albeit flawed, statute. He reasoned that if a flaw in the language of the Articles of War precluded some prosecutions, the language of the specific article itself required legislative revision. To Winthrop, creative lawyering to skirt the due process requirements of notice and strict construction was as great an evil, if not more so, as the flawed Article of War.[142]

Unsurprisingly, Winthrop's position on strictly reading the language of Article 103 was articulated in the 1880 *Digest of Opinions*. And yet, in March 1883, the acting adjutant general criticized Winthrop to Secretary of War Stephen Elkins, pointing out, Winthrop's "views are not only not the views of the Department, but were disapproved by the Secretary of War as being contrary to the best interests of the service." The statement "contrary to the best interests of the service" was a sop to efficiency at the expense of law, and Winthrop noted this in *Military Law*. Documented in the following chapter, following his service in the Bureau of Military Justice, Winthrop prosecuted deserters in the Pacific Division. In one case, he articulated his arguments before Supreme Court Justice Stephen J. Field, who presided as a trial judge. Justice Field agreed with Winthrop's arguments that Article 103 barred a prosecution for desertion where the desertion occurred over two years prior to the arraignment, but that the issue had to be argued before the general court-martial as the federal court did not have jurisdiction to hear the case.[143]

On September 1884, the *Army-Navy Journal* reported the case of a Private Thomas Kirk who enlisted in 1870, deserted in 1872, and was apprehended in New York in 1880. While awaiting trial, Kirk filed a writ of habeas corpus to the federal court and the case was heard by Judge Choate. Choate ruled that he did not possess jurisdiction to hear the case and accepted Norman Lieber's argument that it was for the general court-martial and president to determine whether the statute of limitations had run. And yet, in his ruling, Choate remarked that the strict language of Article 103 applied the statute of limitations to all offenses except the lesser included offense of absence without authority. This case too appeared in *Military Law* as a further strength to Winthrop's position.[144]

The issue was not resolved with Choate's and Field's rulings or with the publication of *Military Law*. Indeed, it was not until 1890 when Congress legislated the very matter Winthrop pressed for, a revision to Article 103, which permitted in its plain language desertion to be considered a continuing offense. As a result, when *Military Law and Precedents* was published in 1895, the discussion involving the statute of limitations found in *Military Law* was absent. While it would be an exaggeration to credit Winthrop with solely being responsible for influencing Congress to amend the flawed article, it is clear that he played a significant part in it. For reasons more fully articulated in the next chapter, Winthrop directly influenced some of the more influential commanders that his position was correct, and the contemporary practice wrong.

Although Winthrop's immediate impact on the practice of military law cannot be fully quantified, there are a number of factors to consider in arguing he made an immediate impact. Many of these factors have already been articulated, but there are others which show Winthrop's impact. Edward Coffman, in his treatise *The Old Army: A Portrait of the American Army in Peacetime, 1784–1898*, credited Winthrop with contributing to the professional growth of the officer corps. Professor Coffman wrote, "Officers were more conscious of their need to know military law, and in the recently published *Military Law* by Lieber's deputy, William Winthrop, they had a text to prepare them for their court duties."[145] Coffman's statement, while neither constituting direct evidence nor providing a full credit to Winthrop's contributions, is nonetheless supportive of the argument that Winthrop altered the practice of military law and as a result directly contributed to the army's modernization.

In 1886, the Artillery School adopted Winthrop's *Military Law* as its law text.[146] The following year, the School for Application of Infantry and Cavalry at Leavenworth adopted *Military Law* as its standard text as well. Both schools taught a mandatory law course. Though the instruction did not necessarily come from a judge advocate, the officer students were tested on the subject and had to discuss the various topics in the treatise. The Leavenworth school initially used Woolsey's *International Law and the Laws of War* as a standard text. But the reading was augmented with *Military Law*, rather than being disposed of altogether. As a result, while officers learned international law from two sources, their knowledge of military jurisdiction, discipline, civil-military relations, and Indian policy came solely from Winthrop.[147]

Almost immediately after its publication, *Military Law* was used by the Supreme Court in *Smith v. Whitney*, a key decision in which the Court held a naval officer was not entitled to a writ of prohibition to restrain court-martial proceedings instituted against him. Relying on *Military Law*, the Court held that since the basis for the court-martial was a purely military offense akin to the sixty-first article of war, the naval officer was not entitled to a writ. In 1890, the Supreme Court denied a soldier a writ of habeas corpus after his conviction for desertion, even though the soldier had earlier fraudulently enlisted by lying about his age.[148]

Other federal and state courts used *Military Law* as guidance before Winthrop's death in 1899. For instance, the Court of Appeals for the District of Columbia cited *Military Law* extensively in determining that a retired officer could be recalled to active duty for the purpose of a court-martial prosecution under the Articles of War. In that case, the retired officer had publicly made a number of insulting comments and odd demands, toward the commanding general, General Schofield. The army recalled the officer and charged him under the sixty-first article. Likewise, the Court of Claims twice cited *Military Law*, including, in a measure of irony, in its decision in Swaim's case. And in 1897, the Nevada attorney general cited *Military Law* to the state's supreme court in arguing for jurisdiction over the state's militia.

With judicial acknowledgment of *Military Law* as the foremost authority on the broad subject, the court not only sustained and protected the character of the practice of military law but also cemented Winthrop's legal philosophy into American law at large. This is a process which continues up until the present day, with the Supreme Court's use of Winthrop in *Hamdan v. Rumsfeld*. Thus, while congressional legislation, such as the enactment of the Uniform Code of Military Justice in 1950, brought the practice of courts-martial in parallel with civilian criminal courts and created appellate courts and rules of evidence almost identical to their federal counterparts, the fundamental character of military trials retains Winthrop's influence. So too does Winthrop's influence continue to affect the executive use of the military, including restrictions on its use.

NOTES

1. Robert L. McKinlay, "Notes on Reform," *Journal of the Military Service Institution of the United States* 1 (1880), 501.
2. William Winthrop, *Military Law* (Washington, DC: W.H. Morrison, 1886), 1:58.
3. Major General James B. Fry, "A Military Court of Appeal," *Journal of the Military Service Institution of the United States* 2 (1888), 438.
4. William T. Sherman, "Letter from General Sherman to General W. S. Hancock, Dec. 9 1879," *Journal of the Military Service Institution of the United States* 1 (1880), 129–130.

5. Major General John Gibbon, "Law in the Army," *Journal of the Military Service Institution of the United States* 1 (1880), 439; Auguste Marmont, *The Spirit of Military Institutions, or Essential Principles of the Art of War*, trans. Henry Coppee (Philadelphia: J.B. Lippincott Co., 1862), 137. Marmont's full name and title was Auguste Frédéric Louis Viesse de Marmont, Duc de Ragusa. He was commissioned into the French Army during the Revolution, served as Napoleon's aide-de-camp, and commanded a corps against the Austrians at Ulm, against Wellington in Spain, and against the coalition which defeated Napoleon in 1814. However, he allied with French monarchists and was eventually exiled to Vienna. He wrote the cited treatise in 1845.

6. William Winthrop, *Military Law and Precedents*, 2nd ed. (Washington, DC: GPO, 1920), 49. Sherman did not advocate lawless warfare and his views on law and the army were complex. For instance, in an article titled "Our Army and Militia," he recommended that all officers read Hugo Grotius' seminal work on the law of war, *The Rights of War and Peace*. William Sherman, "Our Army and Militia," *North American Review* 405 (1890), 138.

7. Irwin McDowell, *HQ Department of the East, Report of the Secretary of War*, 1873, 63.

8. Frank Baldwin, *HQ Department of the Columbia, Report of the Secretary of War*, 1873, 301.

9. For instance, Lieber wrote that "while military law is progressive, it had to remain so within its own sphere." See Brevet Lt Col G. Norman Lieber, "Remarks on the Articles of War and the Common Law of the Military," *Journal of the Military Service Institution of the United States* 1 (1880), 1.

10. Joseph Holt, letter to William Belknap, in *Annual Report of the Secretary of War for 1872* (Washington, DC: GPO, 1872), 130.

11. Holt, letter to William Belknap.

12. Ansell served as the deputy judge advocate general during World War I and later testified before Congress, "Col. Winthrop was first a military man, and he accepted easily and advocated the view that courts-martial are not courts, but are simply the right hand of the military commander." Professor Morgan, a contemporary of Ansell's, later reiterated this criticism during the formulation of the 1950 draft Uniform Code of Military Justice. These criticisms were without merit. When viewed in comparison to the late nineteenth-century civilian practice of criminal law, Winthrop's scholarship was indeed both responsive to evolutionary changes in the law that were occurring during his life, and in several instances more progressive than some of civilian criminal law practices. Moreover, Ansell's and Morgan's criticisms failed to take into account long-standing institutions and influences in the practice of military law. Ansell's denigration of Winthrop occurred in the context of the 1920 Congressional Hearings on Military Justice Reform. *Establishment of Military Justice: Hearings before a Subcommittee of the Senate Committee on Military Affairs on S. 64*, 66th Cong., 1st sess. (1919), 1171.

For an outstanding overview of Professor Morgan's and Ansell's criticism of Winthrop, see, for example, Colonel Frederick Bernays Wiener, "American Military Law in Light of the First Mutiny Act's Tri-Centennial," *Military Law* 126, no. 1 (1989), 123; also, Jonathan Lurie, *Arming Military Justice: The Origins of the United*

States Court of Military Appeals, vol. 1 (Princeton, NJ: Princeton University Press, 1992), 64–65. Winthrop's supporters included the Judge Advocate General; Enoch Crowder, who testified before Congress that Ansell's sworn statements contained falsehoods; and John Henry Wigmore, one of the foremost post–World War I legal scholars, who also served as a judge advocate during the war. Birkhimer served in the Union army during the Civil War enlisting as a private. In 1866, he entered the United States Miliary Academy and received his commission in 1870. In 1888, he transferred into the Judge Advocate General's Department. William Powell, *Powell's Record of Living Officers* (Philadelphia: Hammersly, 1890), 64.

13. William McKee Dunn, *A Sketch of the History and Duties of the Judge Advocate General's Department* (Washington, DC: GPO, 1878), 9.

14. J. W. Clous, "The Judge Advocate General's Department," in *The Army of the United States, Historical Sketches of Staff and Line with Portraits of Generals in Chief*, 6 (New York: Maynard, Merrill, 1896); Dunn, *A Sketch of the History and Duties of the Judge Advocate General's Department*, 6.

15. Clous, "The Judge Advocate General's Department," 34.

16. *Records of Living Officers of the United States Army*, 14. On June 29, 1884, the *New York Times* editorialized Swaim as "not fit to retain the exalted responsible position of Judge Advocate General."

17. Roger D. Cunningham, "Always a Storm Center: The Trials and Tribulations of Asa Bird Gardiner," *Journal of America's Military Past* 104, no. 2 (Fall 2006), 22–24.

18. Wesley Merritt, "The Army of the United States," *Harper's New Monthly Magazine* 80 (March 1890), 497–503; Robert Utley, *Frontier Regulars: The United States Army and the Indians, 1866–1891* (New York: MacMillan, 1973), 6–12.

19. Col. William Winthrop, letter to General A. A. Humphreys, July 19, 1879, in *Annual Report of the Secretary of War*, vol. 2 for 1880 (Washington, DC: GPO, 1880), 1852; Anon., "William Winthrop," *Military Law Review* 28 (1965).

20. Thomas Cash, letter to Joseph Holt, April 14, 1870 (PJH, box 63). On the outside of the letter Holt notated his order to Winthrop to investigate Cash's allegation.

21. Thomas Barr, letter to Joseph Holt, November 29, 1874 (PJH, box 69).

22. Thomas Barr, letter to Joseph Holt, December 20, 1874 (PJH, box 69).

23. Two examples of poor scholarship include Stephen Ambrose, *Duty, Honor, Country: A History of West Point* (Baltimore: Johns Hopkins Press, 1966), and Sydney Forman, *West Point: A History of the United States Military Academy* (New York: Columbia University Press, 1950), 141. Ambrose states, "Smith struggled through four years at the USMA. He was once turned back a class and in his second class year was found deficient in natural and experimental philosophy and dismissed." Ambrose does not note that Smith was twice court-martialed at the academy and failed to mention the fact that Smith's class rank was held back a year as part of the second court-martial punishment. In his treatment of a more famous case involving Cadet Whittaker, Ambrose claims Whittaker inflicted an injury on himself to avoid exams. This is a wholly unsupported claim. Moreover, Ambrose failed to note that the judge advocate review of the case showed a widespread belief that Whittaker was the victim of the academy administration's malfeasance.

Sydney Forman's treatment of black cadets at the academy displays the same sort of benign racism Smith and Whittaker likely faced from the administration. Toward these cadets Forman wrote, "Those who revived the question of loyalty of West Point graduates in the Civil War failed in their object of dishonoring the Academy and were forced to seek new issues. The question of the Negro cadet and his treatment became a favorite new topic."

One exception is William McFeely, who in his biography of Ulysses Grant, thoroughly analyzes the president's role in the academy's treatment of Smith, as well as the general opinions against integrating the academy. However, McFeely blends Smith's two trials as one.

24. William J. McFeely, *Grant: A Biography* (Norwalk, CT: Easton Press, 1986), 375–379; also, *General Catalogue of Officers and Students, 1837–1890* (Ann Arbor: University of Michigan Press, 1891), 414.

25. McFeely, *Grant*, 375–379.

26. John F. Marszalek, *The Assault at West Point: The Court-Martial of Johnson Whittaker* (New York: MacMillan, 1972), 21–23; McFeely, *Grant*, 375–379.

27. William P. Vaughn, "West Point and the First Negro Cadet," *Military Affairs* 35, no. 3 (Fall 1980), 101; Peter Michie, "Caste at West Point," *North American Review* 130 (1880), 610; Henry Flipper, *The Colored Cadet at West Point: An Autobiography of Lieutenant H.O. Flipper* (New York: Homer Lee and Co., 1878), 37. Henry Flipper articulated that Smith cautioned him "not to fear either blows or insults and to avoid any forward conduct."

28. *New York Times*, October 21, 1870, 1.

29. "The Colored Cadet at West Point," *Chicago Tribune*, October 22, 1870, 2; *New York Times*, October 21, 1870. The *New York Times* reported that the court consisted of "General Howard, Lt Col Devin, Lt Col J.H. Dexter, Maj Thomas Haines, Maj Louis Pelouse, Captain A.C. Bainbridge, Captain Michael Sheridan, and Maj Winthrop, Judge Advocate."

30. *New York Times*, October 21, 1870.

31. *New York Times*, October 26, 1870

32. *New York Times*, October 26, 1870. The *Times* reported, "The Judge Advocate closed the case with a lengthy review of the line of defense. He was astounded by it. It was an attempt to escape upon a quibble of dates. The accused knew he was guilty of an offense within two days of the disputed date."

33. Vaughn, "West Point and the First Negro Cadet," 101; McFeely, *Grant*, 379.

34. See, for example, Ulysses S. Grant, *Papers of Ulysses S. Grant*, edited by John Y. Simon (Carbondale: Southern Illinois University Press, 1998), 31–32. Clark wrote, "There can be little doubt that the Secretary of War acting on the suggestion of President Grant did constitute the court, including the judge advocate, with a special view to secure the dismissal of Cadet Smith, and General Howard placed at its head, so that in case a majority of the court should meet the expectations of the President, his name might add weight to the verdict." However, Howard disputed these allegations and it is interesting to note that Howard did not even mention the Smith case in his autobiography.

35. *New York Times*, January 5, 1871.

36. Vaughn, "West Point and the First Negro Cadet," 101.

37. J. W. Smith, "Letter to the Editor," *New National Era*, July 30, 1874, 2–3.

38. See, generally, Darryl W. Jackson, Jeffrey H. Smith, Edward H. Sisson, and Helene T. Krasnoff, "Bending toward Justice: The Posthumous Pardon of Lieutenant Henry Ossian Flipper," *Indiana Law Journal* 74 (1999), 1251–1269.

39. See, generally, Marszalek, *The Assault at West Point*.

40. The letter read, "Mr. Whittaker, You will be fixed. Better keep awake, A friend." Marszalek, *The Assault at West Point*, 230.

41. Marszalek, *The Assault at West Point*, 232. Cautiously, see also, Patrick Finnegan, "The Study of Law as a Foundation of Leadership and Command: The History of Law Instruction at the United States Military Academy," *Military Law Review* 118 (2004), 116–117. Finnegan's account of Gardner is specious. He does not note that Gardner resorted to race baiting and the use of inadmissible evidence, though the record of trial clearly evidences Garnder's race baiting. Instead Finnegan opined Whittaker's conviction resulted from Gardner's prowess as a prosecutor. There are other errors and omissions in the article. For instance, he states Gardner was awarded a medal of honor, but does not note that the medal was rescinded. Additionally, while Finnegan points out that certain judge advocates introduced texts into the course of instruction (e.g., Norman Lieber introducing Thomas Cooley's *Constitutional Law*), he does not explain the significance of these works.

42. John F. Marszalek, "A Black Cadet at West Point," *American Heritage Magazine* 22, no. 5 (May 1971), 44–48; Donald B. Connelly, *John M. Schofield and the Politics of Generalship* (Chapel Hill: University of North Carolina Press, 2006), 258–270.

43. Marszalek, *The Assault at West Point*, 241–242.

44. Winthrop, *Military Law*, 1:525–527.

45. Winthrop, *Military Law and Precedents*, 370–373.

46. Winthrop, *Military Law and Precedents*, 370–373. Though Winthrop placed the blame on Gardner, he also took exception to Attorney General Brewster's labeling of the Whittaker conviction as "illegally obtained." Instead, he referred to the proper terminology as a conviction obtained through error.

47. Winthrop, *Military Law and Precedents*, 370–373. Winthrop also noted that an English statute permitted the use of handwriting experts to compare genuine (e.g., known) handwriting samples with unknown. He also noted the common-law rule was supported by Bishop.

48. J. Granville Gates, letter to Joseph Holt, April 8, 1876 (PJH, box 101).

49. Gates, letter to Holt, April 8, 1876 (PJH, box 101).

50. William Winthrop, letter to Joseph Holt, April 8, 1876 (PJH, box 101).

51. Winthrop, *Military Law and Precedents*, 575. This issue was presented in the context of Winthrop's analysis of the twenty-first article of war which included the offense of disobedience of a lawful order. Although orders from superior officers were presumptively lawful, there were occasional instances that orders issued contravened law and therefore disobedience to the unlawful order was not a punishable offense.

52. William R. Robie, "The Court Martial of a Judge Advocate General: Brigadier General David G. Swaim (1884)," *Military Law Review* 56 (1972), 211–212.

53. See, for example, *Swaim v. United States*, 28 Ct. Cl. 173, 178–179 (U.S. Ct., Cl. 1893).

54. *Army-Navy Journal*, May 10, 1884, 837; *Army-Navy Journal*, May 17, 1884, 864.

55. Robie, "The Court Martial of a Judge Advocate General," 217–218; *Swaim v. United States*, 28 Ct. Cl. 179.

56. *Army-Navy Journal*, August 2, 1884, 1.

57. See, for example, *Army-Navy Journal*, November 22, 1884, 330; also, *Swaim v. United States*, 28 Ct. Cl. at 202–219. Interestingly, the Court of Claims saw the issue of biased officers swerving on the court-martial as a problem had it occurred in a federal court, but the court could not grant the issue review under the restrictions of *Dynes v. Hoover*. That court specifically held, "If this court were sitting as an appellate tribunal in review of the proceedings of the court-martial these objections might be good assignments of error; but it is the opinion of the court that such errors can not be reviewed collaterally, and that these do not affect the constitution of the court-martial, or its jurisdiction of the case before it, or the legality of the sentence which it pronounced." For Miles' service on the Whittaker court-martial, see Robert Wooster, *Nelson A. Miles and the Twilight of the Frontier Army* (Lincoln: Nebraska, 1993), 131.

58. *Army-Navy Journal*, December 13, 1884, 383.

59. Robie, "The Court Martial of a Judge Advocate General," 221.

60. Robie, "The Court Martial of a Judge Advocate General," 221.

61. William Winthrop, letter to Joseph Holt, May 29 1885 (PJH, box 77).

62. Laura Johnson, letter to Mr. Ford, *New York Tribune*, undated (NYPL).

63. Johnson, letter to Mr. Ford, undated.

64. William Winthrop, letter to Mr. Ford, undated (NYPL).

65. George Prugh, "Colonel William Winthrop: The Tradition of the Military Lawyer," *American Bar Association Journal* 42, no. 2 (May 1956), 188.

66. Winthrop, *Miltary Law and Precedents*, 60. This provision still exists under the Uniform Code of Military Justice but it has not been used since the Swaim trial.

67. Winthrop, *Military Law*, 1:83–84; *Military Law and Precedents*, 73.

68. Winthrop, *Military Law and Precedents*, 523. Winthrop also pointed to the fact that courts of inquiry were used not only for determining whether trial by court-martial was appropriate, but also for the vindication of a soldier's character or conduct. However, the placement of Andre and Swaim together does raise the question as to whether Winthrop felt the two cases were comparable. Winthrop also listed General O. O. Howard's court of inquiry in which Howard was accused of negligent oversight of funds while at the Freedman's Bureau. He was exonerated by the court of inquiry which included Sherman as its head officer. Gardner served as the judge advocate in the court of inquiry and gave a forceful argument for Howard's guilt. It did not sway the officers on the court. See, for example, *Proceedings and Opinions Convened under the Act of Congress of February 13, 1874* (Washington, DC: GPO, 1874), 545–592. Also serving on the court of inquiry were General McDowell and General John Pope. Howard was represented by a civilian attorney.

69. Winthrop, *Military Law*, 1:583; *Military Law and Precedents*, 432, 458.

70. Winthrop, *Military Law and Precedents*, 711–712. Winthrop's language was previously quoted in the *Army-Navy Journal* when its editors reported on the conclusion of the trial. See *Army-Navy Journal*, February 28, 1885, 1.

71. *Swaim v. United States*, 165 U.S. 553 (1897).

72. Liva Baker, *The Justice from Beacon Hill: The Life and Times of Oliver Wendell Holmes* (New York: HarperCollins, 1991), 252–257. Baker argued that the common law "shook the little world of lawyers and judges who had been raised on Blackstone's theory that the law, given only by God Himself, was immutable and judges had only to discover its contents." Winthrop did not believe in Blackstone's dicta on God the "Law Giver."

73. Oliver Wendell Holmes Jr., *The Common Law* (Boston: Little Brown and Co., 1881), 1; also, Richard A. Posner, ed., *The Essential Holmes: Selections from the Letters, Speeches, Judicial Opinions and Other Writings of Oliver Wendell Holmes, Jr.* (Chicago: University of Chicago Press, 1992), 12.

74. Winthrop, *Military Law*, 1:41; *Military Law and Precedents*, 41. Winthrop was not the first American to use the *lex non scripta* phrase. Stephen Benet utilized it as well. See Stephen Benet, *A Treatise on Military Law and the Practice of Courts Martial* (New York: D. van Nostrand and Co., 1864), 9.

75. Article 84 required a judge advocate to read the following oath to officers serving on a court-martial:

> You A. B. do swear that you will well and truly try and determine, according to evidence, the matter now before you, between the United States of America and the prisoner to be tried, and that you will duly administer justice, without partiality, favor, or affection, according to the provisions of the rules and articles for the government of the armies of the United States, and if any doubt should arise, not explained by the said articles, then according to your conscience, the best of your understanding, *and custom of war in like cases* . . . So help you God. (emphasis added by author)

76. Winthrop, *Military Law*, 1:43. William Hough, an early nineteenth-century British military scholar and judge advocate whom Winthrop utilized, noted that a custom could not, as a matter of law, triumph over an existing statute. William Hough, *The Practice of Courts Martial and Other Military Courts* (London: Parbury, Allen, and Co., 1834), 326.

77. Baker, *The Justice from Beacon Hill*, 231.

78. Cooley's full work is titled *The General Principles of Constitutional Law in the United States* (Boston: Little Brown and Co., 1882). For analysis of Cooley's influence on the law see Paul Carrington, "Law as the Common Thoughts of Men: The Law Teaching and Judging of Thomas McIntyre Cooley," *Stanford Law Review* 49 (1997), 511–539; and George Edwards, "Why Justice Cooley Left the Bench: A Missing Page of Legal History," *Wayne State University Law Review* 10 (1964), 1570. Cooley's views on military law are best found in his treatise *The General Principles of Constitutional Law*, 156

79. William Hagan, "Overlooked Textbooks Jettison Some Durable Military Law Legends," *Military Law Review* 113 (1986), 163; Charles M. Clode, *The Military Forces of the Crown, Their Administration and Government* (London: John Murray, 1869). For a brief biography of Kautz, see John Fiske, *Appleton's Cyclopaedia of American Biography*, vol. 5 (New York: D. Appleton and Co., 1888), 495. For Kautz

and Winthrop's relations see, for example, *Diaries of August Kautz*, entries as follows: Saturday, October 28, 1882; Friday, February 2, 1883; Sunday, April 27, 1884; September 27, 1884 (LOC).

80. Gerald Leonard, "Towards a Legal History of American Criminal Theory: Culture and Doctrine from Blackstone to the Model Penal Code," *Buffalo Criminal Law Review* 6 (2003), 691.

81. Francis Wharton, *Commentaries on the Law, Embracing the Nature, Source, and History of Law; on International, Public and Private; Constitutional and Statutory Law* (Philadelphia: Kay and Brother, 1884), 317. In his treatment on the laws of war, Winthrop echoed Wharton's view that private military forces had no legal status and hence, protection under this body of international law.

82. See, for example, Joseph Chitty, *Chitty's Treatise on Pleading and Parties to Actions* (Springfield, MA: G. and C. Merriam, 1876); Joseph Chitty, *A Practical Treatise on the Criminal Law Comprising the Practice, Pleadings, and Evidence, Which Occur in the Course of Criminal Prosecutions, Whether by Indictment or Information: With a Copious Collection of Precedents* (Philadelphia: Edward Earle, 1819).

83. See, for example, Stephen A. Siegal, "Judge Bishop's Orthodoxy," *Law and History Review* 13 (Fall 1995), 218–221; also, Leonard, "Towards a Legal History of American Criminal Theory," 748–750. Leonard writes, "Bishop especially strove to incorporate an intensely Christian, Victorian individualism into a treatise that grounded itself in the common law."

84. Francis Wharton, *Philosophy of Criminal Law* (Philadelphia: Kay and Brother, 1880), 22. See also, Leonard, "Towards a Legal History of American Criminal Theory," 767–768.

85. See, for example, *Stogner v. California*, 539 U.S. 607 (2003), and *Ianelli v. United States*, 420 U.S. 770 (1974), both using Wharton; *Lawrence v. Texas*, 539 U.S. 558 (2003) and *Harmelin v. Michigan*, 501 U.S. 957 (1991), both using Chitty and Bishop.

86. Francis Wharton, *A Treatise on the Law of Homicide in the United States* (Rochester, NY: Lawyers Cooperative Publishing Company, 1885), 363. Wharton supported his argument on the nexus between dueling and illegal homicide through both American and British court cases.

87. Winthrop, *Military Law*, 1:841–842; Wharton, *A Treatise on the Law of Homicide in the United States*, 362–363.

88. Winthrop, *Military Law*, 1:841–842; William Smith, *A Dictionary of Greek and Roman Antiquities* (London: Taylor and Watton, 1842), 795. This was a standard dictionary in classroom use during Winthrop's tenure at Yale and Harvard. See also William Blackstone, *Commentaries on the Laws of England*, vol. 1, reprint ed. (London: A Strahan, 1880), 571; and Alexander Adam, *Roman Antiquities: Or an Account of the Manners and Customs of the Romans* (New York: T. Cadell, 1819), 376–377.

89. Winthrop, *Military Law*, 1:5–6, also 45–48; Wharton, *Commentaries on the Law*, 76; Clode, *The Military Forces of the Crown*, 365; Ignaz Ortwein von Molitor, *Die Kriegsgerichte und Milirarstrafen im neunzehnten Jahrhundert mit einem Ruckblicke auf die Kriegsstrafen der Romer, die Kriegsgewohnheiten der alten Deutschen, und die Kriegsgesetze bis zum Beginne dieses Jahrhunderts, mit besonderer Berucksichtigung der Kriegsgesetze Oesterreichs, Preussens, Sachsens, Wurtembergs, Badens, dann Frankreichs, Sardiniens und der Eidgenossenschaft* (Vienna: L. Somer, 1855), 3.

90. Winthrop, *Military Law*, 1:5; Holmes, in *The Common Law*, wrote, "In short, so far as I am able to trace the order of development in the customs of the German tribes, it seems to have been entirely similar to that which we have already followed in the growth of Roman law" (18).Winthrop cited the works of the fifth-century Roman military strategist Vegetius, for his information on early Roman military discipline. Vegetius remains one of the primary original sources of Roman military conduct. See, for example, Flavious Vegetius Renatus, "De Re Militari (The Military Institutions of the Romans)," trans. John Clarke, in *Roots of Strategy*, ed. T. R. Phillips, vol. 1, 65–177 (Harrisburg, PA: Military Service Publishing, 2000). It is likely that Winthrop read Clarke's translation which was printed in 1769.

91. See, for example, Adolphus L. Koeppen, *War in the Middle Ages* (New York: D. Appleton and Co., 1854), 177. For a contemporary interpretation, see William H. Parks, "Command Responsibility for War Crimes," *Military Law Review* 62 (1973), 1–33.

92. Winthrop, *Military Law*, 1:47; Guenther E. Rothenberg, "Maurice of Nassau, Gustavus Adolphus, Raimondo Montecuccoli, and the 'Military Revolution' of the Seventeenth Century," in *Makers of Modern Strategy: Machiavelli to the Nuclear Age*, ed. Peter Paret, 48–49 (Princeton, NJ: Princeton University Press, 1986).

93. Winthrop, *Military Law*, 1:47–49. Blackstone, in his commentaries noted the contribution of Edward I—he titled him "England's Justinian" to the laws of England, including the expansion of military law, Blackstone, *Commentaries on the Laws of England*, 24.

94. Winthrop, *Military Law*, 1:47–49. In Winthrop's time, Gustavus' forces were generally accepted as superior to his Catholic opponents, and he was viewed as a master strategist without parallel. See, for example, Theodore A. Dodge, *Gustavus Adolphus* (Boston: Houghton Mifflin, 1895), 59; William Sherman, "The Grand Strategy of the War of the Rebellion," *Century* 35 (February 1888), 582; and Hans Delbruk, *The Dawn of Modern Warfare*, vol. 4, trans. Walter Renfroe (Lincoln: University of Nebraska Press, 1990), 173–185. For more modern views generally consistent with Sherman's, see Russell Weigley, *The Age of Battles: The Quest for Decisive Warfare from Breitenfeld to Waterloo* (Bloomington: Indiana University Press, 1991), 14–29; Geoffrey Parker, *The Thirty Years War* (New York: Barnes and Noble, 1984), 121–132; also Rothenberg, "Maurice of Nassau," 48–53.

95. William Winthrop, letter to Andrew Johnson, June 12, 1865 (NA RG 153.2.1, folder 14).

96. William Winthrop, letter to Stanton, June 20, 1865 (NA RG 153.2.1, folder 14).

97. Charles M. Clode, *The Administration of Justice under the Military and Martial Law* (London: J. Murray, 1874) 18.

98. Winthrop, *Military Law*, 1:1022–1050.

99. Winthrop, *Military Law*, 1:938–940; *Military Law and Precedents*, 655–656.

100. Winthrop, *Military Law and Precedents*, 179; *Military Law*, 1:240.

101. Winthrop, *Military Law and Precedents*, 189; *Military Law*, 1:252.

102. Winthrop, *Military Law and Precedents*, 189; *Military Law*, 1:249.

103. Winthrop, *Military Law and Precedents*, 185–186.

104. Winthrop, *Military Law and Precedents*, 289; *Military Law*, 1:257.

105. Winthrop, *Military Law and Precedents* 192; *Military Law*, 1:257.

106. Clode, *The Military Forces of the Crown*, 365. Clode also observed, "As military law is generally *lex non scripta*, the Judge Advocate General is the advisor of the general in chief of command, so that he may never enter into a controversy with his subordinate, and by doing so suffer a legal defeat." Clode, *The Military Forces of the Crown*, 361. Ironically, as late as 2005, the politically appointed civilian general counsels to secretary of defense and the secretary of the Air Force sought to undermine the status of the uniformed judge advocate generals, partly in order to advance the administration's policy of forgoing law of war obligations in interrogations and intelligence collection, and of international law obligations in the jurisdiction and trials of captured belligerents.

107. Winthrop, *Military Law and Precedents*, 193; *Military Law*, 1:260.

108. Winthrop, *Military Law and Precedents*, 193–194; *Military Law*, 1:260.

109. Winthrop, *Military Law*, 1:264.

110. G. Norman Lieber, letter to the secretary of war, in *Message from the President of the United States to the Two Houses of Congress* (Washington, DC: GPO, 1885), 435. Lieber also argued the administration of justice was far from perfect so long as the court-martial had no subpoena power over civilian witnesses. Nor did the court-martial possess the legal authority to hold civilian witnesses in contempt for perjury or disorderly conduct. As a result, when an accused needed to have the testimony of a civilian witness, the court was powerless to force the testimony of the witness. It could seek to have an affidavit drawn from a witness who was reluctant to travel, but this was the limits of its authority.

111. Winthrop, *Military Law and Precedents*, 195.

112. 295 U.S. 78 (1935).

113. *Gale v. People*, 26 MI 157, (Mich. 1873).

114. *State v. Irwin*, 9 Idaho 35 (Idaho 1903).

115. *Leahy v. State of Nebraska*, 31 Neb. 566 (Neb. 1891)

116. *People v. Malkin*, 250 N.Y. 185, (N.Y. Ct. App 1928).

117. *People v. Wells*, 100 Cal. 459; 34 P. 1078 (Cal. 1893).

118. *People v. Lee Chuck*, 78 Cal. 317; 20 P. 719 (Cal. 1889).

119. David Dudley Field, "American Progress in Jurisprudence," in *The American Law Register and Review*, 650–651 (Philadelphia: University of Pennsylvania, 1896).

120. Prugh, "Colonel William Winthrop," 189. Lyman D. Brewster, "The Promotion of Uniform Legislation," *The Yale Law Journal* 6 (1897), 133–136.

121. Frank L. Mott, *History of American Magazines, 1885–1905*, vol. 3 (Boston: Harvard University Press, 1957), 1885–1905, 346.

122. Winthrop, *Military Law*, 1:220–222.

123. William Winthrop, *Digest of Opinions of the Judge Advocate General* (Washington, DC: Government Printing Office, 1865).

124. *Gideon v. Wainright*, 372 U.S. 335 (1963).

125. Winthrop, *Military Law*, 1:220–222.

126. Winthrop, *Military Law*, 1:220–222.

127. Winthrop, *Military Law*, 1:406; *Military Law and Precedents*, 289.

128. Cooley, *The General Principles of Constitutional Law*, 156.

129. Winthrop, *Military Law*, 1:413; *Military Law and Precedents*, 293. Winthrop's views on drunkenness accorded with Francis Wharton's, who wrote that when drunkenness induced insanity at the time of an offense, an accused person was not to be viewed as insane, but rather drunk instead. Wharton, *A Treatise on the Law of Homicide*, 492.

130. Winthrop, *Military Law*, 1:414, and *Military Law and Precedents*, 294; Simon Greenleaf, *A Treatise on the Law of Evidence*, vol. 3 (Boston: Little Brown and Co., 1854), 6. Wharton defined insanity as follows: "It must be proved that at the time of committing the act the accused was laboring under such a defect of reason, from disease of the mind, as not to know the nature and quality of the act he was doing, or if he did know it, that he did not know what he was doing was wrong." Wharton, *A Treatise on the Law of Homicide*, 472.

131. Holmes, *The Common Law*, 109. Holmes did make room for the possibility that an insane person could be not liable for crimes, writing, "If insanity of a pronounced type exists, manifestly incapacitating the sufferer from complying with the rule which he has broken, good sense would require it to be admitted as an excuse."

132. *Diary of August Kautz*, December 13, 1883 (Container 2, LOC).

133. Michael D. Pierce, *The Most Promising Young Officer: A Life of Ranald S. MacKenzie* (Norman: University of Oklahoma Press, 1993), 225–229.

134. See, generally, Donald J. West & Alexander Walk, *Daniel McNaughton: His Trial and Aftermath* (Ashford, Kent: Headley, 1977), 1–4.

135. Gerald Linderman, *Embattled Courage: The Experience of Combat in the American Civil War* (New York: Free Press, 1987), 176; Thomas P. Lowry, *Don't Shoot That Boy! Abraham Lincoln and Military Justice* (Mason City, IA: Savas, 1999), 20; Ella Lonn, *Desertion during the Civil War* (Lincoln: University of Nebraska Press, 1998), 145.

136. Don Rickey, *Forty Miles a Day on Beans and Hay* (Norman: University of Oklahoma Press, 1963), 17–32.

137. Rickey, *Forty Miles a Day on Beans and Hay*, 142–155.

138. *Annual Report of the Secretary of War for 1870*, 7.

139. *Annual Report of the Secretary of War for 1882*, 8.

140. The 103rd article of war read, "No person shall be tried before a court-martial for any offense which appears to have been committed more than two years before the issuing of the order for such trial, unless by some reason of having absented himself, or some other manifest impediment, he shall not been amenable to justice within that period."

141. Winthrop, *Military Law*, 1:912. Winthrop was not the only jurist to argue this point. A Senate committee had already recommended that the language of the limitation be altered so as to permit prosecution under a tolled statute of limitations.

142. In distinguishing intent from other acts (e.g., negligence), Holmes remarked, "Even a dog distinguishes between being stumbled over and being kicked." *The Common Law*, 3; and Joel Prentiss Bishop, *Commentaries on the Criminal Law* (Boston: Little Brown & Company, 1877). Bishop wrote, "Crime proceeds only from a criminal mind." Winthrop, *Military Law*, 1:354–357.

143. Chauncey McKeever, acting adjutant general, letter to Secretary of War Stephen B. Elkins, printed in *Message from the President to the Two Houses of Congress with the Reports of the Heads of the Department* (Wasington, DC: GPO, 1883), 38; Winthrop, Military Law, 1:354. Winthrop called McKeever's statements "more fanciful than substantial." *Military Law*, 1:356.

144. *Army-Navy Journal*, September 27, 1884, 167.

145. Edward M. Coffman, *The Old Army: A Portrait of the American Army in Peacetime, 1784–1898* (New York: Oxford University Press, 1986), 379.

146. *Annual Report of the Secretary of War*.

147. *Annual Report of the Secretary of War 1886*, 198; *Annual Report of the Secretary of War for 1887*, 190; William A. Ganoe, *The History of the United States Army* (New York: D. Appleton and Co., 1924), 336.

148. *Smith v. Whitney*, 116 U.S. 167 (1886). *In re Grimley*, 137 U.S. 147 (1890).

11

Marriage and Field Service under the Command of John M. Schofield

I suppose they think your services are more necessary in San Francisco than here, and perhaps they are right. But the decision is a great disappointment to me.

—General John M. Schofield to William Winthrop

After a brief courtship, William Winthrop married Alice Worthington on July 26, 1877. His cousin, Lillie Blake, had introduced the two to each other shortly before their marriage. Alice Worthington was born in 1846 in Washington, DC, to Harvard-educated Dr. Francis Worthington and Jane Tayloe Lomax. Her father was an Ohioan and her mother a Virginia native. Her mother died in 1847 and her father died in 1849. As a result, she was raised by her maternal grandmother in Virginia and Washington, DC. One of the unique features of their marriage is that it brought a Confederate family into Winthrop's life. Alice Worthington's cousin, Lunsford Lomax, was a Confederate general at the close of the war, but despite this, Winthrop and Lomax developed a cordial relationship.[1]

Alice Worthington was clearly Winthrop's intellectual equal, and her lineage was deeply rooted in American political and intellectual culture. She wrote poetry and had an interest in social causes such as health and poverty. She wrote a number of articles and published a treatise titled *Diet in Illness and Convalescence*. She lived with her grandmother during the Civil War in Washington, DC, and saw the growth of executive authority and the expansion of the capital into a military encampment. In her later life, she began to pen a history of American nuns serving as nurses in military hospitals, but her work was not completed before her death in 1900.

Her parents' deaths resulted in two fundamental changes in her life. While her parents were antislavery, her maternal grandmother responsible for raising her, Elizabeth Virginia Lomax, a Virginian, supported slavery. But she did not support secession and hoped the North and South could ameliorate their differences.[2]

The second fundamental way in which Alice Worthington's life changed is that in the 1860s, an Ohio aunt who assisted in raising her father converted to Catholicism and Alice followed suit. In the course of her adult life, she championed causes such as Catholic equality in the military and Catholic charities. When William Winthrop and Alice Worthington married, their ceremony took place in St. Stephens Catholic Church in New York City.[3]

In 1882, Winthrop transferred to the Division of the Pacific, located in San Francisco, as its judge advocate. His departure from the Bureau of Military Justice was an inevitable transfer as the judge advocate general instituted a system of four-year assignments, and Winthrop had been in Washington, DC, since 1863. He was close to finishing *Military Law*, and his career from this point forward was not as influential in the formation and shaping of his legal scholarship as had been his prior experiences in the Civil War and Reconstruction.

Winthrop enjoyed service under the division's commander, Major General John McAlister Schofield. Winthrop grew to admire Schofield as much as he admired Joseph Holt. His relationship to Schofield defined much of his career from 1882 to his retirement in 1895. There was, for Winthrop, much to admire in Schofield.

Winthrop had been at the Bureau of Military Justice during Schofield's brief tenure as secretary of war in 1868–1869, but the two men did not develop a friendship at that time, though they certainly met. They not only were the same age; they also had similar interests and a shared intellectual curiosity of nonmilitary studies such as botany and chemistry.

Schofield had a meteoric military career. Born in 1831, he attended the United States Military Academy as an eighteen-year-old. He did not initially set out to become an officer. His father was a Christian minister, and the young Schofield entertained following in his father's footsteps. He also developed an interest in science, engineering, and the law. Already educated well beyond most of his peers at the age of seventeen, he was employed as a surveyor and mathematics teacher in northern Wisconsin. He hoped to pursue a legal career, but an opening at the service academy caused a Democrat congressman in Schofield's district to actively pursue a cadet. Schofield had, by this time, earned a reputation as a bright teacher, and the congressman turned to him. Once at the academy, he impressed General Winfield Scott with his maturity and bearing. He excelled in physics, engineering, and mathematics, but he maintained his interest in the law. He distanced himself from rote religion and was offended when the academy chaplain preached against "God hating geologists."[4]

Although he was a solid student and a well-regarded cadet, he got into trouble with the superintendent in his third year. While serving as mathematics tutor for prospective cadets studying for the entrance exam, some of his fellow cadets entered into his classroom and wrote obscene questions on the blackboard. The superintendant believed Schofield provoked the incident and admonished him. Later that year a cadet guard attempted to stop Schofield from either sneaking up on him or mistook Schofield's intentions. The cadet guard tore Schofield's coat with a bayonet, and he responded by throwing the guard in a ditch. The administration reacted by threatening Schofield with further discipline. In turn, he demanded a court of inquiry, but the secretary of war summarily dismissed him from the academy. Schofield appealed to Senator Stephen A. Douglas for help, and with the senator's intervention, Schofield was permitted to return to the academy, but he would have to face a court-martial for his conduct.[5]

The court-martial panel consisted of a number of junior officers Schofield later became acquainted with including E. R. S. Canby, George Thomas, and Fitz-John Porter. The board found Schofield guilty of various infractions and sentenced him to a dismissal, but based on his past record, they also recommended his sentence be remitted and he be permitted to graduate and be commissioned. In essence, they recommended the military's form of probation. Ironically, Fitz-John Porter did not support remission, and Schofield knew of this. In 1878 Schofield chaired a board of inquiry into Fitz-John Porter's court-martial. Although the requirement of an unbiased juror did not exist at the time, Schofield could have removed himself from the panel. He did not bear a grudge, however, and recommended Porter be exonerated and restored to rank, earning the hatred of General Pope in the process.[6]

Like many officers prior to the Civil War, Schofield considered leaving the army. He taught physics and mathematics at West Point, drafted a text book, and sought a professorship in a civilian institution. On the eve of the Civil War, he was offered a physics professorship at Washington University in St. Louis. Schofield did not resign his commission, and instead he took a leave of absence. He later claimed that had the war not occurred, he would have resigned his commission and remained at the university.[7] As it turned out, he resided in an area which proved a fertile training ground to command postwar army departments and divisions, as well as administer Reconstruction programs.

When the war erupted, Schofield was still a lieutenant, but as there was a shortage of loyal competent senior officers, he was placed in command of a large militia force in Missouri. The political and legal situation in Missouri was different from much of the rest of the nation. Like that of another border state, Kentucky, the Missouri state legislature had declared the state to be an "armed neutral," and there initially was an uneasy truce between pro-Union and pro-secessionist groups. However, each side formed armed militias, and it became apparent there was a move to federalize the pro-Union militia. On May 10, 1861, Schofield found himself a brevet major in temporary command of one thousand militia soldiers outside of a secessionist enclave near St. Louis. There he served under General Nathaniel Lyons, a controversial abolitionist. Lyons was convinced the secessionists intended to seize a federal arsenal in the city and ordered the pro-Union militia to move against them. Without firing a shot, Schofield obtained the surrender of seven hundred prisoners and transported them to St. Louis, but these men were paroled with the promise not to take up arms against the Union. Some of them subsequently violated their parole and fought against the Union.

After the capture of prisoners, Schofield's professional rise was continuous. He fought at the Battle of Wilson's Creek, a Union defeat. The experience of Wilson's Creek, like much of the Civil War, gave Schofield the belief in the need for a fully professional standing army.[8] On November 27, 1861, Schofield was appointed brigadier general and placed in command of the Missouri State Militia. In this capacity, Schofield became familiar with the difficulties of commanding militia and guerrilla warfare. He pursued the notorious guerrilla William Quantrill. Together with Major General Henry Halleck, Schofield developed a legal regime for military jurisdiction. This regime included the use of military commissions to try captured partisans and guerrilla bands that were not formally constituted by the Confederate government or subject to its military jurisdiction.[9]

In the midst of the guerrilla war, Schofield evidenced his commitment to the law of war. On August 21, 1863, Quantrill and 450 of his men sacked Lawrence, Kansas, killing over 150 men and boys and looting the town. Quantrill's raid on Lawrence, Kansas, was a brutal massacre violating clear, long-held tenets of the law of war. But Schofield believed retaliation an equal problem, writing, "I have not the capacity to see the wisdom or justice of permitting an irresponsible mob to enter Missouri for the purpose of retaliation."[10] Instead, he issued orders removing pro-Confederate families from Missouri border areas, creating roughly twenty thousand refugees.

While the removal of civilians comported with the laws of war, it created difficulties for guerrilla supporters and innocent civilians alike. President Lincoln supported Schofield's actions. He was not as concerned for the rights of Quantrill's followers as he was for preventing "an indiscriminate massacre there, including probably more innocent than guilty."[11] Winthrop later used Schofield's response as an example of lawful measures taken by a commander to curb guerrilla warfare.

As the war progressed, Schofield commanded forces in Arkansas, and in January 1864 he rose to command the Department of the Ohio. In this role, Schofield led an army under the overall authority of General William Sherman and was instrumental in the Atlanta campaign. Schofield's forces did not participate in Sherman's "March to the Sea" and instead turned their attention to southern Tennessee. There he led his army at the Battle of Franklin in November 1864, winning a close battle over General Hood's army. Two weeks later, the Army of the Cumberland under the command of General George H. Thomas destroyed Hood's forces outside of Nashville. Though the victory over Hood was Thomas', it would not likely have been possible without Schofield's earlier victory.[12]

Writing after his own retirement, Schofield reflected that Sherman's March to the Sea campaign was not necessary, though he found it lawful. Schofield recognized the vitality of Sherman's campaign, writing, "By marching a large army through the south where there was and could be no Confederate Army able to oppose it, destroying everything of military value, including food and continuing this operation until the government and the people of the southern states and abroad should find this demonstration convincing." And yet he pronounced Sherman's campaign "an unnecessary destruction of private property." To Schofield, the legitimate focus of military strategy was on the opponent's army rather than the general population. He did not, as with Winthrop, recognize that his strategic view was already outdated, destined never to fully return.[13]

After the war, Schofield briefly served in Virginia during the Reconstruction period. Although he was not enthusiastic about some of the Reconstruction programs, he enforced laws in the theater of operations to which he was assigned, Virginia. He also was sent to France, where he discussed Maximilian's tottering government with Napoleon III. How much influence Schofield's visit had on French policy is debatable, but the use of diplomacy over outright invasion succeeded in the French withdrawal from Mexico without resorting to a major war.

When the dismissal of Edwin Stanton led to the congressional impeachment hearings against Johnson, the secretary of war's office remained vacant. On June 1, 1868, President Johnson nominated Schofield as secretary of war. Johnson did not demand Schofield resign his commission, and Schofield was acceptable to congressional Republicans. His position lasted until March 13, 1869, less than one year in office. But it was during this time Schofield developed strong beliefs regarding the military's subordinate role to civilian government and the need for internal army reform.

The civilian position was difficult for him for reasons of loyalty. Schofield possessed a profound respect for General Grant, then serving as commanding general. He also respected Sherman's military abilities though he did not agree with Sherman's surrender negotiations with Confederate General Johnston. Nor did he approve of Sherman's contentious relationships with Halleck and Stanton. Schofield found the Stanton-Johnson controversy distasteful, and it fueled his desire for an apolitical military. In his day, this was impossible. Grant accepted the Republican nomination while still in uniform, and in 1880 General Winfield Scott Hancock ran for president while still on active duty. Schofield later related that Grant, by mid-1867, distrusted President Johnson. Grant confided in Schofield, "If [Johnson] were acquitted, as soon as Congress adjourned he would trample the laws under foot and do whatever he pleased; that Congress would have to remain in session all summer to protect the country; and that the only limit to his violation of law would be his courage, which had been very slight heretofore, but would vastly be increased by his escape from punishment."[14]

It was not uncommon for military officers to publish their opinions on military matters, but the experience of the impeachment hearings left an indelible mark on Schofield, and two years after his retirement the *Century* published one of his articles titled "Controversies in the War Department: Unpublished Facts Relating to the Impeachment of President Johnson." It was during the impeachment experience that Schofield reaffirmed his core belief that the commanding general had to serve as advisor to the president and that the secretary of war had authority over the commanding general. This did not stop Schofield from seeking reforms within the staff officers, namely, that they were too independent from the commanding general and the division and department commanders. And yet, to Schofield, some of the staff's independence was born from a desire to keep General Sherman from overstepping his authority. At the same time the president and the secretary of war had to coexist as a team. This did not occur, and President Johnson had sent out a number of orders that conflicted with Stanton's previous directives. Schofield did not defend Johnson as he thought Stanton's removal unwise and a violation of the separation of powers. He also believed Johnson too willing to forgive Confederate government officers. But he did not approve of the impeachment hearings either.

After stepping down as secretary of war, Schofield was assigned to the Missouri Department and then to command the Division of the Pacific. In this division command, Schofield oversaw the army's operations in the Modoc wars. Following the Division of the Pacific, he was appointed superintendent of the United States Military Academy, where his leadership proved contentious over the court-martial of the African cadet Whittaker.

Winthrop did not approve of the court-martial. While Winthrop's view of equality proved more progressive than Schofield's, the two men shared a belief in the efficacy of the laws of war.[15]

Schofield's first biographer, Russell Weigley, noted that the general was not a social Darwinian in an age of social Darwinians. Schofield in fact had argued, "the natural law of survival of the fittest may doubtless be pleaded as an explanation of all that has happened, but that is not a law of Christianity or of civilization, nor wisdom." He cautioned the followers of this law, including imperialists, that survival of the fittest "is the law of greed and cruelty, which generally works in the end to the destruction of its victims." Schofield did not praise wars as virtuous endeavors as had von Moltke. Indeed, he found a repugnant connection between war and adherents of ethnic or racial dominance.[16]

He spoke out against a potential war with Chile in 1892, though a number of his peers jingoistically embraced the idea of war with a weak neighbor. The United States had the military power to conduct a war against Chile and the economic and industrial might to sustain an occupation of that country. But Schofield adamantly opposed a war on moral grounds. At the same time he saw Japan's overwhelming success over China in the Sino-Japanese War of 1894 as proof of the necessity to maintain a strong army. Like other officers, he looked at the Prussian victory over France as evidence the United States had fallen far behind its European counterparts. To Schofield, the army had to be designed for defensive purposes. This did not mean the gulf in quality and quantity between the United States Army and those in Europe could be ignored. When he became the army's commanding general, Schofield sought to create a modern army but within the constraints demanded by the Constitution.

Schofield favorably took to Winthrop almost from of their first meeting. Interestingly, Schofield was not enamored with the Judge Advocate General's Department prior to meeting Winthrop. A long-running contentious relationship toward the office began in the late 1870s, but Schofield's ire toward the Department had solely to do with another judge advocate, Asa Gardner.

By the time Schofield encountered Gardner, he had developed a reputation as a bright, hard-nosed prosecutor. But Gardner also possessed a dishonest and unethical side, and Schofield discovered this inherent flaw in 1877 while at the United States Military Academy. Gardner's duties at the academy mainly consisted of courts-martial, but he also taught a law course there. In 1877, he pushed for legislation to mandate the academy have a permanent law professor on its faculty. Schofield was the superintendent of the academy at this time, and while he did not oppose a law professor, he was not enamored with Gardner as the choice. At some point Schofield confronted Gardner with evidence that he specifically vied for the faculty position, but Gardner professed ignorance. This was foolish for Gardner to do since none other than General William T. Sherman confirmed Schofield's suspicion of Gardner's scheming.[17]

During the 1878 Fitz-John Porter inquiry, Gardner rudely treated the higher-ranking court members. In response, Schofield asked the adjutant general if it were possible to have another judge advocate assigned to the case. Schofield, with the concurrence of the other officers, including General Alfred Terry and General George Getty, sought to have McDowell and Pope testify in person over Gardner's strident objection. The board members cross-examined McDowell on a number of inconsistencies with his testimony at Porter's original court in 1863. Pope refused to comply with the inquiry's order to testify, and throughout his refusal he had Gardner's full support.

At one point in the trial, Gardner became so obnoxious that Schofield reprimanded him, and when Gardner attempted to defend himself, Schofield ordered him to be silent. At the conclusion of the case, Gardner was excluded from a number of court's deliberations, and Schofield sealed the notes of the proceedings, preventing Gardner from viewing the notes. Gardner obtained a copy of the sealed documents but could not keep this fact a secret. He also sent General Pope updates as to the proceedings, which alone was not unethical but partisan given the fact Gardner assisted in ensuring Pope did not have to testify a second time. The communications between Pope and Gardner added to Schofield's anger, and the other generals assigned to the inquiry. To add to Schofield's anger, a *New York Times* editorial praised Gardner, condemned Schofield, and displayed facts that could have only originated from someone who took part in the proceedings.[18]

On April 29, 1879, Schofield wrote privately to the secretary of war excoriating Gardner, informing the secretary of his intention to charge Gardner under the Articles of War. The secretary of war asked Schofield to delay charging Gardner. One year later General Sherman interposed and asked Schofield to delay proceeding against Gardner as well. Sherman's reasoning was that as Congress debated the rehabilitation of Porter, charges against Gardner would create a "debate on side issues."[19]

In January 1881, General Getty and General Terry inquired to Schofield why Gardner had not as yet been charged. While Terry opined Gardner had committed "misdeeds," Getty argued, "I thought that during the progress of the investigation into Genl. Porter's case that charges should have been preferred against Major Gardner for disobedience of orders—for contemptuous and disrespectful conduct to the board." Even the following summer Terry vented his anger to Schofield over Gardner's continuation in the army.[20]

The War Department took no action and Gardner was saved, likely as a result of the statute of limitations. On the other hand, though Gardner remained on active duty and took part in important matters such as representing General Sheridan during an inquest or prosecuting Swaim, his reputation was tarnished. Not only did Schofield believe him dishonest, so did Sherman, Terry, Getty, Holt, Dunn, Norman Lieber, and Winthrop. Ultimately, Gardner resigned his commission, altered his name to Gardiner, and was elected as district attorney of New York City after running an antireform campaign. There, he ran into a more formidable foe than Schofield. In 1899, Governor Theodore Roosevelt charged Gardiner with unethical conduct and graft, ending the former judge advocate's public career.[21]

Despite Winthrop's misgivings of leaving Washington, DC, the Division of the Pacific provided a number of professional challenges. After the Civil War, Indian Bureau agents attempted to dictate army policy toward certain tribes. General Schofield was convinced that this was the very evil which perpetrated the murder of General Canby and the subsequent Modoc wars. Schofield and Winthrop believed Canby thought he was obliged to follow the directives of corrupt Indian Affairs officials. His criticisms against the bureau were unrelenting, and from his perspective, the Indian Bureau while under the Interior Department was a hindrance to peace.[22]

Winthrop adopted Schofield's view that the army had a duty to not only contain Indians on their reservation lands, but also to prevent white trespassers from encroaching on those lands. In one instance, he sought permission to override the Bureau of Indian Affair's authority to grant admission to individuals into reservation. In particular Schofield wanted to bar whiskey dealers, who he found "wholly injurious to the Indians." Winthrop advised him of the need to seek this authority from the War Department, though he clearly supported Schofield's intent.[23]

In California a potential for conflict arose when the War Department ordered the army to contain Paiute Indians on their reservation. Originally from the Northwest, the Paiutes and some Shoshone and Bannock allies and settlers engaged in a conflict first in the Utah Territory in 1860. The conflict ultimately brought in California Militia and federal troops but ended in a stalemate in which the Paiutes agreed to an informal cease-fire. Eighteen years later, the Bannocks and Paiutes went to war again. In the time between the first conflict and the second, the Paiutes and Bannocks had been forced onto the Fort Hall Reservation in eastern Idaho. Conditions on the reservation were so poor that by 1868, the Indians were on the verge of starvation and sought a return to their homelands. Moreover, unscrupulous white poachers were the major contributor to the starvation conditions on the reservations. As a result, the Paiutes, Bannocks, and Shoshone viewed settlers as the enemy.

In early May 1878, a number of Bannocks and Paiutes collecting roots on open prairie land became angry at white hog and sheep farmers. One Bannock shot and wounded two farmers. Shortly after, several hundred warriors attempted to raid into Oregon and several Paiute warriors from a reservation in that state joined the original war party. This time the army, fresh from its victory over the Idaho Nez Perce the previous year, campaigned against the Indians across Oregon, Utah, and Wyoming. Appallingly, the war ended with a massacre of 140 Indian women, elderly, and children. After the Indians surrendered they were forcibly returned to their reservations with a promise extracted not to leave. Several of the Paiutes were sent to the Yakima reservation in southern Washington. While the conditions on the reservation were not as onerous as had been the case in 1878, the Indians were far from fairly treated and a trickle of them left the reservation to seek their old way of life on their prior homelands.[24]

In 1882 the Indian Bureau wanted to stem the exodus of Bannock and Paiute from their reservations. The Yakima Reservation was singled out for a demonstration of the army's power to contain its inhabitants. Schofield did not relish the use of soldiers for this task, fearing an outbreak of war once more. In his response to the War Department, which had sided with the Indian Bureau, Schofield complained of a lack of available force to contain the exodus. He also fully believed that in many instances, the Indians suffered injustice at the hands of settlers and the government. Instead, he offered an alternative strategy, arguing, "I beg leave to suggest that the best practical disposition of the matter would be to place these Indians upon a reservation with some of their own kindred people. . . . This would make them more content."[25] Schofield once more showed his desire to use diplomacy rather than force to avoid conflict, and these were not hollow ideas either. He firmly believed in the relationship between conflict and injustice, and he decried the lack of legal enforcement against white abusers. Winthrop found himself in full agreement with Schofield on these points, and the two attempted to end injustices in their own respective arenas.

Like Schofield, Winthrop believed that the laws of war applied to conflict with Indians and whites alike. He advised commanders of their duty to stop whites from encroaching onto reservations. Winthrop opined that relations between the army and "friendly Indians" had to be distinguished by "a particular and scrupulous justice, humanity, and discretion." In that light, he argued that in instances where an officer or soldier committed a crime against "friendly Indians," it was a "peculiarly serious offense," as it made conflict all the more likely.[26]

The other significant legal issue Winthrop confronted was the age-old problem of desertion. At any given time, at least 10 percent of Schofield's assigned forces could not be accounted for. To Schofield, desertion was more than a crime of a single individual soldier; it was a symptom of morale and discipline problems plaguing the army as a whole. Moreover, like McClellan, Schofield strongly believed in an interrelationship between adherence to the laws of war, strategic effectiveness, and military discipline. He was not a martinet as evidenced by his statements on military discipline made while superintendent of the military academy. But he found desertion a particularly vexing issue.

Writing to General Crook, then commanding the Arizona Department, Schofield conveyed his awareness of "128 desertions since June last year." Schofield did not assign personal blame to Crook. "This is perhaps to be expected from the unsatisfactory manner in which the regiments are quartered . . . etc etc, but it does not appear that arrests are in proportion to the desertion and this fact deserves your full attention," Schofield noted. To solve these problems, Schofield turned to Winthrop who advised obtaining railroad company cooperation in notifying officers and United States marshals when soldiers traveled without leave passes or orders.[27]

Winthrop actively protected the extent of military jurisdiction over soldiers, particularly in the arena of desertion cases. However, he held fast to the argument that the statute of limitations strictly applied to all military trials. For instance, when one Private Arno White, a deserter, was captured and detained on Alcatraz by federal law enforcement in early June 1883, Winthrop determined to settle once and for all whether the statute prohibiting desertion was flawed.

Schofield reminded Winthrop, "The Department Commander thinks a ruling of the court on these points is most important for if it is decided by the court that a deserter though over two years absent, can nevertheless be punished for absence without leave by a general court martial can moreover be held liable for his enlistment contract, the effects upon the Army of such a decision will not be disadvantageous." He warned of a loss of jurisdiction being detrimental, writing, "Perhaps if a deserter by keeping out of the hands of the Government two years cannot only bar his trial and discharge himself from the service, the effect upon the Army will probably be to increase desertion very much."[28] Schofield and Winthrop considered White's court-martial a test case based on its special set of facts, namely that White had deserted over two years before his capture.

Like Winthrop, Schofield believed that there was a defect in the 103rd article of war prohibiting desertion. He memorialized his beliefs, opining to the adjutant general, "I believe desertion being a completed offense on the day it was committed first debarred from trial and punishment by the hundred and third Article of War after the lapse of two years. But absence without leave involved in the desertion is a continuing offense until the absentee is returned to military custody."[29]

The Bureau of Military Justice disagreed with Winthrop's analysis, even though only five years prior both General Holt and Colonel Dunn supported Winthrop's views. Schofield was perplexed at what he perceived as the bureau's and War Department's cavalier attitude toward an issue he considered a question of constitutional import. Although the president was the final appellate authority, and the Supreme Court since 1854 accepted the constitutionality of this structure, it gave further impetus to Winthrop and Schofield seeking guidance in the federal courts and the creation of a civil record to augment military justice. Moreover, Schofield rightly perceived that the War Department's attitude was rooted in the advice it received from the judge advocate general, David Swaim, an individual he and Winthrop increasingly had little regard for. Indeed, both Schofield and Winthrop were convinced the hard work of convincing Congress to amend the desertion article ended wholly due to Swaim's inaction.

Frustrations over the case continued with Schofield writing to the adjutant general, "In this connection, attention is respectfully invited to the accompanying report of Major Winthrop, Judge Advocate. In my own official action as in this and other legal matters, I have felt bound to respect the interpretation of the laws as given by the highest courts of the United States." Schofield continued to press his reliance on Winthrop and the civilian courts, stating that "after mature consideration of the subject, not essentially different than the civil courts have rendered in such case . . . no harm can result to the discipline of the Army from the adoption by the military authorities of the plan and manifest interpretation of the statute of limitations given by the civil courts."[30]

Private White had, in fact, argued to a federal judge that he deserted in early 1880, and the statute of limitations for the crime of desertion was two years. White did not contest that he had enlisted in the army in 1876 for a five-year term. He claimed that during the entire time of his desertion, he made no attempt to conceal himself. Thus, he argued the army was partially culpable since at any time it could have arrested him. Moreover, as of the time of the federal hearing, White had not been charged with an offense, nor had a court-martial order been forwarded. The District Court accepted Winthrop's argument that the offense of desertion was specifically a military offense and, as a result, the military maintained jurisdiction over the offender, to include a determination as to whether the statute of limitations had run.[31]

Ultimately, the court sided with Winthrop and it maintained the army's responsibility to determine jurisdiction, understanding that the Supreme Court could later review the case for jurisdictional defects. Schofield was clearly pleased with the result, writing in his annual report to the secretary of war for 1883, "The decision fully sustains the military jurisdiction in all cases of desertion. It also sustains, inferentially, the validity of the claim of the United States to the services of the soldier for the full term of his enlistment, however long he may have been AWOL."[32]

Winthrop's advocacy in this case impressed Schofield. He specifically noted Winthrop's work to the secretary of war in his annual report for 1883. Moreover, the California District Court's determination to side with Winthrop had an influence beyond the Division of the Pacific. In 1885, the United States District Court of Kansas adopted the California District Court's reasoning. In the Kansas case, a deserter claimed the military lacked jurisdiction to try him since he enlisted before he reached the legal age of majority. The deserter made this claim after he was prosecuted and sentenced to four years of confinement. The district court found that the army maintained the jurisdiction over the soldier as fraudulent enlistment was not a bar to prosecution for other offenses.[33]

In addition to Winthrop's dedication to ensuring the constitutionality of specific courts-martial, the desertion case of Arno White also showed Winthrop's frustration at the War Department bureaucracy as well as his own sense of humanity. Schofield had ordered Winthrop to represent the army before the federal courts in the matter. Swaim and the adjutant general believed that Winthrop required their specific permission to represent the army, but their permission was not forthcoming in time for the case at any rate. Winthrop spent twenty-two dollars from his own personal accounts to obtain for the Bureau of Military Justice and the Division of the Pacific copies of the trial transcript as well as the printed favorable ruling from the courts. He also spent his own money to ensure Arno White received these copies as well. Winthrop believed justice and fairness required White have possession of the very materials the government obtained. Winthrop attempted to obtain compensation from the War Department for their copy as well as White's. General Swaim did not approve Winthrop's request for reimbursement based on the fact Winthrop failed to obtain proper permission to represent the government in the first place. Winthrop responded with the argument that he "appeared in the case not as private counsel, but as part of my duty as Judge Advocate of the Department by the direction of the Department Commander." But this was a losing argument, and Winthrop was never paid.[34]

Two years after the White case, Winthrop found himself representing the army in a jurisdictional matter over deserters once more. This time the jurisdictional question had an odd twist to it. One Private McVey had originally enlisted in 1874 and deserted shortly after. He was prosecuted in a court-martial and received jail as part of his sentence. However, he escaped from custody and illicitly reenlisted in March 1877 but deserted one month later. This time Private McVey filed a writ of habeas corpus to the district court in California, arguing his second enlistment was defective as to deprive the military of jurisdiction to try him. The court found no cases to sustain Private McVey's plea for lack of jurisdiction. Instead, the court relied on Winthrop's *Digest of Opinions*, calling it valuable to its decision in upholding the military's jurisdiction. In effect, the court relied on the guidance of the authored work of the government counsel in the case, as well as Winthrop's argument that a deserter cannot profit from his own prior crime.[35]

That Winthrop impressed Schofield should not be of any surprise. Both were thoughtful, articulate men. The Whittaker case notwithstanding, Schofield was likely one of the more sensible interwar regular army generals. He was well read and had a deep respect for the law. For these reasons, he jumped over a number of other Civil War generals and succeeded Sheridan as the commanding general in August 1888. And he admired Winthrop's intellectual abilities. When Schofield received orders to transfer to the Division of the Missouri on November 1, 1883, he requested that Winthrop accompany him. The division was headquartered in Chicago, and this climate likely suited Alice's health better than the foggy enclave of San Francisco. Likewise, when three years later Schofield assumed command of the Division of the Atlantic, he requested Winthrop as his judge advocate. Neither request was favorably acted upon. The judge advocate general, the adjutant general, and the secretary of war had the final authority to determine assignments, and each opposed moving Winthrop before his full four-year tour of duty concluded. Writing to Winthrop on November 9, 1883, Schofield expressed his apologies to Winthrop for the adjutant general and secretary of war refusing his personal requests to have Winthrop assigned to Chicago. Schofield felt the need to explain further, writing, "I suppose they think your services are more necessary in San Francisco than here, and perhaps they are right. But the decision is a great disappointment to me, as it will be to you, and it will be a source of sincere regret to Mrs. Schofield that we cannot have Mrs. Winthrop and you near us again."[36]

Winthrop felt obliged to thank Schofield, but it befuddled him that the War Department would contravene the request of a major general. Although Winthrop thanked Schofield for his help, he expressed "mortification that [Schofield] should have subjected [himself] to have been disallowed a request—it would seem—should have been granted as a matter of course to a commander of your rank, character, and services."[37]

Part of Winthrop's consternation at remaining in the Pacific Division undoubtedly had to do with Schofield's successor, General John Pope. A fellow officer serving at the Presidio, Colonel August Kautz, feared Pope's arrival at the Presidio. On the same date as he notated a discussion with

Winthrop, Kautz recorded in his diary that he "hoped General Pope will be more considerate in his treatment of me than he was at Fort Stanton."[38]

Pope only served as divisional commander through 1885, and while Winthrop did not, in all likelihood, enjoy a lifelong friendship with Pope, he did not have any lasting conflicts with him either. None of Winthrop's letters to Schofield cast aspersions or noted any difficulties with Pope, and this is a testament to Winthrop's professionalism. At any rate, in early 1886, General O. O. Howard replaced Pope, and Winthrop's tour was scheduled to end in the late summer of that year.

By the beginning of 1886, Alice Winthrop's health had deteriorated to a condition that required her to move off the peninsula to San Rafael. However, the upcoming transfer to a new assignment brightened both Winthrops, and there was a possibility of working for General Schofield once more. Schofield was assumed to remain commander of the Missouri Division through 1888, but then General Winfield Scott Hancock died unexpectedly while commanding the Atlantic Division and the War Department transferred Schofield to the Atlantic Division. Once more, Schofield petitioned the War Department to transfer Winthrop to his command. Headquartered at Governors Island, New York City, the prospects of joining Schofield outshone any other opportunities. Winthrop conveyed to Schofield that he would rather join the general in New York than transfer to Washington to serve as Norman Lieber's assistant. In effect, Winthrop was willing to forgo the deputy role for another field tour. From a career perspective this was not entirely unwise. Lieber was only serving as acting judge advocate general since neither the War Department nor the president had pushed his nomination forward to Congress. If Congress denied Lieber's confirmation, he would revert to the assistant position, and Winthrop would return to the Bureau of Military Justice. Winthrop did not begrudge Lieber the chief position. In fact, he respected Lieber's abilities and professionalism. In contrast, he did not respect either Barr or Gardner. Instead, he suspected each of trying to undermine support for Lieber.

Winthrop conveyed to Schofield his desire to transfer at the end of his tour and not seek an early release on political grounds. "I should make the application with less hesitation because of the very discreditable and unmilitary—as it appears to rearrangement resorted to just at the end of Secy' Lincoln's term of office," he opined. Having felt the sting of President Hayes' appointment of Swaim over the desires of Holt and Dunn, Winthrop did not wish to follow a similar path as Swaim. But Winthrop was unstinting in his criticism of political and careerist appointments, singling out Gardner: "The then Judge Advocate of the Division was allowed to go at large, and a young second lieutenant placed in charge of the important duties of JA at Headquarters." Since Gardner had offended

Schofield years earlier, it is likely Winthrop had a receptive ear to this criticism. Winthrop did not reserve his ire for Gardner alone, equating him with Major Barr as "malignant libelers."[39]

To Joseph Holt he wrote, "The Secretary of War has never, it would seem, given any consideration to Colonel Lieber's request last March to have me detailed as his assistant, and the colonel has in other ways been so cavalierly treated and ignored as to Bureau matters, that it is quite evident that the Secretary as to all that concerns our department, is under the malign and intriguing Barr influence." Winthrop added, "I had hoped better of Mr. Endicott's antecedents."[40]

Winthrop did not merely fill his time with professional pursuits. He traveled across the division, ascertaining the conditions of the various Indian tribes. He also spent considerable personal time working on his treatise *Military Law*. But the law was not the only area in which he wrote. He also continued to write poetry and short fiction. He found an outlet for his creativity in writing for a western magazine, the *Overland Monthly*.

The *Overland Monthly* was a San Francisco–based literary magazine. It was first published in July 1868, and its initial authors included Samuel Clemens and Bret Harte. However, in 1875 its editors ceased production as the magazine failed to turn a profit. The *Overland* began a second life in 1883 when it was merged with the *Californian*, a magazine started by the same founders as the *Overland*. After its restart, it included writings from General Oliver O. Howard, who wrote a series on the army's campaign against the Bannock Indians, and Woodrow Wilson, then a young political science professor who published an article titled "Committee or Cabinet Government."[41] In its second run, the *Overland* became a journal publishing a combination of literature and current events.

In May 1883, the *Overland* published a poem Winthrop wrote titled "Jeanne Hachette." In his poem, Winthrop paid tribute to an obscure French heroine during the fifteenth-century struggle between Louis XI and Charles the Bold.[42] Several months later, the *Overland* published one of Winthrop's short stories. Titled "The Seat under the Beeches," the story narrative rambles from the Bureau of Military Justice in Washington, DC, to a fictional land. The story was a tribute to a fictional Englishman who served in a number of conflicts, always on the "right" side: the liberation of Greece as a deputy to Marcos Bozzaris in the 1820s; as an aide-de-camp on the side of the Poles against the Russians in the 1830s in Madrid; with Mazzini in Italy; and against the Bourbons in 1848. Yesterwood had the quality Winthrop found "rare among our military chiefs—initiative; and wherever so placed he could design and execute his own movement or attack, his success was complete and signal." But it was not the company of Yesterwood alone which brought Winthrop to Yesterwood's estate three times in three years. It was a bench on a promontory under beech trees and Yesterwood's niece which brought Winthrop back three years in a row. In the end, Winthrop professes that he has forgotten much of the details of these visits, but that his wife, Yesterwood's niece, could fill them in for the reader.[43]

The *Overland* also published two articles authored by Alice Winthrop. In 1896, ten years after leaving California, she authored an article on Christian altruism titled "The Question of Food for the People." She argued a link between the quality of food available for the working poor and temperance. Aware that food purity had declined for the city population, she sought to reverse the trend in arguing greater quantities of cheap wholesome food were important to alleviating the ills of poverty. Although the Pure Food and Drug Act was not passed until 1906 there was a growing push from muckrakers such as Upton Sinclair for laws regulating the purity of food. While Alice Winthrop was at best a minor author in this area, she did contribute to the awareness of significant health detriments in food processing.

One year after publishing her first article, the *Overland* printed a second, titled "The Catholic Charities of England." While the article did not make suggestions for the United States to adopt the methods of Catholic Charities, it provided a comprehensive overview of those charities. Alice Winthrop's knowledge of the various charities came from firsthand experiences while visiting Britain with William. The article may have been of limited utility, or it may have been of wide interest, but it further evidenced Alice Winthrop's social progressivism. Her egalitarian social beliefs must have complemented William's.

NOTES

1. For a complete Lomax family tree through 1900, see Edward Lomax, *Genealogy of the Virginia Family of Lomax by One of the Seventh Generation of the Direct Line* (Chicago: Rand McNally and Co., 1913). A copy of the *Genealogy* is located at the Virginia Historical Society (VHS) in Richmond. Information concerning Lunsford Lindsay Lomax, Jane Tayloe Lomax, and Alice Worthington is found on pages 39–44. According to Edward Lomax, Lunsford Lomax assisted in the research and writing of the family genealogy. Of Alice Worthington, the *Genealogy* states, "Alice, born June 13, 1846, married Lt. Col. Winthrop of New York, descendant of Governor Winthrop of Massachusetts, July 26, 1877, died October 2, 1900; no issue, she survived her husband but a few months."

Alice Worthington's lineage provides a nexus to her personal pursuits as well. On her father's side, it included Methodist preachers, converts to the Catholic Church, doctors of medicine, nuns, and abolitionists. Her grandfather Thomas Worthington (1773–1827) served as a delegate to the Ohio constitutional convention in 1803 and was elected as its first senator by the convention. He also served as Ohio's sixth governor between 1814 and 1818, as well as one of its representatives in Congress afterward. Thomas Worthington's brother-in-law, Edward Tiffin, an immigrant from England, served as a Methodist Preacher, a doctor, and in the Ohio state government as well. One of Tiffin's notable achievements was the arrest of Aaron Burr, after the former vice president fled from the capital. As Tiffin was the president of the 1803 Ohio Constitutional Convention, it is certainly the case Alice Winthrop's grandfather and great uncle had a significant impact in developing the laws of the state.

2. Diary entries as noted: Diary of Elizabeth Virginia Lomax (VHS); also see entry for December 28, 1860, for Alice's social interaction with Fitz Hugh Lee. Elizabeth Virginia Lomax's diary cited here is from the original. Her daughter and granddaughter published a typeset diary several years after her death. However, the typeset diary omitted several entries. The title of the typeset diary is *Leaves from an Old Washington Diary, 1854–1863* (New York: E.P. Dutton, 1943).

3. For Jane Tayloe Lomax's literary contributions, see Evart Duyckick and George Duyckick, *Cyclopaedia of American Literature*, vol. 2 (New York: Charles Scribner, 1856), 678.

4. John McAlister Schofield, *Forty-six Years in the Army* (New York: Century Co., 1897), 9.

5. Schofield, *Forty-six Years in the Army*, 10–13; Donald B. Connelly, *John M. Schofield and the Politics of Generalship* (Chapel Hill: University of North Carolina Press, 2006), 12–19.

6. Connelly, *John M. Schofield*, 54; Edward S. Martin, *The Life of Joseph Hodges Choate: As Gathered Chiefly through His Letters*, vol. 1 (New York: Charles Scribner's Sons, 1920), 334–335.

7. Schofield, *Forty-six Years in the Army*, 30; Connelly, *John M. Schofield*, 20–22.

8. James M. McPherson, *Battle Cry of Freedom: The Civil War Era* (New York: Oxford University Press, 1988), 351–354.

9. Nicole Etcheson, *Bleeding Kansas: Contested Liberty in the Civil War Era* (Lawrence: University Press of Kansas 2004), 238–242.

10. Schofield, *Forty-six Years in the Army*, 101.

11. Schofield, *Forty-six Years in the Army*, 77; David D. Eicher, *The Longest Night: A Military History of the Civil War* (New York: Simon and Schuster, 2001), 563–564; Etcheson, *Bleeding Kansas*, 240–242.

12. McPherson, *Battle Cry of Freedom*, 811–813.

13. Schofield, *Forty-six Years in the Army*, 311–314.

14. John McAlister Schofield, "Controversies in the War Department: Unpublished Facts Relating to the Impeachment of President Johnson," *Century* 54, no. 4 (August 1897), 580.

15. Schofield, *Forty-six Years in the Army*, 438.

16. Schofield, *Forty-six Years in the Army*, 438.

17. William T. Sherman, letter to John M. Schofield, January 31, 1877 (JMSP, container 88). Sherman wrote to Schofield, "It seems that Maj Gardner applied for the creation of a professorship of law with the understanding of that he was to be appointed professor. The President, after hearing of your letter answered, 'I guess Schofield is right.'"

18. "General Porter's Bad Case," November 6, 1878, *New York Times;* Otto Eisenschiml, *The Celebrated Case of Fitz John Porter* (Indianapolis, IN: Bobbs-Merrill, 1950), 228–241. Eisenschiml wrote that "Schofield was convinced Gardner was looking out for the interests of high ranking officers." Had Eisenschiml researched the correspondences of Joseph Holt, he would have definitively concluded that Gardner had a debt to McDowell. He would have also discovered the decade-long concern McDowell had that the Porter case not be reversed. Unfortunately neither Eisenschiml nor any other scholar of the Fitz-John Porter case seems to have reviewed Gardner's, McDowell's, or Pope's correspondence with General Holt.

19. William T. Sherman, letter to John M. Schofield, March 5, 1880 (JMSP, container 88).

20. William T. Sherman, letter to John M. Schofield, March 10, 1880 (JMSP, container 88); George W. Getty, letter to John M. Schofield, January 3, 1881 (JMSP, container 88); General Alfred H. Terry, letter to John M. Schofield, January 2, 1881 (JMSP, container 88); Alfred Terry, letter to John M. Schofield, July 30, 1881 (JMSP, container 88).

21. Alexander McClure, *The Authentic Life of William McKinley: Together with a life of Theodore Roosevelt* (New York: n.p., 1900), 483; and Gustavus Myers, *The History of Tammany Hall* (New York: G. Myers, 1901), 345.

22. Connelly, *John M. Schofield,* 222–223.

23. John M. Schofield, letter to Michael Sheridan, February 21, 1883 (JMPS).

24. Robert M. Utley and Wilcomb E. Washburn, *Indian Wars* (Boston: Houghton Mifflin, 2002), 267–270; Bill Yenne, *Indian Wars: The Campaign for the American West* (Yardley, PA: Westholme, 2006), 245–248.

25. John M. Schofield, letter to the adjutant general, September 25, 1883 (JMSP, container 51).

26. William Winthrop, *Military Law and Precedents,* 2nd ed. (Washington, DC: GPO, 1920), 337, 874. Schofield's views on the treatment of Indians may be best seen in light of the Modoc war. He argued that while the Indians "were tried and justly executed at the conclusion of the war, according to the laws of civilized war, the white men who, in no less flagrant disregard of the laws of civilization were not called to account for their crime." It was this reality that likely caused Schofield to caustically observe, "Indians could not trust the white man since the latter failed to follow his own laws." Moreover, Schofield was disgusted at the continuing view that "a white murderer was long regarded as much better than an honest Indian."

27. John M. Schofield, letter to the commanding general, Department of Arizona, October 25, 1853 (JMSP, container 51).

28. John M. Schofield, letter to William Winthrop, July 14, 1883 (JMSP, container 51).

29. John M. Schofield, letter to the adjutant general, September 4, 1883 (JMSP, container 51).

30. Schofield, letter to the adjutant general, September 4, 1883.

31. *In re White,* 17 F. 723 (D. Cal. 1883).

32. Schofield, letter to the adjutant general, September 4, 1883.

33. *In re Spencer,* 40 F. 149 (D. Kan. 1889).

34. William Winthrop, letter to the adjutant general, Department of California, August 24, 1883 (JMSP, container 51).

35. *In re McVey*, 27 F. 878 (D. Cal. 1885).

36. John M. Schofield, letter to William Winthrop, November 9, 1883 (JSMP, container 51).

37. William Winthrop, letter to John M. Schofield, November 10, 1883 (JSMP, container 51).

38. August Kautz, *Diary*, entry for December 13, 1883 (LOC).

39. Winthrop, letter to John M. Schofield, November 10, 1883.

40. William Winthrop, letter to Joseph Holt, May 29, 1885 (PJH, box 77).

41. Woodrow Wilson, "Committee or Cabinet Government," *Overland Monthly*, January 1884, 17.

42. William Winthrop, "Jeanne Hachette," *Overland Monthly*, May 1883, 477.

43. William Winthrop, "The Seat under the Beeches," *Overland Monthly*, January 1883, 49–54. Two years after publishing "The Seat under the Beeches," the *Overland* published another poem of Winthrop's titled "Bergamo." In it, he described a small town located on the Italian rail line between Milan and Venice. Like Jeanne Hachette, the Bergamo poem had martial overtones including, "above the embattled parapet, tall palaces ranged in stately show; from lancet windows deeply set, dark eyes dreamed down on Bergamo." William Winthrop, "Bergamo," *Overland Monthly*, May 1885, 468.

12

West Point Professor to the End of a Career

> As you did me the honor to accept a copy of my work on *Military Law* in two volumes, I should be much gratified if you would do the same as to my *Abridgement of Military Law*.
>
> —William Winthrop to President Grover Cleveland

In 1886 Winthrop replaced Lieutenant Colonel Herbert Curtis as professor of law at the United States Military Academy. Surprisingly, this position was not one Winthrop had actively sought. Winthrop's reluctance may have resulted from the academy's slide in reputation into a second-tier institution. No longer could engineering and mathematics, the prized courses of study at the academy, be considered as exceptional. At the same time, the other elements of professionalism then growing in the staff officer schools at Fort Leavenworth and Fort Monroe had not yet been accepted by the academy. Cadet hazing was another issue which drew bad publicity to the school. As a result of these factors, the academy did not generate the same public veneration it had before the Civil War.[1]

On the other hand, the academy's faculty in the late nineteenth century had an almost free hand at running their respective departments. From 1882 to 1886, Lieutenant Colonel Curtis trained a new generation of officers in the importance of constitutional law and the law of war. His primary textual instrument for instructing on the latter subject was General Order 100. When Winthrop took over from Curtis, he added Theodore Woolsey's *Introduction to the Study of International Law*, believing it the most relevant text in international law, and he maintained instruction from General Order 100 so that junior officers who were commissioned from the academy had a basis for understanding the laws of war through their tenure in the army.

Winthrop's inclusion of the *Introduction to the Study of International Law* served a number of purposes beyond simply educating cadets on the subject or the perpetuation of a distinguished scholar's standing as one of the most influential American international law jurists of the post–Civil War. It was a prominent treatise during its publication through six editions and its complexity showed Winthrop trusted the intellectual capacity of the cadets to absorb it. From a modern vantage point, Woolsey's treatise had drawbacks. His chauvinism, common to the nineteenth century, reflected in his statement (in the third edition of the work published in 1874) that he hoped international law would become "a universal law spreading over the land like the gospel." Another example of Woolsey's chauvinism was his explanation that international law was essentially the law of Christian nations which had ascended to a higher state of civilization than other peoples.[2]

Yet, the *Introduction to the Study of International* Law as an educational vehicle had benefit as well. Woolsey did not extol war. Instead, he argued that war was an unnatural state of civilization. He advocated that international law has—as its name implies—a universal character to it, making the law apply to conflicts of all natures, including wars against "insurgents" and "savages."[3] In his treatise, Woolsey repeatedly underscored the importance of respecting noncombatants and enforcing the rules regarding treatment of prisoners of war.

Perhaps most importantly, Woolsey's text reinforced Winthrop's teaching the relationship between adherence to the law of war and a disciplined and effective army. Moreover, it did so in a historic manner, replete with examples which several of Winthrop's contemporary military theorists and scholars viewed as the bedrock of a sound military study. For instance, the text drew a correlation between Gustavus Adolphus' system of military discipline and the Swedish Army's effectiveness against a much larger foe during the Thirty Years' War. Woolsey's use of Frederick the Great, the Duke of Marlborough, and even George Washington served a similar purpose. Indeed, much of Woolsey's text was related to the law of war and the examples he used throughout were already familiar to the cadets.[4]

Winthrop also assigned his own recently published text, *Abridgement of Military Law*, to the first class cadets. While the *Abridgement* lacked the sophistication of its parent, *Military Law*, it taught courts-martial procedures, the law of war, and civil-military relations. Moreover, it served to reinforce the professionalizing of the "constitutional army," providing a counterweight against Uptonian military thinking. It also served as a scholarly bulwark against a potential congressional overhaul of the Articles of War.[5]

The publication of the *Abridgement* and response to it, as well as Winthrop's reaction to criticism, provides another window into his character as well as the importance of his work. The *Abridgement* was not a scholarly undertaking on the magnitude of *Military Law* or *Military Law and Precedents*. It was, for the ten years between 1887 and 1897, the primary text for educating future officers on the army's constitutional place and their duties within it.

Winthrop acknowledged that the *Abridgement* was a scaled-down version of his earlier master treatise, *Military Law*, but its publication drew criticism. An anonymous review in the *Journal of the Military Service Institution of the United States*, but apparently written by his fellow judge advocate Captain William Birkhimer, derided both *Military Law* and the *Abridgement of Military Law*. In criticizing *Military Law*, Birkhimer alleged that its reliance on field circulars, general orders, and opinions of the judge advocate general constituted sources drafted by Winthrop earlier in his career. Birkhimer complained, "These lie buried out of sight, and reach in the files of the Judge Advocate General's office." Attacking the *Abridgement* he continued, "The author has gone to the other extreme, and eschewing what is most useful in the parent work, cites no authorities whatsoever." He also attacked Winthrop's view on the statute of limitations affecting the ability to prosecute desertion, calling it "at variance with Army practice." But the most pointed criticism was, in fact, a defense of legal formalism and a dismissal of Winthrop's use of common law and comparative law. Birkhimer also opined that Winthrop set the bar too high for the prosecution of offenses such as conduct unbecoming an officer and gentleman, by providing examples.[6] This was an ironic criticism since Winthrop aptly defended that particular article of war, and had Birkhimer's view prevailed, Congress might very well have terminated the specific article.

The *Army-Navy Journal* lauded Winthrop, stating, "The excellence of Deputy JAG Winthrop's *Abridgement of Military Law*, has prompted General Wilcox, commanding general of the Department of the Missouri, to adopt it as a standard book of reference at his headquarters and to recommend its use in his command, 'both for its intrinsic excellence, and uniformity of practice and rulings in courts-martial.'" Almost a hundred years later, in 1982, *The American Journal of International Law* credited Winthrop with shaping the American approach to international law through the publication of both *Abridgement of Military Law* and *Military Law and Precedents*.[7]

The most important legacy of the *Abridgement* is that it helped foster professionalism at the lowest commissioned ranks. While it is impossible to quantify its contribution to the army's modernization, it certainly played some part, along with his other texts, in ending the practice of officers charging other officers out of vendetta. By the time the army entered World War I, the days of officers substituting charges against each other for dueling had ended.

Despite Birkhimer's criticism, Winthrop took pride in the *Abridgement*. He sent a copy of the text to President Cleveland, writing, "As you did me the honor to accept a copy of my work on *Military Law* in two volumes, I should be much gratified if you would do the same as to my *Abridgement of Military Law*." In his letter, Winthrop noted that the text had already been accepted by both the academy's academic board and Secretary of War Endicott.[8]

Because the *Abridgement* was in standard use through the early part of the twentieth century, the roster of students who were exposed to it—as well as Winthrop's other works—included many of the army's generals in both world wars. Winthrop did not intend the *Abridgement* to be used to the exclusion of other texts. And one point Birkhimer missed is that Winthrop encouraged students to read Woolsey as well as Halleck, and he still taught the law of war based on General Order 100. Though the criticism leveled against the *Abridgement* was greater than *Military Law* and *Military Law and Precedents*, it is notable that like its counterparts, military courts have cited it well into the twentieth century.[9]

Winthrop's tenure at the academy had another benefit both for himself as well as for the army as a whole. He inherited supervision over two junior instructors, Lieutenant George B. Davis and Lieutenant William Evans. At the time both were officers of the line, but each had enough legal knowledge to qualify as instructors of law. Winthrop was pleased with the performance of both. Evans later attained the rank of brigadier general and the position of adjutant general of the army. Davis remained under Winthrop's supervision for one year. How much of an impact Winthrop had on Davis is speculative, but Davis eventually transferred into the Judge Advocate General's Department and later represented the United States under the direction of Joseph Choate at the 1907 Hague Conference. He also served as a judge advocate to the fielded forces in Cuba during the Spanish-American War.

Davis was a judge advocate in the Winthrop mold. Born in Massachusetts in 1847, he graduated high school in 1863 and immediately enlisted in the First Massachusetts Volunteer Cavalry. During the war he was commissioned as a second lieutenant and took part in over twenty battles, including Brandy Station, Todd's Tavern, Yellow Tavern, and the North Anna Campaign as well as Cold Harbor and the siege at Petersburg. After the war Davis attended the United States Military Academy and was commissioned as a Second Lieutenant of the Fifth U.S. Cavalry in 1871.

In that unit, he was assigned to the Wyoming and Arizona frontiers. In 1873, he was sent to the academy where he spent the next five years as an assistant professor in both the history and law departments. Davis was an avid writer and published scholarly articles in both history and the law. He was instrumental in the research and publication of the *Official Records of the War of the Rebellion*, first published in 1881.[10]

Davis also authored two histories of volunteer cavalry forces and the Army of the Potomac. However, his major literary contributions—aside from the *Official Records*—were his treatises on international law and military law. These were written after Winthrop's death, but Davis credited Winthrop with pioneering military law as a comprehensive study. Had Winthrop not written his legal treatises, it is likely Davis would have become the most cited military legal scholar. Davis' jurisprudential philosophy on military law was similar to Winthrop's in that Davis' use of history as well as comparative law occurs throughout his 1898 text *Military Law*.

After Winthrop's death, Davis also became the army's leading international law scholar, although the two men differed on one fundamental aspect. Davis argued that General Order 100 remained a superior code to constrain the conduct of military operations, and other codes, such as Professor Bluntschi's and the Brussells Conference, were unnecessary. Yet, like Winthrop, Davis believed that military law incorporated international law and practice. Davis' works partly cemented Winthrop's arguments that the military law's *lex non scripta* was evolutionary and had to be interpreted both in a historic and comparative context, into contemporary military law jurisprudence.

When Winthrop first transferred to the academy, General Wesley Merritt was the superintendent. The two men had no prior relations with each other, but generically shared a belief that the army's professionalization was necessary. Unlike Winthrop's relationship with Schofield, it does not appear that Winthrop and Merritt intellectually engaged each other or that the two men had anything but a cordial relationship. Merritt was not an Uptonian acolyte, but he believed that the army had to evolve from a frontier police force to a modern well-trained professional force on a European model. Like Upton, Merritt published a number of articles in the leading military journals and magazines of his time. Notably, in the 1884 *Journal of the Military Service Institution of the United States*, he expressed his view that discipline under the Articles of War should be consistent so that the articles did not undermine the very discipline they were designed to enforce. While he did not mention any nexus between desertion and the inconsistent use of courts-martial, his views accorded with Winthrop's, more so than with Sherman's.[11]

He did not approach Indian relations in the same manner as Winthrop. Instead, Merritt espoused that "in warfare, the Indian, though partially civilized, reverts to his worst savagery." He also believed that humanitarian concerns for Indians were misplaced and often based on the false assumption that there existed a two-hundred-year-old anger that Indian lands were taken by Europeans. Arguing that "the Indian's knowledge of history scarcely stretches beyond one generation," Merritt devalued their culture of oral traditions. Yet, he also lauded the Indians' prowess in battle, and in particular singled out Chief Joseph of the Nez Perce tribe as an astute leader.[12] By the time Merritt became superintendent, warfare against the tribes had almost ceased, so that Merritt was essentially defending a historic record more than preparing for future warfare.

Merritt believed that one of the long-standing offensive hazing events, known as "the rush," had to be terminated by his decree. "The rush" pitted the first class (seniors) of cadets against the second (juniors) class. The second class cadets were ordinarily granted a furlough—or brief leave—from the academy for the first time since matriculating into it, and on their return were rushed by a line of cadets from the first class. On occasion, cadets were knocked over and trampled during the event. When, in 1886, Merritt ordered cadets to no longer participate in it, the cadets openly defied his order and engaged in the activity. It does not appear that any of the cadets were injured, but Merritt was outraged at the affront to his authority and ordered a court-martial.

The cadets initially attempted to hire Benjamin Butler as their defense counsel, but he declined. Though it was well-known Butler disliked the academy, his prior service as a major general as well as his political standing would have made him a formidable defense counsel. It may be that he recommended Winthrop to the cadets, but even if this were true, Winthrop already enjoyed a reputation as a leading legal scholar. Whatever the case, Winthrop was the cadets' second choice, who after receiving permission from Merritt, represented all six. George Davis was selected to prosecute the court-martial.[13]

Winthrop's defense consisted of watering down the government's evidence of intent. He argued that the six cadets were carried away by excitement and no pre-designed plan of disobedience existed. He could not argue that the custom of the rush constituted a defense, though perhaps he hoped the court-martial officers would nullify the evidence and acquit the cadets. This did not occur and the cadets were convicted and subjected to dismissal. However, Secretary of War Endicott refused to approve any of the sentences. Endicott's reasoning was to "discourage the arbitrary methods which have prevailed at the Academy during the past few years, by which has been kept up." When the findings and sentences were made public, it was clear that the cadets were initially found guilty and sentenced to a dismissal, but President Grover Cleveland mitigated the sentences to a reduction in class rank so that while each cadet graduated and was commissioned on time, he did so as a cadet without any rank as such.[14]

The "Rush Cases" were not the only legal issue Winthrop undertook while at the academy. In 1887, Alice Winthrop became concerned with the spiritual welfare of Catholic cadets. The academy chapel provided Protestant Sunday services and it had a Protestant chaplain assigned to the academy, but it did not have a similar religious accommodation for Catholics. While Catholic cadets were permitted to attend Mass, the Catholic priest left something to be desired. Alice Winthrop complained to the archdiocese in New York that one Father Earley collected mandatory monies from cadets in exchange for conducting Mass. She noted to the archbishop that General Merritt was aware of the "injustice" and supported the establishment of a permanent parish at the academy.[15]

Father Earley responded to Alice Winthrop's quest to establish a permanent Catholic Church at the academy by attacking publicly her character. Winthrop complained to the archbishop that Father Earley had notified a number of citizens of his intention to bring a suit against Alice and her friends for libel. Although Winthrop was not concerned about the results of the suit, he recorded, "This may be mere vaporizing or attempted intimidation: at the same time it is by no means improbable that he may have been assured as above by some lawyer of slight repute." He also sought the archbishop's protection from Earley's harassment for his wife and her friends.[16]

To Winthrop, Father Earley was dishonest, and shortly after he first contacted the archbishop, a man calling himself "O'Connor" arrived at the post claiming to conduct an investigation for the vicar general. "The employment of such a lying and treacherous agency for the purpose of entrapping innocent persons and especially unsuspecting ladies, into making admissions with a view to using the same in evidence against them would, in the case of an officer of the army induce his trial by court-martial and dishonorable dismissal from military service," Winthrop notified the archbishop.[17] Father Earley was shortly after removed from any duties at the academy, and in 1899 the academy erected a Catholic chapel.

Merritt's tenure as superintendent lasted eighteen months into Winthrop's tour of duty. His successor, John Grubb Parke, likely appealed from the start to Winthrop as he had authored two legal treatises: *United States Laws Relating to Public Works* and *Laws Relating to the Construction of Bridges over Navigable Waters*. Interestingly, both books were published in 1877 so that it is unlikely Winthrop assisted Parke in writing and publishing either. However, it is fairly clear that Winthrop and Parke enjoyed a friendship.

Although Parke began his college education as a student at the University of Pennsylvania, he left the university for the academy. Parke graduated from the academy in 1849, and as a result of his high class rank, he was commissioned as a second lieutenant of engineers. Parke's interest in the law dated to his army engineering duties, which included mapping the boundary lines between British North America and the United States and surveying a route from the Mississippi River to the Pacific Ocean. The two men were in the Minnesota Territory during the same time. During the Civil War, Parke commanded a brigade under Burnside in North Carolina, and then served as Burnside's chief of staff. Through his station as Burnside's chief, he was innately familiar with the arrest and trial of Clement Vallandigham. Parke was elevated to corps commander during the siege of Petersburg. However, it was in the trial of Congressman Benjamin Gwinn Harris where Parke first came into contact with Winthrop. In that case, Parke served as a member in the court which had unanimously convicted Harris and sentenced him to three years in prison.[18]

Parke joined Winthrop on one of Winthrop's side projects. Beginning in 1888, Winthrop embarked on writing a history and walking tour guide of Revolutionary War forts and redoubts along the Hudson Valley. Completing the project required a number of long-distance hikes through the valley, and Parke joined Winthrop on more than one occasion. While the project was never published, a final draft of it resides in the New York Historical Society, donated by Winthrop's sister Sarah. Winthrop's eloquent prose throughout the draft noted he was related to Reverend Timothy Dwight, who in addition to serving as a Yale president, also served as a chaplain during the Revolution. The draft contained minute details including the types of artillery located at each redoubt. Winthrop also argued for the preservation of historic forts and redoubts against "a certain ruthless bridge and railway company." But the striking feature of the draft is in the life he gave to his historic passion in guiding tourists along a suggested route of travel: "Let us take a boat from West Point and make for the opposing shore. In midstream we rest on our oars to let pass a long tow. Observe the self-importance of the laboring tugs, the passive amenability of the craft in their wake."[19]

Winthrop's tenure under Parke's superintendency was not continuous. In the summer of 1888, the Winthrops traveled to France, Britain, and Germany. Some of his time was spent researching military topics, but they also toured the Louvre and other art museums. During the trip, he maintained his correspondence with Schofield, congratulating him from Paris on his promotion to "General in Chief" on August 14, 1888.[20]

Schofield's ascension to the head of the army did not immediately produce any change of Winthrop's assignment. In early 1889, Lieber reiterated a request to have Winthrop transferred to Washington, DC, as well. With both the commanding general and the acting judge advocate general requesting Winthrop's presence in the capital, the secretary of war had to take some notice, even if, as in Winthrop's case, he did not act on the desires of two of his ranking chiefs.

Indeed, it was initially unclear whether the secretary of war would finally accede to Norman Lieber's and General Schofield's desire to have Winthrop return to Washington, DC. There was no apparent reason for the War Department's intransigence, and Schofield suggested to Winthrop that an assignment to Governor's Island might happen. On March 17, 1890, Schofield told Winthrop that he was unsure of when, or if, the secretary would move Winthrop from the academy, but he wanted to ensure Winthrop did not feel he had failed to measure up in any event. "I need hardly add that the questions involved do not refer to you personally. It will be adjusted to your satisfaction if at all possible," Schofield assured Winthrop.[21] And yet, as soothing as Schofield attempted to be, Winthrop was clearly vexed at the secretary's possible denial. Thanking Schofield for his continued support, he added that he hoped the move would occur as it would be his last assignment before mandatory retirement. Additionally, Alice's health remained a concern, and she had access to a particular doctor in the capital whose expertise had been helpful in the past. Winthrop concluded his letter with more than a hint of exasperation: "You remember my—I might add our—failures on two occasions in the past."[22]

This time, the requested transfer back to Washington, DC, occurred. In midsummer 1890 Winthrop returned to Washington, DC, as the assistant judge advocate. He was deputy to General Norman Lieber, and he enthusiastically accepted this role. He respected Lieber's abilities, and Lieber had spent more time in the Judge Advocate General's Department than had Winthrop. Lieber had, like Winthrop, served as a line officer in the war before his appointment as judge advocate. The two men actually served near each other during the Peninsula campaign. Like his father, Norman Lieber supported Reconstruction. While he did not have his father's scholarly penchant, Lieber made a specialty in studying the army's role in civil stability.

There were minor changes in the Judge Advocate General's Department, such as the disappearance of the Bureau of Military Justice, though Winthrop's duties were similar to those when he served in that bureau after the Civil War. One other difference was that the Schofield-Winthrop relationship placed Winthrop in a position where he often spoke directly with the commanding general.

During Schofield's tenure as commanding general, he frequently vented anger at the various staff departments for failing to keep him apprised of their activities. Some staffs were more egregious than others. For instance, the adjutant general issued orders in Schofield's name without obtaining his permission, and the commissary general transferred personnel, without first informing Schofield or seeking his permission. The list of Schofield's grievances grew in his correspondence so that his letters to the secretary of war soon became flooded with them. Winthrop assisted Schofield in penning those complaints.

But the one staff department Schofield never found cause to complain was that of the judge advocate general. Peace between the commanding general and the judge advocates was largely to the credit of both Schofield and Winthrop. Winthrop remained attentive to Schofield's personal requests as well, advising him on the effect of Section 1244 requiring retirement of officers after forty-five years of service or at age sixty-two. The two men took an active interest in promoting the Army Navy Club, including the city government's incursion onto its property.[23]

Another source of Schofield's frustration came from an officer clearly waiting to become the next commanding general, Nelson A. Miles. Schofield had complained to the secretary of war about Miles' conduct on a number of occasions, and on one of these, Winthrop was at least privy to Schofield's anger. On April 8, 1893, Schofield wrote to Secretary of War Lamont, complaining that the *New York Herald* had printed an article titled "Trouble among Army Officers." The article detailed a spat between Schofield and Miles over the appointment of an investigating officer into a nondescript matter. Schofield was convinced that either clerks in the War Department or Miles had leaked information to the *Herald*. Schofield already did not approve of Miles' conduct in the Wounded Knee Massacre, and he later scolded Miles after writing an article in support of corporate interests after the Pullman Strike in 1894. He noted to Lamont that he wanted Miles reprimanded, and he wanted command over the War Department clerks. Winthrop advised Schofield that he did not have the authority to discipline civilian clerks, but the tenor of the commanding general's letter regarding Miles indicates that he considered bringing charges against him.[24]

Winthrop's other duties included oversight of courts-martial records, advice on civil military relations, constitutional law, and international law. He was likely in his element. General Schofield continued to rely on Winthrop's advice, and the correspondence between the two indicates that on important matters, Schofield found it easier to go straight to Winthrop. However, as a subordinate to Lieber, Winthrop usually ensured that advice was documented and passed to Lieber.

There were a number of strange occurrences. A field grade officer named Overman approached both Schofield and Winthrop offering to plead guilty to a lesser charge. "I advised him of course that the Judge

Advocate General's Office had no authority to withdraw a charge, and that he should properly put in his application and offer in writing to the Secretary of War," Winthrop noted to both Schofield and Lieber. "His manner during this conversation betrayed agitation and anxiety, and his statement, to my mind, was a substantial admission of guilt."[25]

Schofield and Winthrop continued to have reservations about some of the liberal decisions commanders made in regard to following court-martial procedure and respecting the importance of a court-martial both to the army as a whole as well as to the accused soldier. In 1893, Schofield wrote to Winthrop about a poorly prosecuted case, "indicating the greater care needed in the selection of officers for the duties of judge advocate in general courts-martial." The case resulted in a conviction, but was reversed by the judge advocate general with Schofield's concurrence because of the lack of due process afforded the soldier. Schofield wondered if "the Judge Advocate General's office could create a list of officers known to be qualified for such duties or that in making up the details of the general court martial, the Department be consulted as to the qualification of the officers selected for such detail."[26]

Winthrop's most important advice to Schofield during their final years in the army did not involve courts-martial, but rather the 1894 Chicago Pullman strike and the use of federal troops to suppress it. In May 1894 over a four-day period, over one hundred thousand rail workers refused to switch Pullman manufactured rail cars and launched a boycott of other activities. Perhaps unrelated to the strike, an act of arson also resulted in the destruction of several buildings. Under the executive order of protecting the mails, Cleveland authorized the use of federal troops to suppress the strike. Thirteen strikers were killed, fifty-seven more injured, and Eugene Debs was arrested for violating a court injunction against the railway workers union. Unlike the 1877 labor upheaval, the Illinois state governor, John P. Altgeld, did not want federal intervention and believed he could negotiate an end to the strike.[27]

During the strike, Winthrop advised Schofield that soldiers ordered to prevent insurrection and protect government properties were employed as part of the military power of the United States. As a result, no state government official or federal agent other than the president or a military officer appointed to command had any legal authority over the employment and use of the troops. Schofield wanted a tighter rein on the conduct of federal forces, in part because he did not want a repeat of Canby's disastrous meeting with Captain Jack, and in part because he did not want federal troops in the de facto employ of corporations. While Miles would not have been his choice to command the troops, Schofield could not select a different commander as Miles was the commanding general of the geographic division responsible for Chicago.[28]

Winthrop also assisted in drafting General Order 23, which labeled any mob resisting United States laws or destroying United States property (or property under U.S. protection) as a "public enemy." However, this label did not give officers carte blanche to open fire on crowds, as the order cautioned officers that innocent civilians were often mingled in with mobs. Instead, the order only permitted "single sharpshooters, selected by the commanding officer," to "shoot down individual rioters who have fired upon or thrown missiles at the troops." Neither Schofield nor Winthrop completely disagreed with Miles as to the danger of the strikers. Both men considered it an insurrection, but one against the United States laws rather than corporate interests.[29]

Other legal issues involved capital punishment. In 1892 Congressman Newton Curtis, a New York Republican, introduced a bill to abolish the death penalty in federal law. Curtis' proposed bill focused on federal civil law, but it had ramifications under military law as well. Curtis was a novice in neither the American legal system nor military affairs. A Medal of Honor recipient, he served as a Union officer during the Civil War. After the war he held a number of political and legal positions in both the New York government and federal government.[30]

In response to Curtis' proposed bill, Lieber expressed a concern that the Articles of War would require a special amendment. He had Winthrop prepare for Lamont a detailed chart comparing the Articles of War alongside the British articles, which carried a possible death penalty. Winthrop collected pertinent statistical information as well. He noted that from the Confederate surrender to 1892, courts-martial sentenced an accused soldier to death twenty times, and military commissions sitting in an occupation (as opposed to a war court) had done so on nine occasions. Of the twenty courts-martial sentences, only three soldiers were actually executed; the others had their sentences commuted or remitted after a period of time. As for the military commissions, Winthrop reported that only four executions were carried out. These were the Modoc Indian executions, though Winthrop did not continue his criticism of the trial's jurisdiction in his memorandum to the secretary of war.[31]

Both Winthrop and Lieber, with Schofield's concurrence, did not oppose Curtis' bill so long as it applied to the Articles of War during a time of peace, with one exception. They argued for the continuation of the death penalty for murder committed during a mutiny. Both Lieber and Winthrop believed in the necessity for the death penalty's continuation during time of war as well. They expressed a view to limit the death penalty punishment in desertion cases, to only cases where a soldier deserted in the immediate face of an enemy. And, more importantly, both men argued that the death penalty had to remain a proscribed punishment for violations of the fifty-seventh article. This was, as Winthrop argued, the article punishing war crimes.[32]

In some part, the Winthrops' social life remained intertwined with his legal scholarship. His circle of friends included Martin Ferdinand Morris, a federal judge on the District of Columbia Court of Appeals. Morris graduated from Georgetown in 1854, the year Winthrop graduated from Harvard. Morris did not serve in the Civil War and at some point attempted to enter the priesthood, but opted for a law career. Early in his legal career, he served as an associate to Richard T. Merrick and assisted in John H. Surratt's defense. The two men were involved in promoting the Smithsonian Museum and shared a passion for the law. When Winthrop died, Merrick assisted Alice in an attempt to rectify errors in Winthrop's service record.[33]

Prior to his tenure as an appellate judge, Morris served as dean of the Georgetown University Law School. President Grover Cleveland named Morris to the Supreme Court in 1893. In 1898, Morris published *Lectures on the Development of Constitutional and Civil History*, a work based on his prior lectures. The work is historical in its format, and Winthrop assuredly appreciated its contents, but it is interesting to note Morris' thesis that Martin Luther, John Calvin, and John Knox were not reformers. Instead, according to Morris, they constituted a group of intolerant men, prone to violence against others who challenged their faith. Morris' position stood in contrast to Winthrop's *Townsend Prize* essay five decades earlier in which Winthrop lauded the Reformation and argued that the Catholic Church had "oppressed freedoms and killed men." By 1890, Winthrop's position on Catholics had long since changed, and his friendship with Morris was so strong that Winthrop dedicated *Military Law and Precedents* to him.[34]

There were two aspects to the Morris-Winthrop friendship that provide some insight into Winthrop's tenure in his assignment as assistant judge advocate. As Swaim's sentence neared its completion, Cleveland would have to name a permanent judge advocate general. Norman Lieber had seniority and was serving as the de facto judge advocate general, but Morris and George Hoadly petitioned Cleveland to leap Winthrop past Lieber to the top position. They did not petition Schofield, who was serving as commanding general, but it was well known Schofield favored Winthrop. For unknown reasons, Cleveland decided to honor Lieber's seniority, and after Winthrop's retirement in 1895, the president nominated Lieber judge advocate general.

The second aspect of the Morris-Winthrop friendship is that it brought the Winthrops into a circle of Smithsonian board members including the eminent physician Dr. Joseph Toner. Dr. Toner's intellectual interests spanned from collecting genealogies to public health and botany. Like Morris, Toner was an ardent Catholic, and from his early medical practice beginning in the mid-century, he encouraged the construction of Catholic Church–sponsored hospitals. Given Alice Winthrop's interest in medicine and history, it is probable Toner influenced her research into *Diet in Illness and Convalescence* and encouraged her later research on Catholic nuns serving as nurses in the Civil War. At the same time William assisted Toner's genealogical studies in providing him with a growing library of items on the Winthrop family lineage.[35]

Winthrop's other activities included assisting the American Antiquarian Society in preserving the Winthrop family lineage. In 1888, he donated a ceremonial sword to the society which was brought to the colonies by John Winthrop and passed through the lineage to Francis Bayard Winthrop. According to the Antiquarian Society, Winthrop carried the sword with his other kit items through the Civil War. However, it is unlikely that he brought a two-century-old sword into battle at any time. Still, if Winthrop carried the sword in his military assignments and during the war, it evidences a conscious visible link to his background.[36]

Winthrop maintained his interest in international law throughout his career and well into his retirement. He was not reticent at publicly pointing out what he perceived as flaws in the arguments of other scholars, even when the offending individual was a family member. One such occurrence involved Theodore Dwight Woolsey's son, Theodore S. Woolsey. In a *Yale Law Journal* article written in 1893, Woolsey opined that once the United States acceded to the 1856 Declaration of Paris, it was bound to abolish "privacy and privateering." In his own *Yale Law Review* article, Winthrop took exception to Woolsey's opinion on constitutional grounds. He pointed out "Article I, section 8 expressly left to both houses of the legislative branch the authority to make rules regarding the capture of prizes." A treaty did not, he argued, have the ability to strip the Congress of that authority. Winthrop conceded that piracy was unlawful in international law, but the only means to make it so in United States jurisprudence was to amend the Constitution. Winthrop's position was neither conservative nor liberal for its time. It reflected a constitutionalist-based approach to international law; simply, that international law could not trump the Constitution, citizenry had to alter it—as in the case of the Thirteenth Amendment—to effectuate change. Whether Woolsey ultimately agreed with Winthrop's position or even engaged him in debate is unknown, but the response to Woolsey showed a continued vibrancy in Winthrop's legal scholarship.[37]

His relationship with Lieber during their tenure in Washington, DC, does not appear to be anything more than professional. When, in 1894, Lieber rated Winthrop's abilities, he gave his deputy a "good" marking in professional ability. Lieber could have ranked Winthrop as high as "excellent" or "very good" or as low as "tolerable," "indifferent," or "bad." Whether the "good" rating placed a strain on Winthrop's relations with Lieber can never be known because there is no evidence Winthrop protested the rating or that he viewed the rating as an insult. It may be that Lieber down-rated Winthrop because the judge advocate general position still had yet to be filled and Lieber remained acting judge advocate.[38] It was possible President Cleveland could yet jump Winthrop in front of Lieber. On the other hand, the rating may very well have been Lieber's honest assessment. Lieber did not view Winthrop as an inadequate lawyer or officer, and he incorporated Winthrop's scholarship into his own legal writing without criticism, but he was surely aware of criticism directed at Winthrop's scholarship.

One other feature of Winthrop's final years in the Judge Advocate General's Department was his failing health. At the academy he was diagnosed with tonsillitis, requiring surgery, as well as a dislocated knee caused by a fall while hiking. The knee injury may have occurred as he researched redoubts on the Hudson. In early 1893, he suffered from a contusion as well as another dislocated knee. The following year, Captain Leonard Wood, a rising officer serving as an army physician but soon after promoted to general, had Winthrop under his care for "acute bronchitis." Winthrop shortly after was diagnosed with a sprained left foot, followed by another bout of "acute bronchitis."

Winthrop reached the age of mandatory retirement in 1895, which meant that he would not become judge advocate general. Lieber remained a colonel, and his official position was that of acting judge advocate general. It was not until after Winthrop's retirement that Lieber was promoted to brigadier general and confirmed judge advocate general. And a man Winthrop had little regard for, Lieutenant Colonel Thomas Barr, was promoted into Winthrop's position. When Lieber retired, Barr served exactly one day as the judge advocate general before his forced retirement. But by that time, Winthrop was already dead.

NOTES

1. *Annual Report of the Secretary of War* (Washington, DC: GPO, 1995), 777. See also Patrick Finnegan, "The Study of Law as a Foundation of Leadership and Command: The History of Law Instruction at the United States Military Academy," *Military Law Review* 118 (2004), 112–137. For reasons noted previously, Finnegan's article is generic and glosses over the nature of military law and the activities of judge advocates. Finnegan also fails to note that Winthrop introduced two texts into the law curriculum: his own *Abridgement of Military Law* and Woolsey's *Introduction to the Study of International Law.*

2. Theodore D. Woolsey, *Introduction to the Study of International Law, Designed as an Aid in Teaching, and in Historical Studies* (Boston: J. Munroe and Co., 1860), 4–10. Woolsey's chauvinism was not unique by any measure. See, for example, Lassa Oppenheim, *International Law: A Treatise* (New York: Longmans, Green and Co., 1906), 92–93. Oppenheim was one of the leading international law jurists of the early twentieth century. For a well-researched contemporary view of Woolsey and his influence, see, for example, Gordon Hylton, "David Josiah Brewer and the Christian Constitution," *Marquette Law Review* 81 (1998), 417–444.

3. Woolsey, *Introduction to the Study of International Law*, 232–233; Oppenheim, *International Law*, 92–93.

4. Woolsey, *Introduction to the Study of International Law*, 218–222. Woolsey also noted that after Gustavus was killed, the Swedish Army devolved into an undisciplined force led by his successors, Tortensen and Baner. Woolsey's argument on the loss of Swedish prowess solely due to the death of its king was an overstatement for a number of reasons. Sweden had limited resources to conduct a long-term war and as the Thirty Years' War dragged on, it was unable to resupply its ranks with its national army and had to rely on mercenaries. Moreover, Gustavus relied on mercenaries in his own lifetime because of limited resources. Also, the traditional constraints of warfare had, by Gustavus' time, ceased as both sides to the conflict engaged in gross plunder and murder of civilian populations. It was a matter of time before Swedish forces would have retaliated in kind. See, for example, Russell F. Weigley, *The Age of Battles: The Quest for Decisive Warfare from Breitenfeld to Waterloo* (Bloomington: Indiana University Press, 1991), 1–35.

5. *Annual Report of the United States Military Academy*, 1888 (Washington, DC: GPO, 1888), 6–37. In 1886, Senator John Logan of Illinois introduced legislation to enable the Federal Court for the District of Columbia to review "severe sentences," and the authority to revise sentences it deemed unfair. See *Army-Navy Journal*, May 22, 1886. In the *Abridgement*'s preface, Winthrop noted that the book was specifically designed for the education of cadets at the military academy.

6. *Journal of the Military Service Institution of the United States*, 1887, 151–156. Both Prugh and Hagan present Birkhimer as the author of the critical article. See, for example, William Hagan, "Overlooked Textbooks Jettison Some Durable Military Law Legends," *Military Law Review* 113 (1986), 163. Hagan's article has its own errors. For instance, he places Winthrop at the Battle of Gettysburg and notes that Theodore was William's younger brother. Neither statement is correct. He also lists Birkhimer's review of Winthrop as having been written in 1893.

Birkhimer also took exception to Winthrop's position on an action taken by President Hayes in an officer's court-martial. However, Winthrop's position was a stated opinion and not one in which he presented as a matter of law.

7. *Army-Navy Journal*, April 2, 1887, 709; John Raymond and Barbara Frischholz, "Lawyers Who Established International Law in the United States," *American Journal of International Law* 76, no. 4 (October 1982), 816–817.

8. William Winthrop, letter to Grover Cleveland, February 17, 1887 (Papers of Grover Cleveland, Reel no. 109, LOC).

9. See, for example, *United States v. Jacoby*, 11 USCMA 428 (1960); and *United States v. Minor*, 4 CMR 89 (1952).

10. *The War of the Rebellion: A Compilation of the Official Records of the Union and Confederate Armies* is a seventy-volume set of general orders, official correspon-

dences, and other government records relating to the Union and Confederate governments and commands during the war. It is, perhaps, the most comprehensive set of documents ever assembled on any single subject.

11. Don Alberts, *Brandy Station to Manila Bay, A Biography of General Wesley Merritt* (Austin, TX: Presidial Press, 1980), 264. For Merritt's writing, see Wesley Merritt, "Three Indian Campaigns," *Harpers New Monthly Magazine* 80 (April 1880), 720–737; "The Army of the United States," *Harper's New Monthly Magazine* 80 (March 1880), 493–510.

12. Merritt, "Three Indian Campaigns," 720–737.

13. *Army-Navy Journal*, September 11, 1886, 131; also, William Hagan, "The Rush Cases and the Class of 1887," *Army Lawyer* 18 (1887), 18–21. Butler did not mention any aspect of the "Rush Cases" in his memoirs. On September 11, 1886, *Army-Navy Journal* reported that six of the participating cadets were brought before a court-martial. It also reported that the cadets' conduct constituted "one of the most flagrant cases of disobedience and violation of rules and discipline that has been witnessed at the Academy in many years." *Army-Navy Journal*, September 11, 1886, 131.

14. *Army-Navy Journal*, September 18, 1886, 148; *Army-Navy Journal*, September 25, 1886; Hagan, "The Rush Cases and the Class of 1887," 20.

15. Alice Winthrop, letter to Father Hewitt, January 17, 1887 (AANY).

16. Alice Winthrop, letter to Father Hewitt, April 17, 1887 (AANY); William Winthrop, letter to Father Hewitt, May 9, 1887 (AANY).

17. William Winthrop, letter to Father Hewitt, May 10, 1887 (AANY). Winthrop conveyed to the archbishop, "When called upon to exhibit his credentials—some form of written authority from Msgr Preston—O'Connor had none to offer. O'Connor pretended that, in making delicate inquiries of this nature (which he said, he was often employed by the Vicar General)—it was not usual to present formal papers." According to Winthrop, O'Connor was able to interview one of Alice Winthrop's friends, a Mrs. Bernard, "through a deceit." Winthrop, letter to Father Hewitt, May 10, 1887.

18. For biographical information on General John G. Parke, see L. D. Ingersoll, *A History of the War Department of the United States with Biographical Sketches of the Secretaries* (New York: Francis B. Mohun, 1879), 284–291; Oscar F. Adams, *Dictionary of American Authors* (Boston: Houghton Mifflin, 1904), 283.

19. William Winthrop, *Old Forts on the Hudson Highlands* (NYHS, est. 1890). Winthrop began his draft with, "In my walks in the Hudson Highlands, during a sojourn at West Point, I came frequently to make as the object of the excursion some one or more of the Revolutionary Redoubts or other earth works of which remains still exist. The interest spread by these venerable defenses, and by the picturesque surroundings of their secluded sites, soon expanded into a real attachment and many a happy hour I spent on an old parapet, looking down upon the noble Hudson, or across forest and farm toward Dunderburg, or Boterburg, or Anthony's Nose."

20. William Winthrop, letter to John M. Schofield, August 15, 1888 (JMSP, container 36). Schofield was promoted to the head of the army on August 14, 1888, when Philip Sheridan died. For specific facts on Schofield's promotion, see, for example, Donald B. Connelly, *John M. Schofield and the Politics of Generalship* (Chapel Hill: University of North Carolina Press, 2006), 270.

21. John M. Schofield, letter to William Winthrop, March 15, 1890 (JMSP, container 54).

22. William Winthrop, letter to John M. Schofield, March 17, 1890 (JMSP, container 82).

23. John M. Schofield, letter to William Winthrop, January 22, 1892 (JMSP, container 56). Schofield wrote, "I agree that it would be improper though I think it would impair the value of the Club property, if it should ever be for sale. But I doubt not the owner's of the private property, who have a right to be heard in the matter will be able to control it. At all events, it does not seem that I would be justified in taking part in a protest."

24. John M. Schofield, letter to Daniel Lamont, April 8, 1893 (Lamont papers, container 8).

25. William Winthrop, letter to John M. Schofield, June 6, 1892 (JMSP, container 52).

26. John M. Schofield, letter to William Winthrop, May 4, 1893 (JMSP, container 57).

27. See, for example, Harry Barnard, *"Eagle Forgotten": The Life of John Peter Altgeld* (Indianapolis: Bobbs-Merrill, 1938), 185–270, and Henry Jones Ford, *The Cleveland Era: A Chronicle of the New Order in Politics* (New Haven: Yale University Press, 1921), 208.

28. William Winthrop, *Military Law and Precedents*, 2nd ed. (Washington, DC: GPO, 1920), 865–866.

29. Winthrop, *Military Law and Precedents*, 865–866. The order further clarified, "Under no circumstances are the troops to fire into a crowd without the order of the commanding officer." See also John McAlister Schofield, *Forty-six Years in the Army* (New York: Century, 1897), 532.

30. For Congressman Curtis' attempts to abolish the death penalty, see Newton Martin Curtis, *Capital Crimes and the Punishments Prescribed Therefor by Federal and State Laws and Those of Foreign Countries* (Washington, DC: Gibson Bros, 1894); also, Curtis, *To Define the Crime of Murder, Provide Penalty Therefor, and to Abolish the Punishment of Death* (Washington, DC: GPO, 1892).

31. *Report of the Judge Advocate General to the Secretary of War for 1892* (Washington, DC: GPO, 1892), 19–21.

32. *Report of the Judge Advocate General to the Secretary of War for 1892*, 19–21.

33. See, for example, Richard Merrick to Commissioner Pensions, January 11, 1900 (AWPF).

34. James S. Easby-Smith, *Georgetown University in the District of Columbia, 1789–1907*, vol. 2 (Chicago: Lewis Co., 1907), 56–57; Martin Ferdinand Morris, *Lectures on the Development of Constitutional and Civil History* (Washington, DC: W.H. Morrison's Son, 1898), 247–248.

35. See, for example, Judge Morris, letter to Dr. Toner, May 1892 (Papers of Joseph Toner, LOC).

36. *Proceedings of the American Antiquarian Society*, vol. 5 (Worcester, MA: American Antiquarian Society, 1889), 158–159.

37. William Winthrop, "The United States and the Declaration of Paris," *Yale Law Journal* 3 (October 1893), 168.

38. George Prugh, "Colonel William Winthrop: The Tradition of the Military Lawyer," *American Bar Association Journal* 42, no. 2 (May 1956), 188–190.

13

Epilogue: Retirement and Death

> His thoroughness and scholarship have led to as general a recognition abroad as at home, and it is asserted by an English Judge Advocate General that this work changed the course of procedure in English military courts.
>
> —*New York Times* on William Winthrop's retirement

On July 29, 1895, the *New York Times* announced Colonel Winthrop retired from the army. The *Times* lauded his career, writing, "The army will lose the services of an able and conscientious officer." The *Times* editors also focused on Winthrop's contributions to the law, characterizing it as unparalleled and drawing attention to his far-reaching influence: "In addition to his regular duties, Col. Winthrop wrote a treatise on military law, the first edition of which was published in 1886. It has received ready and wide acceptance among military authorities being the only work of its kind in the English language." The paper acknowledged, moreover, that Winthrop was at the time of his retirement the foremost authority on military law; "his thoroughness and scholarship have led to as general a recognition abroad as at home, and it is asserted by an English Judge Advocate General that this work changed the course of procedure in English military courts." While the article noted his other contributions including the publication of the *Digest of Opinions*, his tenure as a faculty member at the United States Military Academy, and his Civil War service, it did not mention his other literary efforts.[1] Perhaps this was a reflection of Winthrop's desire to remain out of any public acclaim while in uniform for matters other than military law.

A number of praises were written about Winthrop during the remaining years of his life. Partly this had to do with the publication of his final treatise, *Military Law and Precedents.* Published in late 1895, it was principally an expansion on *Military Law.* However, in *Military Law and Precedents* there were not only a considerable number of additional sources incorporated into it, but there was also a detailed commentary on the law of war. Winthrop had expanded this section partly in expectation of a future conference between nations which he hoped would result in an agreement on waging war within the confines of international law. The *Boston Advertiser,* in writing a favorable critique, noted the expansion of his law of war analysis, calling it "exhaustive, carefully revised, and without equal."[2] While hardly referenced in contemporary scholarship, Winthrop's presentation and analysis of the laws of war remain significant into the present time as part of the military's *lex non scripta.*

Military Law and Precedents' law of war section was particularly insightful in two areas: defining legitimacy of combatants and the treatment of captured persons. Presaging the use of private military forces, Winthrop criticized the use of armed civilians in wartime. Western military forces had largely abandoned the use of private armies during his lifetime and only recently had their widespread use reappeared. Winthrop was familiar with the franc-tireurs phenomena of the Franco-Prussian War, as well as a number of other instances in which civilians became directly involved in fighting. But these were largely uncoordinated responses to an enemy invasion.

Winthrop argued that the right to carry arms in a military zone, even during an occupation after the conclusion of hostilities, was related to the complete jurisdictional reach of military law. Otherwise, a civilian who bore arms at the behest of a government was nothing more than a mercenary and an unlawful belligerent. To Winthrop, the phrase *subject to the jurisdiction of military law* meant subject to the jurisdiction of a court-martial or military commission. The fact that an individual might be subject to the jurisdiction of civilian criminal law was of no importance.

As early as 1864, Winthrop was concerned with the use of civilians who were not subject to military jurisdiction, and yet engaged in combat operations. In a review of one case, he argued to Holt, "It may be held that Gurley was engaging in hostilities without commission from the rebel government, without lawful authority and without belonging to any organized force, armed and uniformed as soldiers." Winthrop concluded his view that "the laws of war treat such men as entitled to no privileges as prisoners of war, but as liable to be dealt with according to the circumstances of the case." In Gurley's case, the sentence of death was carried out with both Winthrop's and Holt's approval.[3]

Winthrop was not the first to attempt to recognize distinctions in the status of combatants. During the Civil War, General Halleck had, even prior to Lieber's law-of-war committee, sought the professor's advice on the Confederate use of guerrillas and so-called rangers. In a treatise to Halleck titled *Guerrilla Parties Considered with Reference to the Laws and Customs of War,* Lieber posited two types of irregulars—guerrillas and partisans. Lieber was dissatisfied with the widespread use of the term *guerrilla.* He considered guerillas as unlawful combatants and narrowly defined them as self-constituted and serving outside the "general law of levy." Lieber did not, however, address the issue of mercenaries. His central argument was simply that a combatant who was not subject to court-martial jurisdiction was an unlawful combatant.[4]

Neither Lieber nor Winthrop had the benefit of a codified legal distinction for either the term *mercenary* or *irregular,* but both had a profound historic understanding of the differences. Lieber and Winthrop defined a mercenary as a soldier—albeit often from a neutral state—who fought for plunder, pay, or booty, rather than solely for the aims of the state. A mercenary was not subject to the Articles of War or its foreign counterparts, thereby placing him in an unlawful, or unprivileged, status. In contrast, an irregular was a soldier subject to the Articles of War (or its foreign counterpart) who fought in an unconventional manner. While Winthrop believed that the employment of mercenaries was a violation of international law, an irregular's status under international law depended on the individual's conduct in battle. That is, irregulars who violated the laws of war could be tried and punished upon capture. Mercenaries could be tried and punished based on status alone.[5]

Winthrop's concerns with mercenaries were based on the fundamental relationship between adherence to law and military discipline, which he believed eroded when persons not subject to the Articles of War were permitted to bear arms in an armed conflict. Winthrop's analysis on the use of mercenaries, like much of his work, retains its relevance in the modern era as private military contractors are increasingly in use in theaters of operations such as Iraq, and it could hardly be argued he would have approved of their use.

Winthrop's second area of concern, articulated more fully in *Military Law and Precedents* than any of his other writings, regarded the treatment of prisoners of war. The treatment of captured personnel was, in some part, directly related to their status as lawful combatants. Winthrop was familiar with the conditions of the Andersonville and Libby prisons during the Civil War, and he fully supported the trial and execution of Henry Wirz. He also argued the Confederate killing of Union soldiers after their surrender at Fort Pillow "was a crime—the extremest of that period—against the laws of civilized warfare." He noted that combatants and certain noncombatants on capture had to be accorded humane treatment as a result of this status. This was because, as Winthrop noted, international law accorded a prisoner of war with a continuing status of soldier, rather than a criminal. In other words the status was one of containment rather than penal.[6]

To Winthrop, humane treatment meant more than the feeding, clothing, and medical care provided to captured persons. As long as the status of the captured soldier or noncombatant did not violate the law of war, cruel, degrading, and inhumane treatment was not lawful. He argued torture constituted a gross violation of the laws of war, and a captor state had a responsibility to prosecute its own soldiers when they engaged in such conduct.[7]

Public acclaim for Winthrop's contributions did not end with the *Times* article, and in some instances, it came from within the military. He was honored by the Naval Institute in 1897 for influencing naval courts-martial practice and contributing to the practice of international law.[8] In 1896, his fellow judge advocate Lieutenant Colonel J. W. Clous wrote, "Our military jurisprudence was thus founded during the most critical period of our national history by General Holt with the assistance of his able corps of judge advocates. To one of these—Colonel Winthrop—the army is indebted for a treatise on military law in which for the first time are collected for the benefit of the soldier, the lawyer, and the historian, the precedents, decisions, and opinions which have become part of our law military."[9]

Despite the public recognition from the American Bar Association, historical societies, and fellow judge advocates, retirement did not always kindly treat Winthrop. Although he lectured at Georgetown, his efforts at postservice employment were mostly unsuccessful. He attempted to represent clients before the United States Court of Claims. This court was established in 1855 to determine the veracity of monetary claims made against the United States government. Its jurisdiction included "claims founded upon the Constitution." This was the same court which initially heard and than rejected Swaim's argument that his court-martial was improperly convened, depriving him of his pay and status.

There was a prohibition against federal officers representing claimants before the court that had to do with preventing frauds against the government. In effect, Winthrop wanted to serve as a prosecutor against the government. In 1882, the Court of Claims determined retired officers were not eligible to practice before it.[10] Winthrop argued that he was not in a position to "assist in, or connive at frauds against the Untied States." He also challenged the constitutionality of this prohibition, but the Court of Claims ruled against him. The court's reasoning rested on the well-established rule that retired officers were still considered officers of the United States. The court made clear that Winthrop had served honorably, but individual exceptions could not be granted if the rule were to have any efficacy at all. The case result was reported in the *Washington Post,* which quoted Winthrop maintaining his arguments before the court as the correct interpretation of the law and the court in error.[11] Ironically, the Court of Claims found Winthrop's treatises as compelling legal authority in a number of cases, mostly after his death. These cases included questions over pay during desertion and arrest, as well as the nature of jurisdiction over government officials.[12]

Notwithstanding the adverse Court of Claims decision, Winthrop was not in need of further employment. He had a service pension and a family inheritance and no outstanding debts. He owned his home, and he befriended a number of the leading families in the capital, including the Riggs Bank owners. He maintained his friendship with Judge Morris and General Schofield; however, Winthrop and Schofield rarely saw each other. Moreover Winthrop was so well thought of that Georgetown awarded him an honorary doctor of laws. It appears clear enough that Judge Morris effectuated the honorary degree, but the fact remained that Winthrop had, by 1897, been considered in the legal community as the authority on military law.

However, Winthrop's biggest disappointment was in the War Department's refusal to purchase *Military Law and Precedents.* Winthrop's publisher directly contacted Secretary of War Lamont with an offer to supply the various departments and divisions with the work at a discounted rate. However, no interest was forthcoming and Norman Lieber opined that the work's relevance had diminished. Lieber did not elaborate on these views, but it is possible as both Birkhimer and George Davis were writing their own military law treatises, Lieber sought to have the War Department purchase one of theirs instead of Winthrop's. It is also possible that Birkhimer's influence grew after Winthrop's departure and the War Department desired a return to legal formalism. When Winthrop inquired to Lamont as to the War Department's lack of interest, Lamont forwarded the issue to Lieber, but Lieber only articulated that the War Department did not require any updated copies of Winthrop's work.[13]

In 1896, a manual for courts-martial was published by a Lieutenant Arthur Murray, under the secretary of war's authority. This issue may have been the reason behind Winthrop's lack of communication with the Judge Advocate General's Department after 1896. Indeed, when Winthrop died in 1899, Lieber was unaware of his whereabouts and indicated the two men had not spoken in several years. Lieber did not give any reason for the absence of communication between himself and

Winthrop, nor did he leave any reasons in his correspondence as to the cause of their estrangement.[14]

Despite the army's lack of interest in purchasing *Military Law and Precedents*, the treatise continued to be used long after its publication, and indeed continues to be. For instance, the Department of the Interior utilized his work in adjudicating disputed Civil War pensions.[15] Hundreds of courts turned to him, some within his own lifetime. He probably did not foresee that the Supreme Court would cite his treatise on some of the most critical cases regarding executive authority, but he believed that he had provided the judicial branch with the most complete guidance on military law.

Military Law and Precedents was the last legal treatise Winthrop published. However, he continued to write on military matters. In 1898 when war broke between the United States and Spain, he authored a series of articles in two magazines, the *Independent* and *Outlook*. Almost lost to history, these articles provide additional context and clarity to *Military Law* and *Military Law and Precedents*. Perhaps the clearest context the articles provide is that Winthrop intended the principles underlying the laws of war to apply in all conflicts regardless of the nature of the armed conflict.

It is unclear whether he was paid for authoring the articles or donated them to the publications as he earlier had done with his poetry to the *Overland*. Both magazines were at the forefront of the American print media. The *Independent* was founded as a Congregationalist journal, providing analysis of current events. Its editors were generally pro-Republican and its articles reflected this view.[16] Similar to the *Independent*, the *Outlook*—albeit a Methodist-founded journal—printed a combination of news articles, editorial articles, and poetry. Each magazine had a growing circulation, though the *Outlook*'s had grown from twenty thousand in 1880 to one hundred thousand in 1902.[17] Moreover, the *Outlook*'s contributing authors included Booker T. Washington, Jacob Riis, and Edward Everett Hale. Despite their religious foundations, both journals had a progressive editorship. For instance, the editors of the *Outlook* and the *Independent* did not denounce Charles Darwin or evolutionary theory, but rather published articles finding merit in Darwin's theories.[18]

Although the catalyst for the war occurred in Cuba with the destruction of the *Maine*, a United States warship, the United States pursued a strategy to confront Spain in that country's overseas possessions. Spain's possessions stretched across the globe as a remnant of its former empire. For the first time in its history, the United States military was sent to fight a conflict in the Caribbean, as well as in the Pacific. Spain held in its control the Philippine Islands, Guam, Cuba, and Puerto Rico (then spelled Porto Rico), and the War Department at McKinley's direction intended to seize these possessions from Spain. It was, however, unclear at the beginning whether the government uniformly intended to create a vast overseas empire or liberate these regions.

In June 1898, Winthrop tackled the issue of the United States militarily occupying the Philippines in an article titled "The Problem of the Philippines: Racial Commercial, Religious, Political, and Social Conditions." He did not, at any time, advocate permanently occupying the islands or creating an "American empire." He believed that the Philippines ought to gain independence when the internal government achieved stability. At the same time, he conceded that the Philippines, and in particular Manila, was important in expanding American commerce. As a result, Winthrop felt the United States had to gain influence in the Philippine capital. He also acknowledged that the capture of Manila would not, in and of itself, equate to control over the entirety of the Philippine Islands. Winthrop pointed to the British experience in 1762, where 6,300 soldiers supported by the Royal Navy took Manila but were unable to exert influence beyond the city. There were too many islands for the government in Manila to have complete control over.[19]

After detailing the Philippine geography, economy, climate, and demography, Winthrop provided an analysis of the government and various religious factions. His analysis of the population and its religions set the stage for his conclusion that while a successful occupation of the Philippines was possible, it was likely to be costly and difficult. He criticized the Spanish-run Catholic Church on the islands as an impediment to advancing civilization, in part because the various Catholic orders were primarily interested in increasing their opulence and had undergone a century of infighting between themselves. And he was particularly galled that the archbishop of Manila preached a holy war against the United States. The archbishop in fact had warned that American forces would ban the practice of the Catholic faith on the islands.[20]

Winthrop detailed the ethnic and religious differences in the islands. He described Chinese immigrants—he called them "celestials"—as well as the mixed "Chinese-mestizos" as the industrious and professional section of society. The indigenous natives, which he referred to as "Indians," were "the most unprofitable, uncertain, and dangerous element." However, he did not ascribe these traits to bloodlines or eugenics as had been popular to do, but placed the fault entirely on the Spanish, who "taught [the natives] gambling and liquor as we taught our Indians the taste of whiskey." In this article Winthrop continued his shared belief with General Schofield that the responsibility for much of the Native American misfortune rested with white citizens rather than the Indians themselves.[21]

He also expressed particular concern over the Muslim natives of Mindanao and the Sulu Islands. He warned, "Expedition after expedition has been sent against them, and the Jesuit missionaries have labored for their conversion, all to little purpose." He also warned that the diversity of the southern islands, their languages and dialects within the languages, stood as a barrier to successful occupation. In his approach to Mindanao's inhabitants, he argued against forcing conversions to Christianity as this would violate the law of war and strengthen an insurrection against American rule. In effect, Winthrop provided a strategic warning that the United States could not come as permanent occupiers and succeed.[22]

There had been an unsuccessful insurrection against Spain in 1896, and Winthrop condemned the Spanish response to it. Writing, "In the course of their conflicts with the forces of the government, which was instructed to show no mercy, a spirit of atrocious inhumanity was developed on both sides," he noted that prisoners of war were routinely maimed or killed, "without any regard to the usages of civilized warfare." Winthrop singled the Spanish for criticism, writing, "The Spanish to extort confessions, resorted to the thumbscrew and revived the tortures of the inquisition." He countered a Spanish claim that the law of retaliation permitted such measures, arguing that "no law or exigency could justify retaliation pushed to a point so malignant or brutal." In short, Winthrop argued that regardless of the nature of a conflict, to include an occupation, the laws and customs of war applied equally as they would toward a conventional conflict. In this matter, he clearly maintained his belief that armies of civilized nations had to adhere to the laws and customs of war no matter the nature of the war, the scope of the occupation, or the war methods of an indigenous enemy.[23]

Winthrop did not enthusiastically endorse the occupation or colonization of the Philippines after the defeat of Spain. Instead, he raised a number of difficulties the United States had to overcome if the government opted to occupy the Philippines. He pointed out that occupying forces were required to recognize the existing system of government but were permitted to end past abusive practices. He argued that recognition of the Spanish colonial government could not occur since "three hundred years of Spanish occupation of the Philippines resulted in a government so artificial and complicated, so arrogant in its pretensions, so corrupt in the details of its administration . . . so violent in its revenges and brutal in its punishments" that it had to be removed altogether and replaced with a new system of governance modeled after the United States Constitution.[24] He also argued that while the Church could not be removed, its monopoly on faith had to be terminated and "religious liberty had to be enshrined." Clearly Winthrop was not, by this time, anti-Catholic, but he recognized the Catholic Church in the Philippines was too corrupt in its administration to the Philippines gaining independence and a stable government.

In July 1898, Winthrop published an article titled, "Porto Rico and the Capture of San Juan," in the *Outlook*. He advocated landing army and marine forces near the Puerto Rican city so that artillery units could bombard the Spanish defenses from land as well as sea and he further argued for the seizure of the port of Fajardo some thirty miles distant as a base for supply. Winthrop's most poignant caution was to avoid alienating the local population as they were not hostile to the Spanish, and could be provoked into anti-American sentiment. Again, Winthrop staunchly remained committed to the army's adherence to the law of war in its universal application.[25]

Through his writing, Winthrop continued to educate the public on matters of international law through the war. In an article for the *Independent* titled "Our Naval Captures," he assured readers that the navy complied with international law when it seized a number of vessels.[26] In November, Winthrop wrote another article for the *Independent* titled "Fernando Po, a Spanish Prison." Fernando Po referred to an island off the coast of West Africa (now called Bioko), which the Spanish utilized as a prison. As in the case of his other two articles, he provided a historic, economic, and demographic background. However, the gist of his article dealt with inhumane treatment in a large Spanish-run prison. As a result of earlier insurrection in Cuba and the Philippines, as well as political opposition forces in Spain, a number of political prisoners were held on the island. The island's climate caused a high mortality rate. Winthrop encouraged the government to demand the release of the political prisoners as part of any surrender or truce with Spain. This was a demand on humanitarian grounds, as there were no American military prisoners on the island.

Winthrop's final article, published posthumously in the *Independent*, was titled "Our Lesser Insular Appurtenances."[27] Although he took a conservative view of American expansion into the Pacific, he realized this expansion created implications to United States national security. He believed that sea routes to the Philippines had to be maintained or the islands could be isolated by another power. He did not name Japan as the likely contender for control over the islands, nor is there specific evidence he foresaw Japan as a possible enemy. And yet he noted the Midway Islands as essential for a coaling station and naval presence. He also believed the Midway Islands were ideally suited for a transpacific cable. Winthrop further mentioned another island made famous forty-two years after his death, Wake Island. He advocated a permanent naval presence on Wake as well as that island's suitability to serve as a cable relay station.[28]

Winthrop's health deteriorated as he watched the progress of the war. He suffered from "bronchial catarrh" and remained under Leonard Wood's care until Wood left for the war as a line officer to lead the "Rough Riders," with Theodore Roosevelt as his deputy. Indeed, in the years between Winthrop's retirement and his death, he visited Wood at least forty-four times. Even after Wood's departure for the war, Winthrop continued to see an army surgeon.

By the beginning of 1899, Winthrop was in severe pain. Major E. C. Carter, his surgeon, reported that treatments to ease Winthrop's discomforts were of no help. In the three months prior to his death, he suffered from "tracheal, bronchial, and thoracic complaints." Winthrop was unable to function in the capital during the early spring and traveled with Alice to Atlantic City for "ocean air." But this trip did not result in any improvement, and he died of a cardiac failure in his sleep on April 8, 1899. On April 10, 1899, the *Washington Post* reported Winthrop's death in a brief page 3 article. Supreme Court Justice Stephen J. Field had also died on April 9, and his death was more widely reported. The *Post*'s obituary on Winthrop did not detail his Civil War service, writing only that "he served as a private in Company F of the Seventh New York State Regiment, but subsequently made a First Lieutenant in another regiment."[29] The article did not describe his service in the Sharpshooters or his contributions to the advancement of military law. Nor did the *Post* detail his other writings.

Yale University published a glowing obituary later that year. It briefly described his pre-military life and associations. But it also glossed over his Civil War service, not mentioning his tenure in the Sharpshooters. Indeed, the reader of the obituary could be left with the impression Winthrop served the entire war in the Seventh Regiment. Yet, Yale lauded his contributions to law as well as to literary and scientific journals. Moreover, it was the only obituary that recognized the fact the Georgetown conferred on him an honorary doctor of laws degree.[30]

Alice Winthrop lived less than a year after William's death. She spent much of that time frustrated at the Pension Bureau. Her pension reflected William had retired as a captain, and the Pension Bureau downplayed the extent of Winthrop's Civil War wound. She enlisted Major General Leonard Wood to correct the Pension Bureau's mistake. Wood drafted two letters to the War Department detailing that Winthrop had been in his care, and in his medical opinion, Winthrop's heart had never recovered from injuries received while in the service. These injuries dated to the Fredericksburg campaign, entitling Alice Winthrop to a full pension at Winthrop's rank of colonel. She did not seek help from the Judge Advocate General's Department or from General Schofield, who had already retired. However, the matter resolved in her favor, though her death within the year meant Winthrop's pension disappeared altogether.[31]

Winthrop's critics were active in the two decades after his death. On April 6, 1917, the United States formally declared war on Germany. The experience of total war, while brief, brought military affairs to the forefront of the nation in a manner similar to the Civil War. The army prosecuted thousands of courts-martial and calls for reform resulted from a number of injustices similar to those experienced in the Civil War. However, this war was fought without resort to military commissions and the prosecution of senior officers for political reasons. The injustices which occurred largely resulted from a quickly enlarged army, often ignorant of military law procedures. The war did not see officers substituting the court-martial charge for dueling. And the greatest injustices tended to fall on African Americans, something Winthrop would have never countenanced.

General Ansell and Professor Morgan criticized Winthrop in the 1919 Senate hearings on military justice. There, Ansell argued, "Winthrop's orthodoxy has been followed blindly since *Military Law and Precedents* despite Supreme Court decisions to the contrary."[32] Later, Morgan echoed these very arguments. Their argument was in error in many respects. For his time, Winthrop was not orthodox. As noted, his jurisprudential philosophy matched the leading thinkers of his day: Holmes, Cooley, and Wharton. Moreover, the Supreme Court has never taken exception to Winthrop; no single decision exists which labeled his treatise or jurisprudential philosophy as flawed. The expansion of civil rights and the evolution of military justice certainly replaced many of the practices which Winthrop explained and defended. But Ansell's and Morgan's criticisms were nothing more than an attempt to have Congress reform the military justice system by criticizing the existing practices, rather than the actual procedures and fair trial requirements Winthrop embraced.

Winthrop had his defenders, notably the army's judge advocate general in World War I, Enoch Crowder, who argued Ansell was unfair to Winthrop. Crowder had once met Winthrop and was impressed with his work. In 1913, he assigned Major Walter Bethel, the judge advocate assigned to the academy's law department, to revise Winthrop's treatise for a second printing. In 1919, Crowder testified Ansell deliberately ignored the fact that while Winthrop characterized the court-martial as an executive instrument, he also stated that a court-martial was a court of law and justice. Moreover, Crowder's defense of Winthrop included an attack on Ansell's statement that Winthrop was "first a military man." Crowder reminded the Senate that Winthrop had served as a line officer through 1864, but noted, "It is a career limited, so far as military service in the line is concerned; and a very extended and distinguished career as far as legal service in the legal department of the Army is concerned."[33]

Ansell's view of Winthrop was needlessly shortsighted in part due to the close proximity of time between the two men and Ansell's experience as the acting judge advocate during World War I. Ansell did not see Winthrop's successes; namely, that Winthrop's scholarship triumphed over an austere formalism in military law that would have been—had it survived—wholly at odds with evolving standards of justice. Nor did Ansell consider Winthrop's defense of the "constitutional army" served as one bulwark against an Uptonian vision which was incompatible with the Constitution. And it was hardly the case Ansell or Morgan would have endorsed Winthrop's belief in racial equality before the law as evidence of Winthrop's commitment to fairness. By 1919, a number of officers and elected officials called for the complete elimination of African American soldiers from the army.

Winthrop authored for the military and the public two treatises on laws and legal opinions which matched the needs of military discipline to the constitutional place of the army. His broad view on military law and the importance of having officers educated in their legal responsibilities contributed to creating an officer corps less Uptonian and more American. He did not espouse positions which undermined military morale or efficiency. To the contrary, he wedded military principles to the law. In doing so, he pushed for an understanding of the interrelationship between adherence to the laws of armed conflict, the Constitution, and a disciplined force. And he did this in a uniquely American way, one which understood that soldiers, whether draftees or volunteers, could not long tolerate an unjust system or a system which allowed soldiers to commit acts of injustice.

His background beliefs prior to joining the army were one element in explaining the value of his work. As an abolitionist who believed in racial equality, he did not believe in a separate system for minorities. Nor, as he matured, did he subscribe to stereotypes, and through his writing, it is clear that just as race had no place in the evaluation of the competency of witnesses, it also had no place in the treatment of soldiers. Once in the military, his observations on the conduct of commanders such as Hiram Berdan and John Pope reinforced his later beliefs in the need for a professional army.

His role in the trial of the Lincoln assassins, as well as in the presidential impeachment of Johnson, taught him that the military could not (and in particular the judge advocate must not) willfully take part in political matters reserved for the executive and legislature. There were exceptions. Winthrop believed that in the rare instance where the executive acted unconstitutionally or in violation of the law of war, officers could take a public stand where other avenues failed. And he willingly prosecuted a congressman who attempted to assist the Confederacy in a military trial. Although many congressmen supported the trial, and the trial itself was lawful in statute—though of questionable constitutionality—military juntas often occur when the executive diminishes legislative opposition through trials. However, he argued that Harris' trial was based on the congressman's treason and not conscience. But these exceptions were so rare that Winthrop concluded it was unlikely either would ever again occur.

It was partly the Civil War and Reconstruction experiences which led him to argue against Prussian influences, though his unyielding loyalty to the Constitution was the main factor. In Prussia, and later Germany, the General Staff had become an arm of the government—at times seemingly coequal with the legislature. There, the sovereign could decide whether to use the army as a domestic or a foreign hammer without constitutional constraint. In a nutshell, Winthrop strove both for fairness and constitutionality.

And yet, it is a testament to Winthrop's character that he did not use his relationship with Schofield to undermine Lieber and gain the highest position in the Judge Advocate General's Department. Nor did he use his last name to gain promotion to high rank. He was content to serve under Lieber, respecting his position and knowing that Lieber would long outlast him. Winthrop was unusually humble in light of his family lineage and in comparison to a great many officers. Perhaps he felt that haughtiness and arrogance were thoroughly unprofessional traits for an officer. But as the younger brother to a colorful, if occasionally arrogant, gifted writer, he was outwardly modest to begin with. Because of his lack of self-promotion, he became a historic unknown, while his classic treatise was and is cited over and over again.

His influence in courts-martial practice is unparalleled. While there were a number of injustices in military trials after his death, largely as a result of a slapdash approach to prosecutions, a pervasive continuance of racism, and a lack of familiarity with military law during both World Wars, Winthrop's contribution was to lessen these injustices. When, in 1970, Lieutenant William Calley was prosecuted for murdering innocent Vietnamese, Winthrop's influence was in the court-martial and appeal. Indeed, the military appellate court turned to Winthrop in ruling, "Enemy prisoners are not subject to summary execution by their captors. Military law has long held that the killing of an unresisting prisoner is murder."[34] More importantly, when Calley attempted to use the defense of a subordinate following a superior's orders, the military appellate court in dismissing this defense quoted extensively from Winthrop, first labeling him the "leading commentator on military law."

Since Winthrop's death, the Supreme Court has turned to Winthrop for guidance in a number of cases, including *Carter v. McClaughery* (1902), *Ex parte Quirin* (1942), *In re Yamashita* (1946), *United States ex rel. Hirshberg v. Cooke* (1950), *Madsen v. Kinsella* (1952), and *Reid v. Covert* (1957). It was in this last case where the Court first titled Winthrop as the "Blackstone of Military Law" and adopted his argument that "a statute cannot be framed by which a civilian can lawfully be made amenable to the military jurisdiction in time of peace."[35] In *Hamdan v. Rumseld*, decided in 2006, the majority and minority both turned to Winthrop for guidance multiple times throughout the decision.[36] The decision set limits on the executive branch in wartime. In essence, just as Winthrop reminded Andrew Johnson's allies that the law of war and Constitution did not change the presidency into a monarchy during wartime, the Supreme Court using Winthrop did the same.

The Supreme Court's continuing use of Winthrop, as well as other federal courts' use, in determining the constitutional authority of the executive branch is unequalled by any military scholar. A constitutional democracy cannot abandon its laws and survive as a constitutional democracy, though it may survive with another, more tyrannical and arbitrary form of government. Winthrop understood this very point, and he incorporated it into his treatises, knowing these would be digested through the army's educational processes. He believed in a disciplined army wedded to the rule of law and advised by a professional Judge Advocate General's Department.

The successes of a scholar are rarely quantifiable, but his are in several respects. To this day, the practice of military law is predicated on a comparative law approach. The service military courts of appeal, as well as the Court of Appeals for the Armed Forces, use as persuasive authority the decisions of other cases and writing of learned scholars. This has a profound influence on the litigation practices of judge advocates in courts-martial. When in 2004, the judge advocates general of the army, navy, and air force protested interrogation techniques as violating the laws of war, they did so in the best traditions of Winthrop, though he might not have come into their equation. And when Congress and the courts reduce the executive's influence in crafting the jurisdiction and procedures of military commissions in our contemporary conflict, they consciously and deliberatively turn to Winthrop. It is for this reason that he remains, as he was originally titled by the Supreme Court, the Blackstone of Military Law.

NOTES

1. "Colonel Winthrop's Retirement: By It the Army Will Lose a Very Able Assistant Judge Advocate General," *New York Times*, June 30, 1895, 2.

2. For Winthrop's view on the law of war, see, Little, Brown, and Company Publishers, letter to Secretary Lamont, February 25, 1896 (Lamont papers, folder 62). Winthrop's publishers conveyed Winthrop's intent in expanding the section covering the laws of war to Secretary of War Lamont. For favorable review of the book in the referenced newspaper see "The Literary World," *Boston Daily Advertiser*, March 12, 1896, 5.

3. William Winthrop, letter to Joseph Holt, and Joseph Holt, letter to Edwin Stanton, March 11, 1864 (NA RG 153.2.1 folder 7).

4. Francis Lieber, "Guerrilla Parties Considered with Reference to the Laws and Usages of War," *The War of the Rebellion*, ser. 3, vol. 2, 308–309. See also Colonel Carl E. Grant, "Partisan Warfare Model," *Military Review* (November 1958), 48.

5. Winthrop's definition of mercenary was contemporaneous with others. For instance Halleck posited that a mercenary was defined as "foreigners who voluntary serve a state for pay" (Henry Wager Halleck, *International Law of Rules Regulating the Intercourse of States in Peace and in War* [New York: D. Van Nostrand, 1861], 385).

6. William Winthrop, *Military Law and Precedents*, 2nd ed. (Washington, DC: GPO, 1920), 779–790. Noncombatants subject to the 1874 sixty-third article of war such as "retainers to the camp, and all persons serving with the Armies of the Untied States in the field, though not enlisted soldiers, are to be subject to orders, according to the rules and discipline of war."

7. Winthrop, *Military Law and Precedents*, 779–790.

8. Charles H. Lauchheimer, "Naval Law and Naval Courts," *Proceedings of the United States Naval Institute*, 1897, 113–124.

9. J. W. Clous, "The Judge Advocate General's Department," in *The Army of the United States, Historical Sketches of Staff and Line with Portraits of Generals in Chief*, 121 (New York: Maynard, Merrill, 1896).

10. *In re Tyler's Case*, 16 C Cls. R. 223 aff'd 105 U.S. 244.

11. "Retired Officers Excluded: They Cannot Appear Before the Court of Claims," *Washington Post*, December 4, 1895.

12. See, for example, *Webster v. United States*, 179 Ct. Cl. 917 (1967); *Denton v. United States*, 144 Ct. Cl. 840; *Maxwell v. United States*, 49 Ct. Cl. 262 (1914); *Smith v. United States*, 36 Ct. Cl. 304 (1901); and *Cole v. United States*, 34 Ct. Cl. 466 (1899).

13. Little, Brown, and Company Publishers, letter to Secretary Lamont, February 25, 1896.

14. See, for example, Arthur Murray, *Manual for Courts Martial* (New York: John Wiley and Sons, 1896). Murray's manual is short and contains little analysis of the articles of war or courts-martial procedure. It is simply a rule book. However, a simple rule book without analysis could have been the War Department's retreat to formalism in military law.

15. Edward P. Hall, ed., *Decisions of the Department of the Interior in Appealed and Bounty-Land Claims*, vol. 8 (Washington, DC: GPO, 1897). The Bureau of Pensions cited *Military Law* as precedent to support a pension denial to the widow of a contract surgeon (p. 96); civilian assigned to the civilian branch of the army during the war (p. 103).

16. Frank Luther Mott, *A History of American Magazines: 1865–1885*, vol. 3 (Cambridge, MA: Harvard University Press, 1957), 281.

17. Mott, *A History of American Magazines*, 427–430. Mott notes that the *Outlook* was "assailed from time to time on both religious and political grounds. However, on the whole, the Outlook maintained a very high estimation in the public."

18. John Tebel and Mary Ellen Zuckerman, *The Magazine in America: 1741–1990* (Oxford: Oxford University Press, 1991), 87. Jacon Riis (1849–1914) was a late nineteenth-century photographer and muckraking journalist. He was most

known for his treatise "How the Other Half Lives." His articles appeared in the *New York Evening Sun*, the *New York Tribune*, and *Scribners Magazine*. Edward Everett Hale (1822–1909) was a Unitarian clergyman and author who published a number of short stories in the *Atlantic Monthly* and *Scribners*

19. William Winthrop, "The Problem of the Philippines: Racial Commercial, Religious, Political, and Social Conditions," *Outlook* 59 (June 11, 1899), 377–382. See also, Brian McAllister Linn, *The Philippine War* (Lawrence: University Press of Kansas, 2000), 15. Linn's recent work on the Philippine war describes the social, religious, and political environment in a manner consistent with Winthrop's description a century earlier.

20. Winthrop, "The Problem of the Philippines," 380.

21. Winthrop, "The Problem of the Philippines," 380. Winthrop argued against "a mistaken policy to discriminate injudiciously against the Chinese and Chinese Mestizo inhabitants."

22. Winthrop, "The Problem of the Philippines," 380. Winthrop had a unique foresight for a future long-term political upheaval in Mindanao, writing, "It would be in the case of the Indians of Mindanao, who, as we have seen, are Mohammedans and ruled by a Sultan, that our worst dilemma would confront us. Could we succeed in subduing a population which has successfully defied the authority of Spain? In attempting to do so, would we not involve ourselves in a war of long duration?"

23. Winthrop, "The Problem of the Philippines," 380.

24. Winthrop, "The Problem of the Philippines," 380.

25. William Winthrop, "Porto Rico and the Capture of San Juan," *Outlook* 59 (July 1898), 675–678.

26. William Winthrop, "Our Naval Captures," *Independent*, September 22, 1898, 828.

27. William Winthrop, "Our Lesser Insular Appurtenances," *Independent*, July 13, 1899, 1877.

28. Winthrop, "Our Lesser Insular Appurtenances," 1877.

29. For Winthrop's medical condition, see Bureau of Pensions memorandum, March 1, 1900, Officer of the Commissioner. His obituary is found in "Colonel Winthrop Dead," *Washington Post*, April 10, 1899, 3.

30. *Obituary Record of the Graduates of Yale University: Deceased during the Academical Year Ending in June 1899* (New Haven: Yale University Press, 1899), 614–615.

31. On January 18, 1900, Major General Leonard Wood wrote to the Commissioner of Pensions, from Cuba, "I certify that then Lieutenant Colonel William Winthrop was under my care for over a year, during which time he suffered from continued attacks of pain and distress about the heart. Repeated examinations disclosed what appeared to be a valvular lesion. This condition undoubtedly existed for some time and was complicated probably by fatty degeneration. I believe that the trouble commenced while Lt Col Winthrop was in the service and was incident to his wartime service as an officer." Leonard Wood, letter to Pension Commissioner, January 18, 1900 (AWPF).

32. Testimony of Ansell, in *Subcommittee of the Committee on Military Affairs United States Senate, Sixty-Sixth Congress: A Bill to Establish Military Justice* (Washington, DC: GPO, 1919), 75–77.

33. Testimony of Enoch Crowder, in *Subcommittee of the Committee on Military Affairs United States Senate*, 1186.

34. *United States v. Calley*, 22 USCMA 534 (1973). The court quoted from Winthrop:

> But for the inferior to assume to determine the question of the lawfulness of an order given him by a superior would of itself, as a general rule, amount to insubordination, and such an assumption carried into practice would subvert military discipline. Where the order is apparently regular and *lawful on its face*, he is not to go behind it to satisfy himself that his superior has proceeded with authority, but is to obey it according to its terms, *the only exceptions recognized to the rule of obedience being cases of orders so manifestly beyond the legal power or discretion of the commander as to admit of no rational doubt of their unlawfulness* (emphasis in original).

35. 354 U.S. 1 (1957).

36. 548 U.S. (2006). In a telling statement on Winthrop's influence, the majority opinion noted, "All parties agree that Colonel Winthrop's treatise accurately describes the common law governing military commissions."

Bibliography

Note on Sources: This bibliography is divided into four areas: (1) Winthrop's own publications; (2) primary biographical and military treatises; (3) primary legal sources; and (4) secondary sources. The purpose for this scheme is twofold: First, treatises on military affairs published during Winthrop's life were widely used in military education (such as Arthur Wagner's *Organization and Tactics*) and touched on the application of military law to training and policy. Second, the well-known legal works available during Winthrop's life (some of which he incorporated into his own work) shaped the practice of law in his day. This is true not only in regard to legal treatises, but legal commentary as well.

As to Winthrop's works, this biography utilizes the Army's 1920 reprint of *Military Law and Precedents* rather than the original. While the use of the reprint is the choice of the author, it is because there exists far more of this reprint than the original two-volume set and should a practitioner of military law or other interested individual want to reference *Military Law and Precedents* alongside this biography, the reprint makes that task easier. The reprint is paginated differently from the original, but it contains numeric markers within the text which correspond to the original's pages. The text and footnotes are identical between the two versions.

As noted in the introduction, this is the first (and perhaps only) full biography of Colonel William Winthrop. Nonetheless, a prior biographical article was very helpful in getting stated on this biography. George S. Prugh's "Colonel William Winthrop: The Tradition of the Military Lawyer" published in the 1956 *American Bar Association Journal* is by far the best and most accurate compilation of facts regarding Winthrop's life, though he inaccurately characterizes Winthrop as colorless compared to his older brother. He also does not fully mention Winthrop's literary and legal accomplishments. Other biographical sketches lack detail and their errors are already noted. Neither William Winthrop nor Alice Winthrop left to posterity a diary, so that his (and their) emotions, outlooks, hopes, and sources of anger, can be only deduced by their surviving letters and those of his peers.

WORKS OF WILLIAM WINTHROP

Abridgement of Military Law. 2nd ed. New York: John Wiley and Sons, 1893.

"Bergamo." *Overland Monthly*, May 1885, 468.

Digest of Opinions of the Judge Advocate General. Washington, DC: Government Printing Office, 1865.

"Jeanne Hachette." *Overland Monthly*, May 1883, 477.

Military Law. 2 vols. Washington, DC: W.H. Morrison, 1886.

Military Law and Precedents. 2nd ed. Washington, DC: GPO, 1920.

Military Penal Code for the German Empire, or *Militärstrafgesetz-buch*. Washington, DC: Army Department, 1873.

Old Forts on the Hudson Highlands. New York Historic Society, 1890 est.

"Our Lesser Insular Appurtenances." *Independent*, July 13, 1899, 1877.

"Our Naval Captures." *Independent*, September 22, 1898, 828.

"Porto Rico and the Capture of San Juan." *Outlook* 59 (July 1898), 675–678.

"The Problem of the Philippines: Racial Commercial, Religious, Political, and Social Conditions." *Outlook* 59 (June 11, 1899), 377–382.

"The Republic of Holland." *Yale Literary Magazine* (July 1851), 342.

"The Seat under the Beeches." *Overland Monthly*, January 1883, 49–54.

Statistics of the Class of 1851, of Yale College. New Haven: John Wilson and Son, 1854.

"The United States and the Declaration of Paris." *Yale Law Journal* 3 (October 1893), 168–170.

PRIMARY BIOGRAPHICAL SOURCES

Letters and Diaries (with Abbreviations)

United States Army War College, Military History Institute (MIH)
  Sharpshooters Letters Collection
  Hiram Berdan Letters
United States Army, Pension File Application (AWPF)
  Pension Application Documents for Alice Winthrop
United States National Archives (NA)
  Record Group (RG) 153.2.1, Records of the Judge Advocate
General
  G. Norman Lieber Papers
Library of Congress (LOC)
  Benjamin Butler Papers (BBP)
  John McAlister Schofield Papers (JMSP)
  Joseph Holt Papers (PJH)

Edwin Stanton Papers (PES)
Daniel Lamont Papers (PDL)
Grover Cleveland Papers
August Kautz Diary
Joseph Toner Papers
D. W. Little Papers
William McKee Dunn File
Maryland Historical Society (MDHS)
Benjamin Gwinn Harris Papers
Elizabeth Harris, Diary
Missouri Historical Society (MHS)
George Hastings Letters
New York Archdiocese Archives (AANY)
Winthrop Papers
New York Public Library (NYPL)
Miscellaneous Winthrop Family Letters
New York Historical Society (NYHS)
Caspar Trepp Papers
William Winthrop [draft] of Fortresses on the Hudson Valley
University of Rochester (UR)
William Henry Seward Papers
Virginia Historical Society (VHS)
Diary of Elizabeth Virginia Lomax
Jane Tayloe Worthington (Lomax)
Yale University (YALE)
Winthrop Family Letters

Government Documents

Annual Report of the Secretary of War [as referenced by date]. Washington, DC: GPO.

Annual Report of the United States Military Academy [as referenced by date]. Washington, DC: GPO.

Congressional Globe (1833–1873). Washington, DC: GPO.

Journal of the House of Representatives, The Congressional Globe, 37th Cong., 2nd Sess., April 9, 1864.

Proceedings and Opinions Convened under the Act of Congress of February 13, 1874. Washington, DC: GPO, 1874.

Report of the Judge Advocate General to the Secretary of War for 1892. Washington, DC: GPO, 1892.

Subcommittee of the Committee on Military Affairs United States Senate, Sixty-Sixth Congress: A Bill to Establish Military Justice. Washington, DC: GPO, 1919.

United States House of Representatives, *Executive Journal.* Washington, DC: GPO, 1865.

The War of the Rebellion: A Compilation of the Official Records of the Union and Confederate Armies. Publishing under the direction of the Secretary of War. Washington, DC: GPO, 1880–1901 [cited as OR, volume and chapter].

Newspapers

Army-Navy Journal
Baltimore Sun
Chicago Times
New York Times
Washington Post

Biographical Works

Aschmann, Rudolf Karl. *Memoirs of a Swiss Officer in the American Civil War (Three Years in the Army of the Potomac or a Swiss Company of Sharpshooters in the North American War)*. Edited by Heinz K. Meier. Translated by Hedwig D. Rappolt. Bern, Switzerland: Herbert Lang, 1972.

The Bench and Bar of Saint Louis, Kansas City, Jefferson City, and Other Missouri Cities. St Louis: American Biographical, 1884.

Biographical History of the American Congress: 1774–1996. Alexandria, VA: CQ Staff Directories, 1996.

Butler, Benjamin F. *Autobiography and Personal Reminiscences of Major-General Benj. F. Butler: "Butler's Book."* Boston: A.M. Thayer and Co., 1892.

Burnett, Henry. *Some Incidents in the Trial of President Lincoln's Assassins: The Controversy between President Johnson and Judge Holt, Printed for the Commandery of the State of New York*. New York: D. Appleton and Co., 1891.

Clous, J. W. "The Judge Advocate General's Department." In *The Army of the United States, Historical Sketches of Staff and Line with Portraits of Generals in Chief*, 33–34. New York: Maynard, Merrill, 1896.

Curtis, Newton Martin. *Capital Crimes and the Punishments Prescribed Therefor by Federal and State Laws and Those of Foreign Countries*. Washington, DC: Gibson Bros, 1894.

———. *To Define the Crime of Murder, Provide Penalty Therefor, and to Abolish the Punishment of Death*. Washington, DC: GPO, 1892.

Dana, Charles A. *Recollections of the Civil War with the Leaders at Washington and in the Field in the Sixties*. Reprint ed. Lincoln: University of Nebraska Press, 1996 (orig. pub. 1898).

Directory of the Living Graduates of Yale University. New Haven: Yale University Press, 1908.

Flavious Vegetius Renatus. "De Re Militari (The Military Institutions of the Romans)." Translated by John Clarke. In *Roots of Strategy*, ed. T. R. Phillips, vol. 1, 65–177. Harrisburg, PA: Military Service Publishing, 2000.

Fry, James. *A Sketch of the Adjutant General's Department, U.S. Army, from 1775 to 1875*. Washington, DC: GPO, 1875.

Grant, Ulysses. *Papers of Ulysses S. Grant* Edited by John Y. Simon. Carbondale: Southern Illinois University Press, 1998.

Howard, Oliver Otis. *Autobiography of Oliver Otis Howard*. New York: Baker and Taylor, 1908.

King, Horatio. "Judge Holt and the Lincoln Conspirators." *Century*, 1890, 955–957.

Machiavelli, Niccolo. *The Art of War*. Translated by Neal Wook. New York: Da Capo, 2001.

———. *The Prince*. New York: Wordsworth, 1993.

Marmont, Auguste. *The Spirit of Military Institutions, or Essential Principles of the Art of War*. Translated by Henry Coppee. Philadelphia: J.B. Lippincott, 1862.

McClellan, George B. *My Own Story: The War for the Union, the Soldiers Who Fought It, the Civilians Who Directed It, and His Relations to It and Them*. New York: Webster and Co., 1887.

Merritt, Wesley. "Three Indian Campaigns." *Harpers New Monthly Magazine* 80 (April 1880), 720–737.

———. "The Army of the United States." *Harper's New Monthly Magazine* 80 (March 1890), 493–510.

Michie, Peter S. *The Life and Letters of Emory Upton*. New York: D. Appleton and Co., 1885.

Miles, Nelson A. "The Lesson of the Recent Strikes." *North American Review* 159 (1894), 180–188.

Morris, Martin Ferdinand. *Lectures on the Development of Constitutional and Civil History*. Washington, DC: W.H. Morrison's Son, 1898.

Obituary Record of the Graduates of Yale University: Deceased during the Academical Year Ending in June 1899. New Haven: Yale University Press, 1899.

Patrick, Marsena. *Inside Lincoln's Army: The Diary of Marsena Rudolph Patrick, Provost Marshal General, of the Army of the Potomac*. Edited by David Sparks. New York: A.S. Barnes and Co., 1964.

Peet, Frederick Tomlinson. *My Personal Experiences in the Civil War*. New York: F. T. Peet, 1905.

Pope, John. *The Military Memoirs of General John Pope*. Edited by Peter Cozzens and Robert Girardi. Chapel Hill: University of North Carolina Press, 1998.

Powell, William. *Powell's Record of Living Officers*. Philadelphia: Hammersly, 1890.

Records of Living Officers in the United States Army. Philadelphia: L.R. Hammersly and Co., 1884.

Schofield, John McAlister. *Forty-six Years in the Army*. New York: Century, 1897.

———. "Controversies in the War Department: Unpublished Facts Relating to the Impeachment of President Johnson." *Century* 54, no. 4 (August 1897), 577–583.

Sheridan, Philip. *Personal Memoirs of Philip Sheridan*. New York: Jenkins and McCowan, 1888.

Sherman, William T. "The Grand Strategy of the War of the Rebellion." *Century* 35 (February 1888).

———. *Memoirs*. Reprint ed. New York: Library of America, 1990.

Smith, Francis. *The Debates and Proceedings of the Minnesota Constitutional Convention Including the Organic Act of the Territory: With the Enabling Act of Congress, the Act of the Territorial Legislature Relative to the Convention, and the Vote of the People on the Constitution*. St. Paul: Earl S. Goodrich, Territorial Printers, 1860.

Sumner, Charles. *The Selected Letters of Charles Sumner*. Vol. 2. Edited by Beverly Wilson. Boston: Northeastern University, 1990.

Upton, Emory. *The Armies of Europe and Asia: Embracing Official Reports on the Armies of Japan, China, India, Persia, Italy, Russia, Austria, Germany, France, and England*. New York: D. Appleton and Company, 1878.

——. *The Military Policy of the United States.* Washington, DC: GPO, 1916.
von der Goltz, Colmar Freiherr. "Principles of War." *Journal of the United States Artillery* 6 (1896), 33–38.
von Molitor, Ignaz Ortwein. *Die Kriegsgerichte und Milirarstrafen im neunzehnten Jahrhundert mit einem Ruckblicke auf die Kriegsstrafen der Romer, die Kriegsgewohnheiten der alten Deutschen, und die Kriegsgesetze bis zum Beginne dieses Jahrhunderts, mit besonderer Berucksichtigung der Kriegsgesetze Oesterreichs, Preussens, Sachsens, Wurtembergs, Badens, dann Frankreichs, Sardiniens und der Eidgenossenschaft.* Vienna: L. Somer 1855.
Wagner, Arthur. *The Campaign of Konnigratz: A Study in the Austro-Prussian Conflict in the Light of the American Civil War.* Reprint ed. New York: Greenwood, 1970 (orig. pub. 1889).
——. "The Military Necessities of the United States, and the Best Method of Meeting Them." *Journal of the Military Service Institution of the United States* 5 (1883–1884), 238–244.
——. *Organization and Tactics.* 2nd ed. Washington, DC: GPO, 1894.
Winthrop, Elizabeth. *The Life and Letters of Theodore Winthrop.* New York: Henry Holt and Co., 1884.
Winthrop, Theodore. "Our March to Washington." In *The Oxford Book of American Essays*, ed. Brander Matthews. New York: Oxford University Press, 1914.

PRIMARY SOURCES

Military Law and Other Law Treatises

Benet, Stephen. *A Treatise on Military Law and the Practice of Courts Martial.* New York: D. van Nostrand, 1864.
Bishop, Joel Prentiss. *Commentaries on the Criminal Law.* Boston: Little Brown & Company, 1877.
Blackstone, William. *Commentaries on the Laws of England*, vol. 1, reprint ed. London: A Strahan, 1880.
Brewster, Lyman D. "The Promotion of Uniform Legislation." *Yale Law Journal* 6 (1897), 132–140.
Carter, James. "The Proposed Codification of Our Common Law." *Saturday Evening Post*, 1881, reprinted in James Honnold, ed. *The Life of the Law: Readings in the Growth of Legal Institutions.* New York: Free Press, 1964.
Chitty, Joseph. *A Practical Treatise on the Criminal Law Comprising the Practice, Pleadings, and Evidence, Which Occur in the Course of Criminal Prosecutions, Whether by Indictment or Information: With a Copious Collection of Precedents.* Philadelphia: Edward Earle, 1819.
Clode, Charles M. *The Administration of Justice under the Military and Martial Law.* London: J. Murray, 1874.
——. *The Military Forces of the Crown, Their Administration and Government.* London: John Murray, 1869.

Cooley, Thomas. *The General Principles of Constitutional Law in the United States.* Boston: Little Brown and Co., 1882.

Coppee, Henry. *Field Manual of Courts-Martial: Containing the Forms of Proceeding, of All Kinds of Courts-Martial and an Explanation of the Duties of All Persons Connected with Military Tribunals.* New York: J.B. Lippincott, 1863.

Curtis, Newton Martin. *To Define the Crime of Murder, Provide Penalty Therefor, and to Abolish the Punishment of Death.* Washington, DC: GPO, 1892.

———. *Capital Crimes and the Punishments Prescribed Therefor by Federal and State Laws and Those of Foreign Countries.* Washington, DC: Gibson Bros, 1894.

Davis, George B. *A Treatise on the Military Law of the Untied States, Together with the Practice and Procedure of Courts-Martial and Other Military Tribunals.* New York: John Wiley and Sons, 1915.

De Hart, William. *Observations on Military Law and the Constitution and Practice of Courts-Martial.* New York: D. Appleton and Co., 1846.

Dunn, William McKee. *A Sketch of the History and Duties of the Judge Advocate General's Department.* Washington, DC: GPO, 1878.

Eisenschiml, Otto. *The Celebrated Case of Fitz John Porter.* Indianapolis, IN: Bobbs-Merrill, 1950.

Field, David Dudley. "American Progress in Jurisprudence." In *The American Law Register and Review,* 641–657. Philadelphia: University of Pennsylvania Press, 1896.

Fry, Major General James B. "A Military Court of Appeal." *Journal of the Military Service Institution of the United States* 2 (1888), 438.

Gibbon, Major General John. "Law in the Army." *Journal of the Military Service Institution of the United States* 1 (1880), 439.

Greenleaf, Simon. *Treatise on the Law of Evidence.* Vol. 3. Boston: Little Brown and Co., 1854.

Hall, Edward P., ed. *Decisions of the Department of the Interior in Appealed and Bounty-Land Claims.* Vol. 8. Washington, DC: GPO, 1897.

Halleck, Henry Wager. *International Law of Rules Regulating the Intercourse of States in Peace and in War.* New York: D. Van Nostrand, 1861.

Hare, J. J. Clarke. *American Constitutional Law.* Vol. 2. Boston: Little Brown and Co., 1889.

Holmes, Oliver Wendell, Jr. *The Common Law.* Boston: Little Brown and Co., 1881.

Hough, William. *The Practice of Courts Martial and Other Military Courts.* London: Parbury, Allen, and Co., 1834.

Lauchheimer, Charles H. "Naval Law and Naval Courts." *Proceedings of the United States Naval Institute* (1897), 113–124.

Lieber, Francis. "Guerrilla Parties Considered with Reference to the Laws and Usages of War." *The War of the Rebellion,* ser. 3, vol. 2, 308–309.

Lieber, G. Norman. *Message from the President of the United States to the Two Houses of Congress.* Washington, DC: GPO, 1885.

———. "Remarks on the Articles of War and the Common Law of the Military." *Journal of the Military Service Institution of the United States* 1 (1880), 1–5.

———. *The Use of the Army in Aid of the Civil Power.* Washington, DC: GPO, 1898.

Maltby, Isaac. *A Treatise on Courts-Martial and Military Law*. Boston: Thomas B. Wait and Co., 1809.

McKinlay, Robert L. "Notes on Reform." *Journal of the Military Service Institution of the United States* 1 (1880), 501.

Mordecai, Alfred. *A Digest of Laws Relating to the Military Establishment of the United States*. Philadelphia: Thomas and Homans, 1833.

Morris, Martin Ferdinand. *Lectures on the Development of Constitutional and Civil History*. Washington, DC: W.H. Morrison's Son, 1898.

Murray, Arthur. *Manual for Courts Martial*. New York: John Wiley and Sons, 1896.

Oppenheim, Lassa. *International Law: A Treatise*. New York: Longmans, Green and Co., 1906.

Pitman, Benjamin. *The Conspiracy Trial: Trial before a Military Commission at Washington DC*. Washington, DC: Moore, Wilsatch and Boldwin, 1865.

Proceedings of a Military Commission Convened at Fort Klamath, Oregon, for the Trial of Modoc Indians. Washington, DC: War Department, 1873.

Sherman, William T. "Letter from General Sherman to General W. S. Hancock, Dec. 9 1879." *Journal of the Military Service Institution of the United States* 1 (1880), 129–130.

———. "Our Army and Militia." *North American Review* 405 (1890), 121–145.

Wharton, Francis. *Philosophy of Criminal Law*. Philadelphia: Kay and Brother, 1880.

———. *Commentaries on the Law, Embracing the Nature, Source, and History of Law; on International, Public and Private; Constitutional and Statutory Law*. Philadelphia: Kay and Brother, 1884.

———. *A Treatise on the Law of Homicide in the United States*. Rochester, NY: Lawyers Cooperative Publishing Company, 1885.

Woolsey, Theodore D. *Introduction to the Study of International Law, Designed as an Aid in Teaching, and in Historical Studies*. Boston: J. Munroe and Co., 1860.

SECONDARY SOURCES

Books

Adam, Alexander. *Roman Antiquities: Or an Account of the Manners and Customs of the Romans*. New York: T. Cadell, 1819.

Adams, George W. *Doctors in Blue: The Medical History of the Union Army in the Civil War*. Baton Rouge: LSU Press, 1952.

Adams, Oscar F. *Dictionary of American Authors*. Boston: Houghton Mifflin, 1904.

Addresses of the Living Graduates of Yale College. New Haven: Yale University Press, 1872.

Alberts, Don. *Brandy Station to Manila Bay: A Biography of General Wesley Merritt*. Austin, TX: Presidial Press, 1980.

Ambrose, Stephen. *Duty, Honor, Country: A History of West Point*. Baltimore: Johns Hopkins, 1966.

Atwater, Edward E. *History of the Colony of New Haven and Its Absorption into Connecticut*. New Haven: Yale University Press, 1881.

Axelrod, Alex. *America's Wars*. New York: John Wiley and Sons, 2002.
Baker, Livia. *The Justice from Beacon Hill: The Life and Times of Oliver Wendell Holmes*. New York: HarperCollins, 1991.
Barnard, Harry. *"Eagle Forgotten": The Life of John Peter Altgeld*. Indianapolis: Bobbs-Merrill, 1938.
Barr, Ronald J. *The Progressive Army: United States Army Command and Administration, 1870–1914*. New York: St. Martin's Press, 1998.
Barry, John Stetson. *The History of Massachusetts: The Colonial Period*. Boston: Phillips Sampson and Co., 1855.
Bates, Samuel P. *History of the Pennsylvania Volunteers: 1861–1865*. Harrisburg: Pennsylvania State Legislature, 1870.
Beatie, Russell H. *Army of the Potomac: McClellan Takes Command*. New York: Da Capo, 2002.
Blair, William A. "Barbarians at Fredericksburg's Gate: The Impact of the Union Army on Civilians." In *The Fredericksburg Campaign, Decision on the Rappahannock*, edited by Gary W. Gallagher, 142–170. Chapel Hill: University of North Carolina Press, 1995.
Blake, Katharine D., and Wallace, Margaret Louise. *Champion of Women: The Life of Lillie Devereux Blake*. New York: Revelle, 1943.
Blegen, Theodore. *Minnesota: A History of the State*. Minneapolis: University of Minnesota Press, 1963.
Bodart, Gaston. *Losses of Life in Modern Wars*. Oxford: Claredon Press, 1916.
Bond, Wesley J. *Minnesota and Its Resources: To Which Are Appended Camp-Fire Sketches, or, Notes of a Trip from St. Paul to Pembina and Selkirk Settlement*. New York: Redfield Press, 1853.
Boorstin, Daniel J. *The Americans: The Colonial Experience*. New York: Vintage, 1958.
Bouchard, Peter. *One Gallant Rush: Robert Gould Shaw and His Brave Black Regiment*. New York: St. Martin's Press, 1965.
Brauer, Kinley J. *Cotton versus Conscience: Massachusetts Whig Politics and Southwestern Expansion, 1843–1848*. Lexington: University of Kentucky Press, 1967.
Bremer, Francis J. *John Winthrop: America's Forgotten Founding Father*. London: Oxford University Press, 2003.
Brenner, Francis J. *The Purtian Experiment: New England Society from Bradford to Edwards*. Hannover, MA: University Press of New England, 1995.
Bruce, Robert. *Lincoln and the Tools of War*. Indianapolis: Bobbs-Merrill, 1956.
Bucholz, Adrian. *Moltke, Schlieffen, and Prussian War Gaming*. New York: St. Martin's Press, 1991.
Buell, Thomas. *The Warrior Generals: Combat Leadership in the Civil War*. New York: Three Rivers Press, 1997.
Burton, Brian K. *Extraordinary Circumstances: The Seven Days Battles*. Bloomington: Indiana University Press, 2001.
Butler, Benjamin F. *Private and Official Correspondence of General Benjamin F. Butler*. Vol. 1. Norwood, MA: Plimton Press, 1917.
Campbell, Robert A. *The Rebellion Register*. Kalamazo, MI: R. A. Campbell, 1866.
Carlson, Paul H. *"Pecos Bill": A Military Biography of William R. Shafter*. College Station: Texas A&M University Press, 1989.

Carmichael, Peter S. "We Don't Know What on Earth to Do with Him: William Pendleton and the Affair at Shepherdstown, September 19, 1862." In *The Antietam Campaign*, edited by Gary W. Gallagher, 258–288. Chapel Hill: University of North Carolina Press, 1999.

Carpenter, William H. *The History of Massachusetts, from Its Earliest Settlement to the Present Time*. Philadelphia: J.B. Lippincott, 1853.

———. *The History of Connecticut from Its earliest Settlement to Its Present Time*. Philadelphia: J.B. Lippincott, 1854.

Caroll, E. Malcom *Origins of the Whig Party*. Reprint ed. New York: Da Capo, 1970.

Casdorph, Paul D. *Lee and Jackson*. New York: Paragon, 1992.

Castel, Albert. *The Presidency of Andrew Johnson*. Lawrence: University Press of Kansas, 1979.

Catton, Bruce. *Bruce Catton's Civil War: Three Volumes in One*. New York: Fairfax Press, 1984.

Cherny, Robert. *American Politics in the Gilded Age*. Wheeling, IL: Harlan Davidson, 1997.

Clodfelter, Michael. *The Dakota War: The United States Army Versus the Sioux*. London: McFarland and Co., 1998.

Coddington, Edwin B. *The Gettysburg Campaign; a Study in Command*. New York: Touchstone, 1984.

Coffman, Edward M. *The Old Army: A Portrait of the American Army in Peacetime, 1784–1898*. New York: Oxford University Press, 1986.

Colby, Elbridge. *Theodore Winthrop*. New York: Twayne Publishers, 1965.

Connelly, Donald B. *John M. Schofield and the Politics of Generalship*. Chapel Hill: University of North Carolina Press, 2006.

Conversations of the History of Massachusetts from Its First Settlement to the Present Period for the Use of Schools and Families. Boston: Munroe and Francis, 1831.

Cooper, Edward S. *William Worth Belknap: An American Disgrace*. New York: Farleigh Dickinson, 2003.

Cooper, Jerry M. "Federal Military Intervention in Domestic Disorders." In *The United States Military Under the Constitution of the United States*, edited by Richard Kohn, 83–123. New York: NYU Press, 1991.

Cornish, Dudley T. *The Sable Arm: Black Troops in the Union Army, 1861–1865*. Lawrence: University Press of Kansas, 1987.

Cozzens, Peter. *General John Pope: A Life for the Nation*. Champaign: University of Illinois Press, 2000.

Cumming, Carman. *Devil's Game: The Civil War Intrigues of Charles A. Dunham*. Champaign: University of Illinois Press, 2004.

Curtis, George William. "Biographical Sketch of the Author." In *Cecil Dreeme*, by Theodore Winthrop, 14. Boston: Ticknor and Fields, 1864.

Daniels W. H. *Moody, His Words, Works and Workers: Sketches of his Co-Workers, Mssrs, Snakey, Bliss, Whittle, Sawyer, and Others*. New York: Nelson and Phillips, 1977.

Davis, Burke. *They Called Him Stonewall: A Life of Lieutenant General T.J. Jackson, CSA*. Reprint ed. Short Hill, NJ: Burford Books, 1999.

Delbruk, Hans. *The Dawn of Modern Warfare*. Vol. 4. Translated by Walter Renfroe. Lincoln: University of Nebraska Press, 1990.

Detzer, David. *Dissonance: The Turbulent Days between Fort Sumter and Bull Run.* New York: Harcourt, 2006.

Dodge, Theodore A. *Gustavus Adolphus.* Boston: Houghton Mifflin, 1895.

Dougherty, Kevin. *The Peninsula Campaign of 1862: A Military Analysis.* Columbus: University of Mississippi Press, 2005.

Drake, James D. *King Philip's War, Civil War in New England, 1675–1676.* Amherst: University of Massachusetts Press, 1999.

Duncan, Russell. *Colonel Robert Gould Shaw and the 54th Massachusetts Infantry: Where Death and Glory Meet.* Athens: University of Georgia Press, 1988.

Dunn, William McKee. *A Sketch of the History and Duties of the Judge Advocate General's Department.* Washington DC: GPO, 1877.

Durbin, Michael J. *United States Presidential Elections, 1788–1860: The Official Results by County and State.* Jefferson, NC: McFarland and Co., 2002.

Duyckick, Evart, and Duyckick, George. *Cyclopaedia of American Literature.* Vol. 2. New York: Charles Scribner, 1856.

Dwight, Benjamin W. *The History of the Descendants of John Dwight of Dedham Mass.* Vol. 1. New York: John F. Throw and Son, 1874.

Easby-Smith, James S. *Georgetown University in the District of Columbia, 1789–1907.* Vol. 2. Chicago: Lewis Co., 1907.

Eicher, David D. *The Longest Night: A Military History of the Civil War.* New York: Simon and Schuster, 2001.

Ellis, George Edward. *The Puritan Age and Rule in the Colony of the Massachusetts Bay, 1629–1685.* New York: Houghton Mifflin, 1888.

Etcheson, Nicole. *Bleeding Kansas: Contested Liberty in the Civil War Era.* Lawrence: University Press of Kansas, 2004.

Farrell, Grace. *Lillie Devereux Blake: Retracing a Life Erased.* Amherst: University of Massachusetts Press, 2002.

Ferguson, Ernest B. *Chancellorsville, 1863: The Souls of the Brave.* New York: Vintage Books, 1993.

Fiske, John. *Appleton's Cyclopaedia of American Biography.* Vol. 5. New York: D. Appleton and Co., 1888.

Flipper, Henry. *The Colored Cadet at West Point: An Autobiography of Lieutenant H. O. Flipper.* New York: Homer Lee and Co., 1878.

Folwell, William Watts. *A History of Minnesota.* Vol. 1. St. Paul: Minnesota Historical Society, 1922.

Foner, Eric. *Free Soil, Free Labor, Free Men: The Ideology of the Republican Party Before the Civil War.* Oxford: Oxford University Press, 1970.

———. *Reconstruction: America's Unfinished Revolution, 1863–1877.* New York: Harper and Row, 1988

———. *A Short History of Reconstruction.* New York: Harper and Row, 1990.

Foote, Shelby. *The Civil War, a Narrative: Fort Sumter to Perryville.* New York: Random House, 1958.

Forman, Sydney. *West Point: A History of the United States Military Academy.* New York: Columbia University Press, 1950.

Fox, William F. *Regimental Losses in the American Civil War.* Reprint ed. Northridge, CA: Morningside Books, 1974 (orig. pub. 1888).

Freehling, William. *The Road to Disunion: Secessionists at Bay, 1776–1854.* Oxford: Oxford University Press, 1990.

Freidel, Frank. *Francis Lieber, Nineteenth Century Liberal*. Baton Rouge: LSU Press, 1947.

Friedman, Lawrence. *A History of American Law*. New York: Simon and Schuster, 2005.

Fuller, J. F. C. *A Military History of the Western World: From the Seven Days Battle to the Battle of Leyte Gulf*. New York: Funk and Wagnalls, 1956.

Ganoe, William A. *The History of the United States Army*. New York: D. Appleton and Co., 1924.

Garner, James Wilford. *International Law and the World War*. London and New York: Longman, Greens and Co., 1920.

Gilbert, Felix. "Machiavelli: The Renaissance of the Art of War." In *Makers of Modern Strategy*, edited by Peter Paret and Gordon Craig, 11–31. New Jersey: Princeton University Press, 1986.

Goerlitz, Walter. *History of the Prussian General Staff: 1657–1945*. New York: Praeger, 1954.

Grafton, Charles C. *The Works of the Rt. Rev. Charles C. Grafton*. Vol. 4. Edited by B. Talbot Rogers. New York: Longmans, Green, 1914.

Greve, Charles T. *Centennial History of Cincinnati and Representative Citizens*. Vol. 1. Chicago: Biographical Publishing Co., 1904.

Grimsley, Mark. *The Hard Hand of War: Union Military Policy Toward Southern Civilians, 1861–1865*. New York: Cambridge University Press, 1995.

Hanchett, William. *The Lincoln Murder Conspiracies*. Champaign: University of Illinois Press, 1983.

Hall, H. Seymour. "Fredericksburg and Chancellorsville." In *War Talks in Kansas: A Series of Papers Read before the Kansas Commandery of the Military Order of the Loyal Legion of the United States*, 185–205. Kansas City, MO: Franklin Hudson Publishing Co., 1906.

Hall, Kermit. *The Magic Mirror: Law in American History*. New York: Oxford University Press, 1989.

Hart, Albert B. "Salmon Chase." In *American Statesmen*, edited by John T. Morse, 22–29. Boston: Houghton Mifflin, 1899.

Hattaway, Herman, and Jones, Archer. *A Military History of the Civil War: How the North Won*. Urbana: University of Illinois Press, 1991.

Hay, John. *Addresses of John Hay*. New York: Century, 1906.

Hennessy, John J. *Return to Bull Run: The Campaign and Battle of Second Manassas*. Norman: University of Oklahoma Press, 1999.

Henry, Robert S. *The Story of the Mexican War*. Reprint ed. New York: Da Capo, 1994.

Hickey, Donal K. *The War of 1812: A Forgotten Conflict*. Urbana: University of Illinois, 1995.

Hollister, G. H. *The History of Connecticut from the First Settlement of the Colony to Its Present Constitution*. New Haven: Durrie and Peck, 1855.

Holt, Joseph. *Report of the Judge Advocate General on the Order of American Knights, Alias, "The Sons of Liberty," a Western Conspiracy in the Aid of Southern Rebellion*. Washington DC: Daily Chronicle Printing, 1864.

Holt, Michael F. *The Rise and Fall of the American Whig Party: Jacksonian Politics and the Onset of Civil War*. New York: Oxford University Press, 1999.

———. *The Fate of Their Country: Politicans, Slavery Extensions, and the Coming of the Civil War*. New York: Hill and Wang, 2004.
Hubbard, Lucius, and Holcombe, Return I. *Minnesota in Three Centuries*. Vol. 3. St Paul: Publishing Society of Minnesota, 1908.
Huntington, Samuel P. *The Soldier and the State: The Theory and Politics of Civil-Military Relations*. Boston: Harvard University Press, 1959.
Hutton, Paul A. *Phil Sheridan and His Army*. Lincoln: University of Nebraska Press, 1985.
Ingersoll, L. D. *A History of the War Department of the United States with Biographical Sketches of the Secretaries*. New York: Francis B. Mohun, 1879.
Jamieson, Perry D. *Crossing the Deadly Ground: United States Army Tactics, 1865–1899*. Tuscaloosa: University of Alabama Press, 1994.
Jones Ford, Henry. *The Cleveland Era: A Chronicle of the New Order in Politics*. New Haven: Yale University Press, 1921.
Katcher, Philip. *Sharpshooters of the American Civil War, 1861–1865*. London: Osprey, 2002.
Keegan, John. *A History of Warfare*. New York: Alfred Knopf, 1993.
Kelly, Brooks Mather. *Yale: A History*. New Haven: Yale University Press, 1974.
King, George A. *Theodore Dwight Woolsey: His Political and Social Ideas*. Chicago: Loyola University Press, 1956.
Kingman, LeRoy Wilson. *Early Owego*. Owego, NY: Tioga County Historical Society, 1987.
Klement, Frank. *The Copperheads in the Middle West*. Chicago: University of Chicago Press, 1960.
Koeppen, Adolphus L. *War in the Middle Ages*. New York: D. Appleton and Co., 1854.
Kohn, Richard. "The Constitution and National Security: The Intent of the Framers." In *The United States Military under the Constitution of the United States: 1789–1989*, edited by Richard Kohn, 61–94. Baton Rouge: LSU Press, 1991.
Koistinen, Paul C. *Mobilizing for Modern War: The Political Economy of American Warfare, 1865–1919*. Lawrence: University Press of Kansas, 1997.
Lambert, Edward R. *History of the Colony of New Haven: Before and After the Union with Connecticut*. New Haven: Hitchcock and Stafford, 1838.
Landrum, Francis S. *Guardhouse, Gallows, and Graves: The Trial and Execution of Indian Prisoners of the Modoc Indian War by the United States Army, 1873*. Klamath Falls, OR: Klamath County Museum, 1988.
Langbein, John H. "Blackstone, Litchfield, and Yale: The Founding of Yale Law School." In *History of the Yale Law School*, ed. Anthony Kronman. New Haven, CT: Yale University Press, 2004.
———. "Law School in a University: Yale's Distinctive Path in the Later Nineteenth Century." In *History of the Yale Law School*, ed. Anthony Kronman. New Haven, CT: Yale University Press, 2004.
Lapsley, Arthur Brooks, ed. *The Writings of Abraham Lincoln*. New York: Lamb Publishing, 1906.
Lass, William E. *Minnesota: A History*. 2nd ed. New York: W.W. Norton, 1998.
Leech, Margaret. *Reveille in Washington*. New York: Harper Brothers, 1941.

Leonard, Elizabeth D. *Lincoln's Avengers: Justice, Revenge, and Reunion after the Civil War*. New York: W.W. Norton, 2004.

Leonard, Ira, and Parmet, Robert. *American Nativism, 1830–1860*. New York: Van Nostrand, Reinhold and Co., 1971.

Lepore, Jill. *The Name of War: King Philip's War and the Origins of American Identity*. New York: Random House, 1999.

Linderman, Gerald. *Embattled Courage: The Experience of Combat in the American Civil War*. New York: Free Press, 1987.

Linn, Brian McAllister. *The Philippine War*. Lawrence: University Press of Kansas, 2000.

Lomax, Edward. *Genealogy of the Virginia Family of Lomax by One of the Seventh Generation of the Direct Line*. Chicago: Rand McNally and Co., 1913.

Lonn, Ella. *Desertion during the Civil War*. Lincoln: University of Nebraska Press, 1998.

Lord, Francis A. *They Fought for the Union*. Harrisburg, PA: Stackpole, 1960.

Lowry, Thomas P. *Don't Shoot That Boy! Abraham Lincoln and Military Justice*. Mason City, IA: Savas, 1999.

Lurie, Jonathan. *Arming Military Justice: The Origins of the United States Court of Military Appeals*. Princeton, NJ: Princeton University Press, 1992.

———. *Military Justice in America: The United States Court of Criminal Appeal in the Armed Forces, 1775–1890*. Lawrence: University Press of Kansas, 2001.

Mahon, John K. *The War of 1812*. Reprint ed. New York: Da Capo, 1972.

Malone, Dumas, ed. *Dictionary of American Biography*. Vol. 20. New York: Charles Scribner's Sons, 1936.

Marcot, Roy. *Civil War Chief of Sharpshooters Hiram Berdan: Military Commander and Firearms Inventor*. Irvine, CA: Northwood Heritage, 1989.

———. *U.S. Sharpshooters: Berdan's Civil War Elite*. Mechanicsburg, PA: Stackpole Book, 2007.

Marszalek, John F. *The Assault at West Point: The Court Martial of Johnson Whittaker*. New York: MacMillan, 1972.

———. *Burnside*. Chapel Hill: University of North Carolina Press, 1991.

———. *Commander of All Lincoln's Armies: A Life of General Henry W. Halleck*. Cambridge, MA: Harvard University Press, 2004.

———. *Sherman: A Soldier's Passion for Order*. New York: Vintage Civil War Library, 1994.

Martin, Edward S. *The Life of Joseph Hodges Choate: As Gathered Chiefly through His Letters*, vol. 1. New York: Charles Scribner's Sons, 1920.

Marvel, William. *Burnside*. Chapel Hill: University of North Carolina Press, 1991.

———. *Mr. Lincoln Goes to War*. New York: Houghton Mifflin, 2006.

Matloff, Maurice, ed. *American Military History*, Washington, DC: Office of the Chief of Military History, United States Army, 1969.

Mayo, Lawrence. *The Winthrop Family in America*. Boston: Massachusetts Historical Society, 1948.

McAllister, Anna Shannon. *In Winter We Flourish*. New York: Longmans, Green and Co., 1939.

McClure, Alexander. *The Authentic Life of William McKinley: Together with a life of Theodore Roosevelt*. New York: n.p., 1900.

McCrary, George W. *The Political Issues of Our Time: A Speech by Hon, G.W. McCrary, Secretary of War.* Washington, DC: National Republican Publishing Co., 1878.

McFeely, William J. *Grant: A Biography.* Norwalk, CT: Easton Press, 1986.

McKittrick, Eric L. *Andrew Johnson and Reconstruction.* Oxford: Oxford University Press, 1988.

McPherson, James M. *Battle Cry of Freedom: The Civil War Era.* New York: Oxford University Press, 1988.

Meacham, A. B. *Wigwam and Warpath, of the Royal Chief in Chains.* Boston: John P. Dale and Co., 1875.

Millet Allan R., and Maslowski, Peter. *For the Common Defense: A Military History of the United States.* New York: Free Press, 1994.

Millis, Walter. *Arms and Men: A Study in American Military History.* New York: G.P. Putnam's Sons, 1956.

Millis, William. *History of Hanover College: From 1827 to 1927.* Hanover, IN: Hanover College, 1927.

Minnesota, a State Guide, American Guide Series. New York: Hastings House, 1947.

Montross, Lynn. *War through the Ages.* New York: Harper Brothers, 1960.

Moore, A. Y. *History of Hanover College.* Indianapolis: Hollenbeck Press, 1900.

Moore, Frank, ed. *The Portrait Gallery of the War: A Biographical Record.* New York: D. Van Nostrand and Co., 1865.

Morgan, Edward S. *The Puritan Dilemma: The Story of John Winthrop.* New York: Little Brown and Co., 1958.

Morse, Jarvis M. *A Neglected Period of Connecticut's History: 1818–1850.* New Haven: Yale University Press, 1933.

Mott, Frank L. *A History of American Magazines: 1865–1885.* Vols. 1–3. Cambridge, MA: Harvard University Press, 1957.

Murfin, James V. *The Gleam of Bayonets: The Battle of Antietam and Robert E. Lee's Maryland Campaign, September 1862.* Baton Rouge: LSU Press, 1965.

Murray, R. L. *Berdan's Sharpshooters in Combat: The Peninsula Campaign and Gettysburg.* New York: Benedum, 2006.

———. *Letters from Berdan's Sharpshooters.* Wolcott, NY: Benedum Books, 2005.

Myers, Gustavus. *The History of Tammany Hall.* New York: G. Myers, 1901.

Neely, Mark. *The Fate of Liberty: Abraham Lincoln and Civil Liberties.* New York: Oxford University Press, 1991.

Nolan, Dick, *Benjamin Franklin Butler: The Damndest Yankee.* Novato, CA: Presidio, 1991.

Nosworthy, Brent. *The Bloody Crucible of Courage: Fighting Methods and Combat Experience of the Civil War.* New York: Carroll and Graf, 2003.

O'Brien, Fitz James. "The March of the Seventh Regiment." In *Anecdotes, Poetry, and Incidents of the War of the North and South, 1860–1865,* edited by Frank Moore, 228–233. New York: Bible House, 1867.

O'Brien, Frank G. *Minnesota Pioneer Sketches: From the Personal Recollections and Observations of a Pioneer Resident.* Minneapolis: H.H.S. Rowell, 1904.

O'Connor, Richard. *Sheridan.* Indianapolis: Bobbs-Merrill, 1953.

Parker, Geoffrey. *The Thirty Years War.* New York: Barnes and Noble, 1984.

Peskin, Alan. *Garfield.* Kent, OH: Kent State University Press, 1978.

Pierce, Michael D. *The Most Promising Young Officer: A Life of Ranald S. MacKenzie*. Norman: University of Oklahoma Press, 1993.

Posner, Richard A., ed. *The Essential Holmes: Selections from the Letters, Speeches, Judicial Opinions, and Other Writings of Oliver Wendell Holmes, Jr.* Chicago: University of Chicago Press, 1992.

Potter, David. *The Impending Crisis, 1848–1861*. New York: Harper, 1976.

Proceedings of the American Antiquarian Society. Vol. 5. Worcester, MA: American Antiquarian Society, 1889.

Quinn, Arthur. *Hell with the Fire Out: A History of the Modoc War*. New York: Faber and Faber, 1997.

Rafuse, Ethan S. *McClellan's War: The Failure of Moderation in the Struggle for the Union*. Bloomington: Indiana University Press, 2005.

Raymond, Henry J. *The Life and Public Service of Abraham Lincoln, Sixteenth President of the Untied States with His State Papers*. New York: Derby and Miller, 1865.

Reardon, Carol. *Soldiers and Scholars: The U.S. Army and the Uses of Military History, 1865–1920*. Lawrence: University Press of Kansas, 1990.

Reid, Whitelaw. *Ohio in the War: Her Statesmen, Generals, and Soldiers*. Cincinnati: Moore, Wisatch and Baldwin, 1868.

Remini, Robert. *Daniel Webster: The Man and His Life*. New York: W.W. Norton, 1997.

———. *Henry Clay: Statesman for the Union*. New York: W.W. Norton, 1991.

Rickey, Don. *Forty Miles a Day on Beans and Hay*. Norman: University of Oklahoma Press, 1963.

Ripley, William Y. W. *Vermont Rifleman in the War for the Union, 1861–1865: A History of Company F, First United States Sharp Shooters*. Rutland, VT: Tuttle and Co., 1883.

Ropp, Theodore. *War in the Modern World*. Durham, NC: Duke University Press, 1959.

Rothenberg, Guenther E. "Maurice of Nassau, Gustavus Adolphus, Raimondo Montecuccoli, and the 'Military Revolution,' of the Seventeenth Century." In *Makers of Modern Strategy: Machiavelli to the Nuclear Age*, edited by Peter Paret, 32–63. Princeton, NJ: Princeton University Press, 1986.

Rowan, Hinton. *Compendium of the Impending Crisis of the South*. New York: A.B. Burdick, 1864.

Royster, Charles. *The Destructive War: William T. Sherman, Stonewall Jackson, and the Americans*. New York: Alfred Knopf, 1991.

Scharf, J. Thomas. *A History of Maryland from the Earliest Period to the Present Day*. Vol. 3. Baltimore: John B. Piet, 1879.

Schecter, Barnet. *The Devil's Own Work: The Civil War Draft Riots and the Fight to Reconstruct America*. New York: Walker and Co., 2005.

Sears, Stephen. *The Civil War Papers of George B. McClellan, Selected Correspondence, 1860–1865* New York: Ticknor and Fields, 1989.

———. *George B. McClellan: The Young Napoleon*. New York: Da Capo, 1999.

———. *To the Gates of Richmond: The Peninsula Campaign*. New York: Houghton Mifflin, 1992.

Sefton, James E. *The United States Army and Reconstruction, 1865–1877*. Baton Rouge: LSU Press, 1967.

Senior, Robert. *New England Congregationalists and the Anti Slavery Movement*. Ann Arbor, MI: University Microfilms, 1954.

Seymour, Whitney N. "The Bar as Lawmaker." In *The Life of the Law: Readings in the Growth of Legal Institutions*, edited by John Honnold, 5–27. New York: Free Press, 1964.

Shaw, Robert Gould. *Blue-Eyed Child of Fortune: The Civil War Letters of Colonel Robert Gould Shaw*. Edited by Russell Duncan. Athens: University of Georgia Press, 1999.

Showalter, Dennis E. "The Prusso-German RMA, 1840–1871." In *The Dynamics of Military Revolution: 1300–2050*, edited by MacGregor Knox and Williamson Murray, 92–113. Cambridge: Cambridge University Press, 2001.

Simon, James S. *Lincoln and Chief Justice Taney: Slavery, Secession, and the President's War Powers*. New York: Simon and Schuster, 2006.

Simpson, Brooks D. *The Reconstruction Presidents*. Lawrence: University Press of Kansas, 1998.

Smith, Francis. *The Debates and Proceedings of the Minnesota Constitutional Convention Including the Organic Act of the Territory: With the Enabling Act of Congress, the Act of the Territorial Legislature Relative to the Convention, and the Vote of the People on the Constitution*. St Paul: Earl S. Goodrich, Territorial Printers 1860.

Smith, Jean Edward. *Grant*. New York: Simon and Schuster, 2000.

Smith, Theodore C. *The Life and Letters of James Abrams Garfield, 1877–1882*. New Haven: Yale University Press, 1925.

Smith, William. *A Dictionary of Greek and Roman Antiquities*. London: Taylor and Watton, 1842.

Stampp, Kenneth. *America in 1857: A Nation on the Brink*. New York: Oxford University Press, 1990.

Starkey, Marion L. *The Devil in Massachusetts: A Modern Inquiry into the Salem Witch Trials*. New York: Dolphin Press, 1949.

Starr, Chester. *A History of the Ancient World*. Oxford: Oxford University Press, 1991.

Steers, Edward. *The Trial: The Assassination of President Lincoln and the Trial of the Conspirators*. Lexington: University of Kentucky Press, 2003.

Stevens, Charles. *Berdan's United States Sharpshooters in the Army of the Potomac*. Reprint ed. Dayton, OH: Morningside Books, 1995.

Stevens, Robert. "History of the Yale Law School: Provenance and Perspective." In *History of the Yale Law School*, ed. Anthony Kronman. New Haven: Yale University Press, 2004.

Sutherland, Arthur. *The Law at Harvard: A History of Ideas and Men, 1817–1967*. Boston: Harvard-Belknap, 1967.

Swinton, William. *History of the Seventh Regiment, National Guard, State of New York, during the War of the Rebellion: With a Preliminary Chapter on the Origin and Early History of the Regiment, a Summary of Its History since the War, and a Roll of Honor, Comprising Brief Sketches of the Services Rendered by Members of the Regiment in the Army and Navy of the United States*. New York: Field, Osgood and Co., 1870.

Sword, Wiley. *Sharpshooter: Hiram Berdan, His Famous Sharpshooters and Their Sharps Rifles*. Lincoln, RI: Andrew Mowbray, 1988.

Taaffe, Stephen R., *Commanding the Army of the Potomac*. Lawrence: University Press of Kansas, 2006.

Tebel, John, and Zuckerman, Mary Ellen. *The Magazine in America: 1741–1990*. Oxford: Oxford University Press, 1991.

Thomas, Benjamin P., and Hyman, Harold. *Stanton: The Life and Times of Lincoln's Secretary of War*. New York: Alfred Knopf, 1962.

Tidwell, William A. *Confederate Covert Action in the American Civil War: April '65*. Kent, OH: Kent State University Press. 1994.

Todd, John E. *Sketch of the Life and Character of the Hon. William J. Hubbard, Delivered at His Funeral*. Suffolk County Bar, Boston, 1864.

Toole, G. J. A. *The Spanish War: An American Epic, 1898*. New York: W.W. Norton, 1984.

Trefouse, Hans L. *Impeachment of a President: Andrew Jackson, the Blacks, and Reconstruction*. New York: Fordham University Press, 1999.

Urofsky, Melvin. *A March of Liberty: A Constitutional History of the United States*. New York: Alfred Knopf, 1988.

Utley, Robert. *Frontier Regulars: The United States Army and the Indians, 1866–1891*. New York: MacMillan, 1973.

Utley, Robert M., and Washburn, Wilcomb E. *Indian Wars*. Boston: Houghton Mifflin, 2002.

Van Doren, Carl. *The American Novel*. New York: MacMillan, 1921.

Warner, Robert A. *New Haven Negroes: A Social History*. New York: Arno Press, 1969.

Warren, Charles. *History of the Harvard Law School and of Early Legal Conditions in America*. Vol. 2. Reprint ed. New York: Da Capo, 1970.

———. *A History of the American Bar*. New York: H. Fertig, 1990.

Wawro, Geoffrey. *The Franco Prussian War: The German Conquest of France in 1870–1871*. Cambridge: Cambridge University Press, 2003.

Weber, Jennifer. *Copperheads: The Rise and Fall of Lincoln's Opposition Opponents in the North*. Oxford: Oxford University Press, 2006.

Weigley, Russell F. *The Age of Battles: The Quest for Decisive Warfare from Breitenfeld to Waterloo*. Bloomington: Indiana University Press, 1991.

———. *The American Way of War: A History of United States Military Strategy and Policy*. Bloomington: Indiana University Press, 1973.

———. *History of the United States Army*. Bloomington: Indiana University Press, 1984.

———. *Towards an American Army: Military Thought from Washington to Marshall*. Reprint ed. Westport, CT: Greenwood Press, 1974.

West, Donald J., and Walk, Alexander. *Daniel McNaughten: His Trial and Aftermath*. Ashford, Kent: Headly, 1977.

West, Richard. *Lincoln's Scapegoat General: A Life of Benjamin F. Butler, 1818–1893*. Boston: Houghton Mifflin, 1965.

Wilintz, Sean. *The Rise of American Democracy: Jefferson to Lincoln*. New York: W.W. Norton, 2005.

Williams, John H. *Winthrop and Curtis: A Reviewer Reviewed*. Tacoma, WA: J.H. Williams, 1914.

Wilson, James Grant. *Appleton's Cyclodpaedia of American Biography*. Vol. 6. New York: D. Appleton and Co., 1887.

Wilson, James Grant, and Fiske, John, eds. *Appleton's Cyclopaedia of American Biography*. Vol. 6. New York: D. Appleton and Co., 1889.

Winthrop, John. *Winthrop's Journal, History of New England*. Vol. 1. Edited by James K. Hosmer. New York: C. Scribner's Sons, 1908.

Winthrop, Robert Charles, Jr. A *Memoir of Robert Charles Winthrop: Prepared for the Massachusetts Historical Society*. Boston: Little, Brown and Co., 1897.

Woolen, William Wesley. *William McKee Dunn, Brigadier General U.S.A., a Memoir: With Extracts from His Speeches, Decisions, and Correspondence*. New York: Knickerbocker Press, 1888.

Woolf, Eugene. *Theodore Winthrop: Portrait of an American Author*. Washington, DC: University Press of America, 1981.

Wooster, Robert. *The Military and United States Indian Policy: 1865–1903*. New Haven: Yale University Press, 1998.

———. *Nelson A. Miles and the Twilight of the Frontier Army*. Lincoln: University of Nebraska Press, 1993.

Yenne, Bill. *Indian Wars: The Campaign for the American West*. Yardley, PA: Westholme, 2006.

Journal Articles

Allen, Mary Bernard. "Joseph Holt, Judge Advocate General (1862–1875): A Study in the Treatment of Political Prisoners by the United States Government During the Civil War." Ph.D. diss., University of Chicago, 1927.

Alotta, Robert I. "Military Executions in the Union Army: 1861–1866." Ph.D. diss., Temple University, 1984.

Ambrose, Steven F. "Emory Upton and the Armies of Europe and Asia." *Military Affairs* 28, no. 1 (Spring 1964), 27–32.

Anonymous. "William Winthrop." *Military Law Review*28 (1965), i–iv.

Ballam, Deborah A. "The Evolution of the Government-Business Relationship in the United States: Colonial Times to Present." *American Business Law Journal* 31 (1994), 553–635

Bartholomew, Mark. "Legal Separation: The Relationship between the Law School and the Central University in the Late Nineteenth Century." *Journal of Legal Education* 53 (September 2003), 368–401.

Bennett, B. Kevin. "The Jacksonville Mutiny." *Military Law Review* 134 (1991), 157–172.

Bolles, John A. "Why Semmes of the Alabama Was Not Tried." *Atlantic Monthly* 30 (July 1872), 88–98.

Bosco, Carla. "Harvard University and the Fugitive Slave Act." *New England Quarterly* 79 (June 2006), 227–247.

Buell, Clarence C. "The New York Seventh." *Scribners' Magazine* 20 (1880), 63–80.

Carrington Paul. "Law as the Common Thoughts of Men: The Law Teaching and Judging of Thomas McIntyre Cooley." *Stanford Law Review* 49 (1997), 495–546.

Chomsky, Carol. "The United States-Dakota War Trials, a Study in Military Injustice." *Stanford Law Review* 43 (1990), 13–98.

Cunningham, Roger D. "Always a Storm Center: The Trials and Tribulations of Asa Bird Gardiner." *Journal of America's Military Past* 104, no. 2 (Fall 2006), 5–28.

Edwards, George. "Why Thomas Cooley Left the Bench: A Missing Page of Legal History." *Wayne State Law Review* 10 (1964), 1563–1572.

Effron, Andrew. "Military Justice: The Continuing Importance of Historical Perspective." *Army Lawyer*, June 2000, 4–10.

Eldridge, Maureen. "Who's Driving the Train: Railroad Regulation and Local Control." *University of Colorado Law Review* 75 (2004), 549–595.

Finnegan, Patrick. "The Study of Law as a Foundation of Leadership and Command: The History of Law Instruction at the United States Military Academy." *Military Law Review* 118 (2004), 112–137.

Fratcher, William F. "History of the Judge Advocate General's Corps." *United States Army, Military Law Review* 4 (1959), 89–122.

Furman, H. W. C. "Restrictions upon Use of the Army Imposed by the Posse Comitatus Act." *Military Law Review* 7 (1960), 92–106.

Grant, Colonel Carl E. "Partisan Warfare Model." *Military Review* (November 1958), 48.

Green, Thomas H., and Frachter, William F. "History of the Judge Advocate General's Department." *Army Lawyer*, June 1975, 13–16.

Hagan, William R. "Overlooked Textbooks Jettison Some Durable Military Law Legends." *Military Law Review* 113 (1986), 163–171.

———. "The Rush Cases and the Class of 1887." *Army Lawyer* 18 (1887), 18–21.

Hay, John. "Life in the Whitehouse in the Time of Lincoln." *Century* 41 (January 1890), 1–58.

Hennesy, John J. "Father Abraham's Paper Wad, The Army of the Potomac and the Emancipation Proclamation." *Civil War Magazine* 4 (June 1999), 74–75.

Hylton, Gordon. "David Josiah Brewer and the Christian Constitution." *Marquette Law Review* 81 (1998), 417–444.

Jackson, Darryl W., Smith, Jeffrey H., Sisson, Edward H., and Krasnoff, Helene T. "Bending Toward Justice: The Posthumus Pardon of Lieutenant Henry Ossian Flipper." *Indiana Law Journal* 74 (1999), 1251–1269.

Johnson, Elizabeth Winthrop. "Concerning Theodore Winthrop." *Modern Language Notes* 30 (1915), 196–197.

Kane, Lucille. "Governing a Frontier City: St. Anthony, 1855–1872." *Minnesota History* 33 (September 1956), 117–129.

Katta, Kenneth. "Conflicts in Command: An Analysis of Leadership in the Berdan Sharpshooters in the Civil War." *Military Collector and Historian* 53, no. 2 (2001), 50–61.

Katz, Steven. "The Pequot War Reconsidered." *New England Quarterly* 64, no. 2 (June 1991), 208–222.

Kent, William C. "Fighting with Berdan: William C. Kent's Eyewitness Account of the Seven Days Battles." *Civil War Times Illustrated* 15 (May 1976), 5–9, 42–48.

Lamb, Stephen A."The Court-Martial Panel Selection Process: A Critical Analysis." *Military Law Review* 137 (Summer 1992), 103–127.

Leonard, Gerald. "Towards a Legal History of American Criminal Theory: Culture and Doctrine from Blackstone to the Model Penal Code." *Buffalo Criminal Law Review* 6 (2003), 691–832.

Maltby, I., ed. *The Yale Literary Magazine*. New Haven: Yale University Press, 1848.

Marszalek, John F. "A Black Cadet at West Point." *American Heritage Magazine* 22, no. 5 (May 1971), 44–48.

Marti, Donald. "The Puritan Tradition in a 'New England' of the West." *Minnesota History* 40 (June 1964), 5–8.

Michie, Peter. "Caste at West Point." *North American Review* 130 (1880), 601–621.

Nelson, Anne Kusener. "King Philip's War and the Hubbard-Mather Rivalry." *William and Mary Quarterly* 27 (October 1970), 615–629.

Parks, William H. "Command Responsibility for War Crimes." *Military Law Review* 62 (1973), 1–33.

Pindell, Richard. "A Most Dangerous Set of Men." *Civil War Times Illustrated* 32 (July 1993), 41–49.

Prugh, George. "Colonel William Winthrop: The Tradition of the Military Lawyer." *American Bar Association Journal* 42, no. 2 (May 1956), 126–191.

Ranlet, Philip. "Another Look at the Causes of King Philip's War." *New England Quarterly* 61, no. 2 (June 3, 1988), 94–104.

Raymond, John, and Frischholz, Barbara. "Lawyers Who Established International Law in the United States." *American Journal of International Law* 76, no. 4 (October 1982), 802–829.

Robie, William R., "The Court Martial of a Judge Advocate General: Brigadier General David G. Swaim." *Military Law Review* 56 (1972), 211–240.

Shapiro, Samuel. "The Rendition of Anthony Burns." *Journal of Negro History* 44, no. 1 (January 1959), 34–51.

Sheppard, Steve. "Casebooks, Commentaries, and Curmudgeons: An Introductory History of Law in the Lecture Hall." *Iowa Law Review* 82 (1987), 547–644.

Shewmaker, Kenneth. "'Hook and Line, Bob and Sinker': Daniel Webster and the Fisheries Dispute of 1852." *Diplomatic History* 9 (Spring 1985), 113–115.

Siegal, Stephen A. "Judge Bishop's Orthodoxy." *Law and History Review* 13 (Fall 1995), 215–254.

Siegel, Andrew M. "To Learn and Make Respectable Hereafter: The Litchfield Law School in Cultural Context." *New York University Law Review* 73 (1998), 1978–2028.

Simcox, G. A. "Natural Religion." *Nineteenth Century* 12 (1882), 404–412.

Snell, Mark A. "Baptism of Fire, the 118th 'Corn Exchange' Pennsylvania Infantry at the Battle of Shepherdstown." *Civil War Regiments* 6 (2000), 119–142.

Stansfield, George J. "A History of the Judge Advocate General's Department, United States Army." *Military Affairs* 9 (1945), 219–230.

Thayer, Joseph Henry. "Theodore Woolsey, Reminisces." *Atlantic Monthly* 64 (October 1889), 555–561.

"Trumbell's History of Connecticut." *The North American Review* 8, no. 22 (1818), 93.

Tunnell, Ted. "Creating 'the Propaganda of History': Southern Editors and the Origin of Carpetbagger and Scalawag." *Journal of Southern History* 72 (November 2006), 789–800.

Vaughn, William P. "West Point and the First Negro Cadet." *Military Affairs* 35, no. 3 (Fall 1980), 101–103.
Warren, Marc L. "Relief and Review: The Case of Major General G.K. Warren." *Army Lawyer*, 1996, 36–42.
Weigley, Russell F. "The Military Thought of John M. Schofield." *Military Affairs* 23 (1959), 77–84.
Werhan, Keith, "Checking Congress and Balancing Federalism: A Lesson of Separation of Powers Jurisprudence." *Washington and Lee Law Review* 57 (2000), 1213–1291.
Whitney, H. M. "The Analogy between Slavery and Intemperance before the Law." *New Englander and Yale Review* 39, no. 156 (May 1880), 374–385.
Wiener, Colonel Frederick Bernays. "American Military Law in Light of the First Mutiny Act's Tri-Centennial." *Military Law* 126, no. 1 (1989), 123.
Winthrop, Theodore. "Washington as a Camp." *Atlantic Monthly*, June 1861, 103.

www.ingramcontent.com/pod-product-compliance
Lightning Source LLC
Chambersburg PA
CBHW061608180926
51615CB00006B/16